About the A

Thomas Albert Goodwin was born in Hackney, in the East End of London, in 1929. After being evacuated to Oxford during World War II, Tom started work on his 14th birthday as an apprentice 'rivet boy' in a boilermaker's shop. After serving two years in the National Service, stationed for a time in Germany, he returned to London to work, play and ride his motorbike around the English countryside. At age 32 Tom met and married Evie and moved to her childhood home of Johannesburg. After seven warm and wonderful years there, he bravely took his new family (including his daughter Anne and son Stephen) to New Jersey to start a new, safer and freer life in the United States.

After studying engineering while in Johannesburg, Tom began working as a design estimator, ending his 52-year working life as Chief Estimator and Project Engineer with a small company that recruited him on reputation alone.

On completion of this book, Tom and his wife of 40 years moved back to England, settling in Abingdon. He spends much of his leisure time playing golf, reading, tending his garden, writing books, singing and playing the piano.

A Londoner's Life

Thomas Albert Goodwin
1929 – 2000+

GOODWIN HALL
ABINGDON • OXFORDSHIRE

A Londoner's Life

This edition published in 2002 by
GOODWIN HALL
5 Fairfield Place, Abingdon, Oxford OX14 1HA

Copyright © Thomas Albert Goodwin 2002

ISBN 0-9543825-0-1

All rights reserved. No part of this publication may be reproduced, stored in a retrieval system, or transmitted in any form or by any means, electronic, mechanical, photocopying, recording or otherwise, without either the prior written permission of the publisher or a licence permitting restricted copying issued by the Copyright Licensing Agency Ltd, 90 Tottenham Court Road, London, W1P 0LP. This book may not be lent, resold, hired out or otherwise disposed of by way of trade in any form of binding other than that in which it is originally published, without the prior consent of the publisher.

Edited by Anne Hall

Cover design by Wendy Wastie
WW DESIGN COMPANY
34 Park Avenue, Abingdon
Oxfordshire OX14 1DS

Copy checking by Joanna Mitchell
Oxford

Typeset in Melior and Cochin by
EVERGREEN GRAPHICS
11 The Drive, Craigweil on Sea, Aldwick,
West Sussex PO21 4DU

Printed and bound in Great Britain by
ANTONY ROWE LIMITED
Bumper's Farm, Chippenham,
Wiltshire SN14 6LH

Contents

Preface			vii
Acknowledgements			ix
Tribute from Steve			x
Editor's Note			xii
Chapter 1	1929 – 1938	*The Early Years*	1
Chapter 2	1939 – 1945	*World War II*	15
Chapter 3	1946 – 1950	*Apprenticeship at Frasers*	53
Chapter 4	1950 – 1952	*Gun Fitter for His Majesty*	77
Chapter 5	1952 – 1960	*The Wasted Years*	105
Chapter 6	1961 – 1962	*Romantic Times*	123
Chapter 7	1962 – 1969	*Adventures in South Africa*	141
Chapter 8	1969 – 1974	*America, Here I Come*	189
Chapter 9	1975 – 1980	*Working for a Living*	219
Chapter 10	1981 – 1995	*Family Ties*	241
Chapter 11	1995 – 2000+	*The Retirement Years*	269
Afterword			285
Family Tree			286
English – American Dictionary			287

Preface

FOR many years I have wanted to write the story of my life. I know that most people will regard this as ridiculous, even unnecessary. Compared with other autobiographies, written by professionals, politicians, film stars...this one may not be the most interesting, but it has to be unique! The reasons for wanting to write this story are many, one of which is that some future reader may get a chance to learn what it was like going through this period of time, from 1929 beyond 2000 AD. I like that idea. I should like it even better if my future reader is also a member of or related to the Goodwin family. Some of the happenings that took place during the last sixty or more years are being forgotten. Not of course major events like wars starting and stopping, or governments rising and falling, but smaller things that affected the lives of ordinary people, like the Blitz, for instance. My book will recollect these things. After reading some other autobiographies, I concluded that this one, by comparison, could not be any worse – it might even be better. The most important reason, after the obvious one of being host to a future reader, is to satisfy my own selfish ego. Not a bad reason if it makes me feel good. Another reason for writing this is to see if I can do it without any training. So far during my lifetime I have written only letters, and not many of those either. This is my first real attempt to do something halfway intelligent with words.

What shall I call this book? What will its title be? When I first started to think about this project, I had the name of this book all figured out; I was going to call it: *Twenty-seven Years With the Wrong Woman*. A name like that, I thought, would create a lot of interest in publishing circles. I had to think again – do not ask why I chose a name like that; it does not really make any sense except to proclaim many years of marriage, and it would surely meet with objections from a certain quarter – so I dropped it. My next choice popped into my mind immediately: *Three Decades is Enough!* Boy, doesn't that make you think? What a snazzy title! Now, if this were a story of a marriage then maybe the name might fit. But what if the marriage lasted forty years or, (perish the thought), *fifty*! Then the name would not fit the contents.

How about a simple title: *Memories of a Boilermaker*? Not good enough. I was a boilermaker for only twenty-six years, so this kind of title does not fit at all. We could give the book a title that described the contents, such as: *A life history of Thomas Albert Goodwin born August 24th 1929*. I thought that this was a perfect title even if it is a cumbersome, uninteresting, awkward, long, and boring name. I couldn't believe how difficult it was to choose a suitable title. My long-winded search for the title of this book came finally to an end when I asked myself the question: "What am I, and what have I always been?" Why, a Londoner, of course. It's quite obvious that the title should be: *A Londoner's Life*.

How shall I put the book together? Decade by decade would be a good idea. Starting with the 1930s, (I wasn't around for much of the 20s), we will march through these decades, through the 30s, 40s, 50s, 60s, etc, stopping neither for wars, nor for the end of the millennium, until I run out of time.

Having spent about half my life in England and South Africa, and half of my life in America, I will use both English and American phrases in the book. To this end I have included a reference dictionary at the back of the book. Many people confuse being English with being British. They are *not* the same. A person who is English is also British; however, a person who is British is not necessarily English. Britain, or to be precise, Great Britain, is made up of England, Scotland and Wales. The term 'United Kingdom' refers to the countries of England, Scotland, Wales, and Northern Ireland, as well as many tiny islands such as the Scilly Isles and the Isle of Man. The Channel Islands – Jersey, Guernsey, etc – are not part of the United Kingdom, as they are neutral.

I will personally guarantee that the happenings mentioned here took place as described, approximately. When conversations are reported, they contain only the 'bare bones' of what was actually said and are not verbatim. No diary was kept, but I have an excellent memory. In a few instances, names may have been changed to prevent embarrassment to others and myself. Also, I will, occasionally, jump out of the present time slot in order to clarify the meaning or explain an event.

T.A. Goodwin
Piscataway, New Jersey
USA

Acknowledgements

*With heartfelt thanks to my wife, Evie, for all her help and support over the years, and especially for her patience while I was writing this book.
A very special thanks goes to my daughter, Anne, for the time and effort that she devoted to editing this book, and also to her husband Dave. Much appreciation goes to my son, Steve, for all his support and encouragement.*

A Tribute from Steve

WHAT can I say about the 'best dad in the world'? I have so many great childhood memories of Dad. I loved our camping trips to Cedar Creek Campground in Bayville, NJ. It was just the two of us. I remember our canoe trips down Cedar Creek and how sore I was afterwards. We had so much fun heating up our cans of baked beans on the little gas stove, and setting up the big green canvas tent. I remember getting my first real bike, a black Apollo 5 speed with a banana seat. It was a big deal for me, and I remember Dad being as excited about it as I was. Then there was the Green Machine, which I loved to ride in the driveway. I can't even tell you how many times I've heard Dad say it took him all night to put that darned Green Machine together!

Oddly, one of my fondest memories was Dad's unique method of getting rid of loose teeth. He'd take me out to the garage and, with a pair of needle nose pliers, he'd rip the tooth right out of my mouth! You'd think that might have hurt a lot, but it never did, not even a little bit. He always knew just what to do.

Dad knew everything about cars and helped me to work on my first car, a 1971 Satellite Sebring. I loved that car and Dad helped me to keep it running. He also taught me all there is to know about gardening. He truly has a green thumb. Every time I visit him in Piscataway, we walk around the yard and discuss the trees and shrubs.

Dad especially knew what to do when I was looking for advice on how to budget my money wisely. I sat down at the dining room table with him when I started my first real job at ABB Kent and he helped me to draw up a budget. I still frequently use the knowledge I picked up that day.

Looking back, Dad was great with my sis and I as kids, and as an adult, he has become my best friend. We have a mutual fondness for collecting coins. We make a day of going to the coin store and checking our lists, trying to complete collections of Lincoln pennies, or half dollars. More recently, we've taken to going to the driving range and playing Pitch and Putt golf. I love those days. We share a nice, leisurely breakfast or lunch, and then spend the day chatting about the stock market or swapping stories, enjoying the sun, and hitting the golf ball around.

My fond memories of Dad would probably fill a book, and who knows, maybe one of these days I'll walk in his footsteps and put those memories down on paper. I also hope to follow Dad when it comes to raising my own children. When you read this, Dad, remember that I think you really do deserve the title 'World's Greatest Dad'.

I love you.

Stephen Thomas Goodwin
2002

Editor's Note

DAD loves to tell stories, and over the years Dad has shared in elaborate and colourful detail many of the things he's done and the people he's known. These tales were often told while walking around our neighbourhood or along the beach during our summer holidays. I enjoyed these walks; they were often early in the morning when the day was fresh, and were a special time for just the two of us, away from the rest of the world.

I've grown up hearing wonderful stories of Dad's time as a young boy, adventures on his motorbike, endless accounts of his time as an apprentice and boilermaker at Fraser & Fraser, his days in the army. I'll never forget Dad's famous yarn opener, "Did I ever tell you the one about when I worked at Fraser & Fraser, building invasion barges for the war effort, W – W – II, the big one?" Noooo, Dad, not lately!

So when Dad retired it was great to hear that he was going to write a book about his life. He sent me the first few chapters of *A Londoner's Life* to have a look at in the spring of 1995. I began to ask for more detail and clarification and I offered to edit the book for him. I then suggested getting the book professionally produced; I thought a labour of love such as this deserved to be printed and bound.

Reading in detail about Dad's life, from his early childhood through to when he became a grandfather for the fourth time, has shown what a remarkable person he is. Dad's given my life stability and provided me with support when I've needed it, and I'm really grateful to him for that. He's taught me that nothing is impossible, if you really want something and are willing to put in the hard work. He's helped me to see the world with an open heart and a sense of humour.

Working with Dad on *A Londoner's Life* for so many years really has been a great experience. I feel lucky not only to have wonderful childhood memories, but also to have the chance, as an adult, to read about Dad's life in detail.

Although it's been a lot of work getting the book ready for printing, in a way it will be sad to finish. But I also feel a wonderful sense of achievement that we've managed to complete it with about 3,000 miles of ocean between us. What next, Dad?

Anne Goodwin Hall
2002

Dedication

*For
Anne and Steve
and
their children*

CHAPTER 1

The Early Years

1929 – 1938

THE most difficult part of an undertaking like this is getting started, and knowing *where* to start. Old Shackleford, who came into my life about the same time as Anne did, said, "Like Alice in Wonderland, start at the beginning; go on to the end; and then stop." I will try to follow this instruction, but it will not be easy.

I was born on Saturday August 24th 1929 in Hackney Hospital, in the East End of London, the first-born child of Rhoda and Thomas Goodwin. I believed for most of my life that I was named after my Dad, but that wasn't strictly correct. According to the records, he was named Thomas Alfred Goodwin, although he called himself Thomas Albert many times for most of his life. My paternal grandfather had the same names (Thomas Albert), so I could be called Thomas Albert Goodwin III. This is an Americanism that is not (to my knowledge) used in Britain.

Now, let's go back to the beginning. My first home was in Elderfield Road in Clapton, London. Clapton is part of London's East End, a generally poor and deprived area just east of the City of London. The City is where many of the capital's business and financial companies are based - I guess you could call it the equivalent of New York's Wall Street area. Like most families in the East End, we survived on a lot of hard work and very little income. We had a basement flat in a house owned by Mr and Mrs Chalk. Their real name, incidentally, was Chokowski.

The Chalks lived upstairs, and the ground level was a shop. It was the kind of place that my Dad called a 'sweet stuff shop'. Old Chalk sold sweets and candy and cigarettes in this shop along with ice cream and other general items. Dad called him Old Chalk, but he wasn't really old at all. He was probably in his mid to late thirties, but his beard, black hat, Jewish demeanor and old fashioned clothes made him look ancient. Many years later, while reminiscing, Dad told me that Old Chalk had died while still fairly young, in an accident. He was apparently given a lift in a truck, and the truck was involved in a crash.

Mum served at the counter in the shop sometimes and also helped make the ice cream. She occasionally got me to help turn the handle on the ice cream machine to keep me amused when she was busy. I don't know whether my mother got paid directly for working in the shop, or whether she got a cheaper rent on the flat. It doesn't matter which was the case, the point is she helped out.

Mum had always been busy, and I suppose getting married and starting a family made her even busier. She had been a member of the Salvation Army, (the Sally Anne) and had worked at the local Venus Pencil Company before she was married. Once married, she took on her duties as a wife and mother with much enthusiasm. Despite the fact that the flat was tiny, and she had little money to play with, she set about making a comfortable home for her new family. Once I had come along, she worked less in the ice cream shop, as she had plenty to do. In those days no one in that area of London had a washing machine, so all the washing had to be done by hand. This included my Dad's thick overalls, all my nappies and baby clothes, the sheets and towels, and it was like a regular laundry in the house.

Then, of course, there was all the shopping for food. Every morning, my mother would put me in my pram and wheel me down to the market for the day's supply of groceries. There was no such thing as buying ahead, as we didn't have a fridge. So what with that and keeping the flat clean and tidy, Mum had her hands full. She spent a lot of time figuring out how to stretch every penny, and this went on for years. It must have been very difficult for her, but I learned many years later that she had strength of character that could not be matched.

It was a very quiet neighborhood we lived in. No one, absolutely nobody had a car or vehicle of any kind, except a bicycle. There were a few relatively wealthy people who owned a motorcycle or a motorcycle combination, but no one had a car. This meant that it was very quiet compared to the traffic noises one hears today. The greatest noise one could hear was from the birds. Yes, birds! During this period of time (early 1930s) people kept caged birds as pets. One of the favorites was a budgerigar, better known as a budgie. You could walk along the streets of most of east London and hear the birds whistling and chirping from just about every house and flat. In addition to the caged birds, we also had the wild birds that lived in London, notably the sparrows and pigeons. Trafalgar Square is still known for the hordes of pigeons that descend upon the statue of Nelson.

Another memorable feature of the houses on Elderfield Road was the gardens. The English love to make things grow and as the climate is generally mild and damp, the average English person can easily become a natural gardener. The gardens were very small – maybe twelve feet by eight feet – but they were filled to overflowing with roses, chrysanthemums, etc, with espaliered fruit trees against the wall. In my memory, this period of my life as a toddler was quiet, tranquil, and pleasant.

During this tranquil period, my sister Gladys was born in February 1931. It was when Gladys was still very young, less than a year old, that *the very first thing that I can remember* happened. Gladys was lying in a kind of swinging cradle in front of the open fireplace, with a coal fire burning. My mother left the room for a few minutes, which gave me a chance to 'help'. I pushed the cradle to and fro, and all of a sudden Gladys fell out. She started to cry, but luckily she had fallen on the hearth away from the fire, so it was really a lucky escape for her! My mother of course came running to find out what all the commotion was. Funny, but I don't remember the punishment.

In another early recollection of mine, I'm sitting on the kitchen table in our basement flat with my mother sponging my face and hands with a flannel in preparation for a shopping excursion. I was looking up at the airy, which was an area outside the kitchen window about three feet deep and as wide as the window. The ceiling of the airy was an iron grating that was set into the pavement along the edge of the street. People walking on the pavement above could look down into our flat. The ceiling of our basement flat was at about street level, and some children were making a commotion with a barking dog. Nothing exciting happened, except that Mum became agitated and mumbled something about "those cheeky devils".

While we were living in Elderfield Road, Dad made a set of balancing scales for me to play with. He was going to rub off the sharp edges with a file to make it safe, but I got to it first, fell on it, and cut my right shin quite badly. I still carry the scar today after more than sixty years.

Another early memory of mine had to do with a conversation between my parents. One day Dad came home from work and Mum said to him, "Have you got anything for me, Tom?" He said, "Yes, here's a dolly," and he handed her something. Well, I looked for that dolly all over and wondered about it for a long time afterwards until one day the penny dropped! Dad had said 'dollar', a term which was used at the time in England for five shillings, or five bob. So, there was Dad, handing over his wages quite meekly with no argument about it. The five shillings represented Dad's wages for one day. He worked six days a week for thirty shillings, the equivalent of one pound ten shillings.

It was around 1933 or 1934 when I was about five years old, that we made our first move to the buildings in Bow. We lived on the third level, which was the top floor, at 12 Prioress House, Bromley High Street, Bow E3. There was no elevator, so the stairs had to be negotiated every day with the daily shopping bags, vegetables, etc. Our coal – for heating the flat – was manhandled up the stairs in 100 weight sacks. Luckily, the coal man delivered this for us. He took the coal sack on his back, balancing it on the back of his neck and head, and staggered about sixty feet from the horsedrawn coal cart to the stairs, up three levels, and thirty feet to the end apartment before dumping it. There was no place to put the coal except in the bathtub, so, for temporary storage, that's where it went.

Prioress House was located at the north end of St Leonard's Street in Bow. Two streets, Bromley High Street and Saint Leonard's Street, made a three way junction there and that spot is called the Seven Stars. There was a pub by that name on the south west corner, opposite Prioress House, and it took me a few years to discover the connection between the name of the pub and the district. If I were asked as a child where I lived, I would simply answer 'The Seven Stars'.

On the other side of the street, the south east side, there was a church. What's very strange is that everybody knew the name of the pub, but nobody knew the name of the church! Nobody that I knew, anyway. Well, it was here outside the church entrance that the number 208 low decker bus had a terminus. We used to ride that bus from the Seven Stars to 47 High Street in Homerton where my maternal grandparents lived. (Number 47 doesn't exist anymore; a block of flats has been erected on the site.) After leaving the Seven Stars, the bus went to Bow Road, then Fairfield Road (where I was later to get some schooling), alongside Victoria Park and along Cadogan Terrace to the bottom of the hill, where the conductor used to shout "Marsh Hill". This was the bus stop for Hackney Hospital where yours truly was born. A little further on, the bus passes Saint Barnabas Church where Mum and Dad were married and I was christened, then the Adam and Eve pub and 47 High Street, both on the right. Chatsworth Road and Mare Street were Mum's favorite shopping markets and were within walking distance from 47. The bus continued and reached its terminus at Clapton Duck Pond, a total distance of about three miles.

If there was one thing I hated when I was a child, it was riding on the low decker buses. My big problem on the bus was that I would get travel sick, and it was *awful*. I dreaded going on those buses. They stank of diesel fumes from the engine, they vibrated and rattled, and it was always unbearably hot and muggy inside them. Mum would bring along a paper bag and a damp flannel, but I'm sure that made me worse. As soon as the engine started I would begin swallowing!

We visited Nana and Grandad Eley regularly, and apart from the bus ride I enjoyed the visits very much. Elderfield Road, where the bus dropped us off, was only a couple of blocks away from Nana and Grandad's. I guess this was Mum's bailiwick. Number 47 was a very old shop, with living quarters out back and upstairs. Grandad worked in the shop, and in the basement repairing boots and shoes. The family survived, but Grandad was not very successful with boot repairs. He was an old soldier who had served with the British Army in the Boer War (1901) and in World War I (1914 – 1918). The part that they lived in was very dingy, and had no electricity. So there was no electric light, no stove, no fridge, no hot water, and of course no appliances of any kind. An oven was built into the fireplace for cooking and they had to build a fire, winter or summer. Compared to today's standards, Number 47 was no fun to live in. All of the houses on Elderfield Road had similar features so it's not surprising that we moved to the buildings in Bow where we had a relatively new flat, *and* electricity.

My brother Roy was born in this period, in March, 1934. This completed the family: Tommy, Gladys, and Roy, until 1946, when my youngest sister, Carol, was born. When the Second World War finally ended, many families decided to have another child. There was a feeling of celebration throughout the nation, and there were many 'after-the-war' babies.

♫

Let me tell you a little about Mum's family. Mum's parents, Ellen and Henry Eley, had four children: Rhoda, Tom, Nelly, and Gladys. (My father Tom had, among others, a sister Keziah who married my mother's brother Tom Eley. The two families were therefore tied together with two marriages.) Uncle Tom died early, in his late thirties, and Aunt Gladys died even younger, in her late twenties. The first generation of Ellen and Henry Eley's four children produced seventeen children. All of these four original families have grown out of all recognition and exploded in size. I have lost track of most of my cousins, half-cousins, nephews, nieces, (regular and great). There must be literally hundreds of people out there, most of whom I have never seen or even heard of, all members of the same original family.

At this time in the mid-1930s, my Aunt Gladys on my mother's side was living at home as an unmarried teenager. Whenever we visited Number 47 she would take me off my mother's hands and play with me along with my sister Gladys and baby Roy. One day she asked me, "What is two times eight?" I was able to answer immediately with sixteen. Aunt Gladys praised me for this, making me a very happy boy. She was the youngest child in Nana's and Grandad's family, very pretty, and I remember her as being very nice. We played for hours with Aunt Gladys: hopscotch, gobs and bonsters, tippy cat, and many other games.

As I mentioned before, Grandad Eley was an old soldier with long service in the British Army. He retired as a Sergeant Major, which is the highest rank for an NCO (Non Commissioned Officer). He suffered some terrible wounds on his body as a result of action in France during World

War I. Never once, to my knowledge, did he speak of his war wounds. You could say that he suffered in silence. My mother discovered his scars when he was bedridden in the early 50s just before he died of cancer. He wore a waxed moustache in the British Army tradition. He had a straight back, and deliberately held himself straight. His clothes were well brushed, and his boots always brilliantly polished. Whenever he spoke of the *regiment*, he would literally come to attention, and a gleam would appear in his eye. He actually lived strictness, tradition, and *duty*.

Grandad hailed from Derby, and still had an accent, along with a terrifically dry sense of humor. In his cellar at Number 47 he had a knife-sharpening and polishing machine, which he operated by foot treadle. One of his moneymaking ventures was to clean and sharpen cutlery. During this operation the sparks would fly everywhere. One day I was down in the cellar with Grandad cleaning Nana's cutlery, when he gave me a bucket, saying, "Tommy, run down to the oil shop and get a bucket of sparks – we have no sparks left." I was still young enough to fall for his joke, so I went to the oil shop in search of sparks! Needless to say, there weren't any sparks at the shop either.

Grandad Eley could tell stories with such a straight face that you could never be sure if he was really serious or just kidding. He told me once of the time when he was a youngster in Derbyshire. He, his brother Tom (there are a lot of Toms in this family) and his father did the rounds of the local farms, helping with harvesting, etc. At the end of the day, after they had been paid, they were invited to stay for supper. This was a treat, said Grandad, because the lady of the house had a reputation for making delicious meat pies. After supper, Grandad's father congratulated the lady for the excellent meat pies she had served, and asked her what kind of meat she had used.

"Oh," she said, "I use the rats that the terrier catches in the barn."

"Well," said Grandad, "I was so sick that I could not eat for days afterwards." Now he told me this with a solemn deadpan face, and I believed every word of it – and I still do. But, as I said before, he had a terrifically dry sense of humour, and you could be 99 per cent sure that he was not kidding, but never 100 per cent sure!

Grandad Eley seldom smiled and had a sad, solemn expression most of the time. Come to think of it, I don't remember him laughing at all. My Dad always said he had a 'Buster Keaton' face. I am sure that his seriousness was the main reason for his unpopularity among some family members. Those who called him 'Happy Harry', with sarcasm, apparently ignored the fact that he had a hard life, having to cope with three wars, a broken marriage, and long term injuries from the 1918 war. I had a pretty good relationship with Grandad Eley though; it was much better than the almost non-existent one that I had with Grandad

Goodwin. I'll tell you about my Dad's side of the family later. Grandad Eley played his old 78rpm gramophone records for me whenever he saw the chance. This, I am sure, influenced my appreciation of music in later years. Some of the pieces we listened to were 'Pagliacci' (Caruso) and 'Sonny Boy' (Jolson). The Caruso record was about twenty years old at the time, but the Al Jolson record was almost brand new, from about 1928!

♪

During the 1930s my life moved a little faster. Not much, but just a little. We moved from Prioress House to Baker House, a distance of about a half-mile. Our new address was 24 Baker House, Bromley High Street, Bow. Why did we make this move? I don't know. It probably had a lot to do with the rent. We lived on the third (top) floor, again. The coal for burning in the fireplace had to be lugged up the stairs by our poor sweaty coal man and dumped in the bathtub for storage. Similar to Prioress House, there was no elevator, and, of course no fridge, so all shopping was done on a daily basis. Everything had to be carried up or down the three flights of stairs. This made life very difficult for everyone except the children. Singing and yelling in the stairwell made a loud echo, so every day we would make as much noise as possible, just for fun. The other tenants would not only grumble about having to struggle up and down the stairs, but also about the noise, especially the piercing whistling.

There was no such thing as a dishwasher, washing machine or clothes dryer, so if we had laundry to do, we either did it in the sink in winter or in the bathtub in summer, depending on whether or not you needed to store coal. After doing the laundry it became necessary to dry it. That was easy – take it downstairs and hang the washing on the clotheslines provided in the courtyard. We would, of course, have to watch out for children riding their bikes headfirst into our sheets. The last operation for the day was to go downstairs to pick up the laundry, wet or dry, and carry it upstairs. If it was still wet we would just have to hope for good drying weather the next day and try again. Good drying weather means that it's not raining or humid, but windy. It doesn't have to be sunny! Taking the laundry to the bathhouse in Old Ford Road could save a lot of time and trouble. But this meant a bus trip and money for the service. The best deal here was for a wash and part dry so the laundry was damp. This way it was cheaper, and we could finish the drying at home. However, the cost was always a problem.

Dad didn't earn very much money. He worked for his father as a scrap iron and metal merchant. My Grandfather Goodwin started the business T. Goodwin & Sons Ltd in the year 1899. He bought machinery to break up, cleared warehouses of any kind of material and did any kind of work or service for a fee. My Grandfather lived with his very large family at his place of business, 82 Braintree Street, Bethnal Green, E2. Some of Grandad's children grew up and left home, like my Dad who was the oldest, while others were still very young. Nan and Grandad Goodwin had eleven children: five boys and six girls. (Again, the Family Tree will give you the details.) I did not get to know them very well. We didn't visit them like we did the Eleys. Whenever we did visit, we were lectured and told 'be good', and 'behave yourselves'. I have a very dim recollection of listening to Grandma Goodwin talking in her living room. She died shortly after this around 1937, some time before the war started, when I was about eight years old. I remember that their house was very posh, at least to my eyes. There was a parlor, where the piano was kept, which was literally entered on tiptoe. All the furniture and floorboards were polished to a brilliant shine and all the linen looked as though it had just been ironed. The house at 82 Braintree Street was, in fact, very very small.

One time, when I was seven, Dad took me to work with him on a Saturday morning. We walked to Bow Road where we caught a tram (which had an open upper deck – no roof.) to Stepney Green underground station. From there it was a ten-minute walk to Braintree Street. Dad was in his element in the yard there. The most important part of his work was to know the difference between what he called 'metal' and 'iron'. Iron varied from tin cans that were almost worthless, through light steel and heavy steel to cast steel and cast iron. A few pounds of iron either way would be of very little significance when adding up what a load was worth. Metal was a different case. Metal was basically non-ferrous (non-iron) material, such as copper, lead and aluminum. In most cases it was worth much more than iron, but only if it was clean. Being clean meant being uncontaminated with other materials, no matter what they are. So you could have a brass valve with a galvanised iron handle. You would have to separate the parts, if necessary cutting out rusted and broken iron screws with a hammer and chisel, and removing washers to make the metal clean.

There are probably at least 500 different non-ferrous metals in common use, from aluminum to lead, and Dad knew 490 of them. The prices of metals varied day to day in accordance with what happened on the stock exchange. All this was of course scrap metal, but if you sell your metal to a foundry, and they put it in the melting pot, it magically becomes brand new again. However, if we were saving a sack of gunmetal, and a piece of common brass got tossed in by mistake, and the error was not noticed, then the gunmetal would be spoiled, or contaminated by the brass when melted. Local foundries, over the years, got to know their suppliers and whether or not they could be trusted to supply clean metal. This was the gist of the lecture I got from Dad that Saturday morning when he took me to work. It was also the most important part. Of secondary importance was to be careful using tools, don't hurt yourself, and, "whatever your Grandfather says, answer 'yes'."

I worked hard, taking apart small mechanisms that were screwed or bolted together, and carefully carrying the iron and steel pieces along the yard to dump them on the correct pile. During the course of the morning, Dad took me to breakfast at a local cafe. Then we worked some more till about noon. Now I was tired. Then Dad called me, "Tommy, your Grandfather wants to see you. He's in the parlor." I can still feel the discomfort of going into the house alone. It was quiet. Nobody was home except Grandad, and he was waiting for me in the parlor with a large glass of port wine in one hand and a bright, new half-crown in the other. "Your wages," he said, and handed me the coin. A little later, Dad and I got ready for the trip back home. While we were on our way to the tram, Dad said to me, "Don't say anything to your Ma about the port wine."

"Okay," I said.

♫

The 1930s are, to my mind, a little hazy. There were, I am sure, many happenings that took place, which are no longer in my memory. There are, however, a few scenes that still stay with me today. Money was so scarce that a newspaper was used as a tablecloth at mealtimes. However, there was always food on the table, even if it was only fish and chips or pie and mash. There were a few times when we had porridge for our midday dinner, followed by a slice of bread sprinkled with sugar for afters, but this was very rare. Mum managed to get a proper meal on the table practically every day in spite of the lack of money. She aimed for meat, potatoes and greens whenever possible.

I remember one time in particular when there was too much food on my plate. After misbehaving in some way, I tried to gain sympathy by refusing to finish my dinner. There was a big argument. Then tears. Then Dad sent me to bed early in disgrace. But I didn't care; I felt I had won by not finishing my dinner. The next morning everything seemed alright when I went to school. Then at about 10am, my mother marched straight into school. Right into the classroom. With everyone watching. Carrying my dinner from last night that I didn't finish. She explained to the teacher, with the whole class listening, about my tantrum. Of course, the teacher agreed with Mum that the dinner could not be wasted. So, I was trapped. I had to eat it then and there. Every bit of it. With everyone staring at me!

The gas at Elderfield Road and the electricity in Bow were on the meter system. This meant we had to pay for it as we needed it. Sometimes, we ran out before Dad came home from work. We would sit around the fire and Mum would sing songs like *'Clap your hands till Daddy comes home, Daddy will bring us a shilling home'*. This method worked except for at least one time when Daddy came home with no money. He would have to ask a neighbor for a loan, which was an embarrassment, even if it was only a shilling.
    During the 30s we went on one holiday that I can remember – I think it was in 1937. No one got a holiday from his job, except for Christmas Day and August Bank Holiday Monday. Dad came along for the long weekend but then had to go back to London for work on Tuesday, but came back to fetch us at the end of the week. He was able to borrow a car from a friend and take the three children and Mum to a spot on the River Crouch in Essex. There we rented a barge for a week, and shared the cost with Aunt Nell, Mum's sister. Our big excitement that week was looking for pearls in the oysters that were abundant at that spot. We didn't find any pearls, only oysters.
    I was not, at this time in my young life, following the national and world news, but the history books tell us that Winston Churchill warned the British Parliament of the German air menace in 1934, and Oswald Mosley, the Fascist, led an anti-Jewish march in Whitechapel in 1936. I remember Mum saying many times, "Churchill is a war-monger," while Dad would say "He's the one, Churchill's the one. He won't stand for any nonsense from Hitler. In any case, Britain is unbeatable. We've got the best Army, Navy, and Air Force in the world." I guess Mum and Dad were both correct in their summing up of the situation eventually. One thing is for sure: our family was patriotic with a capital P. We appreciated our history going back to 1066 and before. We loved our King, and when he died we loved his successor just as much. We earnestly believed 'British is Best'. In every way. This attitude was prevalent, in my memory, among the so-called working class Cockneys in the mid-to-late 1930s.
    On a more mundane level, I can remember misbehaving one time and getting Mum upset with me. (I think I misbehaved a lot when I was a youngster.) Not only was I naughty, I was cheeky as well. I can remember the punishment as though it were yesterday. She sent me to the local oil shop with a sixpenny piece to buy a cane. The storekeeper asked me what Mummy wanted the cane for – I suppose he thought he was being friendly, but I burst into tears and said, "She's going to hit me with it." The storekeeper must have thought it was funny and started to laugh. He chose a cane, assuring me that it was a good strong cane and would not break.

♪

It is not often that one can pinpoint a particular day in a span of seventy or so years, and know without a shadow of a doubt exactly what one was doing on that day. An example of this would be the assassination of John F Kennedy in 1963. Anyone who was at least four at that time will know what they were doing when they heard that Kennedy had been shot. (I was at home in Johannesburg when I received a call with the news.) My knowledge of a particular day goes back a few more years than that. On January 20th 1936, I was a patient at Shooters Hill Children's Hospital, in south east London. My reason for being there, if I remember correctly, was scarlet fever. During the course of the day the nurses and sisters came around to every child and tied a black ribbon on the child's arm. The nurse who tied on my black armband was crying. When I asked her what was happening, she answered emotionally that the King was dead. The King, George V, was the father of Edward VIII, the Prince of Wales and next King of England. I remember becoming quite upset over the King's death, but only because the nurses were upset. The details of the day before and the day after are gone forever, but January 20th 1936 sticks in my mind like glue. Incidentally, Edward was not crowned King. As you probably know, he abdicated the throne in order to marry Wallis Simpson, an American divorcee. (He was then given the title of Duke of Windsor; his wife being known as Duchess of Windsor.) Edward's brother George became King George VI in time to lead us through the coming war.

During this period before the war, we were living through the depression, which was just as bad as the depression in the USA. The difference between these years and the early 1930s was that I now took an active part in trying to 'make ends meet' at home. Sometimes I went to the fish shop for Mum. To get to the fish and chip shop, I walked to Prioress House and turned right onto Saint Leonard's Street. The fish shop was on the left in the area of Franklin, Washington, Jefferson, and Sherman streets. There was an influence there that I did not realise at the time; I guess some Americans had a hand in naming those streets. Mum did a good job in priming me on what to say when I got to the shop and how to say it. I had to stand in line with five or six local women, some of whom recognized me. When the shopkeeper held out his hand for the money I had to give my little speech. "Four nice pieces of skate, and six penn'orth of chips. Mummy said can I have the fish and chips now and she'll pay you in a day or two."

The man looked at me as though I had crawled out of an apple. "Your Mum owes me for last week; when is she going to pay her debts?"

I answered, "I don't know. She said she'll pay you in a day or two."

With a glare of frustration the man eventually took pity on me. After a lot of moaning and groaning he gave me the package of fish and chips which I carried home in triumph.

Making ends meet was a daily struggle that became more and more difficult as time went on. I didn't blame Mum for not wanting to face the people to whom she owed money. She certainly didn't borrow for fun. There were a few times when we needed extra money, to pay the rent perhaps, or to catch up with clothing needs and insurance. For this, the pawnshop was made to measure. Our local pawnshop was on the corner of Three Mill Lane and Imperial Street, behind Fraser & Fraser Limited, (the company where I worked from the age of fourteen up until I entered the National Service at twenty-one), not far past the fish and chip shop on the left. Mum often took me along, not because she wanted my company, but because she needed moral support. We were very poor, so we had to borrow money, but we still had pride in ourselves and it was difficult to face people.

I reckon the first time that I saw the inside of that pawnshop, or as some called it the pledge office, was around 1937, when I was seven or eight. The favourite item for raising money at the pawnshop was the wedding ring. Most women had one, and there was no disputing the value of it. This is how the system worked: you had to bring something of value to the pawnbroker, a piece of jewellery, a watch, Daddy's shoes, a blanket, a pair of sheets, Daddy's best suit, almost anything you can think of. The pawnbroker then estimated how much the item was worth. Then, he would or would not decide to lend some money, usually a small percentage of his estimate. He then kept the item for which he gave you a receipt. When you had some money again you could redeem your item. You then presented your ticket, repaid the loan, and also paid a fee that became the pawnbroker's profit. If you decided not to redeem the item, or if you could not afford to redeem it, then the item became the property of the pawnbroker. This business was very profitable, with no risk, and a good chance of the broker legally getting something for almost nothing.

The first time I went with Mum to the pawnshop, the broker told her that he was not allowed to deal with anyone under eighteen years of age. So Mum worked out a deal with a woman who sat in that shop practically all the time. Marie sat there waiting for people like me to come in. Then, for a shilling or two she would take the item, deal with the broker, getting as much as possible for the loan, and finally hand me the loan and the ticket. This system meant that I could go to the pawnshop by myself legally without Mum having to be there.

I remember Dad being annoyed once when he discovered that his suit had been pawned. He said, "Pawn the shoes if you must but stay clear of the suit."

"Sorry," said Mum, "We had to pawn the shoes and the suit." It was winter so we could not pawn the blankets, so Dad had to agree.

The broker would not take Mum's coat or her frocks, and there was no way that Mum's wedding ring would be pawned, so there was no choice. The end of the week was usually better. Dad got paid, so we were able to clear up the debts and get our things out of pawn. Once in a while there was a celebration; Dad would take us to the pictures on a Saturday afternoon, although Mum never came. I think she stayed home because of Roy, as he was still only three or four years old. The movies we saw were at the picture palace, which cost about sixpence. It was possible to go to the pictures for a penny; even a ha'penny but these were usually 'magic lantern' or slide shows featuring Charlie Chaplin, and silent movies.

To make things more difficult during this period of near poverty, I wanted a bike. The make, color, and size didn't matter to me. Any old second-hand, rusty, broken-down thing would do. "When our ship comes home," was the way Dad explained it to me. "We have to be patient." In the meantime he said we could make a scooter which would be almost as good as a bike and it wouldn't cost anything. So, we made a scooter from thrown away junk borrowed from the scrap yard, and what a beauty it was. Dad was expert at making something from nothing and this was a good example of his ability. I still have two modern versions of that scooter in the garage of my house in Piscataway, ones that I made many years later for my two children.

Dad often took me to Petticoat Lane for the famous Sunday morning market, where our main job was to buy mint, costing one or two pence. Later, we chopped the mint and mixed in some vinegar and sugar to make our own mint sauce. This was necessary for lamb and essential for mutton, which we had most Sundays for lunch. While we were at Petticoat Lane, Dad browsed around the stalls looking for anything that could be useful. Once he picked up a wireless in kit form. After struggling with it for a few evenings after work he got it to go. We were all very impressed; it was like magic hearing music come from the box with no wires. This was when wirelesses had accumulators as a power source as so many people had gas rather than electricity in their houses. The accumulators had to be charged up regularly, like batteries. In fact, they were similar to the batteries used today in cars.

We are still in the period immediately before the war started. When I say the war, I mean of course the Second World War which for us Brits lasted from 1939 to 1945, and for the Americans from 1941 to 1945. It was about 1938 when Dad took me to the shipping yard of a Jewish merchant, George Cohen Sons & Co, 600 Commercial Road, Bidder St, Canning Town, London. He had a load of scrap steel on Grandad

Goodwin's truck that he was selling to Cohen's. A full load on that truck was about five tons. Dad parked his truck in a spot that was accessible to a crane on the dockside of Regent's canal. The crane was loading the scrap steel onto a ship docked there. There was a seafaring man leaning on a ship's rail, way above us. "*Guten Morgen mein kamerad,*" he called to us. "*Unt vie getes?*" Dad and I just looked at each other. I expected Dad to know what the man had said. "I think he said, 'Good morning my friend and how are you?' The man and his ship are German," Dad explained, "and he comes here regularly to buy steel from Cohen's to take back to Germany." Many years were to go by until the irony of it struck me. Here was Cohen of London selling steel to Germany, and that same steel might have come back in a year or two as bombs! Who knows?

There are a few more things worth mentioning in the last year or two before the war. The most important, in my view, is the problem I had in seeing clearly. I was short-sighted and unable to make out details of things. Worse yet, I didn't tell anybody. In school, if the teacher wrote notes or problems on the blackboard, I couldn't see them so I had to try to copy the questions from one of the pupils without seeming to cheat. This was very difficult but I was able to cover up my deficiency for a long time. Why didn't I tell someone? I guess the answer to that is that kids who wore glasses were laughed at in school, so I was afraid to. Consequently, I suffered in silence, sometimes sneaking out to the toilet so that I would walk near the blackboard to see the question. The longer I kept my secret, the harder it became to talk about it. I can remember the teacher saying to me once, "I can't understand you; you are top of the class one day and a complete dunce the next – why don't you try to concentrate more?"

I came very close once to being found out about my poor eyesight. The teacher held a class with the subject of 'looking and seeing'. Unfortunately, I could only get a seat in the back of the class. A projector was rigged up and the teacher put in a one-pound note. "Can anyone read what it says at the top?" he asked the boy next to me. This is it, I thought, I am now going to make a fool of myself. After he questioned about eight boys, a miracle happened; he passed me by! The point of this looking exercise was to see that the note read 'I promise to pay...' and most people did not see that the *I* and the *P* were intertwined so that it looked like 'Promise to pay...'. I have been carrying this little story in my head all these years. It just goes to show what an impression it made on me, and how worried I was at the time. I have just looked at an American one-dollar bill. I see nothing about promising to pay. The British pound is now minted as a coin so is too small for the promise to pay inscription, but the larger-denomination bank notes still say 'I promise to pay'.

CHAPTER 2

World War II

1939 – 1945

BY 1939, we all knew that trouble was brewing. We had no TV to tell us the news, of course, but there was radio and the newspaper. The big news in the first half of 1939 was that it seemed as though the Great War of 1914 to 1918 was about to be continued. The talk was of zeppelins, bombing raids, Adolf Hitler, and poison gas. The big scare however was the poison gas. In the summer of 1939, probably at the end of July, the local children of Bow E3 all trooped into school one day, not for lessons, but to be fitted with gas masks. That day is still remembered. It was not very pleasant. Roy made a big fuss, and wouldn't stop crying and yelling when someone tried to fit a gas mask on his face. He was six years old, and people were telling him that he *had* to get a mask or the poison gas would kill him. I felt sorry for the teachers who were given the job of making sure that everyone got a mask that fitted properly. Believe it or not, the easiest ones to process were the babies and toddlers.

After a gas mask was fitted, I was shown how to put it on and take it off, how to care for it, and, of course, the mask and its carry case were marked with my name. The stink of the rubber is still, after all those years, in my nostrils. I can remember being very happy to get out of the classroom that day. There was so much activity, children crying, some of the older ones taking advantage and fooling around, and everybody in authority worrying, frantic, and trying to work faster, because the gas bombs could be dropped on London at any time. The rumor was circulating that the Germans had some poison gas left over from the last war. It turned out that the whole gas mask exercise was unnecessary. Poison gas was not released anywhere in Britain either before or during the war. Of course, no one knew this at the time so we had to be prepared – just in case.

I had my tenth birthday the following month. The memory of it has gone from my mind and I can't even remember what birthday presents I got. Or whether I got any. The only thing that was on my mind was that there was going to be a war! Everybody was talking about it, wondering what would happen, when it would start, how long it would last. Roy got confused and mixed together germs and Germans. He knew that both of them were bad. The Government had already decided to evacuate all the children from heavily congested areas such as the East End of London to the countryside and to the less densely populated parts of the country. "We have to look after the next generation," they said, "These children are our future." The plan was to hide as many children as possible by scattering them around the country. This way there would be a smaller percentage of deaths for each bombing raid. The railroads were commandeered by the authorities for this exercise and the plan went into effect at the end of August 1939.

The borough of Bow assigned the three Goodwin children to a train due to leave Bromley on Friday September 1st. Our destination was to be Oxford. What excitement! Would Mum and Dad come with us? The answer to that, unfortunately, was no. Dad's work, the acquisition of steel and other metals, was given the category of 'essential war work', so he would have to stay in London and work. Mum was not pregnant, had no very young children, and was fit enough to work, so she was assigned to the Land Army. This was a group that was required to work on farms and in the fields in what was called 'food production'. Some mothers went with their children on evacuation, but we were not that lucky.

Mum now had a big problem in getting us ready for the evacuation in a few days' time. We had no suitcases, kit bags, or any other carrying case. We had to take our belongings with us to Oxford: how were we going to carry them? We certainly had no money to spend on suitcases. The night before we were due to go, we had a short family conference, lasting about ten minutes. Dad used his stern voice so we knew that whatever this was about, it was important. "You are the oldest, Tommy, and your mother and I won't be there, so you are in charge from now on. Look after Gladys and Roy as though *you* are their father." Wagging his finger at the other two, he said, "Gladys and Roy, you must behave yourselves and do anything that Tommy tells you. Woe betide you if I hear a bad report." This was basically the end of the session, except that Gladys started asking questions about my authority, and how she could dodge it. Then Mum started: "Brothers and sisters should look after each other, the situation is already bad, don't make it worse. If I hear that you misbehaved, there will be ructions." The other two became contrite, and promised to be good.

Later that night, after we all went to sleep, I woke up. I could hear someone in the living room. I got out of bed to find out who it was, because it was late. I found Mum, sitting in the armchair, sewing. She was cutting and sewing some old pillowcases to make carry bags with shoulder straps. "It's alright, Tommy," she said, "I'm making three of these; one for each of you, and they are finished now, so go back to bed."

♪

We all got up early. It was the day we were to be evacuated from the East End of London. Mum made a special breakfast of kippers for her and Dad, and boiled eggs for Gladys, Roy, and me. Dad had to go to work, so he kissed us goodbye. "Look after yourselves and be good," he called out from the courtyard. Mum was already crying, so we suddenly became demure, quiet, and well behaved. We were much too early for the train, so we spent some time organizing and re-packing our pillowcase carry bags. Mum had torn up an old bed sheet to make carrying straps, and to reinforce the corners. The bags looked quite presentable, but we discovered a slight problem. When the bags were filled with shirts, underwear, socks, spare shoes, raincoat, etc, and also personal things like favorite toys, they became very heavy. Naturally, the younger two complained that the bags were too heavy and the straps were hurting their shoulders. After negotiations were completed, we worked out a deal where I carried two bags and Gladys and Roy shared the other one. I guess that was fair as I was ten, Gladys was eight (and a girl), and Roy was six.

When it was time to go, we went to the local school to form up into 'crocodile' lines with families together. Everyone was given a name-tag which had not only the person's name, but also their destination and train number marked on it. This was to ensure that no one got lost. The system worked; we did not hear of anybody getting lost. The crocodile line moved out of the school yard and into Bromley High Street, turning right onto Saint Leonard's Street, past the fish and chip shop on the left, the little park on the right and the pawnshop on the left. Then up the hill making its way towards Bromley-by-Bow Station, which was not only an underground, but also a main line station. The police were out in full force, taking charge of the situation, and holding up the traffic for us. Mum helped carry the bags for part of the way, but when we got to the station she had to let us go. No one was allowed to go into the station except the children with tags, and the authorities in charge. Some of these escorts were schoolteachers; some were church people, among others, who were obviously part of the 'system'. Mum was very upset about the situation, and wanted to come into the station with us but there was nothing we could do about it. Unfortunately, there were lots of other mothers who were crying and making a fuss about the separation, and this affected Roy and Gladys, so it became a relief when the mothers finally bid their children goodbye.

We settled in the train, ate some sandwiches, and sang songs like 'Daisy' and 'Tipperary' all the way to Oxford. We left London late morning and arrived in Oxford about two hours later, after an uneventful journey. Our escorts had cheered us up tremendously with songs and stories, so everyone was in a good mood. Everyone, that is, except me! I had previously managed to buy two comics: *The Dandy* and *Beano*. They were my favorites, one of the characters being Desperate Dan, who would eat cow pies at one sitting. The pies were huge and had horns sticking out of the top. Both these comics were gone. I hunted through all of our things, and ended up almost in tears, but the comics had disappeared. I was to think about those comics many times later; in fact I'm thinking of them now and what a shame it was that I lost them. Happiness consists of such small things.

The children, on arrival at Oxford Station, were all transferred to various temporary rest areas-local schools and church halls – where we were organized into groups according to family, age, and sex. I guess that there were about two or three hundred children on the train. Our escorts did the groupings, which turned out to be a very difficult job. In general, the local people would take children into their homes for an unspecified period of time. Maybe for a week, a month, or a year or more. Who knows? In return, the person taking the child received a cash payment. So much a week. Obviously, a lot of people had been working on this project of evacuating children from the East End of London for a long time. Nobody *had* to take a child. Everyone had a choice. In fact, everyone had too many choices. "One child, no older than two years, please."

"Two children, girls, between six and eight years old."

"One boy, at least twelve years old." The different combinations were never-ending and always changing.

It was easy to see that some people needed a boy to do odd jobs around the house. Some wanted a very young one in order to get their money with the least amount of hassle. The great majority of citizens, however, were there to look after the children, with no thought of personal gain from the situation. Even so, the job was very difficult because some families had more than two children. It was easy to break up four – two and two, but how to break up families of three or five when nobody wants more than two? One child would have to be carried away, alone, and one or two groups of two each would be taken to other foster homes.

We had started our day very early in London, and after a boring and tiring day we finished up alongside about fifty others of all ages in a church hall. The hours crept slowly by, and during the afternoon we had some rain. What a surprise. Then it suddenly dawned on us. *We couldn't go home*! Roy and Gladys cuddled up and went to sleep on a bench. I got dejected about my missing comics. After a while we got to the top of the list and we were interviewed by quite a few potential foster parents. But nobody wanted three. Two was the limit that anyone would take, so what happened now? I couldn't let Roy go to a stranger by himself; that was out of the question. I was sure that he could not handle that situation. Then with Gladys I had a special problem. "Keep your eyes on Gladys," both Mum and Dad had told me the night before, "watch out in case a strange man or older boy tries to talk to her." Don't forget that this was 1939, and I had received no sexual education from school or home. I could not see any problem with strange men talking to Gladys. However, both Mum and Dad had warned me to take care, so I was determined to keep my eyes on her. The third possibility was for *me* to go to a foster home alone. But I couldn't do that, as then I could not watch over Gladys.

We ended up being among the very last to be billeted, on a temporary basis. Our escort, a lady from the WVS (Women's Voluntary Service), remembered a local homeowner named Hazel Hurst, who had earlier promised, under pressure, to help out only if it became absolutely necessary. Well, it was now necessary, so we were bundled into a car and driven to Mrs Hurst's house. It was now dark, probably about 8pm and raining a little. We all stood at the front door – Mr and Mrs Hurst, our WVS lady and the three Goodwin children – all discussing the next move. "I'll take them on two conditions," said Mrs Hurst eventually. "One is that I'll have them for two weeks only and then they move to somewhere else. I'm too old to look after such young children. Two is that you must call me by my correct name which is Mrs Hazelhurst!" This made everyone laugh. We were all invited in for the inevitable cup of tea.

Our first day with the Hazelhursts in Oxford was, for me, very exciting. Mr Hazelhurst sat with me in the kitchen for breakfast while Mrs H looked after the other two. Mr H spread out a map of the area to show me where we were and how to get to the shops, etc. Then he got two bicycles out from the garden shed and took me on a tour of the district. I believe our address was Bartlemas Road. If you walk along Cowley Road towards Oxford and turn in to Bartlemas Road on the right, it was about the third or fourth house on the left. Then if you turn around again and walk back to Cowley Road, turn left, and walk two hundred feet or so, you can look across Cowley Road and see a cinema (which is now a Bingo Hall). This was the area where I was to spend my time. The River Thames was about three-quarters of a mile from Bartlemas Road. This was my link with London. I figured out that if I needed to get back home fast, I could always walk along the bank of the river and I would get to London without getting lost. Dreamer! I was still only ten years old but growing up fast. London to Oxford was about sixty miles as the crow flies, but more than a hundred by river.

On that first day in Oxford, Mr H showed me how to get around the south area of Oxford without getting lost. It was Saturday, but we had a visitor who seemed to know all about us. I was told to attend school on Monday. What a rotten deal! We had been sure that school would be out of the question for a couple of weeks at least. Our visitor, who was obviously from the local school board, explained the situation to us. There were now in Oxford, too many children and not enough schools and teachers. This would be rectified eventually, but right now there was a problem. So, the 'out of towners' would attend school in the morning and the local children would go to school in the afternoon. That way, everybody received at least some schooling.

A British Note, which had been presented in Berlin at 9am on Sunday September 3rd 1939, gave the German Government two hours in which to give an undertaking to withdraw their invasion troops from Poland. As we all now know, this undertaking was not given. On Sunday evening, the King broadcast a message to his people from his study at Buckingham Palace. He said that we had been forced into a conflict, and it was unthinkable that we should refuse to meet the challenge. The King also asked the people to stand calm, firm, and united in this time of trial. Everyone listened to the King's speech. We were all very patriotic, and vowed that we would finish Jerry properly this time and not let him off the hook, like we had done in 1918. We were at war with Germany. The Prime Minister, Neville Chamberlain, chose a War Cabinet that included Winston Churchill, First Lord of the Admiralty, at the age of sixty-four. Later in this war, we were all to fervently say, "Thank God for Winston Churchill."

I counted the years – now I am ten. In six years at the age of sixteen I would be eligible for military service. That was so far in the future that I could safely forget about it. Meanwhile, this was like being on holiday. Half-days at school were great. On my first day, the teacher put me at the back of the class, and then stood right behind me. There was no escape from not being able to see the blackboard now. Within five minutes of starting my first half-day she was able to figure out what my problem was. I couldn't see properly. She took me to the front of the class, and made sure that I could see what she had written on the blackboard. Shortly after, I got spectacles, which made such a difference to me. It's very easy to see where the word spectacular comes from. Now, I could see individual leaves on a tree rather than a shapeless mass.

♫

The Hazelhursts made us very welcome for the short time that we stayed with them. He played the violin and she played viola with a local group of musicians. They practised every day in their living room: classical music, not popular, or jazz. Unfortunately, Gladys and Roy chose this period to go to pieces. They ran a little wild, mocking and giggling, becoming almost impossible to control. I believe that the Hazelhursts understood this as a natural reaction to the recent happenings, so they put up with it, and made no complaints. Mr H was almost completely bald, and had a full beard and moustache. This sent Gladys and Roy into hysterics. They said things like, "Hey, your hair is all upside down." I remember feeling embarrassment over this, but everything became normal again after a day or two.

The Hazelhursts were older people, probably in their fifties, maybe close to sixty. They had a son living at home: Stanley, who was, I believe, an Oxford student of around the age of twenty or so. Stanley showed me the long bow that he was making in his spare time. It was six feet long, so that a man six feet one inch tall could use it in comfort with a half inch or so clearance from the ground. I tried to bend the bow, but found that I was unable to do it. I was too small, and not strong enough. Stanley explained to me how a long bow is usually made to suit one particular person. For best results, it was made to measure. The other type of bow was the crossbow, but Stanley turned his nose up at that. The long bow is a part of English history, he said. The crossbow is foreign.

The Hazelhursts' house and garden were very small. However, that didn't stop them from installing an air raid shelter. While we were billeted with them, they were putting together the finishing touches. The Anderson shelter was about six or seven feet square and five feet high. The Government supplied the shelters at no cost, pre-fabricated from galvanized corrugated iron for the homeowner to install. A hole in the garden had to be dug big enough to take the shelter, and deep enough, so that the earth left over would provide a two-foot deep cover on the roof of the Anderson. Then a door was fitted, along with steps for access. Luxuries could then be taken care of, such as painting, bunk beds, and paraphernalia for making tea, a camp stove, etc.

One day, Mr Hazelhurst put us in the street near the front gate and told us to make for the shelter when we heard the pretend air raid warning. Then he sat in the shelter and made a moaning noise to simulate an air raid. We ran through the house, whooping and yelling, and we all climbed into the shelter, where Mr H was counting the seconds on his stopwatch. "Well done," he said, "less than thirty seconds." Of course this was a game he was playing with us. He was showing us that even though there was a war on we could still have some fun. This little exercise also taught us a valuable lesson about what to do and how to do it when the time came. After the fifth or sixth practice air raid, we casually dropped what we were doing and walked swiftly to the air raid shelter with no fuss.

There were many thousands of these Anderson air raid shelters installed all over the country, and mostly they were put in by the home-owner by hand as there was not enough space to use a back-hoe or tractor. In many cases, including the Hazelhursts, neighbors pooled their resources and helped each other. After the shelter was finished, most people planted ivy, flowers, and other plants to cover it up. Later, when food became scarce, onions, tomatoes, and potatoes replaced the flowers.

As soon as we got ourselves settled in with the Hazelhursts, we had to move. I don't remember the name of the people we got billeted with next, but they lived about half a mile closer to the center of Oxford in a side street on the other side of Cowley Road. They were younger people, probably late twenties, with a couple of children of their own. The man of the house was a pigeon fancier. That's all I remember about them except that they were not very kind to us. They were among the few people who were out to benefit themselves at the expense of the evacuees.

I sent a letter off to Mum telling her that we all were very unhappy with this situation and asking if there was anything that could be done about it. We discovered very quickly that something certainly could be done. About two or three days after I sent the note, we had a ring at the door. Guess what? There stood Mum and Dad. Within five minutes, all our things were packed and we were in a taxi headed towards the home of Mr and Mrs Judkin. Mum and Dad did not argue, or fuss, with our previous guardians. We were whisked away like magic to our new temporary home. The whole operation took no more than half an hour, and then there we were, sitting in the Judkins' kitchen.

The Judkins were stern, no-nonsense people, but kind. They were middle aged, probably between forty and fifty, with no children of their own. They lived in a small two-storey house on the side of a small hill about a quarter or half a mile from where the Hazelhursts lived. Mr J worked at the Cowley Morris Works where they built the Morris motor cars (now owned by BMW). He rode to work on a bicycle but there was a bus for bad weather.

As soon as we became established in the Judkins' home we were given assignments. Jobs to do! My job was to care for everyones' shoes and boots. I don't remember how many pairs there were, but there were a lot. At least fifteen, maybe twenty. Some black, some brown, some special like Mrs J's white and pink ones. I soon learned how to do the job properly. If I put someone's shoes back in the closet with mud or smears on them I got a ticking off from Mrs J, along with a lecture on whether I should have used a rag or a brush, and how to apply the polish stringently without waste. Her lecture usually ended with the promise that she would let Mr J know when he came home from work. Gladys's work consisted of helping Mrs J with bed making and washing up. The bed making, of course, included making hospital corners. Once in a while I would help with the beds, such as, for instance, when the sheets were changed. This was where I learned to make hospital corners and to be very fussy about things being correct.

Roy, being very young, got the job of looking after the Judkins' dog. This included combing, brushing, looking after the dog's food and water and, worst of all, cleaning up its mess. The dog was very big; Gladys and Roy could ride it like a horse, but Mrs J got upset when she saw that, and again promised to tell Mr J when he came home from work. Gladys got the same threat when she did something wrong, like breaking a cup or spilling some water. Poor Mr J! After a day's work he came home to listen to his wife rattling on about what the Cockney kids had done that day. *Then*, he would have to give us a mini-lecture on do's and don'ts before being allowed to collapse, with a pint of beer, into his favorite armchair. Both Mr and Mrs Judkin were kind to us, and they looked after us properly. We always had good food and enough of it. However, we were rebellious to Mrs J, almost for fun. We were, to coin a phrase, winding her up.

The months slipped by and we got close to Christmas. A tributary of the river Thames froze and I listened to the ice creaking as I walked on it. The horse chestnuts fell from the trees. One night, Mr J came home with a handkerchief filled with dark red nuts. "Have you ever made conkers?" he asked. Well, I got the lesson. The other two were not interested, but I learned how to bake the nut on the edge of the fire, just so, how to drill a tiny hole through the thickest part of the nut, and insert a thin piece of cord which gets knotted to hold the nut on the cord.

Now, to play conkers, you had to find an adversary, and challenge him. As you held your conker up by the cord, about chin high at arm's length, he would spin his conker on a cord and finish his turn by hitting your conker with his. If your conker broke, or came off the cord, then he won and added one to his conker's score. But, if your conker survived, you would get a turn to try to break his conker, and if you succeded, you would add one to your conker's previous score, or if it was a new one it became a 'one-er'. A conker match always drew a crowd, just like a fight. It was an aggressive game. Girls did not take part in a conker match, although they did like to watch. With Mr J's guidance, I baked and drilled a really hard conker. This became a *ten-er* before it finally broke up.

Mr J loved a pint of beer but he did not frequent public houses. He would give me a quart jug and tell me to go down the hill to Cowley Road to the off licence next to a pub. I regularly did that trip for his beer, sometimes in the dark. A strange thing happened to me on one of these trips. I was on my way down to the off licence with an empty jug, when a man came out of the dark and said, "Who are you?". I couldn't see his face. There was an enforced blackout every night over the whole country, making it harder for the German air force to figure out where the towns and cities were. When I told him who I was, he slapped my face hard, first with the left and then with the right hand. I was lucky that my glasses stayed on my face; I would never have found them if they had fallen to the ground. I never discovered who that man was or why he hit me. Did he object to me because I was a Londoner? He could tell that from my accent. Was he just having fun at my expense? Was he crazy? Who knows? The puzzle will never be solved.

I had reason to go down to Cowley Road one Saturday for Mr and Mrs Judkin. They wanted a gramophone record of Flanagan and Allen singing on one side 'Run Rabbit Run' and on side two 'We're going to hang out the washing on the Siegfried Line'. The friend I brought with me insisted that we play both sides many times in the shop. "Just to be sure it's not cracked or broken," he said. I got it safely back to the Judkins' house where it was played at least a thousand times. It wasn't up to Caruso standards, or even Jolson, but I enjoyed it and learned every word and almost every note.

♫

Christmas 1939 crept up on us all. Everything was quiet. I discovered much later that this was the time of the 'Phony War'. The Germans were obviously a little hesitant to expose themselves with a hit. After all, we were the group of islands that had taken over so much of the planet that the phrase, 'The sun never sets on the British Empire' was coined. Can you blame Hitler for being so cautious? Europe settled down to a quiet watchfulness. Some of the evacuees returned to their home towns. Slowly. Then, a trickle became a flood. Some went back and stayed. Some, like the Goodwin children, went back home for a holiday. We stayed in London during December, and into January 1940. Dad was nervous in case air raids started while we were in London.

So far in the war, very little had happened. No air raids, no bombs, no troop movements or invasions. It was so quiet that people forgot that there was a war on and relaxed. Back in London before Christmas we became a family again for a few weeks. By the end of January, we had returned to Oxford stayed there until the end of May. During this period, schooling was restricted to two or three hours per day maximum. Many teachers were now in the military services, or on other important war work, so teaching was considered to be less urgent at this time. I guess it was less urgent than defending the country. However, we missed a lot of schooling that we did not catch up on. At the time, I thought it was great having so much free time and so little learning. However, since then I have regretted this lack of education.

I played conkers at every opportunity. What a lot of fun! I also played a lot of marbles in the gutter. It was quite safe; there was no petrol available, so anyone with a car put it up on blocks for the duration of the war. Spring came and went, and it was almost summer time. The news from London was good. The air raid sirens had sounded a few times, but they were all false alarms. We listened to the wireless regularly, and heard the 9 o'clock news. Well, Gladys and I listened to the news, along with Mr and Mrs Judkin, and Roy just pretended that he could understand. The wireless was, of course, our main form of entertainment. Mr J had us gathered together for a comedy program, such as ITMA (It's That Man Again), followed by the 9 o'clock news, which wasn't so funny.

The gas mask was becoming a darned nuisance. It was not very heavy, but it was always there, making a groove on my shoulder with its carrying strap. Since there were no air raids, and no gas attacks, we all began to feel a sense of security and gradually started to leave our gas masks at home when going out.

Mum came to visit us some time in May. She had been working on a farm in what was called the Land Army. Now the situation had changed, and she was going to return to 24 Baker House in London. Gladys and Roy were ecstatic – and I was too. "Can we go back to London, Mum? Please! What does Dad say?" we all cheered. Well, for one reason or another, the Goodwin family went back to London in May 1940. I don't know if this was a good decision or not. It's easy to spot the winner on the day after the races. Many thousands of Londoners made the same decision, and returned from not only Oxford, but also from Wales, Scotland, and other outlying parts of Britain. London was not the only city that evacuated its children to safer places. Heavily populated areas, such as Birmingham and Glasgow, also had an evacuation plan that was in constant flux.

After arriving back in London, things started to happen. Some of these happenings, especially the political maneuverings, such as the re-election of F.D. Roosevelt in the United States for his third term, did not affect my life noticeably. However, food rationing suddenly became a problem. Sugar, butter, and bacon went on ration. Immediately, there were people prepared to pay more for extra rations. The black market was born. Mum and Dad were appalled that cheaters could steal food from others and get away with it. Some got away with it, but some didn't, and they went to jail. "Hooray", said Dad. It is strange how our priorities and needs change with the passage of time. If I were subjected to rationing of sugar, butter and bacon now, I wouldn't care two hoots because it would help to lower my cholesterol!

♪

The next few years of my life were spent in London. From early summer 1940, when I was still ten, until August 1943, I had one year of partial schooling at Botolph Road School, where the evacuation had begun, and one year full-time at Fairfield Road School. The other year, in case you are counting, I cannot fully account for. At this time we were living at 24 Baker House, and if you go across the street today to the Mann & Crossman's pub, the Blue Anchor, and look back across to the apartment building on your left, you'll find my old bedroom window on the third floor, at the end. There was a small grassy lawn under that window which the children used to play on before the war. Once the war started, however, the lawn was dug up, and a steel-reinforced, concrete air raid shelter was built in its place. I can remember listening to the commotion from my bedroom at closing time, and the singing that took place when the publican tried to close his pub with a 'Time, Gentlemen, please'. Everybody always wanted one more drink; everybody also wanted to be a Caruso.

By the spring of 1940, there were about 400,000 children back in London, and the Government tried to register them for a new evacuation scheme. "How many times do we have to do this?" asked Euan Wallace, an opposition politician. "Are we to subscribe to free trips in the country for these children?" he went on. But still nothing happened on the home front. Londoners were expecting imminent invasion during the summer of 1940, but the only invasion we had come from an Englishman, by the name of William Joyce, who later became a traitor by joining the Nazis. He accomplished his invasion over the airwaves, right into our homes. William Joyce called himself 'Lord HawHaw' and broadcast over the radio, boasting of how he and the Nazi hordes would smash Britain very soon. He sometimes named a town or village that was on his hit list, and the town was then bombed. The following day he bragged about the number of people killed and injured. After the war ended, Lord HawHaw was arrested, tried, convicted and hanged for treason. No one was upset by his death.

There were two main schools of thought concerning Lord HawHaw. Some people listened to his radio program with scorn, treating the whole thing like a huge joke. Others refused to acknowledge his existence. There were plenty of other things to concern us. I, personally, remember listening to him on only two or three occasions. If I were going to listen to the radio at all, then I would prefer listening to ITMA (It's That Man Again). This was a tremendously popular program with a lot of likeable characters such as Colonel Chinstrap ("I don't mind if I do"), Mrs Mopp ("Can I do you now, Sir?"), led by Tommy Handley. This radio program did more than its share of bolstering the national feelings of well being. One could truthfully claim that ITMA played an active part in the winning of the war.

Italy entered the war as an ally of Germany in June 1940. This meant, of course, that Italy was now our foe. There were not many Italians living in our area, but those that were became aliens overnight, and were rounded up. Dad knew of an Italian family who owned and operated a tea shop in Roman Road near Globe Road in Bethnal Green. He knew them as 'Dunty', but I believe their name was 'Dante'. Dad was forever talking about the three Dante brothers. One had eyes as big as tea cups, one had eyes as big as saucers, and the third had eyes as big as dinner plates. Dad reminded me that he and I had visited Dante's cafe about three or four years before.

On August 24th 1940, the first bombs fell onto central London. What a birthday present! The Germans had begun their Blitz. Our lives suddenly took on a new pattern. In the late evening the air raid siren, aptly named Moaning Minnie, would sound with the rise and fall of the warning. This meant that German bombers had been sighted, and were on their way. Everyone would gather up personal possessions, including toothbrush, keys, and post office savings book, and make their way to the air raid shelter. The shelter was quite comfortable with bunk beds and makeshift carpets and blankets. Then we would wait. And wait. And wait. Sometimes we waited until the small hours of the next morning for the German bombers to come. In that case we would make up a bunk bed and go to sleep around midnight or so. We always knew when the bombers had arrived. There was a whistling sound of the bomb falling followed by the heavy 'crump' noise of the explosion.

Although it was underground, the concrete shelter used to shake quite a lot when we got a close one, but we were safe inside it. The only way we would have a problem is if we suffered a direct hit. As Dad said, if that happened we wouldn't know anything about it. Sometimes the 'All Clear' would sound off early. Say, 9 or 10pm. That would be nice, because we could go up to our flat and sleep in our own beds, and maybe listen to the radio a little bit. The All Clear had a smooth, single-note, pleasant sound. We loved the sound of the All Clear.

However, there were no guarantees. Sometimes the air raid siren sounded again at an unearthly hour. Like 3am! Then there were moans and groans all round from everyone, even Mum. Of course it was not worth taking a chance. Every night people were dying in their warm, comfortable beds, while their safe, uncomfortable shelters were empty. It became an eternal struggle; go to the flat, get a little comfortable sleep, and run the risk of being woken up in the middle of the night by an air raid warning. Or, go straight to the shelter early, and stay there all night.

A very necessary part of the ARP (Air Raid Precautions) was the preservation of the blackout, and the responsibility of maintaining the blackout rested with the local air raid warden. The blackout meant, of course, no lights. Not only that but no flashlights or torches, no light on bikes, no street lights, no traffic lights, not even matches or cigarettes. Once darkness came, it was dark. The reason for this was to give no help to the German navigators above. Late one evening, during the beginning of the Blitzkreig (Lightning War) onslaught, Dad saw us all safely into the air raid shelter and then told Mum that he had a spare hour or two before he had to go on duty. The various duties included plane spotting, helping to get injured or dead people out of bombed buildings and houses, and taking messages between firemen and medical teams when phone lines were down.

On this one occasion, the situation was at All Clear, and it was about 10pm. Dad said, "Come with me Tommy; we'll make some tea for your Ma." So we went up to our flat and went in. "Don't turn on any lights," said Dad, "until I check the windows first." We both knew that the blackout was in force all the time. After scrutinizing the windows he was satisfied that no light could escape, so he turned on the lights. We put the kettle on to boil and started to get the tea things ready when we heard a knock on the door. It was the air raid warden. "Turn off that light," he said. "You can see it all the way from here to Berlin; turn it off!" We quickly turned all our lights off, and lit an emergency candle.

"That's funny," said Dad. "I was sure that our windows were blacked out properly, but to be doubly sure let's look again." So, we set up a step ladder and tucked in all the corners of the blackout curtains, Dad stubbing his toe a couple of times because it was really quite dark in there. "That's it," said Dad, turning on the lights. "The warden must be satisfied with that."

Five minutes later, we heard the warden yelling about the light leaking from our windows again. Dad was getting very frustrated now. He searched for a toolbox and found a hammer and tintacks and sealed all the blackout curtains around the windows. No sooner had he finished than there was a furious thumping and banging on the door. It was the warden again! "If you don't turn that light off now," he shouted, "I'll have you in court tomorrow." Dad made sure that all lights were out; he told me to stay put, and then he went with the warden down to the street. They counted the window frames from the bottom floor, one, two.

"Look at that," said Dad, "You are looking at the wrong fxxxing window, that's our neighbor on the floor below!" This was the first and only time I ever heard my Dad swear. The water had all boiled out of the kettle; we had made a big mess of the curtains and windows ("Wait till your Ma sees that tomorrow," Dad fretted), Dad had been wrongfully accused, and there was the air raid warning. I had to go down to the shelter, without the tea, and Dad had to go on all-night duty till dawn, after which he was only able to snatch a few hours' sleep before going to work.

The Blitzkrieg continued for some months – although it seemed like years – and was no fun that's for sure. The biggest problem that I had during this period was boredom. On a typical night, I would spend time waiting for either the warning, or the All Clear, or the falling bombs. Or I would sit and wait, wondering why it was so quiet out there. The days were spent trying to catch up on sleep, but I know now on reflection that I did have lots of time for schoolwork and reading that I did not utilize. One of the pastimes I became interested in was knitting. Yes, that's right, knitting. My fingers were thin and nimble enough. I was about eleven or twelve years old at the time. One of the other mothers showed me how to start or cast on, then how to knit: purl and plain, and how to finish or cast off. The first thing I knitted was a scarf made from khaki wool intended for use by our troops during the winter. I made it very long so the lucky fellow that eventually received it could wrap it around his neck and chin three or four times. Then I tried to knit a pullover, but I got into trouble because I seemed to be forever casting on or off and counting how many stitches I had on the needle. Eventually I persuaded a young woman who was an expert knitter to guide me through the complicated bits, and with her help I managed to turn out a reasonably decent pullover. It looked alright when it was finished, but at one stage it looked as though it was made for a man with three arms. It was also rather large. Even for a large man.

I played a lot of draughts but no chess. At that point in my life, I didn't know anybody who could play chess, so I didn't learn the game until many years later. However, I did at this time play the gramophone. It was a handle operated wind-up contraption that played 78rpm discs. I had to wind up the machine before every record was played. It was also necessary to install a new needle for each record. We played this gramophone every night, and got to know some of the old songs from the 1920s and 30s. We had a few records even older than that. People regularly joined in for a singsong, which created a very comfortable and friendly atmosphere. Sometimes people brought along their own records and asked me to play them, a kind of request playing.

♫

When I was about twelve or thirteen years old, I went shopping with my mum at the Roman Road market for my first pair of long trousers. I was still wearing short trousers until then, of course. All young boys did until about this age, when they were getting ready to leave school and start work. We saw a pair of long trousers for sale, second hand and cheap, about a shilling. Mum asked, "Wouldn't you like a pair of grown-up trousers for a change from wearing short ones all the time?" Oh, boy, wouldn't I!

I wore the long trousers every day, showing off in front of the other children, until one day Mum said, "Give me your trousers, I have to wash them." Oh, no! This would mean wearing my shorts to school again. I couldn't do that. Everyone would laugh at me; they would realize that we could only afford one pair of long trousers. In spite of my begging and pleading, mum washed my trousers and I had to go to school wearing shorts for a couple of days. I was mortified, but I got over it.

For quite a long time, we lived out of the shelter. Some people shared their meals with others because it was so difficult to organize shopping trips with the never-ending pattern of warning, All Clear, warning, All Clear. We never knew what was going to happen and when. Sometimes though, during this Blitz period, the German bombers that came over were on their way to designated targets in other areas. Not necessarily our street, or our house. And of course, when bombers were on their way the air raid warning was sounded so we always had a few minutes to get to a shelter. Sometimes if I was running errands at the shops, the warning would sound and I would be obliged to take cover in a stranger's shelter somewhere else. No one would allow a youngster to be out and about while a raid was in progress. Then Mum would worry until we got together again.

Hitler's Blitzkrieg became a permanent fixture in our lives. It seemed as though all of London was on fire. Early in the morning there would be smoke hanging all over the sky and civil defence workers wrapping up their hoses and gear from the previous night's raid. There were work crews trying to make damaged buildings safe. And knock them down if necessary. Then, when people were coming out of their shelters to start their day, the warning would sound once more, forcing people to take cover again. At the end of the day, after dark and once the air raid warning had sounded, the German bombers came in again. An average of 160 planes each night, according to the news reports, dropped hundreds of tons of bombs on London, causing fires that could be seen for miles. The fire fighters had a hard job trying to keep up with the new fires which were appearing all over the place. The attack on London with high explosive bombs and incendiary bombs usually continued all night until just before dawn when the cycle of events started again.

When the Blitz started, Winston Churchill, now British Prime Minister, ordered the systematic bombing of Berlin in retaliation. This period also saw the now-famous Battle of Britain. Anti-aircraft guns were located in strategic positions, and barrage balloons flew in the sky like kites. The barrage balloons were meant to stop the German planes from flying closer to the ground and becoming precise with their bombing. The RAF (Royal Air Force) operated over the south coast of England, trying to stop the Germans from reaching London with their load of bombs. These pilots of the RAF, some of them still in their teens, were the 'few' immortalized by Churchill when he said, "Never, in the field of human conflict, was so much owed by so many to so few." I still get emotionally charged when I think of these heroes and Churchill's tribute to them. In doing their duty, these youngsters marched daily to almost certain death.

While we were huddling together in our air raid shelters, looking somehow for safety, we hardly gave a thought to the German flyers operating their Junkers and Messerschmidts just a few thousand feet above our heads. One of these German flyers at that time was a young man, five years older than I was, named Friedrich. I happened to meet this fellow about forty years later in the 1980s when I attended an engineering co-ordination meeting in the offices of the American telephone company AT&T in Basking Ridge, New Jersey. He was organizing and checking an electrical layout and contract while I was responsible for piping, HVAC (heating, ventilation and air conditioning) and mechanical services on the same contract. We had to check each other's work and be sure that the electrical and mechanical contracts were compatible.

We finished our work, and then over a cup of coffee we chatted and made small talk. After comparing notes about how we had both emmigrated to the USA, we realised almost with a sense of horror that *he*, now known as Fredrick, had actually been dropping bombs on *me*, in the East End of London in the early 1940s. In some ways he was as much a victim of war as I was, as he was forced as a young man into the German airforce. We laughed at the strange situation in which we found ourselves. Sometimes truth is stranger than fiction.

♫

During this period, 1940 to 1943, we moved to a house at 266 Bancroft Road in Mile End. The reason for the move was that Mum was finding it increasingly difficult to cope with all the stairs at 24 Baker House. In addition to this, a house was considered safer than a block of flats. Ironically, our house was later blitzed when bombs landed nearby causing so much pressure that the windows smashed. Luckily no one was home at the time.

The house at 266 Bancroft was a little row house with what I called two and a half bedrooms upstairs. The first thing we did on moving in was build an Anderson air raid shelter in the back garden. There was no front garden; one step took us from the living room to the street. Across the street was a concrete wall about twenty feet high, on top of which was a railroad and shunting station. The shunting gave us a problem. "Forward a bit, 'Arry," called one voice. "Back a bit, Charley," shouted another, and the slack between the goods/ freight carriages was taken up with a bang-bang-bang-bang-bang from the train. Then the shunters called again to stop the train. The first carriage stopped with a crash and then the second and then the third came to a halt all the way down the line with a crash-crash-crash-crash, and the slack between all the carriages was given out. This shunting to get all the carriages into line and onto the right trains usually started early in the morning, about 3am, and finished when it was time to get up.

What with the aggravating noise of the shunting at the worst possible time of night, and the air raid warning sounding at a moment's notice, it's a wonder we got any sleep at all. However, we got used to it. After a few weeks I was able to sleep in the middle of the noisiest environment. By the end of 1940, the Luftwaffe eased off with the London raids, and turned its attention to Coventry, a town about sixty miles north of Oxford. Coventry was obliterated. London therefore had a respite which lasted until December 29th. That day, which was a Sunday, London was caught unaware by a tremendous fire storm raid. The firemen were taking a break, but not the Luftwaffe.

During that raid, St Paul's Cathedral was ringed by fire but untouched by the flames. This was considered by some people to be a miraculous event. This was not the first time St Paul's had been under a threatening attack. The Cathedral had previously received an 800 pound unexploded bomb on its doorstep in September. People talked long afterwards about the Miracle of St Paul's Cathedral.

♫

Harry Jones and I became best friends around 1942. The only other best friend I had ever had previously was Frankie Bozzar, whom I knew as a schoolmate in about 1936 or '37. I remembered Frankie very well because of his initials! What had his parents been thinking? Harry Joneses family must have been rich because Harry had a bike. A shop-bought one, not second hand. This gave me ammunition to start my campaign again for a bicycle, and I became a real nuisance to Mum and Dad. Being a nuisance paid off for me because one evening Dad came home carrying on his shoulder a pile of rusty junk. The junk consisted of a bike frame, a crank with two pedals, two wheels, a saddle and a chain. Dad had rescued this stuff from the scrap iron that was usually sent to the steel works. The tires were worn almost smooth, but, as Dad said, "This will be your own bike, Tommy." With a little bit of help from Harry, Dad and I scraped all the rust and paint from the various parts, and rubbed everything with sandpaper. Then we painted everything with pillar-box red paint, and hung it all up on pieces of wire in the bathroom. Mum made a fuss about the paint drippings, but we cleaned that up with turpentine.

Then we put it all together. The bike looked fine when the paint dried, but it was a little uncomfortable to ride. It was so big I could barely reach the pedals, and when I wanted to stop, I found myself way up, unable to rest my feet on the ground without falling sideways. There was no brake on the bike, but it had a fixed-wheel gear, which meant that the crank and the rear wheel had a fixed gear. No free wheeling! I used to stop the bike by trying to back pedal. This was difficult until I got the hang of it. Then I would get up speed, slow the bike down until I came to a stop, balancing dead still, and then pedal backwards. After a couple of practice sessions, I was able to go forward, backward, or balance with no movement at all. My only problem was getting off the bike after I had stopped. A couple of days later, I was able to mount and dismount in any situation.

I was so excited now that I had a bike. I didn't care if it had brakes or not, if it had gears or not, if it was too big or too small. It was mine. That week I used my pocket money to buy a padlock and chain. The bike may have been twenty years old, but I didn't want to lose it. I taught Harry Jones how to ride my bike, and sometimes we switched bikes for fun. Then I realized what a super bike he had. "When you're fourteen and you start work," said Dad, "you can earn the money to buy a new one. Meanwhile, this one is yours, and it's certainly better than no bike at all."

Harry and I spent a lot of our time near the cut, a straight course that ran through the edge of Victoria Park at Old Ford Road, about a mile and a half from where we lived. We went fishing for roach, gudgeon, and any other fresh water fish we could find there. Harry was nicknamed 'Porky' and I was called 'Slim', which should tell you something about our relative sizes. We dreamed of catching enormous, bone free, sweet tasting fish so that we could take home a delicious supper for both the Joneses and the Goodwins. We caught lots of fish, but nothing that our mothers wanted to prepare or cook for us.

Harry and I had a lot of fun fishing in the cut, but it was much more exciting working in the Jones's basement. Harry was older than I by about six months, so he had already left school. He had a job at Fraser & Fraser Ltd, with a promise of an apprenticeship in a year or two. He was all fired up with the thought of becoming a boilermaker/plater apprentice. There were all sorts of apprenticeships available: riveting, caulking, welding, blacksmithing, anglesmithing, tool and die making, and, the prize of the lot, plating. Lucky Harry was going to be a plater.

During the early months of 1943, I was still attending school, while Harry was working as a plater's mate. He brought home some small scrap pieces of steel boilerplate from the boiler shop, which we measured carefully. Then, after gauging the thickness, we marked off the location of imaginary holes, and imaginary connections to other pieces of plate. We took the dimensions for this marking off from scraps of blue prints of old completed jobs that Harry borrowed from Frasers.

In no time at all, I became hooked on the idea of becoming a boilermaker/plater apprentice when I left school. Harry and I would both be platers, but he would be foreman, and I would be chargehand because I was younger. Harry started to bring home various tools that we borrowed for the weekend, and through constant handling, we learned to be comfortable with most of the platers' tools, especially the dividers. We spent quite a few weekends studying blue prints and drawings, and becoming familiar with all the fine details that make up a steam tube boiler.

♫

The war dragged on. We were still using the air raid shelter most nights. Still carrying our gas masks around whenever we could remember. Still listening assiduously to the 9 o'clock news on the BBC to find out what was happening on the war front. The Americans, after being forced into a full-scale war with Japan, were now at war with Germany and Italy as well. It seemed as if the whole world were at war! During this period we were being bombed on a daily, or I should say, nightly, basis. By the time July 1943 rolled around, while still living in 266 Bancroft Road, I left Fairfield Road School, having attended since August 1942. My teacher at Fairfield Road during '42 to '43 was W.H. Clark, nicknamed 'Nobby', and also 'Clicker' for some reason. Although it was a school for both boys and girls they were taught in separate classes. Although there were no girls in my class at that time, there was a Head Mistress in charge of the school, Miss E.M. Lacy.

One of the boys at Fairfield Road was Ditmore; I forget his first name. Ditmore was nicknamed 'Ditty'. He was a big, tough looking, burly sixteen-year-old. Everyone was scared of Ditty, even Nobby Clark, because Ditty was a bully. I ran foul of Ditty one day. I said something about him and he heard it. He glared, pointed a finger at me, and said, "lunch time". Everyone knew what this meant. It meant that at lunch time Ditty was going to murder Goodwin, that skinny kid with the glasses. Boy, what excitement. There was going to be a *fight*! If it had been someone else, I would have been very happy about it, but I didn't want to fight Ditty. I was scared out of my wits. Lunch time came and about thirty boys with ages varying from ten to seventeen assembled in a vegetable garden at the back of the school. I found myself standing in the middle of a circle of excited schoolboys, all thirsting for blood. Then the whisper ran from boy to boy, "Here's Ditty," and I started to tremble. Ditmore gave a little laugh when he faced me. "You've got a lot of spunk for a skinny kid," he said. "I can't fight you; you're not big enough." Disappointment ran around the group like wild fire. "In any case," he said, "I can't hit a kid who wears glasses, and if you took them off, then the fight would be unfair because you wouldn't be able to see." I couldn't believe it. Am I lucky or what? The feeling of relief that swept over me was tremendous. My skin was cold and wet and slippery. What an escape!

From that moment on I gained stature among the boys. They talked about me as if I were a hero. "That's the kid who stood up to Ditty," they said. "He didn't back off, he was prepared to fight the toughest kid in the school." Someone started a rumor, saying that Ditty had been a little apprehensive about tackling a relatively unknown kid like me. "Still waters run deep," they said. I didn't care what they said. I was very happy to get out of a very tight hole. I would try to keep my mouth shut in future. When I told Dad about it, he laughed. "All bullies are cowards," he said.

♪

One day, during that summer of 1943, Mum asked me when I would start work with Dad. In those days the official school-leaving age was fourteen, so I was eligible to leave school during the summer holidays of that year. "Oh no," said Dad, "Tommy's not going to work with me yet."

Mum started to argue. "He's your eldest son, and he will inherit your business sooner or later. Why don't you take him in, as a learner now, and teach him the business?"

But Dad argued, "It will be better for Tommy if he goes to another company, learns a trade, and becomes independent before he comes to work for me. He can come to me and learn the tricks of my trade any time after he's served an apprenticeship, and has something to fall back on." Mum couldn't argue with that. Dad had practically no education behind him; his schooling finished at the age of thirteen, but he had plenty of street-style common sense.

Dad brought me into the conversation. "My father insisted that I serve an apprenticeship," said Dad, "and I chose to be a cooper. Twenty years ago, that was a good trade, but nowadays barrels are made of steel, not wood, so a cooper is not so much in demand as he used to be. I'm not telling you which trade to take up; I'm just asking you to choose one."

There wasn't much choosing to do. I wanted to be an apprentice boilermaker/plater. That was it! A few weeks later, after making some inquiries at Fraser & Fraser Ltd, I learned that if an apprenticeship were granted to me, I would be eligible to learn the trade during a five-year period, from age sixteen to twenty-one. For the two immediate years, age fourteen to sixteen, I must work for the company as a general helpmate. Mum and Dad paid a visit to the boilershop, and spoke to the foreman, Albert Hunt, who told them that it was not easy to get an apprenticeship unless the boy had relatives, such as an uncle or cousin, already working for the company. "However," said Albert Hunt, "if your boy is keen, willing, and able, then he will get an apprenticeship so long as we don't exceed the limitation. " The limitation was a trade union rule whereby there could be no more than one apprentice serving his time for every seven journeymen working in the boilershop. Like most rules and laws, this one could, if the necessity arose, be bent or enhanced a little. After all, who ever heard of half an apprentice?

I couldn't wait to tell Harry that I was due to start work in August. Dad was very happy that I had shown interest in choosing a trade; so many lads started work as a laborer or a truck driver's mate, which did not require any extra schooling. For an apprenticeship, five years of evening classes was required of me. On the weekend before my fourteenth birthday, I cleaned and polished my bike, pumped up the tires, and attached a saddlebag for carrying my lunch. I was due to start work on Tuesday, August 24th. I hoped that we got through the next couple of days without any air raids.

♫

Today is my birthday. I am fourteen. The date is August 24th 1943. Not only that, but today is my first day of work. My working life will extend for more than fifty years, but I don't know that yet. Let me tell you a little about what, for me, was a very important day in my life. My day started very early, at about 5am, when I left the house at 266 Bancroft Road on my bicycle. I had sandwiches and apples packed in my saddlebag; Ma, of course, had prepared this lunch for me the night before. There was very little traffic on the road, it being so early, and I raced down the road as fast as possible so that I arrived at the gate of Fraser & Fraser Ltd, Engineers & Boilermakers at about 5.20am. The whole place was completely deserted except for one man who was a night guard. When I told him that I was a new employee he burst out laughing. "Shop opens at 8 o'clock," he said, "not half past five. Take a ride on your bike." After we talked a little while, he told me that I could ride to Victoria Park because there was plenty of time. Frasers was located right next to Three Mill Lane, between Bromley-by-Bow Station and The Seven Stars pub. Before I tell you about my first day there, let me give you a brief history of how Fraser & Fraser Limited came into being.

In about 1820, John Fraser began a company that was eventually to become Fraser & Fraser Limited. Its first premises were in Houndsditch. In 1839, the company moved to 98 Commercial Road, with an adjoining house in Batty Street. In those years a great variety of work was produced, including heating plants, vats, mixers, sugar moulds, shot furnaces for the Crimean War, cooking apparatus and ships' galleys. John Fraser carried out all the galley work for Queen Victoria's first private yacht, the *Victoria and Albert*.

After some years at Commercial Road, additional premises were acquired at Bromley-by-Bow, London, E3, mainly for the manufacture of Cornish, Lancashire and portable boilers.

In 1859, John Fraser brought his eldest son, William J. Fraser, into the partnership and then the following year his sons George C. and John W., and began trading from August 31st 1860 as John Fraser & Sons. Ten years later, John Fraser retired and the firm carried on as Fraser Bros.

The eldest son, William J., left the partnership in 1880 to found the chemical engineering business of W.J. Fraser & Company at the Commercial Road premises. George and John then adopted the name Fraser & Fraser, the premises of the new concern being at the Bromley-by-Bow site. In 1894 this partnership of the younger brothers was converted into a Limited Liability Company, incorporated under the name Fraser & Fraser Limited.

For more than 100 years, the manufacture of steam boilers had been one of the specialities of Fraser & Fraser and their predecessors. Marine boilers were at one time supplied to the shipbuilders on the River Thames, shipbuilding being a thriving industry in the middle of the 19th century. In more recent years, the company had developed the Fraser Patent Water Tube Steam Boiler with great success, which was designed by Andrew R. Angus. Many of those boilers were exported to various parts of the world.

In addition to the manufacture of boilers of various types, Fraser & Fraser had for many years manufactured a wide variety of buoys of all sorts and shapes-spherical, conical, and pear-shaped, all of which served different functions. Some were used as mooring buoys, while others carried bells, lanterns, or foghorns, all to give warnings to ships.

Much general engineering work was also carried out in the workshops at Bromley-by-Bow, which extended to about one-and-a-half acres of factory space. Items manufactured there included tar stills, fuel oil heaters, steam separators, evaporator casings, vacuum chambers, food cooking retorts, revolving dryers, heat exchangers, rotary mixers and many other types of equipment, made in various metals including mild steel, stainless steel, monel metal and other similar materials. During World War II, Fraser & Fraser manufactured refueling, landing and rescue craft, in addition to those items generally manufactured.

This was the company I was to join on my fourteenth birthday. Having arrived so early, I made my way to Victoria Park. The weather was warm and sunny, so I relaxed. The sandwiches looked good, so I ate them. The apples went the same way because by now I felt as if I were at a picnic.

I got back to Frasers well before 8 o'clock, and spoke to the guard at the gate, who helped me to make out a time card and showed me how to 'clock in' with it. Then, when I came into the shop, I found lots of fellows wanting to give me advice, which boiled down to the fact that I needed to wait outside the foreman's office until he came in, and be on my best behaviour. I had a look around while I was waiting. The foreman's office was in the middle of the main shop, and was elevated about six feet. In size it was about twenty feet by ten feet by about 8 feet high. It had large windows, so that from the office, one could see over the whole shop. The foreman's office was really a room within a room, if you could call the main shop a room.

The shop itself was pretty large. Probably six-hundred feet wide and a quarter of a mile long. The railroad ran parallel with the shop. The underground trains actually ran above ground in this area to the end of the shop, which ended in a canal and a bridge. In the shop was a large structure, which looked like an upside down boat. The whole shop was enormous and overpowering, like an aircraft hangar, but very busy, with lots of things happening, and people everywhere. There was also a lot of smoke being generated. That was a surprise. How come everyone, or nearly everyone, was lighting a fire in August? It was not to warm up, that's for sure.

It was as dirty a place as you'll find anywhere. Some parts of the floor had a cement finish, but that didn't help much because the whole floor was covered with a solid layer of a mixture of rust, dust, and sand which was stirred up as you walked. The mixture had been accumulating for about a hundred years, due to the countless rusty steel plates that were forever being delivered to Frasers. This job demanded an exertion that made you sweat and the dust stuck to your skin so that you looked as though you had a suntan. No air conditioners here – we didn't even know what they were. The dust and dirt circulated up the leggings of our trousers, making a person filthy all over. I needed a shower every day, but there were no showers, either at work or at home. I used to give myself what I called a stand-up bath. All I needed was a bucket of water, soap and a facecloth, and fifteen minutes of privacy in the kitchen. I often found that the privacy was the most difficult to attain.

I used to wonder how Bob Hotton managed to keep so clean in the Frasers environment. He was a boilermaker/plater doing the same kind of work as the other boilermakers, but he never got grubby. Bob Hotton arrived every morning for work dressed in a suit, shirt, tie, and polished shoes, unlike most of the other workers, who came to work dressed in dirty overalls, and no tie. He always looked as though he had just finished shaving, and just stepped out of a bath.

A smartly dressed man came walking down from the gatehouse: the foreman. After he had changed into a white smock, he came out from his office and gave me a brief lecture on do's and don'ts. "My name is Albert Hunt," he said. "The men call me Albert, and the boys call me Mister Hunt. We expect you to pay attention and work hard if you want to be an apprentice." He then went on to tell me about the boat-like structure being built in the shop. It was an invasion barge, destined for use later when the invasion took place on the coast of France on June 6th 1944. He warned me not to tell anyone about this work, not even my Mum. This was important secret war work, not to be talked about outside the shop. At that time, of course, nobody knew when the invasion (known as D-Day) would take place. Or even if it would.

Albert (we all called him Albert, or 'Hunty' behind his back) led me down to the barge and handed me over to Bobby Moss. "Do as you're told, and work hard," he said, as he walked away back to his office. Bobby grinned at me: "Can you light a fire?". I was put in a riveting gang of four: Albert Lewis – riveter; Bobby Moss – holder up; some other boy – putting in; me – making hot.

The barge was being built upside down, resting on wood and steel supports. When I ducked under to get into the barge, it was like being in a different world. The whole thing was made out of steel angle and channel frames. There was a forest of steel struts, each one necessary to hold the entire structure in place. I guess it was a little like clambering about on an 'inside out' Eiffel Tower. There was an inner and an outer steel-plate skin riveted onto the steel frames, creating dozens of watertight compartments. These compartments were necessary for flotation of the barge. The design of the barge was engineered in such a way that rivets in an almost inaccessible area could be installed before the area was closed off. The complete job was riveted.

Electric welding was frowned upon during that period for any structural or critical application. You could say that welding, or electric welding, was still in its infancy at that time. Riveting had been tried and true for hundreds of years. Electric welding was 'new fangled', and a joint could be broken with a hammer. If you attacked a riveted joint in the same way, it would only stretch. Maybe two or three rivets could be bent or crushed, but the integrity of the joint would remain. During the war-time period we heard of welded ships made in the USA breaking in half and sinking. This would not happen with a riveted construction. However, welding is faster; you get what you pay for. The rivets on our barge were small. Half inch and three-eighths inch diameter. The rivet looked like a bolt with no thread, and the length of the rivet had to be figured by the riveter who considered the various job conditions: 1. The varying thickness of the plate, depending on location. 2. The number of plates at a particular joint. This would be a minimum of two and not necessarily the same thickness. 3. The thickness of the framing being installed at that point. 4. Framing is sometimes installed at a location where there is no joint. This would get one plate, not two! 5. The standard joint. On this job was a lap joint. Sometimes a butt joint was used. This was figured a little differently.

My job was to keep track of all the required rivets, make them hot, and deliver them in the correct sequence to the boy putting in. This required tossing the hot rivet about ten feet through the air. Iron tongs were used at all times to move the rivets around. Speed and accuracy were required from the whole team as soon as I tossed a new rivet because when the rivet came out of the fire it immediately started to cool down.

Bobby Moss helped me to arrange a workspace. First we got hold of a contraption which looked like a barbecue (although in those days I didn't know what a barbecue was). The contraption was actually a furnace for making rivets hot, and was about two-foot in diameter and waist high. The floor area was covered in snake-like hoses providing a tripping hazard going every which way, and all making a hissing noise as air leaked out of dozens of flexible pipe joints. These were 'windy pipes', connected to the plant compressor, providing the air for the pneumatic tools and to keep the furnaces going. For the fire, I used wood, coal, and coke in that order, and quickly learned how to attach a windy pipe and adjust the air pressure to suit the fire that was growing in the furnace.

Bobby showed me how to control the fire in size and intensity and to judge whether it was too hot, or not hot enough. Then we chose a rivet plate from a pile and laid it on the fire. The rivet plate was about eighteen inches diameter, and a quarter of an inch thick. It was covered with holes, probably fifty or so, and the holes were big enough to take the size of rivet.

Now I was set up. I used a small pair of tongs to pick up a rivet and insert it into one of the holes in the rivet plate, and continued until I had ten to fifteen rivets in the fire. The rivet wasn't hot enough until it became a cherry red color, and if it became white it was too hot and would burn, giving off white sparks like fireworks. I had to hop about making sure I had the correct rivet at the right temperature without burning, and following up with rivet number 2, 3, 4, with no break in the flow. I had to be continually moving rivets around on the plate, tossing out the ones that were ready, replacing them with rivets that needed more heat. All this time I was frantically trying to remember which was next, and wondering whether it was hot enough. The tongs I was using were small enough to do the job efficiently, but sometimes my hand got too close to the fire. I discovered, very quickly, that while I was trying to protect my hand from the heat, a critical rivet was burning up.

The noise in the shop was truly deafening. No conversation was possible while work continued. Sign language was necessary for most of the time. Albert, the riveter, positioned himself outside the barge, kneeling on a leather apron, and dragging his windy pipe that terminated in a pneumatic hammer, or what you might call a riveting gun. When a rivet popped up in a hole, pushed up by a boy who was underneath the barge, Albert gave a little 'brrrppp' with his hammer to make sure the holder up was supporting the rivet before he hammered it down. This made the loudest noise you ever heard in your whole life. And this was only one of about fifteen riveting gangs in operation on the barge.

The working conditions for the putter in and holder up were atrocious. They had to put up with the noise, dirt, and heat like everyone else, but in addition to that they had a very confined space to work in. All day. Bobby, the holder up, clambered under the barge, taking with him an extension light (it was dark under there), some short planks of wood, and a couple of dollies, which were tools made from a piece of round steel about two or three inches in diameter and two feet long. He positioned himself so he was working directly beneath the riveter. The holes in the barge didn't always line up, and the riveter would have to hammer in a drift or tapered steel pin to rectify it. This was very dangerous for the holder up underneath, as you can imagine.

After making a rivet hot, I would sometimes hold it up for Albert to see and OK with a thumbs-up. I'd then toss it to the other boy, ten or twenty feet away who picked it up with a pair of tongs and got himself into position to insert the rivet into the correct hole. Then Bobby put the dolly up to the rivet and supported the dolly on a wooden plank resting on his knees and thighs. Then, when the rivet was supported solidly, the riveter hammered it down and closed it. As we advanced along a row of rivets, the riveter gradually moved further and further along the barge; and, of course, further away from me! This meant that there was no base to work from, no place to call home, because we were constantly on the move. The overhead crane moved the furnace, but I had to remove the windy pipe, untangle it, re-connect it and get the fire going again.

The other rivet gangs were also perpetually moving and creating a problem for us when we got in each other's way. One of the big problems was that all the boilermakers were on piecework, meaning they were paid by results. Every riveter marked with chalk and initialled the area he worked on, and he got paid at so much per rivet. If someone got in the way and held us up, we lost time, and therefore money. This created bad feeling sometimes, when two riveters would get into a shouting match.

As the day progressed, it became very warm in the shop. In addition to that it seemed as if I were forever moving the furnace and re-lighting it. A box of matches was essential in this job. I was sweating after the first half hour, and I stayed wet with sweat all day. Lunchtime came and I realised that the lunch that Mum had made for me was long gone as I had eaten it earlier in the park. That did not matter as there was a subsidized canteen with great cheap food. Although the war was still raging, and food was in short supply, the company somehow found enough food for the workers. At that time, there were about 200 or more workers, so there must have been some contact with officialdom.

After lunch, I went back to my workstation, and started to get the fire and the rivets organized, when Albert, the riveter, got my attention. "Hold the rivets," he shouted, "and watch the show you missed this morning." What had I missed this morning? I knew I had been very busy! What had I missed? Then I saw *her*! She came sashaying down from the ladies' rest room, with her friend, toying with a handkerchief in her left hand, and waving to some of the young men with her right. She was in her early twenties, less than five feet tall, weighed 100 pounds and looked better than a film star. The most popular film star at that time was Dorothy Lamour. She was ten times better looking. She was wearing black trousers, black jacket, white shirt, a cute little black bow tie, and black high-heeled shoes. She had jet-black hair, tied up in a ponytail. At first glance, from behind, she could have been a very small, but handsome, bullfighter. She smoked a cigarette in a silver cigarette holder.

Everyone in the shop gave a collective gasp, and 200 pairs of eyes were on her as she made her way to one of the steel supports that had a vertical steel ladder. All work had come to a complete halt. The ladder led up about thirty feet to one of the overhead cranes. She removed the cigarette, tossed it to the ground with a seductive gesture, and ground it under her heel. She then took off her shoes, slung them over her shoulder, and climbed the ladder. Slowly. Step by step. When she reached the crane, she slipped into a seat, clicked the crane into gear, and disappeared into the shadows. "Hey, Goodwin!", Albert the riveter was calling me. "Rivets. Inch-and-a-half. She will do it all again tomorrow." Suddenly, the shop became alive again, and filled with smoke from all the furnaces.

My first day at work was drawing to a close. I must admit, I wasn't sorry. It was a heck of a job. I had cuts, scratches, and scorched skin on both hands. I was filthy dirty, and bleary eyed from the smoke. I had a ringing in my ears from the noise. The day before I was fishing down at the canal with Harry Jones. Was that only yesterday? It seemed like a year ago. But, I think to myself, there is a war on, and we all have to do our bit. So, I did my bit at Fraser's. At the first opportunity I'll ask Hunty for a transfer to the Plater's shop. That must be better.

That night I fell asleep at the dinner table. I don't remember that bit, but Mum and Dad told me about it later. Many times!

♪

I settled in quickly at Frasers. The job was routine and boring but there was no escape from it. All I could think about was *rivets*! Too darn hot, it was burning. Not hot enough, too cold. If the rivet was not hot enough, then it was not soft or pliable and it was harder for the riveter to knock it down. Sometimes, Albert got half way through knocking down a rivet that was not quite hot enough, and he couldn't finish it properly because it was too hard. Then he would have to cut the rivet out with a chisel, and start afresh with a new rivet.

After a couple of weeks had gone by, Bobby Moss told me to switch places with the boy who was putting the rivets in. This made a pleasant change for me after working that fire every day. Bobby and I got along fine working together in the crowded confines of the barge. I regarded him as my boss, seeing that he was more experienced, and older. He was at least twenty, maybe twenty-five, and was deferred from serving in one of the armed services temporarily because of his job.

After a few days, we had a slight accident that took me out of the riveting gang. The boy on the fire tossed a hot rivet to me, and I pounced on it, gripping it with my tongs. Then, when I turned my upper body to position myself, I found that I was facing the wrong way. I had the tongs in my right hand but I needed to insert the rivet with my left. I tried to change hands but that was a mistake. I should have tossed out the rivet and started again. As soon as I fumbled with my tongs, I dropped the rivet, the cherry-red hot rivet, right into Bobby's lap. He jumped a foot into the air, banging his head on the steel framing. The rivet, meanwhile, burned though his apron, through his trousers, and scorched his underpants, right between his legs. It then burned through the other side of his trousers before landing on the floor. He screamed like a stuck pig, and all hell broke loose. He was shouting and yelling, and frothing at the mouth like a lunatic. He called me all the names he could think of. His tirade eventually wound down with a threat: "I'm going to kill you, Goodwin".

I didn't wait for any more. That was enough. I got out from under the barge and ran. When I got to Hunty's office, I was in tears and scared out of my wits. Hunty was able to calm Bobby down, and the episode finished when Bobby promised to leave me alone. It was discovered later that his skin was scorched but not burned. We were very lucky. "When we consider the consequences of keeping you in the riveting gang," said Hunty, "it would be best to move you to some other place."

The next day, Hunty called for me to go to his office. "I'm going to put you in the welding shop," he said. I saw my opportunity right away. I told him that I wanted to be a boilermaker/plater, not a riveter or welder. "No room for you in the plater's shop right now," he said. "You must be patient and learn all aspects of boilermaking, even welding. Go to Fred Larkin, the welding chargehand, and work with him. Do what he says."

Working as a welder's mate was boring. This was nothing like the work that Harry Jones and I had played at in his basement a few weeks ago. All the thinking in regard to the job had been done already in the plater's shop. All the materials had been procured; the cutting, drilling, bending, and marking of the components had been done. Fred Larkin would tell me to call for the plater in charge, who duly arrived in the welder's shop, followed by a boy carrying drawings and tools. The plater set the job up by putting the various parts of the job together in accordance with the requirements shown on the drawings. The plater carried the responsibility of making sure that the welder did his job correctly. If something went wrong with the job, no matter what, the welder would throw up his hands and say, "Hey, you're the plater on the job; this is your problem."

Like everyone else, platers and welders were paid by results, so when mistakes were made, it usually meant that someone would have to do his work again for no extra cost. This sometimes resulted in argument and bad blood. While a job was being put together, I found myself hanging around with very little to do. "Hold this bracket while I tack weld it," or "Fetch those pieces over here." Sometimes, "Put up a screen to protect everyone from the welding light." Although I wasn't exactly useless, I came close. Working with Fred Larkin, who looked just like Arthur Askey, a famous radio personality, was not my idea of starting a five-year apprenticeship and continuing as a welder. There was a saying: 'What is a welder? Answer – A welder is a riveter with his brains kicked in!'

After a few weeks in the welder's shop, I decided that I would not be a welder. I spent some time as a mate with each welder, and was not impressed with any of them. Apart from Fred Larkin, who was chargehand, or boss of the welding shop, there was Bert Moore, Tom Wilson and his son Ron, Albert Reason, and a few more that I don't recall. They weren't bad fellows in general, but every day they did a boring job, so they became kind of lazy.

One Monday morning we came into work and found the invasion barge that I had worked on now the right way up. It had been turned over on Sunday to be prepared for shipment to who knows where. The barge was swarming with people, mostly painters, who were putting finishing touches to the mechanisms, and painting it battleship grey. The front of the barge had a drop-leaf design, so that when the barge ran up the beach in France, the front hinged section would be dropped, allowing the vehicles and soldiers to charge forwards, creating a beachhead.

When the barges were finished, they were taken out of the shop and delivered at night. One afternoon they were there-next morning they were gone. There were at least two of these barges built by Frasers during the war, but no one knows the fate of any of them. It's quite possible that one or more of them took part in the Normandy invasion. Who knows? I like to think that my tiny effort made a difference.

Every day at lunch time some of the boys and apprentices who worked at Frasers gathered together on the roof of a pipe and angle rack to play cards. While the weather was decent it was nice to sprawl in the sun, and try to get some kind of tan. Curly Priest was the kid in charge. The ages of the boys varied from fourteen, the youngest, up to about twenty. Conscription age was eighteen, but some were deferred until their apprenticeship was finished. Sometimes the air raid warning sounded, and the rule was very clear on that. Boys up to eighteen must go down into the shelter during a raid. Men and boys over eighteen were responsible for themselves.

The favorite card game that we played on the pipe rack was very simple. The dealer shuffled and then cut the cards making about six or seven piles, all face down. Any one who wished to bet then put money on one or more of the card piles. The dealer was left with the pile of cards that nobody had bet on. Once the betting was finished, the piles were turned over and the money, doubled by the dealer, went to the person with the highest face card; either the better or the dealer. Curly was invariably the winner, and the winner of each round became dealer.

Some of the other boys were Eric Cole, Peter Collard, Tommy Clements, and Sid Kirrage, amongst others. I was able to strike up friendships that would last for some years. I had lost contact with all my old pals and school friends, due to the war and the evacuation scheme. Sid and I became really good friends as time went on. I remember one Saturday afternoon we went to the movies and saw a picture called 'A Song to Remember'. Cornel Wilde played Chopin, and some other actor played Liszt. On the way back from the movie, Sid was able to whistle, from memory, the theme song by Chopin, 'Polonaise in A Major'. Then when we got home, I played it, one finger at a time, on the piano while Sid corrected me with his whistling. I was able to play the outline of the piece after a few weeks' effort, including the part that goes 'Tiddly Om Pom' with the left hand. Unfortunately, I taught myself to play always on the black notes, in the key of F sharp, in the same fashion as Irving Berlin. It looked convenient at the time, but it was no way to play the piano. Now, at my advanced age, I am still trying to undo those errors that I made in the 1940s.

After the last of the invasion barges were shipped out, Fraser and Fraser Ltd reverted back to the business they had built over the last one-hundred and twenty years, making boilers. In addition to boilers, Frasers also fabricated storage tanks, Trinity House buoys, ships' bulkheads, and all kinds of steel-riveted and welded structures. I noticed that there were only a few platers who were entrusted with making a boiler, and they already had an apprentice each. It looked as though there were too many boys after too few jobs.

One of the jobs available was helping the blacksmith as a hammerman. For this job, I learned how to use the pneumatic hammer, the same hammer that had taken off Bill Maize's fingers a few years before. I managed to get in and out of the blacksmith shop with no problems and spent six months making chisels, small tools, and various miscellaneous forgings. Hunty then put me in the anglesmith shop. Ullie Slaymark was the anglesmith, which means that he was in charge. There were two helpers: Albert Lester and Dan Platt. When these three were standing together, they looked like extras from a Walt Disney movie. Ullie was six feet tall, forty-ish, handsome, and he sang a piece of opera or an Irish ballad at every opportunity. Albert Lester was five feet nine tall, fifty-ish, scrawny, and silent. Dan Platt was five feet six tall, sixty-ish, plump and jolly with whiskers like one of the seven dwarfs in Snow White. All three wore identical clothing: khaki shirt with sleeves rolled up, brown work-trousers with braces, a leather apron, brown boots, and a brown checked cap.

There was plenty of workspace available in the anglesmith shop. This was necessary, because large steel pieces were made red hot in one of the three furnaces, and with the use of various tools, presses, jigs, and wooden mallets, the work pieces were hammered, bent, squeezed, and forged into shape. I felt very important on the day that Hunty brought me to Ullie. Both of them tried to persuade me that I would be the ideal person one day to take over Ullie's job as anglesmith. They told me that it was a very important job, that I would be the only one doing it, and that I would become the highest paid journeyman working at Frasers. I was coaxed by both of them: important job, no other man in the whole shop could do this, and high pay.

For nearly a year I worked with Ullie, Dan, and Albert Lester in preparation for starting an apprenticeship as an anglesmith, and I must admit that I learned a heck of a lot from them. Some of the things I learned were not to be found in a book. However, the skin on the palms of my hands started to blister because of all the hammer work I was doing. Dan told me, with a little shyness, that if I peed on my hands, and rubbed them together as though washing, the skin would soon toughen up and repair itself. Well, what do you know? It worked in two days!

♪

My apprenticeship was due to start in August 1945, and I still wanted to work as a plater. This was in spite of the fact that I hadn't yet worked alongside a plater. During this period, 1943 to 1945, I lost track of my old friend Harry Jones. He didn't make the grade as an apprentice, so he left Frasers and took a job as a truck driver's mate. Nowadays, in the new millennium, we see that the truck driver often works alone, and he loads and unloads his deliveries with the help of a built-in crane or motorised tailboard. Back in 1943, we had very little motorised anything, so a helpmate was necessary for a delivery truck driver.

In general, during wartime, it was not possible to change one's job. All working people were registered in a government sponsored program, and this program was considered to be more important for the war effort than the wants and needs of the worker. So, to change job, you had to have special permission from the authorities. Harry Jones was able to change his job because he was not helping the war effort at Frasers. However, his wages went up like a rocket when he left. Apprentice wages are and always have been notoriously low, whichever trade you choose.

During my year working with Ullie, Albert, and Dan, I learned to set up and rebuild the main furnace. This was built to suit the job in hand, which varied in size quite a lot. A typical furnace size for a flanged end was about six feet long by two feet wide and two to three feet high off the floor. This was built with firebrick masonry, and a fire was made within the furnace. Then, while the job in hand was getting hot, we would prepar and rehears all the movements that would take place once the job was the correct temperature. The real art of conducting this procedure was to make sure that while the portion of the job to be worked on was hot, the remainder of the job stayed cold. By cold, I mean cool enough to touch with fingers without being burned.

A fast pace was necessary at all times. If this operation were conducted in a leisurely fashion, then the heat would leak from the hot area to the cold area. After a few minutes the job would be too hot to hold. If this happened, then we would have to abort and start over again. Nobody wanted that. It would be like losing three or four hours, multiplied by three and a half (I was the half), which equalled a lot of lost money in wages alone.

I am very glad, in retrospect, that I did not take the anglesmith apprenticeship. The fumes from the furnace, coupled with cigarette smoke, breathed in daily by Ullie, Albert, and Dan were, I believe, instrumental in shortening their lives. There was, of course, in those days no safety gear available like filters, gloves or ear protectors. One thing I did learn, however, was how to move very heavy pieces around using only a crowbar, and solid rollers. While I was in the anglesmith shop, I enjoyed operating the hydraulic press, which was located in the center of the shop. (There is a sketch of the hydraulic press included in the photograph section.) The press shown in the sketch is an exact copy of the one I operated in Frasers. It was about twelve feet high, with the operating handles on the right hand side of the machine about three feet high. I wonder how many dished and flanged ends this press shaped since it was built?

The hydraulic press must have been very old, because the encyclopaedia that I copied the picture from is dated 1907! Incidentally, it's from a Harmsworth Encyclopaedia that my father bought me in Petticoat Lane for ten shillings (now 50p). After taking this encyclopaedia with me to South Africa and then the USA, I gave it to Anne, who is now looking after it and, I hope, enjoying it. It includes a discussion about the advisability of constructing a channel tunnel between France and England. "Let us not forget Napoleon Bonaparte," said the writer, rather pompously. This shows me how close we are to history. Old Boney, as Bonaparte was nicknamed, was finally laid to rest, but Adolf Schicklgruber continued the war on all fronts.

Sometimes I went to work and arrived just in time to be greeted by an air raid warning. This meant, of course, that I had to go directly to the air raid shelter. I wanted to be eighteen, so that I wouldn't have to go in the shelter. But I didn't want to be eighteen, because so far I wasn't eligible to be called up in the army. I would go when called, of course, but I wasn't looking forward to it.

June 1944 was, I believe, a turning point in the war. On June 4th, the Allies took Rome, and then it looked as if Italy would drop out of the war pretty fast. Two days later, on June 6th 1944 the Allies invaded France from across the English Channel. D-Day! What a relief. I was at work when I heard the news. All the men and boys, and the few women, raised their hats, caps, and bowlers, and cheered, and applauded everybody and everyone. Albert Hunt came out of his office and had to calm everyone down. "Steady lads," he called. "This is an exciting day, but the war is not over yet." We all went back into the shop feeling a little sad.

One of the men – Ullie, I believe – had mentioned the fact that many, many soldiers were going to die that day, and the only way that we could support them was by working harder to get the war material out to them. We all had electricity in our fingers, and started really hopping about. At that time, I was working in the anglesmith shop pressing out tank tracks. A government official had visited Frasers a few days before. He had watched me press a tank track, and had written 100 per cent on it in chalk. That gave us all a boost.

♪

Early in the morning of Tuesday June 13th 1944 at about 4.30am, the air raid siren started to wail. Everyone had been expecting some retaliation from the Germans after the Normandy invasion a week before. Roy, who slept in my room, went down to the shelter in the back garden. After much calling from Mum and Dad, Gladys also went down to the shelter. Then I heard the plane. Both Mum and Dad yelled at me to come down quickly because the bombers were close. I quickly grabbed my box. My worldly possessions were in that box: house key, wristwatch, post office savings book (balance: about two pounds), identity card, and a few shillings in cash. I looked out of the window and saw the plane very clearly; there were flames coming out of the back of it, but then there was no noise. It was as if the pilot had switched the engine off. The plane blew up with a terrific explosion. I escaped injury, but Oh Boy, that was close. Mum was almost having hysterics by now, so I got into the shelter as quickly as possible and we all calmed down. Luckily, we had left all the windows in the house wide open, so that they wouldn't smash if a bomb landed too close.

Shortly afterwards, the all clear sounded and we got up ready for work as normal. After a plate of porridge and a cup of tea, Dad and I rode our bikes over to Grove Road to see the damage. The plane had landed on a railroad bridge that crossed Grove Road, which was about two streets from where we lived on Bancroft Road. It was too close for comfort, we thought. There were some people putting a barrier across the road, one of them an air raid warden. "No one got hurt," he was saying, "but there is no pilot; he must have bailed out by parachute before the crash."

Later that day, the newspapers came out with a headline story that said something like, "German plane crash in East End, pilot missing." It turned out that this plane was the first V1 secret weapon that crashed in London's East End. One other had gone down in Gravesend ten minutes before. The V1, which was quickly nicknamed 'Doodlebug', was a small single engine plane, as cheaply and as simply constructed as possible, and packed with high explosives. There were no pilots on the plane, so you could say that the V1 was an unmanned flying bomb. The Germans called it '*vergeltungswaffe*', meaning retaliation weapon.

These Doodlebugs came from a launching ramp in a place called Peenemund, Germany, which is east of Denmark in the Baltic Sea. The Doodlebug had some kind of 'automatic piloting system', which the German engineers adjusted and set very carefully. Fuel was carefully measured out and then poured into the tank. Then the Doodlebug was pointed in the right direction, and launched. The trip from Peenemund to London was about 600 miles. Believe it or not, these Doodlebugs flew, by themselves, to London, ran out of gas, and dropped to the ground, blowing themselves up in the process. At first the bugs came over one at a time. Then they came in groups of four, then six, then ten. Then the sky opened up, and they came over in one damned great big lump.

On the night of June 15th, more than 200 of these Doodlebugs were fired and about seventy reached London, causing varying amounts of damage. In the period from June to September 1944, 6,700 Doodlebugs were launched against Britain, but 3,400 were shot down by Ack-Ack guns or destroyed by RAF fighters.

There was a weird situation here. The Doodlebug had, of course, no defence against anything, and if left alone would crash in a random place causing perhaps no damage except a hole in the ground. However, if the Doodlebug was shot down over land, then the damage caused could possibly be more serious. There was no way to ascertain this, and so Civil Defence could not work out the best course of action to take: shoot them down, or leave them alone. Sometimes, the engine, or the engine controls, would go haywire for some unknown reason. This happened once while I was at work at Frasers. During the afternoon, a Doodlebug came into our area. A raid was on, so some of the boys went down into the shelter. After the bug had passed over, we all came out of the shelter. Then we noticed that the bug was on a circular course, it was coming back again, so down the shelter we went again, then up, then down. That Doodlebug circled Frasers five or six times until it finally ran out of fuel and crashed down by the River Thames, less than a mile away.

The V1, Hitler's secret weapon, became almost a joke. Even its name, Doodlebug, was funny. Londoners quickly got used to the V1. If it passed overhead with its engine running you were safe! It would crash somewhere else. If, however, its engine stopped and you heard it starting to dive, then it would very likely crash-land close to you. A Doodlebug fell in the garden of Buckingham Palace, and one fell on London Zoo.

Londoners were not worried about Hitler's V1. But then came the V2! The V2 gave you no chance to worry about it. It just happened. From September 1944 to March 1945 more than 1,000 V2s fell on Britain, with half of them landing on London. The V2 was a rocket, or a gigantic firework, one of Adolf Hitler's toys. It was forty-five feet long, weighing thirteen tons, and carried a one ton (2,000 pound) explosive warhead. These V2 rockets were launched from sites in the Netherlands, rose about sixty miles into the air, and plunged vertically into the London target area 200 miles away. The only reason for these rockets to be used, of course, was to kill and maim as many civilians as possible.

The V1 was abandoned by the Germans in the early autumn of 1944. The V2 was stopped only when the Allied ground forces overran and captured the assembly points and the launching sites in March 1945. There was never, as far as I know, any talk about a V3. A lot of people talked and behaved as if the war was coming to its end. We noticed the difference, as the Luftwaffe attacks became less and less frequent. Later, after the war ended, it was speculated that the German scientists had been trying to manufacture an atom bomb. If this had been successful, who knows how things would have worked out? Germany already had a rocket capable of delivering a warhead across the Atlantic.

Things happened very quickly after that. Mussolini was killed by Italian partisans, and Hitler committed suicide on April 30th 1945. Berlin surrendered to the Russians on May 2nd, and Germany finally capitulated on May 7th. Victory in Europe Day (VE Day) officially ended the war in Europe on May 8th 1945.

The end of the war was such a relief. Everyone dropped tools and went home. Who cared about work? *The war was over!* Bonfires were lit in the street, and people sang patriotic songs like 'Rule Britannia' and 'There'll always be an England'. Of course I joined in for all I was worth. Mum made pots and pots of tea, and kept the pot boiling until way after midnight. We all behaved as if there was no tomorrow. One of the women down the street took her ration book to a small grocer's shop and banged on the door until the shopkeeper came out. Then she cashed in a whole month's worth of meat and cheese to keep the party going. One of our neighbours did a weird dance around the bonfire; although he was very drunk he was surprisingly able to stay on his feet. After dancing around the fire three or four times, he put his hand to his mouth and let out an ear-piercing whistle. "Here you go, Adolf Bloody Schickelgruber," he yelled, "up your bloody arse," and he flung his hand up into the air in a Winston Churchill V-for-Victory salute. Dad looked at me, and winked. I knew what he was thinking. He was thinking of the ARP (Air Raid Precautions) warden who caused Dad to swear because of the blackout curtains in Baker House. That was all finished and done with.

A new song came out, and immediately became a hit. It started, "When the lights go on again all over the world". I don't remember how long the VE Day festivities continued, but I do remember that, in the East End of London, people took their kitchen and dining tables out into the street, and partied all day and into the second night. Someone raised the question of who was going to pay for all the food and drink that was being consumed. I heard that the local shopkeepers, grocers, and publicans would help. Mum said she didn't care how much this party cost us, and that we all deserved a good long break. I was very happy that the war had ended without me having to go into the military during wartime.

VJ Day, or Victory in Japan, wasn't to come until later that year, in August. The United States dropped two atomic bombs over Japan, which immediately surrendered, and World War II finally came to an end on August 14th 1945. The war dead were estimated at thirty-five million, plus ten million in Nazi concentration camps. What a dreadful price to pay for peace. The celebration that took place on VJ Day was very quiet compared to the one on VE Day. I guess the reason for that was because the war with Germany became a personal fight. The war in the Far East was so far away that we were not able to hate the Japanese in the same way that we hated the Germans.

As an aside, ten days after VE Day, a little girl living in New Jersey, USA celebrated her fourth birthday. Her name was Evelyn Dorothy Landsberger. Her parents, Elfreda and Harold Landsberger, were immigrants from Europe. Elfreda was a baroness from Vienna, Austria, and Harold from Breslau, Germany. I will tell more of Evelyn as my story progresses.

Keziah Goodwin, my paternal grandmother

My grandfather, Thomas Albert Goodwin

Ellen Eley; Nana lived at 'Number 47'

Grandad Henry Eley served the British Army in two wars

This was Mum's favorite picture of my dad, at about 16

Dad working in the scrap iron yard of 82 Braintree Street, Bethnal Green, c1935

Mum in the garden of the new flat in Benfleet Court, Hackney, c1968

Mum and Dad enjoyed a happy marriage for over 50 years. This was taken c1955

At about 7 months old, 1930

School picture taken at Botolph Road School, just before I was evacuated to Oxford in August 1939. I'm in the back row in a white shirt, 4th from the left

Another school photo, from 1940, age 11

My brother Roy in school uniform, at about 9, c1942

Our house at 82 Braintree Street, just before it was demolished in the mid-1960s

My sister Gladys at about 18, taken c1949

Mum with Roy, in his mid-teens, and Carol, about 2 years old, c1949

The Fraser & Fraser boilershop; steelplates and Albert Hunt's elevated office to the left, furnaces to the right

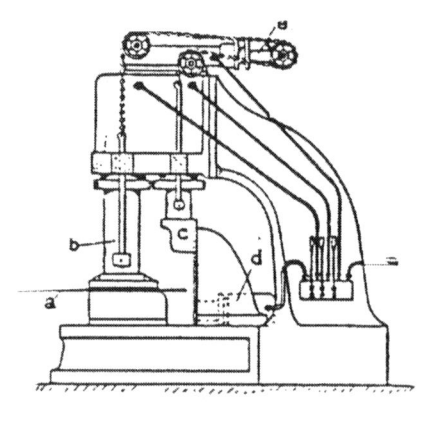

A hydraulic flanging press, operated during my apprenticeship with Fraser & Fraser

(photo: courtesy of Harmsworth Encyclopaedia, 1907)

My 1929 Matchless motorbike, which I rebuilt from scratch when I was 18

Ready for a night out with Ron Rollinson (Young Rollo), 1947

With my friend Heinz Samland (left), whom I jokingly called 'Sieben und funfzig' (57), in Osnabrück, Germany, 1952

Taken while serving in Osnabrück, on Easter Sunday, 1952

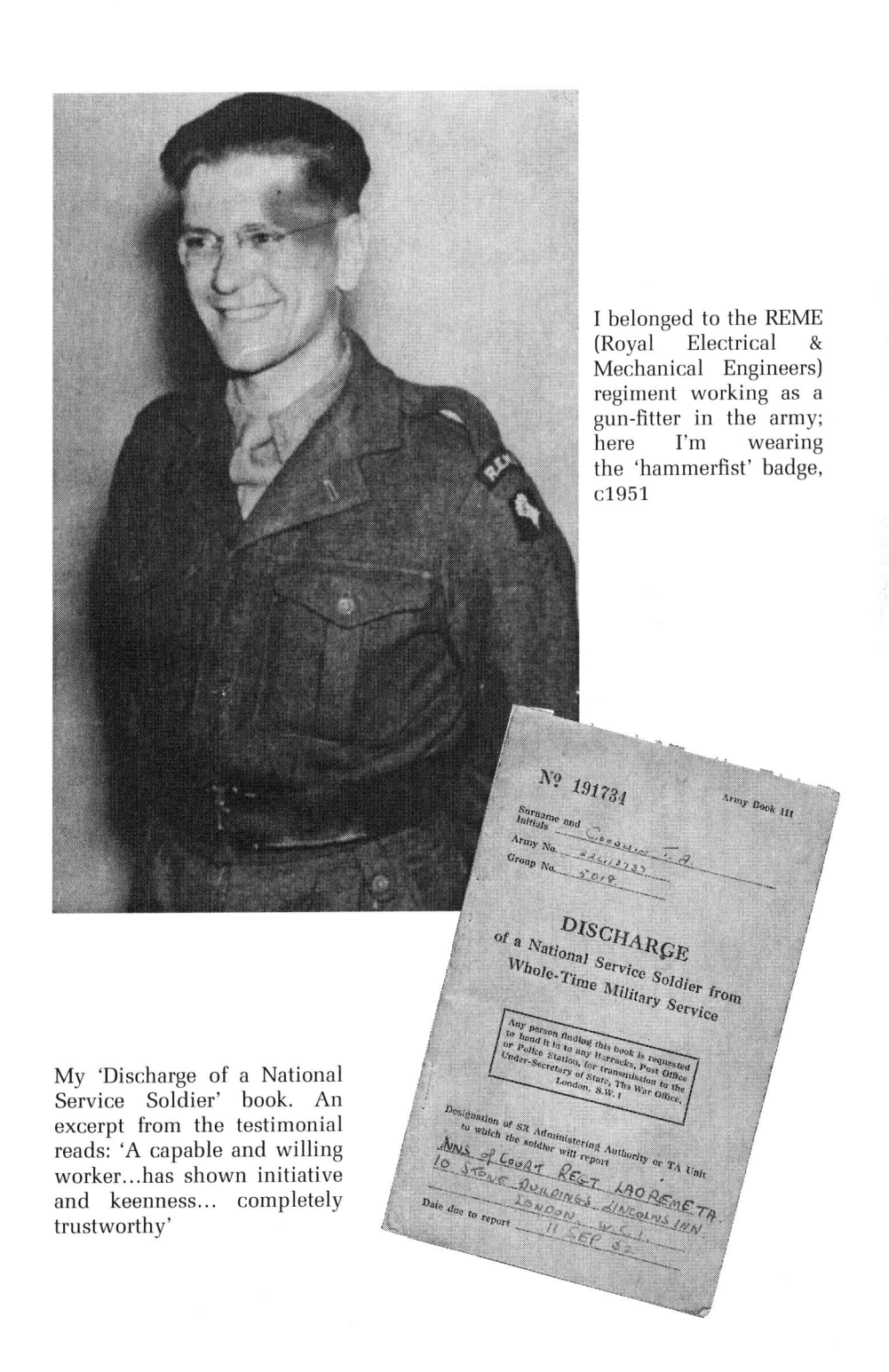

I belonged to the REME (Royal Electrical & Mechanical Engineers) regiment working as a gun-fitter in the army; here I'm wearing the 'hammerfist' badge, c1951

My 'Discharge of a National Service Soldier' book. An excerpt from the testimonial reads: 'A capable and willing worker...has shown initiative and keenness... completely trustworthy'

With Dad, Carol, and a friend, in the scrap iron yard of 82 Braintree Street, with the racing car I built out of an Austin 7. I drove it for about four years during the 1950s

No rain today for a change, mid-1950s

On the beach in Margate during a company 'beano' (day out), mid-1950s

On the way to the seaside for a company beano with Fraser & Fraser; Rollo and I are in the middle row, Eric Cole is 2nd from the right at the top, c1947

Pals from Frasers: Reggie Nickelson, Young Rollo and Ron Gorman (Ginger), early 1960s

My favorite picture of Evie, taken in Dawlish on the south coast, just before we got engaged, Easter 1962

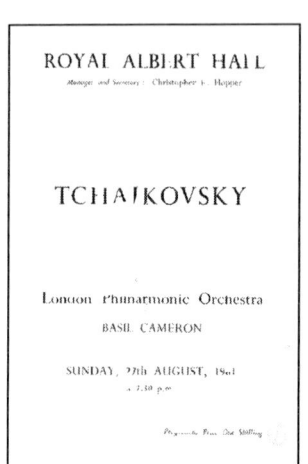

Concert program from the night Evie and I met at the Royal Albert Hall in London

Evie, age 2, on a Christmas card designed by her mother, Elfy, 1943

Our wedding day, 11th August 1962

Our favorite picture, taken in the Volkspark (People's Park) on our honeymoon in Vienna, 1962

A sad farewell to family and friends at Southampton before sailing to South Africa. Back row from left: Gladys, her husband Lesley, me, Dad, Rollo. Front row: Linda (Gladys' daughter), Carol, Mum and Eileen (Rollo's wife), 1962

Photographed on Board
R.M.S. PRETORIA CASTLE

On the boat to start our new life in South Africa, 1962. Evie loved being 'On Board Ship'.

Evie with her sisters Trixie (left) and Monica, and her mother Elfy, 1964

Elfy in her garden in Johannesburg in the early 1960s

Our house, 75 Second Road, Kew, Johannesburg

Walking around the edge of the pool I built for us in 1964

My sister Carol married Terry Wallis in Bethnal Green, London, in April 1965

CHAPTER 3

Apprenticeship at Frasers

1946 – 1950

WE entered a period we knew as 'after the war'. All the things that we wanted and dreamed of would, we thought, magically become available 'after the war'. It didn't quite work out like that, of course, but the devastation all around us it looked like a good fresh start should be made. London in general and the East End in particular had suffered from the extended periods of bombing in the early years of the war, and consequently there were many bomb sites and damaged buildings, both private homes and industrial premises. However, as the war had come to an end, and the men, women and boys who had served in the armed forces were returning to their families and civilian life, life for me became carefree and happy. There was much excitement, and people began to look forward to a better future, although rationing of food and clothing was to continue until the early 1950s.

One of the first things the British voters did was throw Prime Minister Winston (still Mr) Churchill out of office in favor of Clement Attlee. I was so surprised, since as far as I was concerned, Churchill was a war hero who did more than any other man to bring our country to victory. In my humble opinion, he deserved better treatment. Well, that's politics for you! In any case, what did I know? I was only fifteen.

Shortly after VE Day, I was summoned, along with five or six other boys, to attend a meeting of the Boilermakers Union, London branch number 12, at the Lion Hotel in West Ham, E15. The reason for the boys' attendance was so that local union members of the Boilermakers' Society could be given the chance to question, and approve, new members who were applying to be apprenticed to the trade. In addition to me, there was Reggie Nickelson, Tommy Clements, and Sid Kirrage, from Frasers, and three or four other boys from another company, Towlers, in the area.

I remember that I dressed up for the occasion with a tie and my best jacket and trousers. Mum and Dad both gave me advice on what I should do, and how I should behave; in other words: don't lark about. The meeting took place in an upstairs room at the pub. We were called into the meeting room one at a time to be questioned by the membership, who numbered about twenty-five or thirty. The questions were not a problem for me. They mainly had to do with common sense, but one question made me think. Are you prepared to go to night school two or three evenings a week for the next five years? *Five years!* And I wasn't sixteen yet. But I didn't think for too long. I promised to go to school.

My questioning continued for about five or ten minutes more with inquiries about my family and what kind of work my father and uncles did. I realised by now that those boys with relatives in the trade were preferred. They had a father, or a cousin, or an uncle who would speak for them, and influence the members in their favour. In my family, I was it. We had no boilermakers in my family. After the questioning was finished, I was told to wait with the other boys in the private bar. We were all too young to drink alcohol in the pub, so we drank cream soda to celebrate the successful conclusion of the questioning.

All we had to do now was wait for a decision by the Boilermakers' Union. I discovered that a company would employ any boy accepted by the union as an apprentice for five years. During the course of the evening, I was able to listen in to the union members conducting their meeting. They were all Cockneys, as I was, with a rich accent. Whenever someone had something to say, he would stand up, clear his throat, and address the meeting with, "Wurvey President, Wurvey Secretary, and Bruvvers all". ("Worthy President, Worthy Secretary, and Brothers all".) Then he would continue with what he wanted to say. It seemed to me like a group of fellows aping the Members of Parliament in Westminster.

We tried very hard not to laugh, but with Reggie hunching his shoulders, making an obscene gesture with his right hand, covering it with his left hand and calling it a secret Boilermakers' signal, and whispering "Bruvvers All", it was impossible to keep quiet. Reggie didn't worry too much about his behaving at what was for me a critical meeting. His position as an apprentice plater was just about guaranteed. His father, grandfather and brothers all served in different capacities at Frasers and were well known as the Nickelson hierarchy. I felt like a contender in some sort of contest, and that made me an adversary of Reggie's. Well, that could not really happen between Reg and me. He was and still is one of the nicest fellows I know, and we were always good mates.

My problem was that I had to worry about getting an apprenticeship spot, and he didn't. I shouldn't have worried, though. When the results were made known, it turned out that each and every boy who applied for an apprenticeship was successful. The old, time-honored rule of having no more than one apprentice for every seven journeymen had been temporarily but completely suspended. Even though the war was now over, there was still the problem of servicemen and women who would have to stay in the forces for a reconstruction period. The work force needed to be built up quickly to replace all those lost. What a wonderful surprise. Every boy got an apprenticeship, even the ones who were considered not quite up to snuff.

Dad came to Frasers with me on August 24th 1945 for the ceremony of the signing of the apprenticeship agreement over a half-crown stamp. This agreement, which was also signed by Stanley B. Leech, the Works Manager, spelled out not only the duties of both parties, but also the wages to be paid. In my first year, wages were eight pence an hour; the fifth year wages were one shilling, seven pence an hour. This meant that I would start my apprenticeship earning the magnificent weekly sum of thirty-three shillings (one pound, thirteen shillings). I gave Mum a pound for my food and lodging, and kept the rest for lunches at work, and incidentals, such as sweets, cold drinks, occasional visits to the movies, and bus fares to night school at East Ham Technical College. The fees required by East Ham Tech were paid either by Frasers or the Boilermakers' Union.

I started to save as much as possible because I wanted a bike to replace the red painted, obsolete piece of junk that I was presently still riding. Even though the bike was still in working order, now that I was to be an apprentice, I felt that I deserved something a little newer. That bike had seen me through a lot. Towards the end of the war, I had a scare while riding my old red bike home from work. A radio report had been mentioned on the news about a V2 that had landed on a public house near Bancroft Road in Mile End. We lived in 266 Bancroft! I remember that ride as if it were yesterday; all along Bow Road, Mile End Road and right on to Bancroft Road. I felt absolutely sick and worn out by my exertions, but I couldn't slow down. All I could think of was the house smashed to pieces and my family lying there. And so close to what seemed to be the end of the war, too.

When I got to the house, I was amazed to find it still standing, and the street quiet and tranquil. Dad came in, looking for a pair of overalls. A V2 rocket had come down a few streets away, he told me, right on a public house. It was Friday, and the pub was packed with people paying their Christmas Club money. The Christmas Club was an East Ender's method of saving up for Christmas, without being tempted to spend the money. The publican of a local pub usually employed the organizer of the Club as a service to his customers. Dad put on his overalls, and went back to the bombsite to help dig the people out and remove the bodies.

He wouldn't let me go with him. "No," he said, "You don't want to see that; it'll give you nightmares." Weeks later he told me of the clothing being literally blown off some of the victims, and of people being buried alive in the rubble and badly injured. He convinced me that it was best not to see such carnage.

♪

I don't remember the details of working my first day at Fraser & Fraser Ltd as an apprentice boilermaker, although I'm sure that it was very similar to the other 500 or so days I had already worked there. I had now worked at Frasers for two years at fifty hours a week. As an apprentice, I was assigned to work alongside one of the journeymen, on a permanent basis. My governor was Charlie Garner, who originally came from Manchester, and now lived in a rented room in Bow. Charlie was forty, active and sprightly

The first thing that Charlie taught me was how to deal with Bill Brown without losing my sanity. Bill Brown, known as 'Old Browny' was in charge of all the steel plates, in all sizes from a typical ten foot by four foot by a quarter inch thick to a typical forty foot by ten foot by one and a half inches thick. Old Browny never let any piece of material go out of his jurisdiction without a struggle. The first thing to happen on any job, or contract, was that the plater, in this case Charlie, would study the plans, blue prints, and drawings that the drawing office had prepared. He would then make a list to give Old Browny of all the materials required to build and finish the job. Browny saw me coming from Charlie's workspace, so he knew who I was and who I worked for. He put his knuckles on his hips, stood with feet apart facing me, and said, "What do you want?" After I gave him a list of plates that we needed, and told him they were for Charlie Garner, he started to complain and moan. "I have three jobs ahead of yours," he said, "you'll have to wait your turn like everyone else, and who are you, to be giving me orders?" He carried on at me for no reason that I could see, and finished his tirade just as Charlie appeared on the scene, wondering what the noise was about.

Old Browny shut up immediately, turned his back, and carried on with what he was doing. I was left standing there, wondering what the Dickens that had all been about. "Every so often," said Charlie, "You'll meet up with a lunatic like him, who tries his hardest to hurt you for no reason at all. This kind of person we call a 'Browny', in honor of old Bill here." The name stuck. Whenever I meet up with a truly cantankerous, bad tempered old goat like he was I can't help thinking of Old Browny.

Charlie spent a lot of time with me going over the details of the job, one of which was a cone. The cone was about three feet high, two feet large in diameter, and three inches small in diameter. This cone was to be made from quarter inch thick steel plates, which were considered to be thin, compared to a boiler header, for instance. "Don't let these 'boiler' boilermakers fool you," said Charlie. "We have to work out the development of patterns for our cone now, and we have to make our own patterns. The boilermaker, making just boilers, simply goes to that pattern rack over there and chooses a set of patterns, or templates, from among the dozens of previously made boiler patterns. Some of the platers in this shop are unable to develop a complicated structure like a cone, or a square-to-round. But you will be able to do it, and that will make you more useful."

After we worked out the cone pattern (which looked like a ladies fan) we had to bend and fold it from a flat, steel plate to its finished shape. This was done with the aid of a bending, or folding machine, little by little with radius bends. We were both having fun. This reminded me of working in Harry Jones's basement, with chalk-line, center punch, set square, and dividers. But this was different. This was the real thing.

Charlie was very easy to work for. He described each operation in minute detail before we carried it out, so that when we started a 'run', we both knew exactly what was going to happen at each machine, especially as far as safety rules were concerned. And, if Charlie ever found an error on the contract drawings, which we were instructed to regard as Gospel out of the Bible, there was no place for anyone to hide. Not for Bert Parkin, the chargehand who was supposed to check all contract drawings, or Hunty, or the designer in the drawing office.

Whenever Charlie found something that didn't make sense on the drawings, he quickly went into action. He would pick up the offending drawing between thumb and forefinger, as though it were diseased, and march through the boilershop, with the bedsheet-sized drawing fluttering and flapping behind him. He'd march through the shop by the longest route, so that more people could see, puffing away at his meerschaum pipe and making a small cloud of smoke like a steam train. I would follow along behind. When we got to Hunty's office, we would watch the comings and goings of whoever was guilty this time. Twenty minutes later, Charlie would saunter back to his work station, calling out as he went: "That would have been an expensive mistake, it's just as well I discovered it before it was too late."

♪

Frasers must have realised that they had a shortage of tradesmen due to the war, and I guess they tried to rectify the problem by appointing more apprentices. Traditionally, apprentices had served a five-year term, and they had always been male. I'll bet that you could search back 500 years and you wouldn't find one female boilermaker plater apprentice in the records. Well, Frasers had two lady platers in their boilershop now, from about August 1943. In addition to that there were lady drillers, lady welders, lady labourers, and lady crane drivers. It was curious to see how quickly the men gathered round to show the ladies all the tricks of the trade, especially when the men put a protective arm on the ladies' elbow. Lots of mild flirtation took place under the guise of apprenticeship. All the platers felt a need to show the ladies the best and safest method of shearing steel plates, for instance. The ladies enjoyed the close proximity, too. I remember one lady telling me that this training was just as good fun as learning to play golf.

Just as we thought that all the apprentice openings had been filled, there arrived two more boys in the plater's shop. Although I don't remember the exact dates that they became apprentices, I do remember these two in particular as they have been life-long friends of mine for nearly sixty years! One of them was a small lad, the other a big one, and as different from each other as chalk and cheese. The smaller one of the two was called Ronald Rollinson, who had actually joined Frasers in 1944. I got to know him at that time, and had we immediately become good friends. He, too, had left school at fourteen, but had worked in an office for about a year before deciding that he didn't like office work and wanted to learn a trade. He was three weeks younger than I was, so I called him Young Rollo, and still do today.

The other fellow was called Ronald Gorman. Ron was a large, red-haired exuberant fellow. He had a natural air of quiet superiority, which put him in a separate class from the rest of us boys. We all thought of him as a bit of a mystery for several reasons. Firstly, he lived in Westminster, so what was he doing in the East End dock area? Secondly, his father was a policeman. It was rare to have a copper in the family. Someone had seen him talking to S.B. Leech, the Works Manager, in the shop one day. Leech didn't talk to anyone in the shop unless they were important. And lastly, rumor had it that he had a relative who was high up in Frasers. Of course, all the rumors could easily be discounted if you put it down to chance. Fraser & Fraser had the reputation of being one of the best boilershops in the country. Why wouldn't a copper in Westminster send his son there to learn a trade? Let's put it down to chance, and say that Ron Gorman, nicknamed 'Ginger', had nothing going for him except his considerable ability. He and I also became friends, and still are to this day.

♪

Usually the bus to night school at East Ham Technical College was almost empty by about 7pm, and a group of seven us, including Johnny

Slaymark, Sid Kirrage, Tommy Clements and Young Rollo, invariably climbed to the top deck and seated ourselves at the front of the bus. Then, out came the pipes, and we started off with what we called our admiration society. We boys were forever buying new pipes so that we could brag about them on the bus. Then there came the lighting up ceremony, and the smoke filled the top deck of the bus like a fog. We never knew, at that time, that smoking tobacco could cause cancer. Although, if we had known, I'm sure we would have smoked anyway.

We had a lot of fun on our bus to night school; we got to know the bus conductor, and made friends with him in spite of all the smoke we made. One winter night it became foggy as I left the house. By the time we all got to Stratford the fog had become a thick 'pea-souper'. As we continued, it got worse, until the bus driver found himself unable to see the kerb. The bus conductor then gave us instructions; one or more boys were to stand at each corner of the bus, and shout to the driver the bus location relative to the street and kerb. We all helped the driver to crawl along the street about 100 feet to the next bus stop where the bus could pull off the road a little to be safely left. The bus driver and the conductor thanked us, locked up the bus, and set off to find a telephone to call for help.

We were then left on the edge of the road, half way between home and East Ham Tech., trying to decide whether to continue or go home. The decision was made to go home, as soon as possible. Before we all got going, some of us announced that we would take a leak in the little park next to the bus stop. About four or five of us spread out for a little privacy, Then someone kicked me and my trousers became wet. Can you believe that Sid Kirrage thought I was a tree, which he kicked before urinating all over my trousers? I was so mad, I could have punched him. What made it worse was that he laughed. He thought it was funny. They all did. Today, I think it's funny too.

The five years I spent at night school disappeared in a flash. I know that I did calculations, sketches, and drawings in reference to boilers, because I still have some of my homework books in my den in Piscataway. The math that I worked on so carefully, week after week, making rows and rows of numbers, I could have completed in an hour or so if I'd had a cheap, hand held calculator. Unfortunately, the calculator had not been invented in the 1940s.

In addition to the small group of seven apprentices previously mentioned with tobacco pipes, there were about seven others that were doing their time, making about fourteen apprentices in total, at that time. I don't remember all their names, or all their faces, but there were, to name a few: Harry O'Brien, Johnny Ashlin, Eric Cole, Georgie Goldsmith, and, of course, Ginger. Out of these fourteen boys only two became devoted to motor cycles, Young Rollo and I. Not one of those boys ever bought a motor cycle or a car, although Ginger occasionally rented a car when he needed one. What a difference there is today, in the USA, when youngsters, after reaching the age of seventeen, rush to get their driver's license, by-pass motor cycles, and start driving a car immediately.

♪

After the war, in 1946, Grandad Goodwin died and my father, being the eldest son, inherited the house and yard at 82 Braintree Street. Dad got a shock when he discovered that the house and yard were *rented* and there was money owing on the rent! My Dad had to quickly safeguard the business by buying the property immediately. Poor Dad. His inheritance put him deeply in debt. The house at 82 had three bedrooms, the parlor, a living room, and a kitchen. The kitchen had a sink with a cold water tap only. There was no bathroom, but there was a toilet in the yard.

Mum was so delighted to own her own home at last. She was very houseproud, forever polishing the brass door handles, and scrubbing the floors and the front doorstep. However, she never cleaned the windows: Dad always did that for her, ever since they had been married, and later on, when there was a little more money coming in, Mum paid a window cleaner. One thing that Mum insisted on having was a bathtub, but where to put it? These houses had been built in the 1800s, and were designed for the working class, who presumably did not take baths. Eventually, Dad put in a bathtub in one of the three bedrooms, which happened to be where Roy and I slept. It certainly became very crowded in the room! Dad also put in a hot water geyser, which served both the bathtub and the kitchen sink. Now Mum didn't have to boil water on the stove, using endless amounts of coal, each time she needed to do the washing up. And even more important – it meant we didn't have to go down to the neighborhood bathhouse once a week for our baths, as we used to have to do when the bathtub was full of coal for most of the year!

♪

I reached a restless period around 1947, when I was about eighteen years old. The war was over, we moved house to 82 Braintree Street, Bethnal Green, after the death of Grandad, and I was the right age to be conscripted into the military services. At the age of eighteen, I was still an apprentice, and destined to remain one until I reached twenty-one. The authorities had made an exception of people like me: trainees, apprentices, and students, by postponing my military service while I was still in training.

Up until then, I just had a bicycle. Sid Kirrage and I had gone on camping trips by bike to that part of Essex that is on the north bank of the River Thames estuary. Thurrock rings a bell in my memory, as does Canvey and Benfleet, all about an hour and a half from the East End. We had cycled around the area a few times about 1944 to visit Sid's aunt, who lived on Canvey Island with her children. Her husband was away in the army.

Sid and I manufactured a little trailer on two wheels made from pieces of aluminum that I got from Dad's scrap yard. We each had a bike and we rigged up a towing bar that could be used on either one. Those trips were lots of fun. We always knew that there was someone close by in case we encountered a problem. However, we soon discovered that no one was allowed to get close to the water. The military had taken over the whole shoreline, including rivers. We came upon a roadblock one day, manned by soldiers, who told us to keep away from the water because of the 'invasion preparations' which were still in force even after the war.

Sid's aunt always made us very welcome, and gave us beds to sleep in. She also loved to play cards, Pontoon being her favorite. Pontoon was also called Black Jack or Twenty One. We played one Saturday afternoon, after riding bikes down from London that morning in the pouring rain. In addition to Sid and his aunt, who was about forty-five years old, there were the aunt's three children, a girl of about nineteen or so, and two teenage boys, six of us altogether. I discovered immediately that this was my lucky day; after a couple of hours, I was winning about two pounds: a lot of money. I felt a little uncomfortable about taking all this money, but they assured me it was no problem. I had won fair and square.

We continued playing into the early evening, when I found that I was winning more than five pounds from Sid's family. We stopped playing a while to eat supper, which was a simple boiled potato and spam meal. I offered to give back my winnings, and call it a day. "Oh no," they said, "let's play some more, you have to give us the chance to *win* it back." This was when I started to feel really uncomfortable. I wanted to quit and get out of the game with modest winnings, maybe ten shillings or so. But they wouldn't let me. We played on to 8, 9, 10 o'clock in the evening, and I found it very difficult to deliberately lose. However, with much skill I managed it without being caught. They finally allowed me to count my winnings of less than a pound at about 1am, and prepare to go to bed. I learned a very good lesson that day. Do not play cards for money with close friends or relatives.

I started to want a motorbike more and more. I had some money that I had saved from my paltry wages over the last four years, about twenty pounds, and Dad promised to lend me more, if I needed it. "I don't know anything about motorbikes," said Dad. "If you want help or advice about choosing one, ask my brother, your Uncle Joe." I spoke to Uncle Joe, telling him about an advertisement for a 'JAP' motorcycle in the newspaper. I asked him if someone was really trying to sell a Japanese bike after all that had happened recently in the Far East. That would not be easy, I thought. "No," said Joe, "This was a bike that had been rebuilt by the James Arthur Prescott Co, it has nothing to do with Japan." When he told me that JAP bikes were among the best, we decided to go and look at it.

What excitement! By this time tomorrow, I might be the owner of a JAP motorbike. Uncle Joe and I took a bus, and walked part of the way to the district near Victoria Park where Harry Jones and I used to go fishing in the canal. We found the address easily enough, and after knocking, we explained to the man who appeared at the door what we had come about. "JAP," he said, scratching his chin, "now that was a great bike, perfect for a youngster like you, but unfortunately I've already sold it this morning, so it's gone." We couldn't help noticing that there appeared to be two or three motorbikes parked in the passage as well as a couple more chained to the iron railings in the front garden. Uncle Joe glanced at me, at the same time raising his eyebrows slightly. This meant, in a kind of secret body language, "Would you be happy to take one of these instead?" My Uncle Joe had warned me ahead of time to leave all the talking and all the negotiations to him, so I just nodded slightly to him and waited.

In the next half hour, Uncle Joe discovered that the man was a local mechanic who specialized in motorcycle repair, and who had worked on a bike belonging to a close friend of Uncle Joe. "This meant that I could trust him," Uncle Joe told me later. The bikes in the corridor were in the house for repair, but there were a couple in the back garden that were available at the same price as the JAP. It was obvious that this fellow was running a little business out of his house, and enjoying the arrangement, too. One bike caught my eye; it was a New Imperial, and the registration plate was BNM 75. In the UK, any vehicle, whether it is a car, truck, or motorcycle, gets, when new, a set of registration plates along with a logbook. The plates and the logbook stay with the vehicle for life as a permanent record. All previous owners are listed with their names and addresses, so it is always easy to check up on details, if necessary, of what previous owners have done to the vehicle.

Uncle Joe and the mechanic chatted about the New Imperial, which not only looked good, but had good engineering features, one of which was that the engine and gear box were connected together in what was known as 'unit construction'. On most motorcycles, the gearbox was driven from the engine by primary chain. In the unit construction arrangement, gears meshing drove the gearbox and the engine, so there was no primary chain. It was a 150cc OHV (overhead valve) engine. After Uncle Joe had persuaded the mechanic to take the cylinder head off so that we could check the valves, we bought it.

We went immediately across the street to Victoria Park where I received about half an hour of instruction and practice in the very quiet environment of the park, before venturing onto the main streets. I can't remember how much it cost – probably about twenty to forty pounds – but I do remember how much fun I had with that bike. It wasn't very fast; the top speed was about 50mph, but it was reliable and easy to handle.

♪

As I said before, up until now Sid and I had spent a lot of our free time riding bicycles all over the southern Essex area, and camping in different spots. Now, with my motorbike, I could go much further afield. Places like Dover, Dymchurch, or Dungeness. Sid wasn't keen on riding pillion, in fact he just wasn't keen on motorbikes at all, but Young Rollo was. As soon as I got my motorbike, Rollo started to badger me for rides on the pillion, and in front in the saddle. It wasn't long before Rollo bought a motorbike of his own: a Triumph 250cc OHV single cylinder, which was built around 1934.

I remember one of those trips that Rollo and I took in pretty fine detail. It was in the spring of 1947, and Rollo was going to visit his Aunt Rose who lived in Gosport, a harbor town fairly close to Portsmouth on the south coast. We decided to go on one bike, the Triumph, and I would ride pillion to save petrol. On the way back, we were cruising along at a comfortable speed of about 60 or 65mph (there was no speed limit in those days) when we heard a metallic 'clink' noise, and the engine cut out. This was during a period when the roads were not as crowded as they are today. There were fewer people on the highway, and it seems to me now that people were willing to stop and help anyone who was having a problem of any kind.

We took the spark plug out of the Triumph, and saw right away that something was wrong. It looked as if someone had been bashing it with a hammer. Rollo and I looked at each other, as if to say "Now what?" After two minutes had gone by, a motorcyclist pulled up, and asked if he could help. "Yes," said Rollo, laughing, "Straighten that out for me," and he handed over the scrunched-up spark plug.

"I have some spares," said the motorcyclist, shining a flashlight into the spark plug hole, "but it looks as if you have a real problem here, there is a hole in the top of your piston."

There was absolutely no way we could do any kind of repair,

temporary or otherwise, without a fully equipped engineer's workshop. "No chance of that," said our newfound friend, "It's 5pm on a Sunday afternoon now so you'll have to wait until tomorrow morning." Our friend, who was riding a large combination, motorcycle and side car, offered to give us a tow to help get us out of trouble. After studying our maps, we found that we were about sixty miles from London, but only twenty miles from Guildford, which had a railroad directly to Waterloo station in south London.

So the arrangement was that our friend rode his bike, with his wife in the sidecar, and Rollo sat on the pillion holding one end of a ten foot piece of rope, while I rode behind on the now dead Triumph, holding the other end of the rope. This was the most hair-raising experience. I had one hand to guide the handle bar of the Triumph, and the other hand to hold the tow rope. If I had any kind of a problem, I was to *let go of the rope!* We found a quiet back street, and practised for a little while so that we could accomplish the towing operation without me being killed. We did it, at a speed of 20 or 30mph, with all lights on, and eventually got to Guildford.

We were much too early for a train. Having no railroad timetable, we didn't know what options, if any, we had. We wasted a lot of time walking around the town looking for some kind of cheap café or teashop. We were getting hungry, and, in addition to that we had very little money to splash on food. We still had to buy railroad tickets. We eventually got some eggs and chips in a café and made our way back to the station. We got to the platform when we heard a voice call "Hey you". We looked around and saw the stationmaster gesturing in our direction. "Do you have petrol in the tank of that motorcycle?"

"Of course," we both said. I felt a feeling of apprehension wash over me.

"Well, get the bloody thing off my platform, and out of my station," he said. "You are breaking the law by bringing petrol into my station." We didn't know that, but no matter, we had to obey him. Now you come to think about it, I guess it was kind of stupid to bring petrol into a railroad station.

We took the bike out onto the street, and discussed what we could do to get rid of the petrol. In the aftermath of the war, rationing was still in force for some foods and for petrol, so it was difficult for us to deliberately throw it away. We approached two or three motorcyclists who were hanging around, and offered to give them the petrol, but they didn't want to get involved with us. I'm sure we looked suspicious, trying to give away petrol that was on ration. We couldn't dump it into the street drain, as that would have created the makings of a firebomb if a passing stranger had flicked a cigarette butt into the drain. We had about two gallons of petrol, so we decided to spread it, little by little on to the surface of the road, away from the kerb. We figured that the petrol would evaporate safely, and it did.

We heard the loudspeakers from inside the station: 'The train bound for Waterloo will be arriving in a few minutes. This train will be the last one to London until tomorrow morning.' Wow, panic stations! We had to loosen the threaded connection at the tank, as the bike was too heavy to turn upside down to get the petrol out, and drain the petrol through a quarter inch diameter pipe. It was just as well that we had some tools. During this period of my life, I used to walk about with a screwdriver in one pocket, and an adjustable spanner in another. We finally got rid of all the petrol from the tank, went into the station to buy our tickets, and then discovered that we were on the wrong platform. Never mind, we manhandled the bike up a stairway, walked it across a bridge, and heaved it down the stairway onto the platform just as the train was pulling into the station.

We heard a familiar voice behind us. "I hope you young gentlemen have a ticket for that motorcycle, you need three tickets total if you take it on the train." It was, of course, the stationmaster. I wedged the bike half in and half out of the train, pretending I had a problem with it, while Rollo chased over to the ticket office and came back with another ticket. Now we were in business. The stationmaster helped get the bike into the carriage, told us to be careful, and bid us a very good night.

It was a short ride to Waterloo, but by the time we got there it was pretty late, so we decided to push the bike to my house, which was closer than Rollo's. We went over Waterloo Bridge, into the City, passing St Paul's Cathedral. We walked on to Bishopsgate past Liverpool Street Station, turning right onto Bethnal Green Road, and all the way down Bethnal Green Road to Cambridge Heath Road, where the pub called The Salmon and Ball was located on the right. A few more yards and we were home. Anyone who knows that area will know what a walk we had that night. A few days later Rollo and I went to a spare parts dealer and asked him for replacement parts for the piston, which had a hole in it, and the valve, which was bent and twisted like a corkscrew. He eyeballed the samples we had brought in, and said with an impish smile, "Well, lads, I can easily bend a new valve into that shape, *if* you want me to, but you'll have to tell me what size hole you want drilled into the piston!" Very funny. We took the new parts home and mended the bike, and it ran for months after that.

♪

Young Rollo's Uncle Bill from Dagenham had two old motorbikes that he wanted to get rid of. Rollo and I gave Uncle Bill two pounds for them and I borrowed my Dad's truck one Saturday morning to pick them up and bring them to the Rollinsons' pre-fab house in Bow. We found ourselves the proud owners of a whole bunch of miscellaneous bits and pieces, including two frames, two petrol tanks, two engines, four wheels, and all the necessary levers and cables to make up 95 per cent of everything required to rebuild two motorcycles.

One of them was a 1929 Matchless, and the other a circa 1936 Rudge. The Matchless was easy to rebuild, the most difficult part being that we had to manufacture and assemble a new steel plate frame for the engine, and a new exhaust pipe and silencer, because the originals had been lost. We managed to sell the Matchless after rebuilding it and getting it on the road so this gave us a feeling of accomplishment. We actually made a small profit on the deal. However, there was a surprise when we took the cylinder head off the Rudge. The machine had a 250cc single cylinder engine, equipped with four overhead valves, two inlet, and two exhausts. We had never before seen a gasoline engine with four valves per cylinder. The standard is two. (Recently, in the 1990s, a car manufacturer advertised a 'new' innovation of four valves per cylinder. Without doing any research, it looks to me as if the Rudge Company sneaked one in, back in 1936!)

The bike was, as my Dad would say, a 'go-er'. The standard 250cc motorbike was good for about 50mph at that time. After a thorough going over, which included not only polishing the inside of the crank case but also polishing the insides of the inlet and exhaust ports, all four of them, our Rudge could travel on a level road at about 80mph. Rollo and I used the Rudge as a reliable convenience. When I went to Catterick Camp in 1950 to start my two-year term of military service, I wrapped it up in plastic and left it in my Dad's scrap yard. Then, each time I was home on leave, I would unwrap the bike, kick the kick-start – once – and it would start. No nonsense. I think we sold the Rudge eventually. It was the kind of bike you remember for a lifetime. Rollo and I talked many times about starting a small business as motor cycle repair mechanics, but it was only talk. We never did, although we probably had enough know-how and experience between the two of us to do it.

♫

It was during this period, 1947 – 48, that we suffered some setbacks on a national level. One was the Berlin Airlift, which caused concern for everyone that a new war could start up at any minute. Number two was the 'big freeze' of the winter of 1947 – 48. This was pretty bad. I don't know how the rest of the country fared, but in London we had a hard time. Coal was in short supply, and I can remember being cold most of the time. Problem number three was the government. Our new Labour government was in the process of nationalizing everything and everybody, including the coal mines, the railroads, the trucking industry, and the health service. I thought, at the time, that the new nationalized health service would help me. I needed eye tests, and up-to-date spectacles on a continuing basis, and I was entitled to them, according to the new laws.

After my glasses were broken in a football game, I went to the doctor to start the ball rolling for new ones. He gave me an eye test, and told me to stay at home until the new glasses became available, as it was dangerous to ride a bike or a motorbike, and to operate any of the machines in the boilershop without proper glasses. But I needed these glasses today, now, otherwise I couldn't go to work, and I couldn't earn money. "Sorry, laddie," said the doctor, "the glasses will be six to eight weeks in the making, so you will have to be patient." Mum was with me at this interview, and she asked if there was any way that we could speed up the process. "Oh yes," said the Doctor, "if you *pay* for them, then you can get them right away, in a couple of days. Of course, if you can't pay for them, and you can't afford to take the time off work, then you can apply to go on a welfare scheme."

This appeared to be such a crackpot situation that I couldn't believe it. We stopped all negotiations right there, and I borrowed five pounds from Dad, and paid for the new glasses. I worked overtime to pay off the loan. I then became independent and paid for my glasses whenever I needed new ones. Maybe I was lucky to be self-sufficient, and not depend on other people, but I was learning all the time how to look after myself.

I remember seeing a cartoon in a newspaper (probably The Daily Mirror) at about this time, which showed two ships tied up at a dock. One ship was bringing people into the country from all over the Empire. All the passengers on this ship had a medical condition of some kind: some needed glasses, some needed false teeth, the women were pregnant. The second ship was readying itself to sail back to various places in the Empire with the same people after they had availed themselves of the new British health service. They were now flashing dazzling white false teeth, or wearing new glasses, or holding newborn babies, and showing wallets stuffed full of the money that they didn't have to spend. The cartoonist, his editor, and some of his readers obviously felt a sense of frustration about this situation.

♪

Back in the boilershop, I worked with Charlie Garner as an apprentice for about a year, or maybe two, and I learned a lot from him about the use of a hammer. When you want to flatten a mild steel plate that is buckled, you have to be very careful not to make it worse by hitting it in the wrong place. Let's say that you started with a completely flat plate, and you laid it on a heavy, solid work slab. By lifting one side an inch or two, and then dropping it onto the slab, the plate would land onto the slab sounding like a car door closing with a gentle 'thump'. No rattles – you could tell that the plate was flat. Now, if you were to start hammering in the center of the plate, the material would stretch a little, and become buckled. The more you hammered the center of the plate, the more buckled it became, looking something like a biscuit tin lid. Have you ever tried to hammer one of those things flat? To flatten our plate, we had to stretch other parts of it by an equal amount, and if you did it right, the plate would magically become perfectly flat again. Charlie showed me, on more than one occasion, a demonstration of how to make a steel plate flat by 'stretching' it with a hammer. "I get a shilling for doing this job," he said, with tongue in cheek, "a penny for hitting the plate, and eleven pence for knowing *where* to hit it!"

Charlie left the company around 1947, when I was eighteen years old, and with three years still to go in my apprenticeship. My new governor was Ernie Mace, a cheerful, friendly, *happy* fellow. He was a little younger than Charlie, and about ten years older than I was. During the war, Ernie had served in the Royal Navy as a boilermaker on a repair ship. I had not heard before of Naval repair ships, but Ernie described the system to me.

When a Navy ship needed repair or service after seeing action afloat, it would not be wise to send it to a Navy yard for repair unless absolutely necessary. That would be the first place to be bombed by the Germans. So, the Navy rigged up support ships as floating factories that could go wherever they were needed, and make repairs while afloat. These ships were equipped with all the tools and materials required to keep the fighting ships going. They had sets of rolls with which to make curved plates to suit the lines of a ship, guillotines and shearing machines, bending and folding machines, and welding machines galore to do any and all types of repairs.

Ernie told me that when he reported for duty at a Naval establishment early on in the war, he was assigned to a particular ship, and he presented himself to a receiving officer. When the officer discovered Ernie's job and function, he called out, "There is no union card valid in the King's Navy. No boilermakers on this ship, only the King's matelots." Ernie told me that the navy men went out of their way to make erstwhile civilians welcome on board. In the same way, later, when I was assigned to work alongside Ernie as an apprentice, he made me welcome in the boilershop.

All the platers in the shop kept a careful record of all the jobs they worked on during the week, and the number of hours spent on each job. Once a week Albert Hunt, the boilermaker foreman, made his rounds of the shop, and spent some time with each plater to verify what portion of each job was to be 'booked' for this week's wages. For this purpose, each plater kept a ledger (under lock and key) which was secret to everyone except Hunty. Ernie was the only plater to open up his book to his apprentice, to let him see the whole story. I was very lucky to work alongside a fellow who trusted me immediately. He beckoned me to his 'desk', which was similar to a large lectern, except it was made of metal, and on which one could lean comfortably while viewing drawings. No chair or seat was required for this arrangement. Ernie showed me the contents of his book and there was a listing of Ernie's current jobs, along with the value of each job (the contract price to Ernie) and how much had been 'used up' so far in wages. It was quite possible for a plater to fall into debt if he was careless. He could work a complete week (about fifty hours at that time) on one particular job that was taking longer than expected, and find that there was not enough money left in his contract to pay his wages at the end of the week.

The plan was to do a little *more* work during a week than was necessary so as to get ahead of the game. Then after two or three weeks there would be enough money in the kitty to pay either a bonus, or to take a day off. The first week with Ernie was fun. We worked with one eye on the clock, and one eye on the ledger, and after our first week together, we made our wages for the week, plus a day's wages in hand, just in case we had a problem the next week. I got a bonus from Ernie practically every week during the time I worked for him. The other boys got wages only, no bonus.

Among my duties as an apprentice, there was the lighting and care of a five-gallon fire bucket to provide some heat in winter. I was also required, along with the other boys, to be in the shop half an hour early every day in order to light the fire and to warm the governor's overalls. There was a canal at the lower end of the shop, and in winter, the moisture and damp drifted up to where we were working. When warming up the overalls, the steam came pouring out of them.

One morning, Ernie came into work early, and caught me drying and warming up his overalls at the fire. "This is no good," he said, "we will catch pneumonia if we're not careful. What we need is a watertight locker to put our overalls into at night. I'll speak to Albert Hunt about it." Hunty told him to go ahead and make one, using scrap pieces of thin plate from the back of the guillotine. He also told Ernie to cover the wages involved from one of our current jobs.

We built a locker about six feet high, three feet wide and two feet deep, with shelves inside, and a door with a hasp and padlock for security. We got all the bits and pieces ready for welding and took them to the welder's shop. Fred Larkin welded it together for us. It was quite heavy when it was finished, so we needed help to bring it back down to the plating shop. I went off to find Jim Blake, the chargehand for the laborers, but he said he couldn't spare any of his men. "I could do it first thing in the morning," he offered. When I went back to the welder's shop, I found Ernie waiting impatiently. "Come on," he said, "let's try and move it ourselves." We tried to pick it up, but it was too heavy for us – we couldn't shift it.

As we stood around scratching our heads a few fellows walked by, among them Herbie Nickelson and Johnny Slaymark. "Hold on there a minute," called Ernie. "My great-great-great-grandfather has just died, and we need some help getting him down to the canal so that we can put him on his barge." First there were frowns, then blank looks, and then smiles all around as the penny dropped, for we suddenly realized that this locker looked exactly like a coffin! We picked it up, the four of us – Ernie, Herbie, Johnny and myself – and positioned ourselves one at each corner.

We then took a walk through the whole factory, slowly and in step, with our caps off and placed over our hearts. Someone borrowed a bowler hat from one of the old-timers, and placed it on top of the 'coffin'. We started our slow march through the welders' shop, turning into the engineers' (fitters') shop, where everyone stopped work and stared. I suddenly realized that this was a real giggle. Some people didn't get the joke, or the fun of it all, until four or five seconds had passed, and then they absolutely *hooted* with laughter. Hunty must have received a phone call from the engineers' shop, because as we marched towards his office, we saw two figures standing at attention. They were Hunty himself, and Bert Parkin, a chargehand. They were *both* bareheaded, which was an unforgettable sight. I, for one, had never before seen Bert's bald head, as we all wore caps – they were part of the 'uniform'.

We manhandled the locker down the stairs outside Hunty's office and slowly marched down the main assembly shop, where the invasion barges had been built. Everyone joined in and laughed when they saw Ernie pretending to blubber into a huge handkerchief. The young boys all danced around, while the older men stopped work and took a smoking break. We carried on with our march past the anglesmiths' shop where Ullie and his two mates stood to attention. Then Ullie gave a shrill blast on his whistle, the one he kept on a string round his neck as a danger signal if anything ever went wrong in the shop. The whole shop now wondered what the heck was going on, and I was very happy to tell anyone who wanted to know that we were taking Ernie's great-great-great-grandad down to his barge on the canal. The whistle blast had served as a signal that the fun was over – it was time to get back to work.

I can honestly say that that thirty minute episode was the funniest situation I have ever taken part in, without any rehearsal.

♪

I worked very hard on my apprenticeship, and took a pride in being able to fabricate all kinds of weird shapes out of steel, stainless steel, copper, or aluminum, varying from round, square, conical or tapered. All the fabrications or shapes that I made started off as a flat sheet or plate (hence the trade name plater). To divide the trades, the sheet metal worker handled sheets of about twenty gauge (thin like a biscuit tin) to ten gauge, (approximately one-eighth inch). The plater, apart from being a member of a different union – the Boilermakers' Union – handled all thicknesses of plate from one-eighth inch thick and up. Among my favorite shapes was a 'square to round', which started of course as a flat plate, and finished up as a tube which is round one end and square the other. This square to round was necessary some times as a transition in duct work or smoke stacks, which are not coded in the same way as a boiler steam drum, or steam headers.

I watched very carefully one day when Herbie Nickelson arranged for me to help him to prepare a boiler according to Lloyd's of London insurers guildelines. This was known as preparing the boiler to 'the code'. Reggie, Herbie's brother and apprentice, was not at work that day. Herbie told me to tell Old Browny (not ask – tell) to get plates which were stamped with a particular steel mill number out from a stock pile. These plates were hung up on the crane like a gigantic shirt on a clothesline. The plate size was about forty-foot by ten-foot or more. There was a man from Lloyd's Insurance Company who checked the numbers stamped on the plates, and carefully examined the surfaces and edges with a flashlight to be sure there were no flaws. It should be remembered that at the end of the fabrication and manufacturing stage, the boiler would go into service under a high steam pressure. In the past, steam boilers manufactured from poor quality materials had, on occasion, blown up, causing loss of life. The Lloyd's man, whose job it was to proclaim that the numbers on the boiler plate matched the numbers from the steel mill, and to ensure that the steel was unblemished, made very, very sure that these materials were the best available, as specified.

Once the plates were 'proved' to the Lloyd's inspector's satisfaction, they were then marked off with a chalk line to the approximate sizes of the various components, including all sorts of bits and pieces such as man-hole collars, stiffeners and gusset plates. The Lloyd's man had in his pocket a steel stamp which he applied to the boiler plate in various places with a hammer so that after fabrication, the stamp mark, along with the inspector's initials and logo, were permanently marked on every piece due to become part of the boiler.

Old Browny would set up his oxygen/acetylene gas cutting equipment, which was arranged on wheels and tracks (we called it 'Old Browny's choo choo'), and cut the boiler plate up into its component parts. The reason for this performance was to prove that each piece of the boiler came from the original plate that contained the steel mill numbers. The worst that could happen would be that after fabrication, a piece of the boiler, no matter how small, would not have the inspector's stamp. In my memory, this never happened. Some pieces were stamped as extras when the inspector was available, so that if a mistake happened, we could ask the inspector to come back to the shop, inspect any left over pieces still attached to the original, and stamp them before cutting.

The platers and plater apprentices who were chosen to work solely on boilers were very proud of that fact. The plater had to be very careful when identifying and marking all the materials. He also had to be extra careful to make no mistakes in fabrication. Otherwise, there was nothing fantastic about being a boiler plater. I consoled myself in not being a number one boiler plater by being able to make any kind of heat exchanger, vessel, tank, or ductwork section. Some of the top platers were unable to develop the various patterns that came easy to me. To be a boiler plater in charge, I would have to extend my service at Frasers for another twenty years after my apprenticeship was finished. That would make me forty! Would I want to be making boilers at Frasers at that age? I didn't think so. Who knows what I might be doing when I was forty? Perhaps I'd take a plane trip to America! (ha-ha.)

♪

In the wintertime Bob Hotton's apprentice, Sid Kirrage, would come into work early to light the stove and warm up Bob's work clothes. Each boilermaker had a floor space that he called his own. The three most important aspects of that space, as is still the case today, were 'location, location, location'. Bob had probably the best location in the shop, being close to the main shop runway where the slingers and laborers handled Bob's material into, and out of, his work area. His presence, quiet but firm, was such that people regarded him with respect, and listened to him. He had only to make a request of the laborers for the movement of some material, and Bingo, it was done. Lesser, younger people, like Ernie Mace for instance, would get backchat from the slingers, and would be told, "We can shift your material close to your area, but you'll have to move it the rest of the way, or wait till tomorrow when we have more time."

Bob would mark off his plates for size, and locations for drilling, and give permanency to the chalk marks with a center punch. He would then do all the necessary cutting, bending, rolling, and shaping. It seemed like no time at all went by and Bob Hotton's project was finished and waiting for the painters. Meanwhile, he stayed clean all day despite the environment. I guess that the plater who had the worst location of all was Bert Slaymark. Bert was a relative of Ullie – a cousin I believe – but they were as different from each other as chalk is from cheese. Bert was a bit of a bully as far as the boys and apprentices were concerned. His favorite trick when chastising someone was to take his two-foot rule and hit the boy right behind the knees causing him to buckle and fall down. Bert was notoriously bad tempered so most people kept out of his way. Unfortunately though, Young Rollo was Bert's apprentice and had no choice but to work with him when directed by Hunty. People would ask Rollo "How do you stand it? How can you work with a git like that?"

Rollo would answer by saying, "You get used to him, and he's not really that bad."

The best bit of news that ever hit Frasers was when Bert Slaymark and Bill Brown had a fight. A real one, which started when Bert ordered some steel plate materials from Old Browny and forgot to say 'please'. They were both as bad tempered as a bear and it seemed as if both were having a bad day and were looking for trouble. The excitement was intense as the two of them struggled, punched, sweated, and swore like combatants. Within minutes Hunty was on the scene, trying to cool them off. He wasn't very successful. These two, by now puffing and blowing like fighters, set off on what looked like a race around the boiler shop. Each tripped and fell one after the other while they were running. It was difficult to figure out who was chasing whom because by now there was a crowd of at least a hundred watching the fun.

When it all finally calmed down, old Tom Baxter, the first aid man, refused to treat them together because he was scared of receiving a stray punch on the nose. The final outcome was that Hunty and Ullie Slaymark held onto Old Browny while Bert was cleaned up and sent home, then Tom Baxter dealt with Old Browny.

Bert and Old Browny still had to work with each other, so Hunty, the foreman and Ullie, who was the Boilermakers' Union Shop Steward at that time, got together a few days later with them and got the two culprits to shake hands and promise not to fight any more. Like a couple of schoolboys. They hated each other from that time on, and passed notes to one another whenever it was necessary to communicate about their work. The whole situation could not have happened to two more worthy people. They were both embarrassed in front of the whole shop, but, you know what? Neither one knew it.

I spent about three or four years as Ernie Mace's apprentice after

Charlie Garner left. Charlie was a champion at making cone type constructions. He could set a regular plate-bending machine in such a way that many bends of less than ninety degrees would, under his magic fingers, transform two or three fan shaped plates into a cone. Ernie inherited various jobs including making cones after Charlie left the company. Ernie would say to me "When Charlie was here we called him the Cone King. Now, I think we can safely call you the Cone Prince. Why don't you get going on the cones for our various jobs?" People noticed that there was only one person in the shop who made cones – me. So I tried to make every one with a perfect shape, and I got lots of compliments. Hunty noticed. He gave all the cone work to Ernie, knowing that it would filter down to me.

♫

There were two old fellows working in the company, who had been there forever. One of them was Alex, a mechanical maintenance engineer. His job was to make sure that all the equipment and major tools were working correctly. He would take out, sharpen, and replace the blades on the shears and guillotine, for example. He was reputedly close to being ninety years old, and the only reason he worked for so long was because he was needed; firstly during the war, and later because there was a shortage of returning workers after the war ended. When Old Alex was finally retired from work he came in on his last day with a bottle of Scotch and invited his old friends in to his dingy office/store-room for a 'going away' drink. About two weeks after he left, we heard that he had died and many of us believed that he had simply given up on life because he had nothing other than his job to live for. I couldn't believe that anyone could love his job so much and I remember thinking to myself at the time that it was a shame that they had retired him; he would have been quite happy to die on the job.

The second 'old fellow' was Bill Bevington (Bevo) who worked a drilling machine and a plane. The drill was, of course, self-explanatory; it drilled holes. The plane was in the shape of a platform that was made to travel back and forth over the edges of the boilerplate that were being worked on. Old Bevo had a selection of chunky pieces of tool steel, one of which he would choose and grind to the shape required on the edge of the boilerplate. After Old Bevo had set up the tool steel, the platform was then set in motion by an electric motor and a belt drive. It was fascinating to see the operation with the plane in motion. The boilerplate being worked on was bolted to a substantial steel frame under the platform. Then Old Bevo, by means of a set of levers, would make the plane move forward and back, forward and back, and each stroke of about twenty or more feet planed the edge of the boilerplate. To retain control of what was happening, Old Bevo would hop onto the moving platform, and ride with it. This was a very dangerous job, and it became more and more dangerous as Old Bevo got older. A man of thirty, forty, or fifty years of age can hop on or off moving platforms without a problem, but when that man reaches the age of sixty, seventy, or more years, then it's time to retire him before a dangerous accident happens.

Old Bevo was old. His drilling belt-driven machine had the date 1885 cast into the frame and the story goes the drill was delivered brand new to Fraser & Fraser as he started his apprenticeship. You could say that they both, Bevo and the drill, started work at Frasers at the same time. This put him in the range of eighty years old, more or less, a ripe old age for anyone to be still working at any kind of job. Especially a job like his which demanded so much skill.

One Friday afternoon, a shrill whistle sounded throughout the boiler shop signalling that a meeting was to take place at Bevo's workspace to honor him on his enforced retirement. Some people said a few words in his praise, about what a grand fellow he was and had always been for more years than anyone else could remember. Ernie Mace and Herbie Nickelson told Old Bevo that we would love to give him his drill as a going away present as both he and the drill had earned their keep over the last sixty or so years, and it would look very good in his back yard. Someone else called out to remind everyone that Old Bill Bevo could goof off, but the drill must keep on working. Ullie's cap was passed around the men and boys for a collection and some of the men gave Bevo presents, such as a tobacco pouch filled with the best tobacco, and a new pipe. After the money collected had been counted, it was discovered that, sadly, the collection amounted to no more than two or three pounds – about a shilling for each year he had worked. I have often wondered exactly how many boilerplates Old Bevo drilled and planed during his working life. He surely deserved more than that.

During my apprenticeship years, around 1949, I lost sight of the fact that a few years before, I had been offered the top boilermaker's job as apprentice with Ullie, and had turned it down. If I had taken that job, I would have been turning out hefty boiler forgings and steam headers. I would also have had the respect of the whole shop. There I go again, day-dreaming. Ullie was my hero, a kind of second father, and I worked with him on many projects on a short term basis.

I worked with many other men and boys at Frasers between 1943 and 1950, with never a fight or an argument to spoil the relationship. Well, there was that slight altercation with Bobby Moss regarding a hot rivet that fell onto his lap, but even that situation ended with good feelings. Not only did I take away an apprenticeship that was to stand me in good stead for the rest of my working life, but I also made lifelong friends, and we still spend many a happy hour talking about the 'good old days'.

CHAPTER 4

Gun Fitter for His Majesty

1950 – 1952

MY twenty-first birthday happened in 1950, August 24th in case you have not been paying attention. Dad came to Fraser &Frasers with me that day for the big signing ceremony to cancel our agreement with the company. My apprenticeship was finished. I had no further obligations to Frasers, nor they to me. I had been anticipating my release, but when it came I remembered that His Majesty King George VI had other plans for me for the next two years. I would have to do my National Service in the Armed Services, and then spend another three years part time in the Territorial Army, doing one weekend a month and other odd days. I had been instructed to attend the local army recruiting office, and undergo a medical and general intelligence examination some time in July 1950. This included a test for color blindness. I was amazed to discover that about half of the young men presenting themselves that day could not read or write. I got through the reading and general intelligence tests with no problems, but I came unstuck with the eye test. I was instructed to read the letters on the card. Putting my glasses on, I told the doctor "D...A," etc.

"No, no," said the doctor, "no glasses, take your glasses off."

"All right," I said, "but without the glasses I can't see what's on the card." With that he scribbled something onto a pad, gave a big sigh, and, looking up to heaven, said, "Why do I always get landed with the dodgers, pretending to be blind and trying to escape their military service?"

I tried to explain that I really couldn't see the letters without my glasses, but he didn't believe me. I was given a note directing me to make an appointment with a specialist in London. I wasn't very happy with the treatment I received, but this was the army. There was no recourse, no one to listen to complaints. The sergeant in charge, hearing something of what had transpired, muttered under his breath, "Orders sonny, orders. You have to learn to obey orders, no matter what." After the eye test I received a new pair of steel rimmed spectacles from His Majesty's Government. Free! The first and last that I have ever received, so far.

I was sent shortly after this to Catterick Camp in the north of England. At that time going into National Service was taken for granted by all young men - it was just a fact of life, and everyone accepted it. For years I had looked forward to finishing my apprenticeship so that I could start drawing full pay from Frasers. This dream was wiped out when I started on army pay, which was a pittance. However, Dad had promised that when I returned from military service, he would form a new company, which would include him, Roy and me, and would be limited by shares. This company was to be called T. Goodwin & Sons Limited. When I left for camp, Dad wasn't able to see me off at the station. He was too busy – he had to rush off to see a client. Things had really started looking up in his business since the end of the war.

It was Sid Kirrage who saw me off at Kings Cross when I went to Catterick Camp. Sid's father, who had been wounded during the First World War came along to wave goodbye, to give me last minute instructions on how to behave while in the army, and to buy me a pint.

Catterick Camp, or Catterick Garrison, is located in Yorkshire, 229 miles north of London. I went by train from King's Cross. I believe that at that time the line was called LNER (London & North Eastern Railway). The London train went express to Newcastle, north of Catterick, and a local train carried passengers a few miles south to Darlington. This area is pretty rugged with moorland wherever you look, and scarcely a tree or a bush to be found. If you get enjoyment from hiking through very remote areas in a perpetual downpour of cold rain, then this is your kind of place. However, there are lots of places marked on the map as 'Danger Areas' in the locality, because of the army manoeuvres and war games that take place.

On arrival at Catterick, I was given my kit, which consisted of two sets of everything including boots, uniforms, and overalls. The overalls were the important item for training. I was also given a bag in which to carry my kit. Hence kit bag. There were a lot of items in my kit, one of which was a sewing needle and thread. Guess what color the thread was? Khaki, of course!

We were greeted by Sergeant Dow in the NAAFI, the Navy, Army, and Air Force Institute. The 'Naffy' was a kind of universal club to which all military people were welcome. Whether in Scotland or Hong Kong, all Naffys looked alike. You could buy drinks, cigarettes, reading materials, and all kinds of snacks. "My name is Sergeant Dow," he said, in a manner that was at the same time cajoling and threatening. "I am your drill Sergeant. For the next six weeks I will also be your mother. You will call me Sergeant, not Mister, not Sir, not Sarge. *Seargant*! Please do not forget this." The new recruits, numbering about thirty, including myself, fidgeted and stirred as if they were just a little uncomfortable. The Sergeant continued with his so-called welcome speech, finishing with promises that we all would be as fit as fiddles in a few weeks.

I was assigned to a barrack room along with about a dozen other fellows. I discovered immediately that I was the odd man out. Most of the fellows were eighteen years old, which was conscription age, whereas I was twenty-one, due to apprenticeship deferment. This gave me a bit of a problem. One of the most important rules to live by – if you want to survive in the army – according to Sid's father anyway, was: do not draw attention to yourself. I soon found that if a group of soldiers of the same rank (private) were thrown together, the oldest soldier would become the leader of the group, and also responsible for the actions of the group. I had no choice but to become unofficial leader in my barrack room. Of course, if a Lance Corporal, or a Corporal or Sergeant came in, then I was out-ranked right away.

We all settled down by 9 or 10pm, and it became story time. Everyone had to tell a funny story. This was not a requirement; it just happened. It was dark; all our lights were out, and it became very quiet. We could hear the softly droning voice of each soldier telling his story. One of the soldiers was crying; he had never before been away from home overnight, and he was worried about tomorrow. Most soldiers in the barrack room came up with a story of sorts, and we finally came to the last one. It was in the form of a question and answer and we, the listeners, were supposed to provide a comment. The story went like this: 'Q. What did they do with the man who couldn't shit? A. They put him in a cage and called him the wild man of Borneo!' The fellow who came up with this story thought that this was terrifically funny and he almost had hysterics laughing about it. He thought it was so good that he told us the story again the following night, and again the night after that. He wouldn't shut up about it. We got this story night after night until training was finished, and we were all scattered to different regiments. This storyteller would not elaborate on his story in any way, but just gave the same simple question and answer recital every day. Every day, we all had a good laugh, no matter what had happened during our training.

The most important goal in life, for a British soldier in Catterick Camp, was to be the possessor of highly polished boots. Your best boots had to be gleaming so that you could see your face in the reflection. Sergeant Dow conducted an inspection every morning at 6am, at which time he expected to see my bed made up in a particular fashion, I needed my face clean and shaven, and my whole kit laid out on my bed in accordance with a photo nailed to the barrack wall. This photo showed an ornate arrangement with shirts folded just so, and laid on the bed in a precise way, socks folded and positioned exactly, and all the kit, including overcoat, laid out in meticulous fashion.

We were allowed to claim "Laundry, Sergeant" for any missing items that we were not wearing. The Sergeant's inspection, known as 'Sergeant on Parade', was made in preparation for the officer on parade at 8am. With this timing, it was virtually impossible for the duty officer on parade to discover anything that was not up to scratch. Sergeant Dow made sure of that. The boots were given pride of place on the bed and were examined much more closely than any other item. The boots were expected to be gleaming as though illuminated.

You could not achieve this mirror-like surface without 'elbow grease' and 'spit and polish'. The elbow grease was no problem. Just keep polishing for hours and hours. The spit and polish was no problem either. Just wrap your index finger in a clean soft cloth, dig your finger into a tin of black boot polish, spit onto the boot and make little tiny circles with your finger onto the boot. The problem was that it took so long, and it was so boring. After working on my boots for an hour on my first day in camp, my right shoulder ached, and my finger was numb.

It was time to take a break. I went to the Naffy with one of my new buddies for cigarettes and tea, and found a long line of new soldiers trying to buy boot polish, brass polish for buttons and buckles, and cleaning cloths. Some of these new soldiers had no money to buy this stuff. "That doesn't matter," said the man in charge, "Sign for it and we will stop it out of your pay." A soldier's pay was ridiculously low, less than a pound a week if I remember correctly. Some of these fellows went into permanent debt on their first day.

There are two names that I can remember from my army training period – one, of course, being Sergeant Dow. The other name was Gillard. A soldier with one day of service automatically had a rank of Private. We all became a friend of Private Gillard. He was what my Dad used to call a 'rough diamond'. Gillard started his military service by asking the Sergeant if it was possible to see a doctor; his feet hurt when he tried to put on his boots. You could see that Sergeant wasn't very happy with this request, but there was nothing he could do at this stage. A week or so later, when it seemed as if Gillard was on permanent sick parade, Sergeant Dow vowed, in public, before the whole squad in our barrack room, that he would make a soldier out of Gillard, "if it's the last thing I do." That was a rash promise, because Gillard declared secretly a day later that he had no intention of serving his two years in the army. "I've made a good start," he said, "so far I spent more time in the doctor's waiting room than on the parade grounds." This was a turn up for the book; the regular soldiers, including Sergeant Dow, were forever bragging to us National Servicemen how they had spent more time in brothel queues than we had in the army.

Gillard went on to beat the system. By wearing his new army boots without socks on a self inflicted march over hill and dale, he managed to rub enough skin off his feet to make it look as if he had a genuine problem when trying to march, or even walk. He went on sick parade every morning, and Lord knows what he told the doctor, but whatever it was, it worked. Gillard applied for, and received an 'Excused Boots' pass. A soldier that doesn't wear boots at any time very quickly becomes good for nothing. This was exactly what Gillard wanted. If he could become permanently useless then he could apply for a discharge on medical grounds. While Gillard was still Excused Boots, he claimed compassionate leave due to various problems at home, which could be solved only by his presence.

Gillard received his discharge when two or three weeks had passed. We were standing outside our barrack room waiting for one of the corporals to take us to the parade ground for march exercises, when the sergeant called out to us, "Party" – the signal to straighten up and be ready to come to attention and salute a passing officer. "Party – Atten – *shun*". In accordance with our training, we stood at attention, slamming the left foot to the ground, with raised chin and head. In other words we were all aquiver, like a pack of puppy dogs, waiting for the next order. I saw someone strolling towards us, and assumed it to be an officer; it had to be an officer – who else could it be? The figure was dressed in civilian clothes and hauling a large suitcase, which had obviously been packed in a hurry because some of the contents were spilling out and dragging on the ground.

It was Gillard. He had his discharge certificate in his pocket, was on his way back to Civvie Street, or civilian life, and was being saluted by Sergeant Dow and the boys from barrack room twelve. That night, after lights out, and after the telling of our 'funny story', we discussed Gillard's achievement, and eventually concluded that he had worked nothing less than a miracle in a very short period of time. The authorities had been 'had' by Gillard, and the best part was that they never knew about it. Well, maybe the sergeant guessed!

♫

Our training period lasted only six weeks, but it was the toughest period of my life. A typical day started at about 5am, with ablutions: shaving and showers, all accomplished with cold water. This was followed by a quick run to the cookhouse for a cup of cocoa. Then I would do my daily chore according to a schedule that was pinned to the barrack room wall. This chore varied from cleaning some of the windows, to washing the floor, to cleaning up part of the toilet and washroom. This was followed by the precise make-up of my bed, tucking the sheets and blanket neatly and laying out my complete kit on my bed. Then I would be marched by a regular NCO (Non-Commissioned Officer) to the cookhouse for breakfast.

Breakfast was a feast. Eggs, any style except boiled. The cookhouse didn't do boiled eggs, but they did fried eggs, scrambled eggs, poached eggs, any kind you can think of and as many as you wanted. Then there were sausages, fried tomatoes, special dishes like liver and tongue as well as bread, rolls, butter, jam and marmalade, and enough tea to launch a row-boat. Oh yes, I nearly forgot; bacon and fried potatoes were also dished up. If you were still hungry, or just greedy, after that lot, you could get in line again and have more, as many times as you wanted. On some mornings we were given, in addition to the regular breakfast, specialities such as steak or fried chicken which had not been used up from the previous night's dinner menu.

Every fifteen minutes or so the officer of the day sauntered through the cookhouse, fully dressed in uniform and cap. (The new recruits were allowed to go to breakfast wearing overalls and no cap.) The officer, usually a second Lieutenant, had a brief chat with some of the men eating breakfast and asked questions on a friendly basis rather than the traditional officer – recruit relationship. The officer would ask, typically, "Are you satisfied with the food? Is there anything you would like to change?" This was a little different from the picture painted by Sid's dad who described a situation where the new soldier had no rights, and no one would listen if he had a problem. I guess the British Army changed its image over the last generation.

My typical day continued with dressing properly, and making sure I was clean. It was essential to be clean at all times. If you made a mistake, you paid for it. After seeing a young soldier pay the price of being charged with 'filthy flesh', I became very cautious and prudent and made sure that it could not happen to me. This young soldier became overwhelmed with all the duties and work that had to be completed before breakfast. Like most of the soldiers in the camp, he was just eighteen. His big problem was that he overslept. He managed to finish his cleaning and scrubbing duty, and laid out his kit on his bed, but by the time he got to the cookhouse, he was in a real hurry. While eating his eggs one day he managed to leave some of the egg juice in the corner of his mouth. One little touch with the back of his hand would have cleared it away. A glance in a mirror would have solved his problem. But twenty minutes later a screaming and shouting commotion came from the parade ground where Sergeant Dow was telling the whole world, (and one soldier in particular) what happens to soldiers who come on parade unwashed, and filthy. "There is no excuse," he said, "for coming on parade in an unclean condition. There is also no punishment for being filthy, just a correction."

Our soldier in distress was marched at double speed across the parade ground to the guardhouse where he was told to undress, but to leave his underpants on. Then, supported by two NCOs, he was washed down with a garden-type hose and scrubbed, head to foot, with soap and scrubbing brushes. From what I can remember, there were probably 200 or 300 soldiers watching. The poor guy, sobbing the whole time, ended up looking like a lobster. When the ordeal was over, he was covered with towels and blankets, and whisked away to the first aid room for a thorough medical check. I believe that this whole scenario was made to look as brutal as possible deliberately, so that, from then on, there would be no doubt as to who was in charge. It worked. Every morning thereafter, we all checked the mirror before going on parade, and developed the habit of wiping our faces with a damp flannel, which was kept moist in the locker for just that reason. The young soldier who was scrubbed suffered no damage or ill effects from the treatment he received. The bristles on the brushes were not quite as stiff as we had imagined them to be, so the mental anguish and embarrassment were the worst part of his punishment.

The early part of the day was spent on the parade ground, which was a barren, flat tarmac area, about 300 feet square. I discovered that marching, march movements and having control over my own two feet were much more difficult than they look. We started off shambling, dawdling, and slouching along, some out of step, some stooped, and some upright. The NCO in charge of us dozen or so from barrack room twelve summed us up in one word: 'shower'. Calling us a shower was as close to swearing at us as he could get. It was used instead of the word 'shit'. In 'King's Regulations', which was a Government published manual that dictated permissible behavior in the military, swearing and foul language to a recruit was forbidden. King's Regulations were what you might call an encyclopedia of rules and laws pertaining to army life. No one was exempt from this. (There is, incidentally, an immediate change from King's Regulations to Queen's Regulations on the ascent of a Queen if and when the King dies.)

On the parade ground, an NCO put us through our paces. "Atten——as you were. Atten——as you were. Atten——*shun*! Stand at——Ease! Atten—— (wait for it, wait for it) *shun*!" During this, someone released muscle spasm and quivered out of turn at the wrong second. "*Shower*!" screamed the NCO. "I've never seen such a shower on this parade ground as you lot." He then stamped his way over to one of the perpetrators and positioned himself so that his mouth was no more than half an inch from the unhappy victim's nose. Then with spittle flying everywhere, he proceeded to insult the victim by using words and phrases which were acceptable under King's Regulations. Sometimes the NCO would give specific instructions or orders for a foot movement which, for one reason or another, we did not follow exactly, so he would repeat the order a little louder – then louder again until he was screaming at the top of his voice. It was as if he thought we were deaf!

Sometime during parade ground exercises we were marched to storage to pick up rifles. The rifles were Lee Enfield .303 caliber, which means that the diameter of the bullet was .303 of an inch. Rifle exercise on the parade ground consisted of learning how to handle the rifle, learning how to use it as a weapon but not firing it, and learning the best methods to kill with a fixed bayonet. It became quickly apparent that this was not a little boys' game. We were learning how to kill, and the first thing we learned was, "Go for the throat with the bayonet."

Our training during the afternoons usually consisted of classroom style activities, such as working on small arms: pistol, rifle, or Sten gun. The idea was to be able to take these guns apart and rebuild them while blindfolded. There were also lessons for those who needed them, in the three R's (Reading, 'Riting and 'Rithmatic), or any subject the soldier might need. We also were given interviews that were intended to reveal the best job for any particular recruit. Square pegs were supposed to be fitted into square holes, but, predictably, the system often went wrong, and those who had been bus drivers in Civvie Street became cooks in the army, while cooks in Civvie Street became motorcycle dispatch riders.

I had no complaints about my treatment. Somebody decided to give me extended training as a gun fitter. The guns would be 75mm, which means they fired 75mm diameter shells, (about three inches diameter). I would have to take some courses: blacksmithing, welding, bench fitting, in addition to a specialised course dealing with the Centurion Tank which was armed with a 75mm gun. They were going to try to turn me into a gun expert. This training was to take place in the south of England, with the specialised course being held at Lulworth Cove in Dorset, after a short mechanical course in Andover. I felt excited about becoming a gun fitter, and having the title of Craftsman (Cfn) instead of Private. I was destined, after my courses, to become a member of the REME (Royal Electrical and Mechanical Engineers), and would be loaned to a tank regiment that required my services. This, of course, would all take place later, after my basic training was complete.

Although basic training in the British Army around the year 1950 was tough, it could have been worse, or better depending on your point of view. My brother Roy, who went through the famous 'Black Watch'

Scottish Regiment's training program, always maintained that his experience was torture. Well, who knows which of us went through the most turmoil during basic training. My experiences at Catterick were tempered a little by the fun I had. Was it fun? Well, I thought it was sometimes.

There were about twelve of us in barrack room twelve. All full of fun and ready for a joke. However, we were not quite ready for the joke played on us one day. When trying to climb into bed we discovered that our bed sheets were tied together. What a nuisance that was. It took half an hour to undo it all. During the next day, we found that our collapsible beds had been collapsed, and stacked neatly in a spare, empty barrack room, fifty feet or so away. This was now beyond the category of 'joke'. We were ready for war. After finding out which people did which chores during the day, we were able to pinpoint two barrack rooms as possible culprits. But we weren't sure who was guilty, and whether it involved the whole room, or just one or two fellows. We used a little Sherlock Holmes logic, and discussed which barrack room of the two had the noisiest and most aggressive swine in Catterick Camp. It was going to be impossible to repay them all adequately, so we decided to concentrate on the one who had been cat calling and goading us the most. One of the comments he had made to me that morning at breakfast was, "How did you soldiers in number twelve sleep last night?"

We made our plans during the afternoon, and posted a guard in number twelve to make sure our enemy could not try anything again. At 4 o'clock the next morning, our alarm clock sounded, waking six conspirators in our barrack room. Wearing soft shoes, we sneaked to our enemies' barrack room, and waited to see if anyone was going to wake up. The moon was shining, so although the lights were all out we could see quite well. Four or five of them were snoring, but they were all fast asleep. We all knew which beds to go to, so quietly we went from bed to bed, putting everything that we could lay hold of into four pillow cases we had brought with us. These bulging pillow cases now contained just about everything our enemies owned, except, perhaps, the pyjamas they were wearing. Then we hid the four bags behind some junk in the loft of their own room. Part of our plan was to carry out our opponent, while still in his bed, and plant him in the middle of the parade ground. This would have been tremendous fun, but we all got cold feet at the last minute with the thought that he might wake up at the wrong time, and lash out at us. So we scrapped that idea, checked our watches, and slipped back quickly to our barrack room.

We got dressed, shaved, and cleaned up, did our morning chores, laid out our kit on our beds, and went to breakfast leaving a couple of fellows on guard in case of retaliation. As luck would have it, our enemies overslept! This was an added bonus for us. They couldn't shave, wash, brush their teeth, dress, or comb their hair. Nor could they do their daily chore, lay out their kit, or go to breakfast. When they woke up late, this was the final straw. They didn't know what to do. They eventually pulled themselves together and started to search the area around their barrack room, not dreaming that their belongings were hidden inside their room. Sergeant Dow, striding around the camp in preparation for his early morning inspection, caught sight of the performance that was unfolding around our enemies' barrack room. They were all talking at once, and running about like headless chickens.

When the missing kit was found, a shout went up, but it was too late. The sergeant could see only one thing: a crowd of two or three-week-old recruits making a hell of a commotion, unshaven, undressed, and late for parade. He put the whole barrack room on a charge immediately, without asking a single question. When a soldier is charged with an offence, he is brought before the commanding officer by the soldier bringing the charge, in a kind of informal court. Both sides give evidence and speak their piece, after which the CO makes his judgement and hands out any punishment. This system is used for minor offences, such as drunkenness or horseplay. If the offence proves to be rather more serious, then the soldier may be required to appear before a military Court Martial or a civilian court. Our erstwhile opponents from the barrack room were given a light punishment: a few days of 'Jankers' (extra time on work duties, usually peeling potatoes). They kept out of our way after this, and we kept out of theirs.

I managed to get Jankers on one occasion during basic training. While I was on clean-up duty, I was smoking a cigarette and flicking the ash onto the ground while I picked up pieces of paper and rubbish. An officer who was walking past saw me, and charged me with littering. This taught me another lesson; if you are smoking in public, make sure that the cigarette is in your left hand in case you pass an officer who needs to be saluted.

The six weeks or so that I spent in Catterick Camp were tough, but on the whole, an enjoyable experience. Every few days a march was arranged after breakfast. The march was very popular with the soldiers while it was conducted over a five mile course, but when it was increased to ten miles, a lot of fellows started to complain about it. I found it exhilarating to be out in the wind and rain. What a difference it was from being in London where I hated being out in the rain.

Then, for 'relaxation', a five mile run was established for those who were interested. The run grew in popularity, and eventually became virtually a race. This 'race' was held every third or fourth day, and I took part whenever I could, although I never got anywhere near the winner.

The best I could do was to get around the course and finish about fifteenth out of about fifty. Most, if not all, of these runs, were held early in the morning, and we usually stopped at the cookhouse for a cup of cocoa to set us up for the exercise. It was here at Catterick that I discovered what is meant by getting a second wind. After trying to speed up my pace, when I had covered about two miles, I noticed, suddenly, to my surprise that my arms and legs were pumping by themselves. My breathing was smoother and more regular and I felt good from head to toe. I remember thinking to myself, "This must be my second wind." It was as though I were a machine that had been liberally oiled. Many years later, when Anne was in High School, she and I had early morning walks together. The same feeling of having a spring and bounce in the step came over me many times.

During my time at Catterick Camp, all conscripts undergoing their six weeks of basic training were confined to barracks. In addition to that, all conscripts were required to wear uniform at all times, whether in camp or out. This meant, of course, no civilian clothes for me. However, once my basic training (in the USA they call it 'Boot Camp') was finished, I was able to roam a little. Along with a newly found friend (whose name I can't remember) I made my way into the local pubs where my buddy and I soon drank what little money we had. We spent every last penny on beer and cigarettes, and became broke on our first day of freedom from camp. The next evening, we went into town again and challenged a couple of locals to a game of darts. We won the darts game along with a pint of beer each. Then we tried our luck with a different pub, racking up two or three pints each in our favour. Before the end of the evening, I realised that my partner was a real champion darts player, calling "fifty-seven", and then aiming for and getting triple nineteen, or calling "two", and then aiming for and getting double one. Sometimes we were challenged to a game of 'Shove ha'penny', or bar billiards, but wisely we stuck to the darts, keeping ourselves in beer and fags until pay day.

When the weekend rolled around, our whole group got a forty-eight-hour pass from Saturday morning until Monday morning. I didn't have enough money for a return train ticket to London, but my darts playing mate invited me to stay the weekend at his mother's place in Manchester, so long as I bought my own rail ticket. What a nice weekend that was. We played a round of golf (nine holes) on the Manchester public golf course – the first time I ever touched a golf club. We visited Manchester dog track, winning about five shillings, and finished both days, Saturday and Sunday, with a couple of pints, and a generous helping of cheese and potato pie, made and cooked by my friend's mother. The golf was hilarious; I had never played before, and my friend was a novice to the game, so the scores became astronomical. It was a relief to be away from Catterick Camp and Sergeant Dow for a day or two, and to know that we were going to move on and start to learn something at last. When we got back to camp, we discovered a fresh group of recruits who looked as scruffy as a bunch of tramps. We were 'old soldiers' now, with six weeks of training behind us. We tut-tutted, and shook our heads, glancing up to heaven and saying: "What a shower!"

♫

Within a few days of finishing my basic training at Catterick I got my marching orders. I packed up all my stuff into my kit bag, and made my way to Andover, west of London, where my gun fitter courses would take place for the next month. On my first day, I was given a lecture on blacksmithing with an emphasis on how to make quick emergency repairs to practically anything made of metal. My first project was to make a pair of tongs. With tongs I could grip a work piece, and place it right into the fire. I could also retrieve a red hot piece and hold it whilst hammering it into shape. On our first day all the young men taking the course were shown how a blacksmith with minimal tools and materials could set himself up to do repairs. I remembered then, as I do today, how to set about making a set of tongs, which is the primary tool needed by a blacksmith in order to do his job.

For starters, I had a blacksmith's fire, known as a forge, plenty of coal, some pieces of steel bar, and various sized hammers. Choosing a piece of steel bar stock, I made one end of it red hot, and with the hammers and anvil, shaped it into what looked like the right hand leg of a pair of scissors. Then, taking another piece of bar stock, I hammered into shape what looked like another leg of a pair of scissors, except that this was a left hand side, and, holding the two pieces together, I could see the beginnings of a pair of tongs. I needed a chisel to trim away the excess material, and a punch to make holes on the tongs. I was able to fashion the chisel at one end and the punch at the other end of a four-foot long piece of stock. This looked like the tool I needed, but it was too soft to serve as a chisel or a punch capable of cutting steel. The steel to be cut would of course be red hot and the cutting steel (chisel or punch) would be cold.

The terms hot or cold in this case were relative, and it's always wise for a visitor in a blacksmith shop to keep his hands in his pockets so that he can *not* try to pick anything up. Once the colour has gone from a formerly red hot work piece, or tool, the blacksmith calls it cold. It looks cold. In actual fact, if you were to touch it, it would probably take your fingers off. To make the tools serviceable, they needed to be hardened at the cutting edge by a process known as 'case hardening'. After case hardening the tool would be very hard like glass and would shatter like glass if used in this state. So, another process called tempering was used in such a way that the cutting edge stayed hard and the remainder of the tool was left soft. I was able to finish off the tongs that needed a pin, and this strange looking contraption, believe it or not, worked as a fully-functioning set of tongs.

After a few days in the blacksmith shop, where my work was judged to be satisfactory, I was sent to the fitters' shop to accomplish some of the trade called 'bench fitting'. I was given space on a workbench that contained a vice. I was also given some pieces of steel about three-quarters of an inch thick, a brace and bit drill, a hacksaw, and a set of files like the type used for removing metal from a steel plate. There were several work pieces to be made as part of the course. One was a clamp made of two parts. It had to be quite small, about six inches by four. The two parts were to be fitted together, one sliding upon the other as though it was a factory-made tool. To this day it sits in my toolbox in Piscataway, and I still use it occasionally as a clamp.

My previous work experience at Frasers stood me in good stead in these mechanical courses. I was able to meet my objective of making various test pieces ahead of the time allowed. The course included other training periods and lectures, one of which was welding. Electric welding at that time was generally regarded as relatively new, or modern. After watching the welders at Frasers for the last five years, I figured that I could do this with one hand tied behind my back! Gas welding, where oxygen and acetylene gases are used to provide the welding heat, had been in use for many years. Gas welding was not as useful or as quick in operation for mechanics as electric welding. The third type of welding in relatively common use was the 'smithy's' weld. For this type of weld, the blacksmith would take two pieces of steel bar, and bring one end of each to a white heat. Then, quickly so as not to lose the heat, the two pieces were brought together overlapping on the anvil, and hammered together, which really created a longer bar from two or more short ones. The blacksmith's weld, as described, could be used for welding together solid steel bars, but could not be used for welding pieces of pipe together as the pipe would crush when you tried to hammer the two hot ends together. The blacksmith's weld really belonged in the last century, as there was not much call for it in this modern year of 1950.

Before I finished with the mechanical course, I had to learn the skills of soldering and brazing. These methods of joining metals together were used mostly on non-ferrous (non-iron) work such as copper, brass, or bronze. To distinguish between soldering and brazing, one must remember that a soldered joint gets a low temperature solder that 'sticks' a joint together, while for a brazed joint a high temperature is required to 'melt' the joint, providing a much stronger welded system.

After finishing the mechanical portion of the gun fitters course, I was sent to Lulworth Cove, which is on the south coast about fifteen miles west of Bournemouth. The tank museum was nearby at Bovingdon Camp near a little town called Wool. If you ever find yourself in this area, drive down to Lulworth Cove on the B3071 and have a pint in the pub on the right hand side, a mile or two before you get to the sea. This is where I got blind drunk on my twenty-first birthday, but more about that later! Meanwhile, go back on the B3071 to the A352 and head west to Dorchester. Dorchester is a very interesting town and well worth seeing. There are museums, Roman remains, ancient cottages and houses and a life-sized statue of the famous author Thomas Hardy. In the tank museum, on one of my visits, I was shown a tank relic from the war, in which the gunner had apparently failed to fire the gun correctly in the proper sequence. The result of this error was that the shell exploded while still in the barrel of the gun and the gun barrel peeled open like a banana. This gun barrel was constructed of the finest steel, and was about two or three inches thick, but when exposed to such tremendous force it behaved like butter. I learned one very important lesson as I examined this tank that had become a coffin for all those inside: don't mess about with a tank gun that has been triggered, but did not fire. That's a simple rule.

Now that I was in 'tank heaven' I started to learn all about tanks, and, in particular, tank guns. The guns we were using at that time were of 75mm bore (three-inch diameter shell). The tanks weighed about sixty tons. My trainee colleagues and I took guns apart, rebuilt them, then took guns apart, rebuilt them, till we were sick and tired of guns, especially tank guns. In addition to rebuilding guns, we made use of our new found abilities with file and hacksaw by 'cannibalising' critical gun parts. This meant stealing a part such as a firing pin from one gun and making it fit some other gun. We also spent time drafting on a drawing board, and making sketches of various gun parts. Our objective was for every gun fitter to become self-sufficient, and able to ensure that all guns were capable of being fired under the worst possible conditions, namely under enemy fire.

I think that the course was very successful, at least in my case. I became supremely confident that, no matter what happened, I could 'fix' a broken gun. My birthday arrived and this was my twenty-first! I was the oldest recruit in my barrack room, everyone else being eighteen. Two or three of my new friends suggested that we celebrate the magic twenty-one with a trip to the local pub. My birthday was, I believe, on a Thursday, so we waited until Saturday to commemorate the day, just in case something went wrong and kept us from Friday morning's parade. That was a clever move. We all cleaned up and shaved and made our way to the pub, a mile or two down the road. No one had a vehicle of any kind, so we walked.

It's a tradition in an English pub that the first one to walk in the door buys the first round of drinks. They all arranged it so that I walked in last. I thought that this was very good of them, as I would be the last to buy drinks. The first one up to the bar ordered 'rum and chaser, four times'. This meant that everyone got two glasses: the first one, a small glass of rum, and the second a pint of 'scrumpy', which was a local alcoholic cider with a reputation for being very potent. Having a rum and chaser each was similar to having what Reggie Nickelson always called a 'gulpers and sippers'. We gulped down the rum in one swallow, and sipped the cider slowly. Before I knew what was happening, I found myself on my second rum and chaser, and then my third. Suddenly, I was up at the bar with a pound note in my hand; it was my turn to buy drinks. At this point, I'd had enough to drink, probably too much, but I couldn't let these youngsters drink me under the table, so I kept drinking. We all continued to have a whale of a time, graduating from talking and telling jokes, to singing at the tops of our voices.

Some time must have passed without me being aware of it and suddenly I was wondering how I had got into the water! One minute I was in the pub, warm and dry, with a drink in each hand, the next I found myself in the sea up to my chest. Not only that, I was fully dressed. Luckily my glasses were still in position, so I could see in the dark by moon and starlight that the other three fellows were whooping and splashing in the water. Then the penny dropped; I must have had so much to drink that I passed out on the way from the pub to the beach, and then 'came to' when I went into the water. I was amazed to find my boots and socks neatly bundled and dry on the beach. Even though I was as drunk as a lord, and walking in my sleep, I was able to keep my boots and socks dry!

The four of us made our way back to camp, noticing that the pub was still open for drinks, but no one suggested any more rum and scrumpy for tonight. They just said, "happy birthday". The following day, Sunday, I was due to meet up with Young Rollo in Bournemouth but I'm sorry to say that I stayed in bed until Monday morning parade. That was the biggest and best hangover of my life – so far. Nowadays, I choose my drinks a little more carefully, stay with Scotch as much as possible, and keep away from fancy combinations like rum and scrumpy.

♪

My training course continued to the point where I sat for examinations, and, having passed them successfully, I became an official gun fitter. I moved to a regiment called REME, which is short for Royal Electrical and Mechanical Engineers. My new qualifications entitled me to be called a Craftsman (Cfn) rather than Private (Pvt) and I received considerably more pay. Another benefit was that I was now on the level of first and second lieutenants and was looked up to by sundry sergeants, corporals, and junior officers.

I was transferred to a tank regiment and given charge of a squadron or two of tanks. The tank crew, who were not under my command, serviced the tanks and guns. My job was to make any and all repairs to the guns, and write a weekly report on the condition of all the guns in my charge. If a particular gun had not been serviced and cleaned to my satisfaction, it would show up in my report as being 'improper'. When this happened, the culprits who wanted to justify a dirty or rusty gun, but who were too lazy to clean it, would line up at my door offering all kinds of bribes for a 'clean gun' report. I never took a bribe from any soldier in connection with his gun. My policy was to roll up my sleeves and help him.

There is not much room for people in a tank. You wouldn't go joyriding inside a tank for fun. A tank is designed to smash up other tanks, and to kill people as fast as possible. Although a tank was very large, there was room for only three people: a driver, a gunner, and a commander. The driver, who had no windshield, went into the tank first, and manoeuvred himself into the driver's seat. There was no steering wheel! The tank was made to turn right by the driver pulling on the right-side hand brake. Pulling on the left-side hand brake would accomplish a left turn. To go straight ahead he would release both brakes. Although the driver had no windshield, he did have a periscope. That advantage was cancelled when you consider that there was no reverse mirror. The driver was what you might call legally blind.

The second person to climb into the tank was the gunner. As his title implies, he is the one who loads and unloads the shells and sets the gun. For instance, he sets the elevation of the gun to suit the distance the shell will travel, based on the information given to him by the commander, who enters last. The gunner has almost no space in which to work. The driver is under his feet, and the commander who stays up in the cupola, or turret, is almost standing on his shoulders. The order of exit was the reverse of the entry: first the commander, next the gunner, and the last out would be the driver. If during a battle the gunner or commander were injured or killed, it would be just about impossible for the driver to get past them, and out of the tank.

One warm, sunny afternoon before my course had finished, I was on duty with one of the instructors at the firing range, when he asked me, "Look after things here while I'm away for an hour or two." Although we were technically on duty, there was really nothing for us to do except to be there when a group of gunners nervously fired their first shells, or rounds, across the valley into the hillside. A full size mock-up of a cardboard truck was being dragged back and forth on the side of the hill by a contraption of ropes and electric motors. It looked very realistic from the distance, which was about a quarter of a mile (1,300 feet) away. There were five or six tanks lined up on my side of the valley, about fifty feet from where three or four other trainee gun fitters and I were lounging on the grassy hillside.

Suddenly, the day became filled with excitement. There was abrupt movement at one of the tanks firing at the mock-up cardboard truck, and three people came up out of the tank and ran towards where we were sitting. One of the men called out to me, "I say there, are you a gun fitter?" This was a second lieutenant, one of the so-called 'chinless wonder' members of the upper crust. I mumbled something about being a gun fitter "next Thursday fortnight", but the humor was lost on him. "My gunner triggered the gun in this tank," he said, "but the damn thing didn't fire. Hop up there and take a look at it, there's a good fellow."

I could not believe that I heard correctly. This was the very thing that I knew I shouldn't mess with, and here I had an officer telling me to mess with it. "I'm a trainee gun fitter," I shouted, "I haven't had training for this kind of situation, it could be very dangerous."

He answered, "What would you do if this was a real tank battle? Ask the bloody Germans to wait while we get our gun ready? No, this is preparation and training for war. Now, get up on that tank, climb inside, and make the gun work. That is your job."

Everyone was watching. There must have been about twenty soldiers in the area, all staring at me. There was no escape from this situation, unless I refused point blank to get into the tank, which might mean a court martial. I found myself walking over, quite nonchalantly it seemed, to the tank with the jammed gun. What could have gone wrong to stop the gun from firing? Maybe the gun's firing pin was a fraction of a millimeter off-center, and if I touched it or moved it the gun might blow up in my face, like the one I'd seen recently in the local tank museum. Was this tank about to become my coffin? I don't remember my exact thoughts, but I was panicstricken and full of dread.

I climbed up to the gun turret, and carefully lowered myself into the deserted tank, being careful not to touch anything on the way. I wanted one more cigarette before I got blown to smithereens, but it wasn't a good idea to have smoke billowing out of the tank, so I forgot about smoking, and tried to concentrate on the inside of the tank. I saw that the gun had previously fired and recoiled into its large pair of springs. The next move would be for the gunner to load another shell, or missile into the breech of the gun. That had taken place, so the gun should now be ready to fire. Why hadn't it fired? Suddenly I could see the problem, and what a simple little malfunction it was. After a firing takes place and the gun recoils, the spent shell is ejected into a canvas bag, or container, which is connected to the gun. Somehow the canvas bag had folded into a loop, and worked its way between two coils of the recoil spring. With the bag wedged into the recoil spring, the spring could not completely return to the firing position. I brought my head down to the same level as the breechblock and squinted along the length of the firing pin. Bingo! The pin was a quarter of an inch higher than the firing area on the shell. There was no way the gun could fire with the firing pin in the wrong position.

I was sweating and clammy by now but what a relief that there was nothing wrong with the gun. Now what? Jump out of the tank laughing and cheering, and proclaiming that nothing was seriously wrong? Or get a moment of glory for myself by playing it up a bit? What would you do? I climbed out to the top of the turret and called out to the gun fitters, who were all sitting with wide open mouths, "I need a screwdriver and a crow bar please." With these tools, I was able to lever between the coils on the recoil spring. The canvas bag, which caused the problem, fell harmlessly out of the way, allowing the breechblock to close fully when I removed the two levers. Now the gun was ready to fire. I caught the eye of the officer who had insisted that I go ahead with my so-called training for war, and called out to him, "I request permission to fire the gun, Sir." He raised his arm, and pointed his thumb sky-wards, at which I went back into the tank, aimed at the target across the valley, and fired.

When I came out of the tank, I was greeted with cheers, applause, and a barrage of questions from everyone. "What was wrong? What was the crow bar for? How did you fix it? How did you know what to do?" I managed to parry all the questions with a wise look, and a wink. That was going to be *my* secret; let them guess.

♪

I soon finished my gun fitter's course at Lulworth Cove and REME transferred me immediately to the 3rd Carbineers, sometimes called the Carbineers, as a REME Craftsman. They were a regiment of tank that had at one time been horse mounted. In one stroke, I became a kind of special oddball. I belonged to the REME regiment, and I would go wherever they sent me in the British Empire, but in this case, I was 'attached' to the 3rd Carbineers.

The 3rd Carbineers were also known as the Prince of Wale's Own Regiment and The Prince of Wale's emblem was carried on the regimental flag. One of the distinguishing features of dress in the 3rd Carbineers was that the webbing and belts on the uniform were black, not the standard khaki used in most other regiments. I had to adhere to this ruling and blacken my webbing with boot polish. I also wore a brass badge on my right shoulder, which showed a hammer and sickle, signifying a tradesman rather than a soldier. On my beret I wore a REME badge showing a chained horse rearing over the world, backed up with a stroke of lightning, which indicated enormous speed. On my left shoulder I wore a mailed (what is 'mailed'?) fist, which indicated that I was a member of the 6th Armoured Division.

I joined the 3rd Carbineers the day I left Lulworth Cove, and made myself comfortable in my new barracks close to Aldershot. The regiment was to become, in addition to being a member of the 6th Armoured Division, a part of the BAOR (British Army Of the Rhine.) The barracks were in turmoil as they were in the process of moving from their present location near Aldershot to Osnabrück, in Germany.

I was assigned immediately to make an inspection of all the tank guns in one of the squadrons, and if I remember correctly, a squadron consisted of eight or ten tanks. My job became very easy; all the tanks and guns in my squadron were fairly new and in excellent condition, which meant that repairs were unnecessary on any of them. I met up with another gun fitter who, like me, had just finished a gun fitters course. He and I had also both finished apprenticeships in the engineering trade, and we both came from relatively poor families. His name was John Wight and he came from Lancashire.

He and I became good friends right away, and we organised our workload so that if one of us became overloaded with duties, then the other would help out. John told me of a job offer he had recently received from his uncle who was a part-owner of some rubber plantations in the Far East. He said there was room for me to take part in this adventure; we would travel together, all expenses paid, to the Far East, and work as managers of the workers on a plantation. The workers, of course, would all be local people. This offer was a big 'fork in the road' for me at that time. If I took the job, my life would change completely. "Don't make a decision now," said John, "wait till our military service is finished, then we can talk about it." Military service for both of us was two years. Then I would have to think carefully about following in the footsteps of so many of Somerset Maugham's characters, or returning to London.

♫

For the remainder of my two years of National Service, I went with the 3rd Carbineers regiment to Osnabrück, Germany. I suppose I was considered lucky to be posted in Europe. My friend Tommy Clements was sent to the Far East and took part in the Korean conflict, contracting malaria along the way, which bugged him ever after.

My journey to the regiment's new home began with a boat trip from Harwich on the east coast of England to the Hook of Holland in the Netherlands. This was the first time I had ever travelled on a troop ship and, I hoped, the last. We trudged on board ship, each man carrying his own tightly packed kit bag, and slithered and slipped down, down, down into the bowels of the damp, uncomfortably hot ship. When we finally got to the bottom, we discovered that there was no space to turn around and go back. We were packed in, literally like sardines.

After a little while, at about 11pm, the engines started, and we sailed to what was probably the middle of the North Sea. There we stopped, and we sat there until noon the next day, when one of the officers came struggling through the mass of humanity with orders to eat and drink. We had been given special rations and containers of water when we boarded ship, so we didn't need to be invited to breakfast.

Some of the fellows were badly seasick. This was due to the heavy swell of the water, which moved our ship from side to side, forward and back, and up and down, even though the engines were off, and theoretically the ship was not moving. I had a dose of seasickness but I managed to keep my food down. The feelings that I had day were similar to the feelings I used to have when visiting Nana in Homerton, and riding the Number 208 low-decker bus. After what seemed an interminably long time, the engines started, the ship made way and the trip finally came to an end when we docked. However, we still had to wait a few hours until we were given the order to make our way to the upper deck, with its cool breezes and relatively fresh air.

Our next move was to march down the Dutch streets, through the town to the railroad station where an empty passenger train was waiting for us. A sizeable crowd of local residents, mostly small boys, gathered silently to see what, if anything, was going to happen. There was no sign of any welcoming gestures, no smiles, and no applause. Some of our lads said that the troop ship must have been lost, and we had landed in Germany not Holland.

We heard the familiar voice of our sergeant, telling us that we may stop, rest, and smoke, on a ten-minute break. Then, as if at a signal, all the locals scurried in and out of their houses carrying drinks and titbits. They were making us welcome after all. The drinks varied from water through orange juice to beer, and the titbits were pieces of cheese, biscuits, and cookies. A large proportion of the locals spoke excellent English, which was a surprise to us, and some of them were waving small Union Jacks. The officer on duty increased our ten-minute break to twenty minutes, and all of a sudden everyone had a lot to say. The general consensus among the Dutch was that they were very happy to see the British Army of the Rhine on their way to ensure that the

Germans would do what they said they would – keep the peace.

By the time we all got checked in from a massive checklist, which seemed to go on forever, it was starting to get dark again. Was this our second night since Harwich, or third? I was beginning to think to myself, 'Who cares?' All I cared about was going to bed and sleeping. After the train ride into Germany, we had a bumpy ride in a standard army truck to Osnabrück. We were 'home'.

The barracks were brand new. A far cry from Catterick camp in the north of England. We had a parade ground (the first requirement for any military establishment), a NAAFI, garages for the tanks and a large cook-house. In addition, there were dozens of barracks and miscellaneous leisure rooms where one could play darts, billiards, and snooker, or just lounge in a comfortable chair with a book. This was to be my home for a couple of years, like it or not, so I thought that I might as well like it from the start, even though I was in Germany.

The local town, Osnabrück, was a mile or two from the Osnabrück Barracks. It didn't take long to find the local beer garden, the equivalent of the local public house. Every night, in contrast to the delights of the beer garden, there was a necessary duty to perform in the camp: guard duty. The reason for nightly guards was, of course, to keep the camp safe from prowlers and break-ins. But everyone hated guard duty with a passion. A dozen or more men would assemble at the guardhouse wearing their best uniform and highly polished boots and be assigned particular time slots from 6pm to 6am. Everyone carried a loaded rifle and a loaded pistol. The officer of the day carried out a stringent examination of each soldier and his weapons. There was no excuse for carrying a firearm that was not cleaned and lightly oiled, or for the soldier being unshaven or unclean. A soldier could spend a whole day polishing and cleaning his equipment and himself and then find himself on a charge because some dust had settled on his otherwise perfectly clean boots or gaiters.

The whole camp had a perimeter iron fence, which was difficult for the man in the street to clamber over. If you were on duty from, for example, midnight to 2am, and a person suddenly appeared before you, then you had better watch out. This would not be one of the soldiers who lived in the camp taking a stroll near the perimeter fence before going to bed! But it might be the guard responsible for the integrity of the next section of fence, or it might be the officer of the day checking up on you, or it might be someone who was not satisfied with the way the war ended. " Halt – who goes there?" you'd growl, making yourself sound as gruff as possible. Then you'd discover that this was one of the fellows who had been out on the town without a pass. He wanted to sneak back in without having to sign in late at the guardhouse. What a relief, you think. There was no danger, although you could have been dragged in to having to explain what was going on.

Occasionally, the alarm would sound, and the whole camp would wake up to a terrific hullabaloo of bells, whistles, and flashing lights. If this happened while you were resting in the guardhouse, between tours of duty, then it was very likely that you had relaxed slightly by unbuckling your belt and gaiters and removing your boots. Then, within a minute or so, at the sound of the alarm you would have to be 'on parade', fully and properly dressed. Can you imagine the panic? This was a good way to snare soldiers for cookhouse duty!

I was scheduled for guard duty over a period of a month or so, with a frequency of two or three duties a week. Then, somebody in authority discovered that I was a REME Craftsman and therefore ineligible for guard duty. It was only those in the regiment, not those 'attached' to it as I was, who would go on guard duty. My life in the 3rd Carbineers suddenly became much more tolerable now that I had lots of spare time.

Lots of local German people were employed by the British authorities to service the buildings in the camp, and to work in the cookhouse. Most of these people could speak pretty good English, and of course, they all spoke German. I wanted to buy a radio to put in my barrack room, but I wanted a German-speaker to go with me and choose the best radio set for the best price without being overcharged. One day a young German singled me out calling for "Herr Goodvin". He offered to go with me to help choose a radio at a shop in Osnabrück. He seemed very friendly, and anxious to help, so I decided to trust him. I corrected him with the spelling of my name, and asked for his. "Heinz Samland," he said. I knew the German for most of the numbers so I thought I would have a bit of fun at his expense. "In England," I said, "You would be called '*sieben und funfzig*'" (translating as '57'). This floored him completely. He didn't know what I was talking about, even when I mentioned the Heinz 57 varieties brand name. For as long as I knew him, which was about two years, he was *sieben und funfzig* to me. (Even today, nearly fifty years later, I can't look at a Heinz can in a supermarket without thinking of him.) Heinz and I went into town that day and I bought a radio, a Telefunken, for seventy-five Deutsch marks. I eventually gave the radio to Heinz when I was demobbed in 1952.

I was able to learn some simple conversational German from the Samland family, and Heinz's mother, father and two sisters helped a lot by inviting me to Sunday lunch and bombarding me with German. The sisters flirted with me at every opportunity, causing lots of laughter and hilarity around the table. The girls were about eight years old or so, making them far too young for me. No girlfriends here!

During the summer of 1950, preparations were being made for what we called 'manoeuvres', or what some called 'war games'. All the countries and regiments from around the world taking part were given an area of their own marked on maps, which were organized into colors. For example, the 3rd Carbineers became one of the regiments to make up the Blue army. The Canadians, along with others, became a part of the Green army, which attacked (really attacked, with live ammunition) the Blue army.

There were objectives for different armies and groups. A neutral establishment, known as the Headquarters group, watched the comings and goings of all the different armies. When objectives were deemed to be accomplished by the Headquarters group, the 'Front Line' location was changed accordingly, and, if a successful invasion were to take place, then 'prisoner of war' camps were set up where the prisoner would lose all his equipment and personal possessions. These war games were certainly not games. I prefer to use the much more realistic term manoeuvres. The reason for this whole exercise, I believe, was to make certain people (the Russians in particular) take notice.

I started my first day in the Blue army under orders to load emergency equipment and tools onto one of the many regimental trucks that was set up as a portable workshop. We had a little team: a sergeant in charge, a driver of the truck, a mechanic with knowledge of the tanks and tank engines, and me, with knowledge of tank guns. Four of us who were capable, apparently, of keeping tanks and their guns operating successfully in wartime conditions. We were given a location in a long line of twenty or so other trucks, and warned that we must stay in line. Our orders, which came by way of an officer riding up and down our convoy in a jeep, included the admonition to follow the truck in front. When he goes, you go. When he stops, you stop. We quickly discovered that when the convoy stopped, there was not enough time to boil water to make tea. Very frustrating! However, the main requirement was to carry out orders, rather than make tea.

After travelling about twenty miles in the truck convoy, we were eventually flagged down to stop and make camp for the rest of the day. We parked the truck in a wooded area and immediately covered the truck with camouflage material, which was part of the kit that we carried. After half an hour's work and cutting a few leafy branches, the truck was invisible from a distance of about forty feet.

"First things first." called the sergeant, who was a 'regular' with twenty years or more of active service. "Two things we have to take care of before it gets dark. A communal latrine and a safe place to sleep." The latrine was easy the way the sergeant described it. He chose a spot that was far enough away from our camp for us not to be bothered by any odors. He also pointed out that we should avoid any tree roots, especially large ones. Then, each man in turn grabbed a shovel and started to dig the outline of the latrine. First the driver, then me, then the sergeant, with each man digging for no more than two minutes per session. Each man, of course, tried to outdo the others. At the end of sixteen minutes (timed with the sergeant's stopwatch), we had a five-foot deep trench, two foot wide by six foot long. A couple of pre-fabricated wooden platforms completed the rough and ready job. This method of having a fresh worker every two minutes really worked! Later, of course, when we broke camp, we made sure we filled in the latrine before moving on.

The safe place to sleep turned out to be a shallow trench, about twelve inches or so deep, and two foot wide by six foot long. As the sergeant pointed out, sleeping in a 'bed' like that with most of your body below the surface of the ground provided protection against stray bullets and the blast from large guns. I must admit that it was no fun sleeping in a muddy hole alongside the bugs and worms, although I slept like a top until 5am when I awoke to find myself being bitten by about 100,000 mosquitoes around my forehead and on my face. It had been raining overnight. We gained a heck of a lot of experience on our first day of manoeuvres!

The Blue army that we were attached to spent the following day and night in camp making itself comfortable. We received unofficial orders through the grapevine that we were to stay put for at least the rest of the day. "Good," said our sergeant. "Let's spend our time building a water heater so that we can make tea when in convoy." We couldn't build a fire because no fire, or even the semblance of a fire, was permitted on the truck at any time. So when the convoy stopped, we figured on having a maximum of five minutes in which to off-load our heater onto the road, fire it up, watch for steam, and extinguish it, reloading everything including our four cups of boiling hot water. As part of our kit on the truck, we had several pieces of copper tubing of various sizes, from a quarter inch to two inches diameter. We also had a box filled with connecting elbows, tees, valves, and caps.

Our first attempt at putting together a workable boiler did not work too well. It was far too large; the copper tubing was two-inch size, and it should have been one-inch maximum. There was not enough heat transfer area as it needed more tubes of a smaller size. We spent a couple of hours soldering all our bits and pieces together, until we came upon the correct formula, which worked, but was also not too large.

The contraption, which was about twelve inches square, sat on a two-inch deep tray and was simply bristling with tubes. The tray was filled with three or four cups full of sand and there were two systems for heating the cold water. The first one raised the water temperature from cold to about 100°F or so. The second one took our water temperature to boiling point. We had a real little boiler, which was petrol operated. Now, to get our cup of tea as fast as possible, we poured half a cup of petrol into the sand, then four cups of water into the water pipe, being careful not to mix them up. Then, we had to put the tray onto the kerb side, strike a match, and toss it on to the sand. Within less than two minutes, we had boiling water. To stop the operation, we simply dumped a shovel full of sand onto the contraption, and tossed the whole thing onto the back of the truck to be cleaned and prepared for the next time. All this for a cup of tea!

Our regiment spent a lot of time advancing and retreating, which meant that we were forever making and breaking camp. Each new camp, of course, meant a new latrine to be dug, whether anyone used it or not, and a new sleeping area. Then there was a sudden break in the monotony, when our senior officer, a major, came to our sergeant with orders from Headquarters. The time was 2am, but we all scrambled to liven ourselves up. We were to break camp and drive by the shortest route to a particular map reference where we would meet up with two tanks. It seems that one tank had a broken-down engine, and the other had a broken-down gun.

The four of us were to take charge of the two tanks and get them both back to Osnabrück camp along with our truck. Then we were to replace the engine on the one tank and replace the gun on the other. After the switch had taken place, we were then to drive both tanks to the firing range, and fire both guns to prove them. Our sergeant had three people under his control, a driver, a motor mechanic and me. I don't remember who drove what, but I do know that between us we managed to get everything back to camp, by using one of the tanks as a towing vehicle.

I found myself delegated to take care of the tank with the broken-down gun. It wasn't really broken-down, but our major had taken a pencil rubbing of the serial number which was stamped right on the gun barrel, so I didn't have a choice. He would know whether or not I had switched the guns. I would have to completely dismantle a perfectly good gun and replace it with a completely new gun from the arsenal. Our sergeant and the motor mechanic went to their beds after calling out, "Get the driver to help you with the gun change-over, and call us in the morning." We had started this little exercise on Thursday morning at 2am, and it was Thursday midnight when we started to take the gun apart. It took us about fifteen hours to take out the old gun and its parts and replace it with the new one.

I learned a lesson about people from this exercise. The lesson was that a willing helper is worth much, much more than a lazy so-and-so who would rather go to bed than help his comrades. The situation was not serious. It was almost funny if you think about it. The driver and I drove the two tanks to the driving range, and met up with our sergeant and the motor mechanic. The mechanic intimated to me that he had not changed the engine on his tank, but the sergeant had guaranteed that the switch had been made. I fired both guns under the supervision of our major, hitting one target, and missing the other. The major gave a flippant salute. "Well done, sergeant," he called out.

I spent about two years in Osnabrück camp, including the month or so running around the countryside on manoeuvres. While there I ventured to take a few train rides in my spare time to nearby towns. One of these trips was to Munster, where Young Rollo was serving in the King's Royal Rifles as a dispatch rider. Lucky devil, I thought. He gets to ride a motorbike for his National Service. We kept in touch during this time through letters and postcards, not via telephone as we do today.

One day I went to meet Rollo on an early train, getting to Munster well before noon. We made a tour of the small town, ate some lunch and spent the afternoon drinking in the various beer gardens. We had a good drink, but we didn't get drunk, just a little sloshed. My train was due late afternoon, about 6pm, and I thought that the journey back would be a good opportunity for me to get a little shut-eye.

The train was filled to capacity. All German civilians, but I didn't feel uncomfortable about that situation. They were mostly women and old men. I was about to doze off when the old man opposite, in the other window seat, started to talk to me. He spoke a tiny bit of English and I responded with a tiny bit of German. We eventually arrived at the point where we both knew that he was a baker and that I was a boilermaker (*kesselmacher*). As we talked about where we came from (I mentioned Osnabrück) there was a sudden commotion outside and the train stopped. An official who worked for the railway came running past our carriage and on the way he popped his head into our window and called out to us that the steam boilers on the train had broken down. By now it was quite dark and people outside were moving back and forth, flashing their hand-held torches.

A young German fellow, sitting diagonally across from me and probably about my age, started talking to the old man. He was quite voluble and as he talked he kept nodding his head in my direction. He was obviously talking to the old man about me, and whatever he was saying it was definitely not to my benefit. I don't know why, but a cold feeling came over me as I sat there. I remembered a recent newspaper story of an incident which had taken place in Germany about three weeks before. A British soldier, travelling alone on a train, had been tied up and left on the tracks; when the next train came along he was cut in half. The old man told me that the young man was annoyed because the British soldier, namely me, with training on steam boilers, did not offer to help start up our broken-down steam train.

I looked around to see if there were any allies in the immediate area. Two or three British soldiers would be a godsend right now but all I could see was a carriage loaded with unhappy Germans who were, by now, all glaring at me as if blaming me for the breakdown! I went to the corridor and strutted back and forth, putting on a big pretence to show that a few German peasants didn't worry me.

After what seemed like hours, but was in fact most likely twenty minutes, the train started up and began to rattle slowly along towards Osnabrück. I stayed in the corridor for the rest of the trip; I didn't want the other passengers to hear my heavy breathing or see my hand shake as a result of the stress the young German had caused me. The train slowed down as it approached my station, and I breathed a huge sigh of relief as people began to pull down their cases and coats from the luggage rack above.

I glanced across to the elderly baker, who returned my glance with a smile while mouthing "*Auf Wiedersehen*". The young man, who half an hour ago frightened me so much with his aggressive attitude, walked past me with a clumsy salute saying "*Gute Nacht*". I realised that nothing was going to happen. The young man was not going to lead a bloodthirsty mob to attack me. The baker waited for me to shake my hand saying, "Please forgive our young friend for his bad manners; he is upset because there are foreign soldiers in his country. In spite of what you may think, you are a foreign soldier. He, I hope, will learn." Fancy that – me a foreign soldier! I hate to think what my Dad would say about that.

CHAPTER 5

The Wasted Years

1952 – 1960

MY two years of National Service passed swiftly. The King, George VI, died and his place was taken by his daughter, Elizabeth II. We were now ruled by a Queen. King's regulations became Queen's regulations overnight. Prince Philip, the Queen's husband, did not become King in the same way that Albert did not become King when he married Queen Victoria a hundred years earlier.

In order to get demobilized (de-mobbed) from the army, I was shipped back to England and sent to Andover for a few weeks to be 'processed'. The only thing I had in Germany that was of any value was my radio, which I gave to Heinz before I left. The clothes that I stood up in, consisting of two uniforms and one overcoat, technically belonged to the Queen, but the quartermaster responsible for getting me through the discharge system warned me that I would need my uniforms during the next three and a half years in the Territorial Army. My shirts, socks, and underclothes were all mine.

The Territorial Army was not something I had reckoned on. Being in the 'territorials' was like being in some kind of men's club. I was on call for more than three years, and during that time, I was expected to show up for at least two evenings every week for lectures and discussions on the subject of 'the modern army'. In addition to that, a member of the territorials had to be available for manoeuvres two weeks a year. This effectively fouled up any vacation plans that I might have had for the future, although at that time not many people that I knew took regular holidays anyway.

All this was bad enough, but the worst part was that in practice, the two evenings a week were spent playing snooker and billiards, drinking cups of tea, and telling yarns about army experiences. But the time had to be spent with the military, so I spent it. I must admit that I eventually got used to what I call my 'wasted' Tuesday and Thursday evenings and I began to enjoy the club atmosphere. My new regiment was called the "Inns of Court" and was located at 10 Stone Buildings, Lincolns Inn, London, WC1.

When I was preparing to return to England from Osnabrück, I suddenly realised that the army had looked after me so well over the last two years that I wouldn't have to concern myself with lodgings or a job if I signed on for a further five years or more. I must admit that I was sorely tempted by my Regimental Sergeant Major (RSM) at the time. He spelled out to me the various courses that I would be taking if I signed on, which would be equivalent to a civilian degree in engineering. My pay would also increase dramatically, even though I was already the highest paid National Serviceman in the regiment at the time. I was eligible for a pension, guaranteed by the British Government, which I could draw at forty. In addition to this, of course, was the companionship that can only manifest itself among soldiers and fighting men when facing a common enemy.

My RSM tried very hard to get me to sign on. One of my reasons for not staying in the army was that I wanted, eventually, to be married and raise a family. Army life and family life, in my mind, didn't mix. "Nonsense," said my RSM, "come and have lunch with me and my family on Saturday, and you will see how a family survives in the modern army." I agreed to visit, and at the appointed time I knocked at his door. He opened it himself with a flourish, at the same time introducing his wife, a beautiful young woman of about my age, and two children, a boy and a girl, squabbling over some toys in the background. What a surprise! I don't know exactly what I expected his family and living conditions to be like, but I certainly didn't expect what I found. When on duty, the RSM was as tough as nails, giving orders to all and sundry and taking charge, whatever the situation. When he was displeased, he let it be known by raising the pitch of his voice. Several junior officers (second lieutenants) fell foul of him, embarrassed by his sarcastic tongue almost to the point of tears, even though they out-ranked him. To see this soldier, this tough, brutal loudmouthed individual suddenly turned into a pussycat was almost funny. I came into his house with a smile.

The house was very nice. Much better than what a boilermaker could afford in London. "This is the married quarters," he said. He went on to describe to me how a family stays together even though the soldier may get posted to various parts of the world, and to where the regiment is needed. We spent the afternoon rolling about on the carpet with the children, talking about army service, and drinking beer. I had never seen such a transformation in a man. I thought that this could be my life style if I signed on, and I felt a tinge of envy that he had all the things that I wanted, especially a beautiful wife.

The first thing a fellow must do in order to start building a family of his own is of course, to find a wife. This is not as easy as it sounds. A fellow can't go to the supermarket and buy one. Nor can he position himself in Petticoat Lane with a sign around his neck proclaiming: "Ladies: reliable, respectable, and decent man available as husband". No, no, no. If he tried either one of these methods, he would wind up on a funny farm!

So. Where did that leave me? A foreign wife, with foreign relatives would not make for connubial bliss. Far better to have an English, or British, wife and of course I would have a better chance of meeting someone suitable in England than anywhere else in the world. Needless to say, for a very long time I wasn't very successful at finding and keeping a partner who looked halfway decent, and was also keen on me.

The first girl to get my attention was Sally Rollinson, Rollo's cousin. We genuinely liked each other, and started to 'go out' together while I was still in my teenage years. I guess I was about eighteen when we first met. Young Rollo and I were in the habit of visiting his Uncle Harry in Stratford in the East End for the purpose of bringing bottles of home made wine back to Rollo's Dad. Another uncle of Rollo's lived in Stratford and Uncle Sid also made wine, which was potent stuff. Uncle Harry often opened a bottle, "Just to be sociable," he claimed. An added attraction for me to make the trip to Stratford on a regular basis was that Uncle Harry had two daughters, Sally and Iris. Iris was spoken for by Reggie Nickelson, but Sally was free; she had no boyfriend to complicate the situation. Sometimes she and I would spend time at the roller skating rink, or at a movie, but the most interesting discussions I had were with her father, Rollo's Uncle Harry. He and I talked of all kinds of things while I was waiting for Sally to 'get ready' for our outing.

Whenever we went on a trip we went by motorbike, and her favourite place to visit was Southend on Sea, which was on the coast about forty miles from London. We would ride there, eat some chips, drink a couple of cups of tea, and then ride back for more tea. Oh boy! What fun. The ride was terrific, exciting, and fast. It was also dangerous. We did not wear crash helmets in those days. Riding a fast motorbike with the wind in your hair and a girl hanging on like grim death behind was as close to solo piloting a plane you could ever get. Especially when it was raining!

Sally and I were not compatible as far as music was concerned. I had been in the habit of going to one of the West End concert halls to listen to a program of Brahms, Beethoven, or Schubert. I tried to coax her into joining me once or twice, but I was wasting my time. She had absolutely no interest in listening to anything classical. She wasn't the only Rollinson to feel this way. Some years later, after listening to a performance at the Albert Hall of Schubert's Unfinished Symphony, Rollo was heard to say, "Thank God he didn't finish it!".

The average Eastender, in my experience, did not spend any time listening to music, and for that reason I sometimes felt like an odd man out with my friends. Sally and I broke up our relationship when I packed my suitcase prior to returning to camp after being on leave. "You are taking your civilian clothes with you back to Germany," she said. "That tells me that you might be going out on dates when you go back." This may or may not have been true, but at this stage of my life I found it difficult to argue.

While still deciding what to do after returning from my two years of National Service in Germany, I picked up where I left off at home. Mum and Dad were both pleased to have me back at 82 Braintree Street where I had my old room, which I used to share with Roy. I believe that we still shared the room until Roy married and moved away.

♪

Another time waster that I exploited to the utmost during the 1950s was drinking. I didn't drink booze like rum, gin, or scotch but preferred drinking beer – to excess. I can remember a few times when I drank eight English pints in the space of two or three hours. The standard procedure for a good night out among ordinary people like boilermakers, or tradesmen in general, would be for the men to meet in one of the local public houses and start the evening by having a 'whip round'. This meant that all the men contributed money to a kitty. The kitty was doled out as needed for drinks as the evening progressed. Any women belonging to the group didn't contribute; they had free drinks.

There was usually some form of entertainment in the pub, depending on which pub was chosen. Darts was popular, along with shove ha'penny, although shove ha'penny was a little old fashioned and usually reserved for the older fellows. The most popular pubs were the ones with live entertainment: piano, singer, or small group. The most popular choice was a pub with a singer at the piano, always a man. The singer and piano player would drag out all the old songs along with the popular songs of the day. Slowly but surely, and one after another, the patrons would start to sing along, until someone would call out on the microphone to a singer, "I see one of our favorite singers at the bar, whetting his whistle – I think he's going to give us a song."

Once somebody had broken the ice by singing a solo, others would follow in quick succession, and in no time at all half the people in the pub had a go on the microphone with their favorite song. Some of the singers were pretty good and able to harmonise with the rest of us. The ones who were not up to scratch were booed away from the mike. It was a lot of fun being among friends, experiencing the warm glow that a couple of pints of beer can bring, and singing your heart out with songs like 'Nellie Dean', and 'Heart of my Heart'.

But I must say that gambling was the worst time waster that I came across. I first started playing cards during the 1940s at Frasers and refined my card playing skills whilst at Osnabrück. Then I progressed to what they call 'working man's gambling' and became snared into trying to pick a winner at the dog track. I even had a turn at the horse track, considered a wealthy man's gamble. Racing was called 'the sport of kings'. That was probably to make it a bit more acceptable. Far better to admit "I lost a few pounds today whilst playing the sport of kings", than "Today I lost money gambling on the horses". Whether you subscribe to the first or second statement makes no difference. You will end up losing. Unless of course you are a bookmaker, and then no doubt you will make a decent living at the racetrack.

In my experience at various racetracks as a punter I lost steadily, week after week, year after year. It's true that I made some spectacular wins on a few occasions, but the losses far exceeded the wins. In fact, sometimes the winning streak was worse than losing. The win would bolster your ego and boost your confidence, making you bet even more because, dear punter, when you win, you begin to feel infallible. You might back two or even three winners in quick succession, and those winners might have good odds, say ten to one rather than even money. But you must have enough cash in your pocket to enable you to place a decent sized bet. If you have a potential five to one winner and you would like to win some real money, it wouldn't do much good to back it with two pounds. Your winnings would total a princely ten pounds, hardly enough to pay the entrance fee at the track or treat yourself to a sit-down meal, or buy a round of drinks at a party.

My Dad had the right attitude to gambling, especially dogs and horses. "It's a mug's game," he would say. "If you start to gamble, be prepared to lose." Dad stuck to this adage until well into his 60s, at which time he would have what he called an occasional 'flutter', and back his 'fancy'. He usually lost, of course.

My time spent with the territorials was not the only time I feel I wasted during the 1950s. I started gambling, and found that once I had started it was very difficult to stop. I was betting on the dogs and horses. I also smoked like a chimney and was never seen without a cigarette in my mouth. In fact, I used to start smoking my first fag of the day while shaving in the morning. That wasn't easy to do without choking. I learned to draw the smoke, gulp it down into my lungs, and then blow it out through my nose without touching the cigarette. All this while I was shaving and my face and hands were covered with soap. Today, I have a crease running down from my left nostril to the left side of my mouth. This groove, etched into my skin, is the result of a few years spent blowing smoke out of the left side of my mouth whilst keeping the right side closed. I was copying the actions of people like James Cagney who smoked incessantly on the movie screen.

♫

Dad's business as a scrap iron and metal merchant was slowly thriving. He incorporated it and included both Roy and me as directors of the new company, which was named T. Goodwin & Sons Limited. It would have been nice if I could have benefited from this company but unfortunately it was not to be. Roy and I, being younger and more aggressive than Dad, wanted to expand our scope of work to include repairs to any kind of engine or mechanical device. Dad was against this so we never got a chance to see if it would work. I wanted to buy a welding set and a cutting torch so that we could start by streamlining the demolition part of our business.

Roy and I were wasting our time arguing about it. Dad wanted everything to be the same as it was originally when Grandad Goodwin died and Dad took over. Dad would not even open a bank account for the firm. The last straw for me was when we tried to agree on wages and benefits. Under Dad's rule, Roy and I would live at home free and be paid pocket money of, if I can remember accurately, five pounds a week. What a shame. At the time it looked as if it would have been a good opportunity for the company to grow and for us, one day, to become successful, maybe even wealthy. I worked out an arrangement with Roy that I would return to my trade of boilermaker, pay Mum and Dad for my lodgings, and let Roy help Dad to run the business. If the 'family' business ran into trouble, I would be available to help them as much as possible.

Fraser & Fraser, Engineers and Boilermakers was still there right next to Bromley-by-Bow underground station, and I lost no time in going to see Albert Hunt regarding a job. "No problem," said Hunty. "Carry on where you left off. I'll put you with Ernie Mace, you and he can work together and we will see how it goes." I walked around the boiler shop and said "hello" to all my old buddies and workmates. I wore my army uniform on purpose in order to swank a little and show off.

I was surprised to see how dirty and noisy the place was, but everyone told me it had always been like that. I had a long chat with Ernie Mace, and I found that our original relationship was to continue, he as the master mechanic, and I as the apprentice or helpmate. This was not what I was hoping for. I had served a complete apprenticeship, taken extra courses and training in the army, and I was now more than twenty-three years old. I reckoned that I deserved more than this. I decided to stick it out for six months and if nothing changed, I would go job hunting. Although Ernie and I got on fine together I wanted independence, so I began looking for another job. One day I buttonholed Hunty with a "Good morning Albert, how are you today?" smile. We chatted about army life; he had been too young for the First World War and too old for the Second. He had experience however from his boys who, like me, had served in the army. "When," I asked him, "are you going to regard me as a man rather than a boy?" This debate continued for ten minutes or so and ended when I told him that I was very unhappy with the situation of having to work under Ernie's jurisdiction. We ended our little chat when I told him that a Thames-side barge building company, Badcock Company, had offered me a job building and repairing the company barges as well as manufacturing miscellaneous steel products.

Albert Hunt couldn't believe his ears when I told him that I would be leaving at the end of the week. No boilermakers in living memory had left Frasers except to join the armed forces, and they had all returned or were in the process of returning. "You may regret leaving," he told me finally, "but you are always welcome to return at any time."

My gambling increased dramatically as soon as I started work at Badcock in 1956. This was because I met up with Bill Spurling , commonly known as "Steamboat Bill". Bill had heard of the new man starting with the company – me – and wanted to be assigned to him as 'mate'. Bill had missed an apprenticeship due to the war but was now trying to make up for lost time, and he needed someone like me to coach him. The foreman, Jones, duly assigned Bill to be my mate with the proviso that Bill must be a member of the Boilermakers' Union and abide by their rules regarding apprentices and trainees.

Bill was a former merchant navy man whose ship had been torpedoed in the North Atlantic early in the war. He survived an hour in the freezing water before being picked up by a Royal Navy boat and rescued. Bill then served in the merchant navy for another year when his ship was torpedoed again! Once again his ship went down, once again he landed in the freezing North Atlantic water, once again he was rescued, and survived. Bill Spurling must have been the luckiest man alive. "I have been so lucky," he would say whenever we went racing, "my horse must win!"

On the way to the races we would stop at a roadside pub for a late breakfast of bread rolls with cheese and onions, and beer. I would study the map to make sure we were on our way to the right racetrack, and Bill would check the day's paper to study the form of the horses in each race.

By the time we arrived at the track, Bill had a possible winner picked out for each of the six races. One winner was all we needed for the day. Bill figured out our day's expenses for petrol, entrance fee, food, and parking. He added five pounds to the total, and this amount was the total winnings we should try for on the first race. If our first possible winner lost his race, then we had to recalculate how much we had to speculate so that we would finish the day as winners. I remember a day at Epsom, when we figured the first race winner. "This is it," said Bill, "This is the one that you can safely call a dead cert winner. I'm going to put ten quid to win on this horse." Imagine our surprise when we checked out the odds and found that the bookies' price was ten to one. An outsider. Bet one pound to win ten. The horse won his race easily. This was the best win we ever had. Bill won £100, which was a heck of a lot of money in those days, and I won £10 after backing the horse with a pound note. We sat in the grandstand with the toffs drinking beer for the rest of the day, backing the other five hopefuls we had picked earlier only with odd half-crowns or shillings. None of them were hopeful winners. We were both lucky and clever that day!

♪

There were many minor adventures that took place in my life during the 1950s, some of which I regarded as a waste of time. Gambling, drinking and smoking took up a lot of my time, as did the riding of my motorbike, which I enjoyed right up until I finally sold it in 1955 when I came off my bike at 70mph doing a 'speed wobble'. This was the last time I had done any serious motorbike, but the experience was enough to put anybody off motorbikes for life. It started early in the morning when I packed a lot of camping gear consisting of tents and sleeping bags into my bike's pannier bags. I had been on a camping trip to Land's End, the furthest point west in England, with Young Rollo. We decided to do the return to London in one day stopping only for food and petrol. He was riding his new 350cc Triumph Twin and I was on my 350 Royal Enfield. I had heard of speed wobbles from other riders and the generally accepted cure was to open the throttle and accelerate as much as possible. This, I had been assured, would solve the problem immediately.

My problem, I know now, came from loading my luggage badly. The heavy pieces consisting of tents and sleeping bag, I packed behind the center line of the rear wheel. If you reflect a moment on this you will see that this will tend to lift the front wheel or at least make the front wheel lighter. We came to a section of road that was dead straight across Salisbury Plain. Rollo, who had the faster bike, took off like a bat out of hell and disappeared in the distance. I was following at a slower speed, about 70mph. I guess it was my lucky day because there was no traffic on the road at all except Rollo and me.

I felt a quiver on the front wheel and handlebar. I glanced down and saw that my speed was exactly 70mph. Suddenly the quiver became a shake, then the shake became a wobble. It went through my mind like a streak of lightning; this is a speed wobble. Accelerate. Turn that throttle. Then I realised that I couldn't go any faster, I was already doing flat-out top speed. Now what? Decelerate? Slow down just a little bit? *Mistake*! All at once I felt and heard and saw the handlebar crashing to full lock three times before I noticed that the sun was in the wrong place and rolling up and down, up and down. Then I saw my bike, all by itself, about two hundred feet in front of me with the engine still running, lying on its side.

I kept perfectly still for a long time, worried about what damage might have been done. The only special protection we had in those days was gauntlet gloves, leather jacket and goggles. No crash helmet, no special trousers or boots. My right hip hurt a little, but when I explored with my fingers I could feel that it was just a graze. I heard a small truck coming but I couldn't see it. My glasses were gone. I got to my feet and saw the truck; it was a type of army vehicle often used as a runabout. I waved my arms and shouted for the driver to look for my glasses, which were somewhere on a two-hundred-foot stretch of road. Rollo was nowhere to be seen and the road was still deserted for about half a mile in both directions. The army driver and his buddy put me and my bike onto the grass verge and found my glasses. "You're lucky to be alive," they both said. "It was just as well you rolled into the foetal position, and kept on rolling, otherwise you would be dead now that's for sure." I didn't know how I did what I did, but somehow, automatically, I curled up and protected myself. I can't claim to have done anything clever, and from start to finish it took no more than about twenty seconds.

I sat and smoked half a pack of cigarettes over the next forty-five minutes waiting for Rollo to return. When he came back he was hopping mad. "Where the dickens have you been?" he shouted. When I told him about my adventure he calmed down. There was surprisingly little damage done in this episode. First there was the graze on my hip and secondly my bike had suffered a broken lamp glass and bent foot-rest. We continued to London at a slower pace and arrived there before dark. It was shortly after this that I bought my first car, a second-hand 12hp Standard Coupe. I replaced that with a Hillman Minx.

♫

However, the 50s were not a complete disaster. After working in Badcock's barge yard and the family business, I went to work for Hobal Engineering for five years starting in September 1956, and then in 1961 for Brown Lennox for one year. Hobal Engineering's name was an amalgamation of Hobbs and Balbes, who started out in business shortly after the war as a partnership manufacturing ice cream sticks. Yes, you read it correctly. They made those little wooden sticks that get frozen into a bar of ice cream.

Hobbs and Balbes together heard of a stainless steel manufacturing company that could not complete its contract on a half-finished storage tank. Hobal came into being, finished the tank, made a fantastic profit and started to specialize in stainless steel equipment. While working at Hobal, I became a member of the Hobal cricket team. We played against other companies in the area, plus a few from the Isle of Dogs. This of course was during summer. In winter we got together at lunchtime and used the local swimming pool for relaxation.

On several occasions while working for Hobal, based in Plaistow, I was sent to install our factory-fabricated dairy equipment into farms all over the south of England and parts of Scotland, taking with me a crew of five or six men of various trades such as welders and fitters. One such job was located near Bath and we left London early on a Monday morning, in order to get a jump on the job. I kept a timesheet of everyone on the job, including myself, because each man was paid by results. I had a contract price to provide all the labor to complete the job, and paid all the wages out of the contract price for the job. Then, if we finished the job and still had money left in the contract price, that money was shared out as a bonus for finishing ahead of time. Each man received a share of the bonus, according to his wage structure. The system was designed to ensure that everyone, no matter how little he earned, got a fair share.

Everyone on the job worked to capacity starting at 6am, taking half an hour off for lunch, then continuing work on the job until 9pm. The reason for such a hectic schedule was that the owner had been promised an up-and-running dairy within one week of our starting work. This meant that we were scheduled to finish on Sunday night so that the owner could press his 'On' button on Monday morning!

But this gave me a problem. My whole team wanted to see a big soccer match on Saturday in nearby Bath, and we couldn't be in two places at once. One of my fellows suggested that we go to see the match on Saturday afternoon then work around the clock until the job was finished. I thought that this was a very good idea. After all we hadn't been told about the shortened work schedule until Thursday. Based on other dairy plants that I had installed elsewhere, and on how much work there was still to do, I figured we could complete the job on time as long as we kept our concentration going.

We worked on Saturday morning until lunchtime, then we all piled into the company truck and made our way to the local soccer club and saw the game. When the game was over we all sang our way back to the dairy. There was a message waiting for me to call the boss, Mr Hobbs. When I made contact with him, I heard his voice, in a sarcastic tone, asking, "Did you enjoy the football?" He then went on to tell me that several people had noticed the work crew going to a football game, when they were supposed to be working. He implied that we had gone to see the game on 'company time', in other words, we were going to charge him for that time even though we hadn't been working. I assured him most emphatically that we had marked our time cards very clearly that we had stopped work at noon, and would not charge the company until we resumed working that evening.

He reluctantly accepted my version of what had happened, but I knew he didn't believe me. No matter what I said, I could not protect myself from his criticism, and it rankles me to this day that he more or less accused me of lying to him.

After this incident, I continued to work for the Hobal company for a couple of years, and whenever I was involved with Mr Hobbs he would give me a knowing wink and ask which football team I was currently supporting. I must say that, in retrospect, I quite enjoyed my time at Hobal Engineering. It was in this period that I quit smoking, cut down on drinking, and stopped gambling completely. The final straw came one Friday night, when I gambled and lost my whole week's wages. At the end of the evening, I left the stadium, and found my car a couple of streets away. As I started the engine, I realised that my wallet was empty, my pockets were empty and my Post Office savings account was empty! I had no money, and payday was a whole week away. I would have to scrounge money from someone to get through this period. Then what? Take my wages to West Ham and bet them away again next week? This was when I called it a day. I figured that I couldn't go any further down this slippery slope called 'gambling'. I decided then and there to quit, and as I had recently also stopped smoking, for the first time in years I was 'clean', and I felt really good about it.

♪

During the late 1950s, I received an invitation to a dinner party being held at a local hotel. The reason for the celebration was to get all the Fraser & Fraser people together, and although I now worked at Hobal, I was included as an ex-Fraser employee. One of the organizers of the dinner was Sid White. Sid was a driller in the boiler shop who worked alongside Johnson (Johno). Both Sid and Johno were almost completely deaf. That's what comes of working in a boiler shop all your life. In addition, they were both completely bald. They worked with their drilling machines on opposite sides of the boiler shop drilling holes that were destined to be filled with rivets. Two or three times a day, Sid and Johno would need to talk to each other and the one would wave to the other to get his attention. Johno would come up to Sid, meeting him in the middle of the shop, put his right hand on Sid's left shoulder and yell in Sid's right ear. Then, Sid would put *his* right hand on *Johno's* left shoulder and yell in *Johno's* right ear. This was how they carried on a conversation. To the rest of us in the shop they looked like two large birds pecking at each other, first the one side, then the other!

Sid White called me on the phone about the dinner. (Dad's telephone number, ADV-3730, was still in service at this time.) He seemed quite anxious to make sure that I would be at the party, and that I would be alone. I was surprised that he took notice of me at all. He was at least twenty years older than I was and we had never been close friends. On the night of the party, I discovered why he had singled me out. I arrived a little late and right away went to the bar for a drink. All my old buddies were there: Rollo, Ginger, and Reggie among all the others. Just then a young woman came up to me, held out her hand to shake mine, announced her name as Patricia, and said, "Hello Tom, I'm pleased to meet you. I've heard so much about you from my Dad."

I wondered, "Who the Dickens is this? Am I supposed to know her?". She linked arms with me and guided me across the room to the dining tables. "You don't know me, do you?" she said.

"Well," I thought, "she's certainly very friendly, I shouldn't worry too much about how she knows me." When we sat at the dining table I noticed that everyone had a place card with his or her full name except Patricia and me. We sat alongside each other with a joint card proclaiming "Tom & Pat". When she saw the look of surprise on my face, she burst into laughter.

"The fellow you know, Sid White, is my father," she said. "I couldn't resist having fun at your expense." She told me that her father had made some of the arrangements and she had helped him with the place cards. She told me that her father had painted such a rosy picture of me, telling her what a nice fellow I was, and what a handsome chap I was, that she was determined to put us together in the seating arrangements and find out for herself what I was like.

We engaged in a lot of small talk during which I learned that she was twenty-one and unattached. She was also presentable and good looking, but the best feature about her was that she was such good fun to be with. When we got to know each other better, we discovered that we both liked to do things on the spur of the moment and catch each other unawares. We started and continued what some people might call a close relationship, which lasted about eighteen months. Mum, who most likely knew me better than anyone else, probably fell onto her bended knees, giving thanks to Almighty God that at last her eldest son had finally met a woman he could get on with. This attitude, even if it were true, was short-lived.

We then burned out very quickly, and although I hate to say we got bored with each other, I believe that is what happened to us. I was glad to be working at Hobal at this time and not at Frasers where I would have undoubtedly had to field all kinds of questions from Sid White. Questions like, "Why did you break up with Pat, what went wrong?" Pat lived far enough away for it to be impossible for us to meet by accident. Neither of us (to my knowledge) tried to contact the other from that day to this. The situation came under the lawyer's statement of 'Case Closed'.

It was at about this time that I was asked if I'd like to go on a 'Beano' as a guest with the lads from Frasers. A 'Beano' was an outing to the seaside organized and paid for by the company. It was my friend Ginger who, many, many years later, reminded me of this one particular, but not necessarily typical outing. I've taken the following description from a letter written to me by Ginger in January 2000.

Sometime either in the late 50s or very early 60s we went on a works outing to Margate, a seaside town on the south coast. It's a trip I remember well. We met up at Frasers at about 8.30am and were soon on our way. The day was very hot and we had the roof of the coach open. The journey was going well and with beer stowed on board to quench our thirst, everything was fine, with the prospect of a good day in Margate. However, when we arrived at Rochester/Chatham the roads were blocked with traffic and there we sat and sweltered for some little while. Time was passing and we were all becoming a little hot and impatient. The traffic was not moving and we did not want to spend our day stuck in a very hot coach. We suggested to the driver that we would walk through the town, have a quick pint at each pub we passed en route, and wait for the coach on the other side of town when he had cleared the traffic.

All went well for a little while until the police unblocked the traffic jam and the coach was not allowed to stop until it had arrived beyond the other side of town. Collecting all the bodies together again through the town and getting them back to the coach took quite some time, and we didn't reach Margate until about 4pm. In those days coaches had to leave town by 5.30pm, so our day trip to Margate was a very short one. All Ginger can remember of that one-and-a-half hours in Margate was that Young Rollo and I took a dip in the sea, and I don't recall even that much! I've always wondered if that was due to the fact that we had had about a dozen pints of beer before we even got to Margate!

♫

I eventually left Hobal Engineering Limited in Plaistow in March 1961, but only because the company relocated out of the London area. I had the opportunity to go with them, but for some reason that I cannot now fathom, I decided against it.

After leaving Hobal Engineering I went to work for Brown Lennox Company Limited, of Millwall, London. The company was accessible by road and bus, being located on the River Thames in the area called the Isle of Dogs. The Isle of Dogs has since undergone drastic changes, including a beautiful new development called Canary Wharf. During my time at Brown Lennox I made another two good friends, Bill Taylor, and Andrew Caithness Meldrum Robertson, known as Andy. At the time when I joined the company, Andy and Bill, along with two other general laborers, made up a team. Andy, as a boilermaker, was in charge, and Bill, as a burner/welder, helped with the assembly and tack welding of the various tanks, buoys, and steel manufactured items that were being handled by the team. I was asked to join the team, which would now number a total of five: two boilermakers, one burner/welder and two laborers to fetch and carry, move materials, and operate the various cranes.

After being introduced by the works manager, Andy described the system to me. "Brown Lennox pays the laborers their wages," he said, "but we pay them a tip to encourage them to work harder for us." Andy showed me the list of all the jobs his team was presently working on. Each job had a set of drawings and specifications for our use, in addition to an estimate of the total number of hours our team would be paid to complete the job. "We get paid by results," said Andy. "If we complete a job and find that we haven't used up all the allotted hours, then the remaining hours left over are ours, belonging to us!"

I liked the system and I especially liked the idea of working against the clock! One little refinement that made the system even more attractive was that we didn't have to accept any job that we were offered. If we were given the details of a job or contract and we decided that there were not enough hours to enable us to finish it, then we could (and sometimes did) hand the whole package back to the works manager. He would try to re-negotiate with the company estimator or hand the job to another team of boilermakers and helpers. If this ever happened then someone would shout, "Can't do it for the price," and, amid winks between the leaders of the teams, the works manager would sadly return the job to the company estimator's office. "They can't do it for the price" would be the report.

You will probably realise from this that the poor old company estimator was in a very difficult position. He originally figured the complete job including other materials such as electrical work, and painting. If one part of his estimate was too low then he would be blamed for the loss of company profits. But if it was too high then the boilermakers would take full advantage of the situation and 'book in' all the hours they could find. Each hour was worth somewhere in the region of fifteen shillings, making £30 for a forty-hour week, and that represented pretty good wages in 1961.

Andy, a proud Scotsman from Dundee, welcomed me into his group as an equal and Bill Taylor, a rather laconic Londoner agreed. We were a team. We worked together successfully, and found that we were able to finish a couple of large jobs very quickly thereby building up a large balance of hours. The working week was forty hours and after a month or so we booked in our forty hours each per week without having to exert ourselves. My job became both lucrative and easy. The three of us became very good friends as time rolled by. Instead of going to work on a daily basis, it was like going to a club.

Andy, who had originally migrated from Dundee to London due to lack of work, went back to his wife who was still living in their Scottish home. He returned to Dundee to take advantage of the work situation, which was improving by 1962. Our team at Brown Lennox continued with me taking Andy's place and with Bill and I the proud possessors of several completed jobs that we could book in at any time.

The works manager called me into his office one day and handed me a set of drawings for a new job. "This is a real special one," he said. "I want you to be very careful with it." After glancing over the drawings for a couple of minutes, I saw that the design was for two large tanks of the kind that go on tanker-trucks, the type that one usually sees transporting some kind of fluid, such as petrol. The only thing that was special about this job was that it had to be galvanized inside and out after fabrication. I pointed this out to him, and we both agreed that this did indeed make the tanks special. All fabrication including cutting, drilling and welding of these tanks would have to be completely finished before the galvanizing procedure took place. No problem, as long as we all remembered that galvanizing was the very last thing to happen. "Just thought I'd mention it," said the works manager. "You can't successfully do any welding on a galvanized tank."

The job was easy. I spent half an hour doing some simple math to figure out the sizes of the various parts that made up the tanks. Then some hours were spent on the cutting and the same again on bending the steel plates. Bill Taylor and I put the job together in less than a week, which was about eighty hours total, and then we sent the tanks to the welders. The tanks were six feet in diameter, circular-construction, and twenty feet long. They each had a bolted manhole at the top for access and cleaning, and an internal ladder. They also had some hefty brackets welded on for future use when the tanks were bolted to their respective trucks. The two tanks were hoisted onto the loading bay, then shipped out to the galvanizing shop.

A week later, the tanks were back in our shop on the loading bay, all clean and freshly galvanized awaiting delivery to the customer, and they sat there for about a week. Then, one day, the works manager handed me a set of drawings. "You won't believe it," he said. "We have an order for two more of those galvanized tanks. Identical."

It's always cheaper by the dozen they say, so I thought we should be able to make some money on this job. The first thing I did was to go over my original 'simple math' to prove all the various sizes for cutting. To my surprise it looked as if the two new tanks were to be a foot shorter than the originals. I checked it again and all of a sudden my stomach went ice cold. The new ones were not a foot shorter, I had made the old ones a foot too long! How could that be? I scrabbled among pencils and paper and found a piece of paper where I had written 'Twenty feet total length made up of three eight foot sections which had to be cut to suit'. I grabbed a measuring tape and quickly ran over to the loading bay. I couldn't believe it, they were twenty-one feet long. I had made a mistake. Not only that, it was a mistake to beat all others. Twelve inches! I'd never made nor heard of such an error!

"Goodnight Tom," someone called out, "don't stay all night." I picked up the tape, tore off a fresh piece of paper, and licked my pencil stub. This can't be right, I thought. I went over it again, and again, and one more time to no avail. I had two tanks twenty-one feet long and an order for two more tanks twenty feet long. What was I to do? How would I get out of this mess? If the first two tanks had not been galvanized I could have cut, welded, and repaired. Forget about that. I was going to have to face the disgrace of being sacked. Just then, I heard the echo of footsteps in the shop. It was the works manager. "We're closing the shop for the weekend," he said. (It was Friday.) I mumbled something about tidying up and went home to spend a weekend worrying about my tanks.

On Monday I came in to work early, having made up my mind that all four tanks would be the same length (twenty-one feet), and decided that this was to be my secret alone. Then I rolled my sleeves up and set to work finishing the total job. This meant, of course, fabricating the two new tanks a foot longer than called for but all four would be an identical twenty-one feet long. I hoped that the owner would be glad of the extra few gallons he would be able to carry in each tank. I also hoped that the extra length would not be a problem to the people who would have to fit the tanks to the trucks.

That was my biggest gamble so far. I wrote a confession about the situation and gave it to Bill Taylor – to be opened whenever I left the company. My secret was now out! However, I have never to this day heard another thing about the matter, so I guess that no one ever found out.

It was at about this time, when my confidence was at a pretty low point, that Ginger told me about an ad he had seen in the paper. The ad was for 'first class fully experienced boilermaker platers, able to take charge of complete projects overseas with no supervision.' We talked about it, and contacted Young Rollo to see if it was worthwhile all three of us applying. "Oh yes," he said, "I'll give it a try." We decided to apply and were told to meet up with the company representative the next Sunday morning in Chelsea.

I was driving an old 1925 Ford that I had recently refurbished, using it for fun in place of my regular car, a 1950 Hillman Minx. I drove Rollo to Ginger's flat and there we all climbed into the Ford. The car was more than old; it was ancient, with a squeezable honk-honk horn on the outside of the driver's door and a top that went up or down, depending on the weather. We had plenty of time so we took a spin around central London before we started. When we got to Buckingham Palace, we drove around the circle three or four times honking our horn just for fun before heading for Chelsea for our interview.

The fellow we were to meet, Jack Thornton, was driving a Jaguar, a top-notch model right out of the box. "Climb in fellows," called our host, "we're on our way, so you can park your car here, and I'll bring you back later." We headed west out of London and stopped at a little pub for a pint. Ten minutes later we all climbed back in the Jag and continued driving west until we pulled into another tucked-away pub for another drink. As we were being driven from pub to pub to pub, Jack was asking dozens of questions about our abilities, our qualifications and our experience in the engineering and manufacturing trades.

After our fourth pint (and our fourth pub) it was beginning to sink in. This was our interview. We finished up after half an hour of hard driving, in a pub by the river, close to Henley on Thames. "Come on fellers," said Jack, waving a five-pound note, "they'll be closing in a minute." As we walked into the public bar, the publican started with his persuasive monotone "Time, gentlemen please", signalling closing time. "Never mind," said Jack "we'll go to my office."

With that he started his engine up again and wended his way through a series of back streets finally stopping at a large property containing several offices and an enormous parking lot. He had keys, and led us to a sumptuous office on the second floor. "No beer, I'm afraid," he said opening a liquor cabinet, "but we have scotch, rum, brandy, whatever you fancy."

Jack settled us into a very comfortable situation with leather armchairs, bottles of booze galore and promises of employment in Jamaica manufacturing equipment for the sugar trade. We were promised the moon! "Whatever you fellows are getting now, I'll double it," he said. The only problem was that the person making the promises was as drunk as a lord. Did he mean what he said, or was he just stringing us along? He spoke of a contract, but today wasn't the time or place for contracts. We let him know that another, sober, interview would be in order at some other time.

Then the three of us had to go. Doris, Ginger's wife, was making a lunch for us, a large one in the style of a Sunday dinner, so we drank up and promised Jack we would keep in touch with him and think about his generous offer, and let him know one way or the other. Meanwhile, would he please take us back to Chelsea where my old Ford was still waiting? We retrieved the car and bid him goodbye. Oh boy, what an interview that was. When we finally got to Ginger's flat Doris was waiting for us and was she mad! I never knew she could reach such a high note. It was about 4pm and we had been due back between 12 noon and 1pm. We had a very late cold lunch that day, but the dialogue was very interesting. Needless to say, we never contacted Jack again.

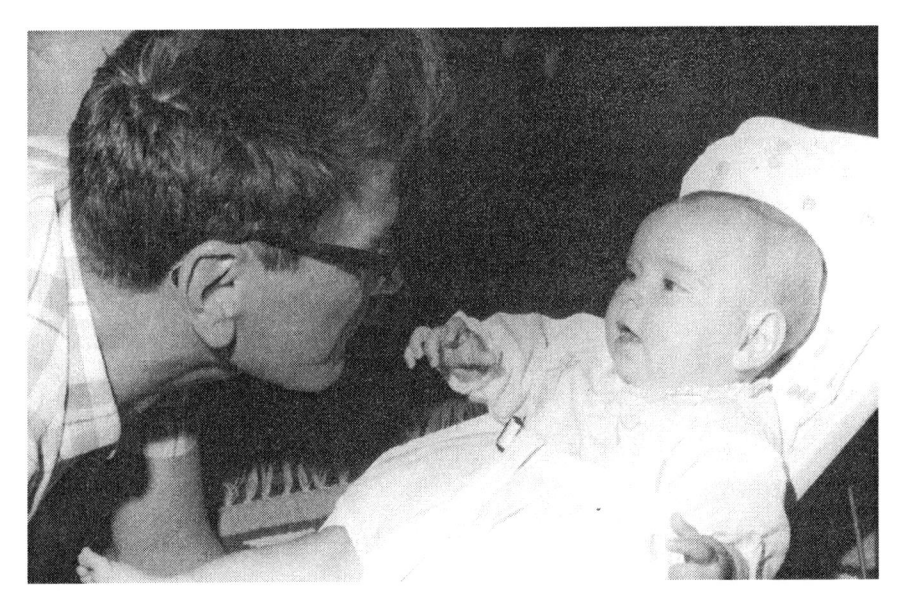

With Anne, born in June 1966

'The House That Tom Built'; I started building in 1967 and finished in 1969

Our family is complete when Steve is born, June 1968

Anne and Steve, sitting in the back garden, 1969

Evie with Anne and Steve in front of our house in Second Road, Kew, 1969

Our last holiday in South Africa before emigrating to the USA, Umhlanga Rocks, Natal, 1969

The old Chevy I bought when we first arrived in New Jersey in 1969; it 'drowned' in a local flood, but I rebuilt it and it ran for another 50,000 miles!

Our house, 215 Wyckoff Avenue, Piscataway, New Jersey, taken in the spring when our crabapple tree was in full bloom

Winters in New Jersey are very cold, but the children loved playing in the snow

Anne, age 4

Our 10th Wedding Anniversary, 1972

Reading with Anne in my favorite reclining chair, 1972

Mum and Dad visited us in Piscataway for a long vacation in 1972

The two sets of parents get together at our house; from left: Mum, Harold (Evie's dad), Elfy and Dad, with Anne and Steve, 1972

We spent many of our vacations at the beach; this was taken at Chincoteague, Virginia, 1973

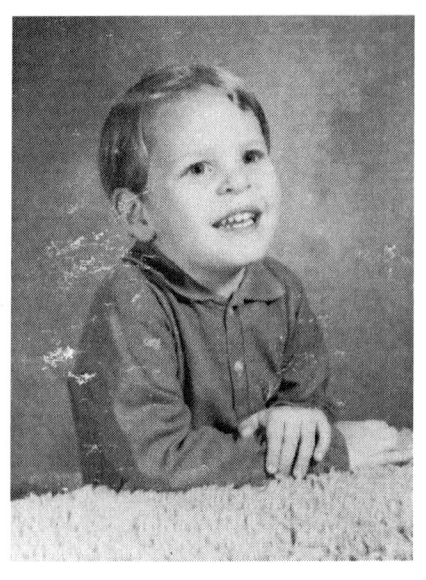

Steve, age 5

My favorite picture of the children, playing with the geese at Waterloo Village, 1973

Father and son having fun in Cherry Hill, Easter 1974

This one was included to show I was up on 'Bum Art'; taken in Washington DC, 1974

'Waiting for Santa Claus'; Christmas with Elfy and Gerhard Freund in Cape Town, South Africa, 1974

Eugene, he called himself 'Gene, short for Genius', my foreman at the Ortho site in Raritan, 1974

Construction at Aquaduct Racetrack that I helped manage for Dick Brady, and where I won $110 on the horses when the job was finished, 1975

Taken while visiting the Statue of Liberty, with the New York City skyline in the background, 1976

Still looking very much the Englishman in my 'titfer-tat, hat', 1977

I've enjoyed many years of singing in choirs and choruses

With Steve on a visit to London, in our new 'titfers', 1979

This photo appeared in London's 'Hackney Gazette' to commemorate Mum and Dad's 50th Anniversary, 1979

Gathered around the dining room table for my 50th birthday party with, from left, Trixie, Harold, Anne, me, Steve, Ruth Skaller, Henry (Harold's brother), Elfy and George Skaller (Harold's cousin), 1979

Showing off my new birthday watch

My good friend Austin Horn, with his wife Hella at their home in Johannesburg, 1983

Evie with her father in Woodstock, New York, c1985

With Steve, who was just about to graduate from high school and Anne, who had just started college, 1985

At a Hawaiian 'Hula' party, mid-1980s

Dressed up as the Duke of Edinburgh and Queen Elizabeth II, 1986

'Mad Dogs and Englishmen...', visiting Stratton, Vermont in 1988

Going to a Halloween party, 1988

Shopping in London, 1988

In charge of things at Elling Bros, where I worked for 12 years

CHAPTER 6

Romantic Times

1961 – 1962

UP until and during 1961 I regularly visited two of the best known concert halls in London, the Royal Festival Hall and the Royal Albert Hall. I often walked the distance, starting at Braintree Street in the East End and walking through central London and out the other side. The journey from Braintree Street to the Albert Hall was about four miles and to the Festival Hall about half that. I enjoyed the walk and it was a break from driving the car.

The London Philharmonic Orchestra, under the direction of Basil Cameron, was going to play in the Royal Albert Hall on Sunday August 27th 1961 at 7.30pm. The program was Tchaikovsky, nothing else. They were going to play among other things the '1812 Overture' (really gripping stuff), and the very popular piano Concerto Number 1 in B flat minor. The piano soloist was to be John Ogden, the famous 'youngster' born in 1937 who was by now world class. When I saw the newspaper advertisement for this concert I decided to go and listen. My morning was taken up with lazily dressing in my best suit and strolling to what I regarded to be my local pub, The Rising Sun on the corner of Globe Road and Roman Road. Traditionally, in the East End of London, the men congregated in the local pub on Sundays for an hour or so (between 11am and 2pm) while the women stayed home preparing lunch, or what we called 'Sunday dinner'.

The pub was noisy, crowded, uncomfortably warm, and it had a smoky atmosphere; almost everyone in the pub was smoking like a chimney. I didn't notice all these bad conditions when I walked into the pub, everything seemed to be perfectly normal to me; pubs were always like this. I caught sight of Rollo and his girlfriend Eileen Goldsmith near the bar. They had been dating for about a year or more, becoming what is nowadays called 'an item'. Reggie Nickelson was in the pub, but not his wife Iris. I supposed she was at home doing Reggie's Sunday dinner. I waved to them and sidled over to our little crowd. "What are you having Tom?" called Reg.

"Brown Ale," I replied. We all knew now, in observance of an unwritten law, that Reggie was 'in the chair' for one round of drinks before it became my turn to step up to the bar to order drinks for our party.

Eileen started to describe the gathering that was due to take place that evening at her mum and dad's place. Someone in the Goldsmith family was having a birthday or anniversary or something and I was invited to be there to take part in any and all festivities. "That's a shame," I said, "I can't make it."

"What do you mean you can't make it?" they all said. "What's so important that you can afford to miss a party like this?"

"A concert," I said, "a Tchaikovsky concert that happens only once in a blue moon." Well you should have seen their faces. With mouths wide open they stared at me as though I had gone completely crackers. They didn't have to say anything; I could see it in their eyes. Who in his right senses would miss a party in order to listen to a classical concert?

"Where is this concert?" asked Eileen, "Will they show it again?" I tried to explain that this was a one-time deal. If I missed tonight's concert, I might have to wait months or more before something like this was available again. When I told them that the concert was going to take place in the Royal Albert Hall, Rollo laughed and said that I had better start walking now if I didn't want to be late. "You're not going to walk it today Tom, are you?" said Eileen, "It's much too hot today for walking."

"No," I replied. "I'm planning to go by car, the good old PPG7." In those days we would often refer to a car by its license number. This was because the license number stayed with the car for its life. We chatted about our various bits and pieces of news, who got married, who changed his job, etc and before you could say 'Jack Robinson', it was my turn to get drinks at the bar. The Sunday lunchtime drink at The Rising Sun had become a ritual among Fraser employees past and present. Sid Kirrage often came for a drink. He's the one who wound up marrying Alice Brimstone. Who is she? you might ask. Alice, who lived next door to me in Braintree Street, would have become my wife if my mother had had her way. Luckily, I escaped matrimony that time. "Time, gentlemen please," called the bartender. We checked the time; it was after 2 o'clock and time to go home for dinner.

In spite of my friends coaxing me to go to their party, I stuck by my guns and got my car out of Dad's garage in plenty of time for the concert. When I got to the Royal Albert Hall, I saw that there was a line of people queuing up to get tickets. I had to park my car around the back of the building. The building, which can hold 8,000 people, was originally built in honor of Prince Albert, Queen Victoria's husband and Consort. I had to join the queue, which consisted of about fifty or sixty people all standing in the late-day sun. It was about 6pm on a summer's evening.

Two young women came slowly walking along the line of people. They seemed to be looking for someone. They walked past me so I took no notice of them, thinking they were probably looking for their boyfriends. Five or ten minutes went by, and the same two girls came back up the line. This time one of them marched right up to me. "Excuse me," she said, "Would you be interested in a single ticket?"

I didn't hesitate at all. "Why, thank you very much," I said. "That will save me from having to queue up."

She handed me a ticket, which was marked seven shillings and sixpence, so I took a one pound note from my wallet and offered it to her. She became slightly flustered, saying to her friend, "We must give change, Alex, twelve shillings and sixpence. Let's give the gentleman his change first and we can organize our purses later."

Having pocketed my ticket, I realized that I now had lots of time, so I decided to take a short walk. There was a pub on Kensington Road on the left as I strolled towards Queens Gate. I popped in for a half a pint and then walked back to the concert hall. It was quite a climb to the 'Gods' as the upper seats were called but this was where my ticket led me – up up up to the cheapest seats in the Gods. When I found my seat it came as a pleasant surprise that I would be sitting next to the girls who sold me my ticket. As expected, the seats were numbered.

The girl sitting on my left was called Evelyn Landsberger; she was the one who had approached me in the ticket queue. The other one was Alex. Alex was a student from Greece who could speak very little English. I wasn't able to converse with her beyond something like, "Hello, I'm Tom." Evelyn, however, was very easy to talk to and to converse with.

She was from South Africa, which was not among my favorite countries at that time. In addition to being from South Africa, Evelyn told me that she had been born in the USA, which I found very interesting. We chatted and talked about so many things that I was almost disappointed when the tuning 'A' came up from the orchestra. During the first part of the Tchaikovsky concert, I found myself wondering: if she was born in the USA, how did she get to South Africa? 'This young woman is one of the most interesting people I've ever met', I thought.

There was an interval of fifteen minutes or so, and I asked the young ladies if they would like a coffee, or an ice cream. Yes please, they both smiled! The second part of the concert was a rousing success with the conductor tying himself up in knots and the extra percussion in the '1812' really sounding like guns on a battlefield. When it was all over, we joined the crowd of people flowing onto the stairways and down the stairs. "I have my car with me," I volunteered. "May I give you a lift home?" The two girls whispered to each other, asked me to wait a moment, then disappeared in the direction of the ladies' room.

After a few minutes they reappeared at my elbow with Evelyn saying "Thank you, Tom, we would appreciate a lift home."

We walked to the car, and following Evelyn's instructions I started to drive it towards Hyde Park Corner. Suddenly Evelyn blurted out "Oh my gosh, we're going the wrong way." Surprisingly, this didn't bother me at all, going the wrong way at 10pm at night with two strangers! If it had been two men that I gave a lift to, I would have been annoyed. As we drove along, going the wrong way, Evelyn showed me the building where she worked for the Chrysler Corporation. Her boss was an American, Sherman Busch, who was vice-president of sales for Africa.

We were eventually able to make a U turn in the traffic, getting back to the building where the girls lived. Evelyn shared a bed-sitting room with Christine Horn on the ground floor. It was the nicest room in the building, a front room with a bay window. Alex shared the basement flat with Lorette Walder whose concert ticket I had bought. When Lorette had discovered at the last minute that she couldn't make the concert, she had begged Evelyn to sell her ticket. After all, this was the price of a dinner she reasoned.

When we got back to the building Alex invited Evelyn and me down to her flat for coffee. After a very pleasant half hour, I rose to go upstairs to the street level for my car. As Evelyn had to go up the same stairs to get to her bed-sitter, we found ourselves walking up together. At the front door I saw a brief moment to be alone with her. I turned and said, "I'd like to see you again, are you free one evening this week?"

"Yes," she said, "I'm free on Thursday." So we arranged that I would come round at half-past seven and we would go to Battersea Park to see the deer.

When I said " Good night, Evelyn", she smiled.

"I like to be called Evie with the first E sounding almost like an A." She told me this was a pronunciation that was from her mother, who was a Viennese from Austria.

I drove away, turned left at the next street, and then suddenly pulled up sharp with the realisation that I didn't know her exact address. After driving around the block I had it! 41 West Cromwell Road, Earl's Court. I jotted it down on a tiny sheet of a note pad so that I wouldn't forget. And I didn't forget; I still have that very, very important piece of paper!

♫

The fact that Evie and I got to know each other on the steps of the Albert Hall in the summer of 1961, in spite of the coincidences happening that day, was nothing short of miraculous. Firstly, Lorette Walder, who lived in Evie's bed-sitter, had agreed to go to somebody's house party outside

London that evening. This meant that Evie and her friend Alex had an extra ticket for the concert at Albert Hall. They originally offered the spare ticket to a young man who lived in their building, but he excused himself by claiming he had to do his laundry. Good old Lorette, if she hadn't gone to her party I couldn't have bought her ticket for the concert. And of course, Evie might have found some other unknown person in the queue at the concert and sold *him* the ticket. The ticket, by the way, cost seven and sixpence, the equivalent of a marriage licence in those days – quite a lot of money. And, if I hadn't so stubbornly refused to go to Eileen's family gathering, I could have been in the midst of an Eastender's party with all my old friends, rather than sitting next to Evie in the Albert Hall.

All of these things conspired so that the end result was that Evie and I met and went out together on our first date. The date was August 31st. We went on a ride to the south side of the River Thames and toured Battersea Park, which was well known for its free-roaming deer. Evie particularly wanted to see the deer. When it got dark we strolled through the portion of the park which was laid out like a fair ground. There were sideshows galore, where paying customers threw darts or rolled balls or slid pennies down a ramp, all trying to win prizes that were worth peanuts.

One of the sideshow operators caught sight of us strolling arm in arm, and called out, "Hey, my darlings, you haven't been married very long, I can see that." Little did she know that this was the first time that we had been out together – we must have had a certain look about us! We walked into a large tent where they were serving tea. We sat for quite a long time swapping stories and histories. Evie had been born in the USA, in 1941. I felt a spasm of disappointment when I heard that. She would be far too young to be my partner. Rollo would criticise, Mum would chastise if I were dating someone almost twelve years my junior. Such a large age difference could cause nothing but problems and embarrassment for me. It dawned on me that this was not going to be a good relationship. Much better to cut it off before we got too involved.

However, during our conversation, Evie remarked that she knew that I had just recently celebrated a birthday. "How on earth did you know that?" I asked.

"Oh easy," she replied. "When you were telling me about being evacuated, at the outbreak of the war, you said then that you had just turned ten. After that, I put two and two together." This little gem of logic impressed me no end. She had figured out that as this was now the end of August, and the war had started on September 3rd 1939, it was obvious that I had had a birthday at about this time. This was no child, I thought; we are on the same mental level. My mind was now in a complete turmoil. As we talked and talked about this, that, and the other, it became increasingly clear to me that I did not want to cut this relationship off. I wanted to be involved. Who cared what Rollo or Mum thought or said? In any case, Rollo's girlfriend Eileen was about ten years younger than he was, so who was he to pass judgement? In spite of my feelings I decided to take things slowly at the start.

On one of our early dates I called on Evie and asked where she wanted to go that night. "Let's drive out to the airport," she suggested, "and see the lights." Before air travel became commonplace most people travelled long distances by sea and visiting an airport was still rather exciting. We went out to the airport and found a parking lot near the buildings where we were able to leave the car and continue on foot to the viewing platform. After watching the planes come and go for half an hour, we'd had enough so we made our way to the restaurant and checked the menu that was pinned to the door.

The food was top quality – couldn't be better. However I felt a warm flush rising into my face when I saw the prices. The cheapest plate was more than a pound. I knew that I had a one pound note in my wallet plus some small change, maybe ten shillings or so. There was no escape for me. "We don't seem to have enough money with us tonight," I said. "Let's try the snack bar downstairs." That proved to be absolutely packed out, probably with all the people who couldn't afford the posh restaurant either.

Evie said she knew of a 'very inexpensive' place on West Cromwell Road. "Why don't we go there?" she suggested.

So, we set off walking towards the car park, and, in a little while we came upon a wire fence. "There's the car," we shouted together, "on the other side of the fence!" We carried on walking towards the car until we found ourselves on the wrong side of the fence. We discovered that the fence had only one entrance then doubled back! We had to start again from the beginning. "Well, young lady." I said jokingly, "I hope you enjoyed this date with me of a walk around the car park." With that she burst out laughing.

"I was about to say the same thing," she said, "We must both have the same weird sense of humor."

We eventually found a place where we could afford to eat. This was under a sign that proclaimed "Real men don't eat quiche". I ate the quiche. It was good.

♫

Not long after Evie and I met, we decided we would get together with Rollo and Eileen. We arranged to meet for an evening meal at The Lass of Richmond Hill. This was a popular pub in the Richmond area. Evie and I arrived a little early and found lots of room to sit in the dining room. In fact it looked as if we had the whole place to ourselves. I went to the bar, and ordered a couple of drinks while we waited. We then noticed a middle-aged couple sitting way over on the other side of the room. Evie started to giggle. "What's the matter?" I asked.

Evie said, "That couple over there, they've hardly said a word to eachother over the last ten minutes. Isn't it sad when married couples run out of things to say to each other?" We tried to watch them without them noticing us, and said that we couldn't imagine not having enough to say to each other.

We heard Young Rollo's booming voice as he and Eileen entered the dining area. "Come on then, what's all this giggling and larking about? Let's get some drinks in." After introductions we settled down with our drinks, ordered the food, and listened while Evie told us about herself. She was born May 18th 1941 in New Jersey, USA. Her mother was from Vienna in Austria and had been attending a university in Italy when the war broke out. Her father, originally from Germany, had been working in Italy. They were both unable to return to their homelands because of the war. Evie's parents made their way to England where they married. They then went on to the USA once her father had secured some work there. After Evie, there was another child, a sister born four years later called Beatrice, known as Trixie.

From photos of the era, they were a handsome family but in 1948, Evie's parents divorced. At that point in time, Evie was seven years old and Trixie was three. Evie's mother then married a man who was living in South Africa and, taking the two little girls with her, went with her new husband to a new life in Johannesburg.

This was where Evie's formative years were spent until the age of nineteen, when she sailed to Southampton from Cape Town. Her twentieth birthday fell the day before her ship steamed into Southampton. Her intention was to spend a little time in England, get a job, save up and go to see her father in America, whom she hadn't seen in about fourteen years. She was still a US citizen, so whilst in England she was classified as 'foreign' or 'alien'. She had to register with the police and needed a work permit which had to be renewed yearly.

"This is the story of my life so far," said Evie, "and here I am with my registration, my work permit, my bedsit and my job with the Chrysler Corp which pays enough for me to survive and save for my trip to America." After this story was completed, we all agreed that this was the most impressive recital that we had ever heard. For someone, especially a young girl of only twenty, to successfully make such a trip, alone, from one side of the planet to the other was totally unheard of in our experience.

After our first few dates, our relationship 'took off'. Our pace of dating increased until we were seeing each other almost every night. We were completely oblivious of others, and what they might say. Ginger, who lived half-way between Braintree Street and West Cromwell Road, complained to me several times that I was wearing grooves in the roadway of the Embankment outside his block of flats with my car. To coin a phrase, we were what they commonly call 'in love' and we didn't care who knew it.

At this time, a close friend of Evie's mother, Erica Cie, was living in London. Without any evidence to the contrary, I guessed that full reports on Evie's new boyfriend were being forwarded to an anxious mother in Johannesburg. Erica wheedled out of us (with a raised eyebrow in some cases) our relative ages: twenty and thirty-two. Exactly where I lived: East End of London close to the slum area. What kind of a college degree I had: none. What I did for a living: I was a boilermaker! This was not a resumé that would inspire confidence, and I was very aware of the danger that Evie could be summoned back to South Africa at short notice and be lost to me. In our several meetings with Erica, I tried to boost my image, being a perfect gentleman at all times, especially at the table, and showing whenever possible my knowledge of the composers and music that Evie and I were fond of. Erica eventually warmed to me and became very friendly.

During the summer of 1961, I was working at Brown Lennox of Millwall and doing very well as far as wages were concerned. On the strength of this, I promised to buy a washing machine for my mother before the end of the year. She was overjoyed at the prospect and never stopped talking about it. "My Tommy is buying me a washing machine for Christmas," the story went, until all her friends and neighbors were tired of hearing it. She knew that I had a new girlfriend, so one day she suggested that I bring her home for Sunday dinner. I went to fetch Evie from the underground station and as soon as I brought her into the house, my mother took one look at us and said, "There goes my washing machine." She could tell, just by looking at the two of us together, that I would be spending all my money and all my time with my new girlfriend! She told me many years afterwards that there was just a certain look in our eyes and she knew that this was serious. And of course, she was right.

The story about never getting her washing machine became one of my mother's favorite stories. Whenever we talked about the time she first met Evie, she would remind us of the fact that because of Evie she never got her washing machine! We would always have a good laugh at that.

The time Evie and I spent together between September and the end of the year was like one long holiday. We spent time with Ginger and Doris in their flat. We were invited to parties to celebrate first Young Rollo's and Eileen's engagement and later Eileen's twenty-first birthday.

On Sunday September 10th I remember that we went to the Farnborough Air Show. On the way back to London after watching a magnificent flying display hosted by the Royal Air Force, we became tied up in a traffic jam. We found our way somehow to a café, where they were advertising egg and chips, sausage and chips, steak and chips, and, glancing at each other and laughing together, we burst out, "Chips and chips". We agreed that our sense of humor was synchronised. We had the same sense of fun.

Another memorable occasion took place on Sunday October 1st. We loaded the car with all kinds of picnic food, wine and a wind up gramophone and drove to Claygate. We found a spot that was practically deserted and there we spent the afternoon eating, drinking, listening to music and talking.

I remember an incident that showed me exactly how the situation in South Africa had influenced Evie's thinking. In between our dashing about, with drives in the countryside and listening to various concerts, we sometimes went to the cinema, or as they say in London 'up the pictures'. 'The King and I' was one movie we saw, 'Breakfast at Tiffany's' was another. One evening we came out after the movie was finished and decided to stop in a snack bar for coffee. We tried two or three places with no luck as everyone seemed to have the same idea. Eventually we found a coffee shop of sorts, which looked as if it had few available seats. In one corner there was a table which had two seats available together but where we would have to share the table with some other people. I called to Evie, asking her to hold the seats while I went to the counter for the coffee. When I got back to Evie with the two cups of coffee I found her standing in the middle of the shop. Someone else had taken 'our' seats. "That's a shame," I said "Now we must drink standing up. Why didn't you sit down at that table?"

"I couldn't do that," she answered, "one of them was black. One doesn't sit down with a black person in South Africa."

I could see her point after we had discussed the issue. Her training over the last thirteen or so years was ingrained very deeply and it was deemed 'wrong' for a white person to have any kind of social contact with persons of a different color. "However," I said in closing our discussion, "This is not South Africa, it is England, so we should obey English rules and practices. In other words, when in Rome do as the Romans do."

When Evie and I had known each other for a few weeks she invited me to have supper with her. Not at a restaurant or café, but in her room. She wanted to cook a meal for me to say thank you for the times I had taken her out. I don't remember the menu, but I do remember that it was to be a proper meal with meat, vegetables, desert and coffee. I accepted with alacrity, and we fixed a day and time. Evie shared her room, of course, with Christine Horn, so she had to make arrangements with Christine so that they wouldn't be in each other's way.

The time had been agreed upon as 7.30pm, but I turned up a little early and knocked on the door just before 7pm. After some scuffling and a muffled, "Who is that?" the door opened revealing Evie dressed in a bathrobe and with curlers in her hair. I could see that she wasn't very pleased about this so I apologized quickly for being too early. All the time I was apologizing and talking about why I was so early, I could see her eyes darting back and forth in aggravation. "Look," she interrupted. "Why don't you go to the pub around the corner, have a couple of drinks, and get back here about 7.30pm. Better still, make it twenty to eight. We are losing valuable cooking time while we are standing here talking about it." There is a valuable lesson to be learned here. Don't expect your new girlfriend to work under pressure while preparing for a date – and cooking her first meal for you!

When I came back her face was calmness itself in place of the flustered look she had previously worn. She had, in addition to the food, also purchased a bottle of wine for the occasion, and there was a candle burning to make the table look more festive. I have since discovered, in the years since then that Evie will burn a candle at the drop of a hat.

The dinner was a huge success, at least until we got to the dessert. That was an instant chocolate pudding, the type of thing that you whip up with a spoon or a mixer until it becomes smooth like a cream. Then you put it on one side to be served later. Alas, when Evie served it, the pudding was found to have lumps, not a smooth texture at all, and the lumps were large enough to make one gag. Evie tried very hard to turn this dessert into something edible, but it couldn't be done. We had to throw the whole thing away. I tried to take the blame for this disaster on my arriving too early and upsetting Evie's schedule. No doubt it was my fault. Nowadays, whenever Evie dishes up one of those instant chocolate puddings, we have a giggle and remember the first one.

One of the happiest days that we spent together was Sunday December 31st. The whole world was white, and the snow was all soft and fluffy on the ground. I drove to Evie's bedsit with my camera and we took lots of photos. The snow had stopped and the weather was mild so we decided to drive to Richmond Park. Evie couldn't remember seeing snow before, but she could remember the peculiar crunching sound it makes when one walks on it. It reminded her of the time she lived in America as a small child.

We drove through the gates into Richmond Park and cruised down a slight slope at about ten or twelve mph along the road into the park. There was no one driving behind us and four or five cars in front of us all going the same way as we were. The park is quite large and the road that we came in on formed a huge circle before the road ended in an exit. Every so often the cars in front stopped for a while to view the deer who were permanent residents of the park. This suited us fine. Evie loved to watch deer in their natural habitat. She loves deer, especially the small Bambies.

We slowly followed the road around the park and I noticed that the road, instead of sloping slightly down was now sloping slightly up. The driver in the lead car skidded a little and stopped moving although his wheels continued to turn. The same thing happened to the second car in line, then the third, and suddenly the car in front of us stopped moving and I had to brake. All of us were sitting on a patch of ice and when we stepped on the accelerator pedal the only thing that happened was that the rear wheels span. The car did not move. The other drivers organized themselves into pairs, pusher and driver, and it looked as if this was the only way to get out of trouble. "You get behind the steering wheel," I told Evie "and I will get out and push." This caused a major problem and brought Evie close to tears. "I have never driven on snow," she said, "I don't think I could drive on snow, let me push and you drive." And that's exactly what we did, she pushed and I drove. Once we got the car moving I was able, by careful operation of the accelerator pedal, to keep the car running up the remainder of the slope, while poor Evie followed on foot. Believe it or not, Evie enjoyed this whole episode very much. She called it 'team work'.

During the remainder of 1961 and the beginning of 1962 not a week went by without us being invited to some sort of celebration. There was my younger brother Roy's wedding to Margie, Rollo and Eileen's engagement party, a whole slew of birthdays, the christening of Ginger's son, Peter, and of course, the Goodwins' for a Christmas party that included my sister Gladys and her family. During one of these parties, Evie and I became quite warm and stepped outside for a breath of air. When I took off my jacket, Evie gave a squeak of laughter at the sight of the braces that I was wearing in addition to a belt to keep my trousers up! "You're so old fashioned sometimes, nobody wears braces any more," she said. I discreetly removed them at the first opportunity and shortly afterwards gave all my braces away. I have never again worn, or even touched, braces.

Although we were not actually engaged in January 1962, we had by then what you might call an 'understanding', which means we intended to marry, but the event had not yet been officially announced. In other words, it was a secret. The reason for this secrecy was that Evie was still a minor and subject to the will of her mother. I insisted that we wait until Evie became twenty-one, at which time she would become legally free to marry anyone she chose. I felt at the time to be more of a guardian than a suitor. She agreed to this secrecy and we continued to be girlfriend and boyfriend for a little longer.

If we were to marry, one of the problems we had to face immediately was where we were going to live. There was a real housing problem in the south of England, a legacy left to us by Adolf Hitler as so many houses and buildings had been destroyed during the war. My former colleague from Frasers, Arthur Ling, waited for seven years before getting a council flat. I went to make application for a flat anywhere in London and was told by an official to come back when I was married with two children. Then he could put me on the list. There was absolutely no way I could get a council flat. A privately owned flat or house in London would have been fine, but I quickly discovered that if it was suitable then I couldn't afford it, and if I could afford it, it was in a slum! We went to Australia House to be interviewed as Australian immigrants but that was no good – Australia had a worse housing problem than England did at that time.

While this was going on Evie planted a seed in my mind concerning South Africa. She wanted to go back. She also wanted to be with me. On the other hand, I had no desire to live there. The Sharpeville incident, in which many black citizens were gunned down by the police, had only recently taken place so the country was in bad standing with the rest of the world. Although I had never been there, I considered it to be brutal and not a fit place to start a family. However, to lose Evie was out of the question, so we made a deal. We would live in South Africa for two years, and then we would decide on a permanent home. This seemed the best temporary measure that we could both agree on.

In April 1962, Evie and I decided to take a holiday in the little seaside town of Dawlish, in Devon, about 180 miles from London. We went by train, arriving in the afternoon well rested. We had no car with us of course, so we relied on shank's pony for getting around and exploring the town, which had a small stream running through it on its way to the sea. The hotel was very smart, almost luxurious, but we immediately discovered an error in the booking of our rooms. Evie had written to the hotel requesting rooms for herself and for her friend, signing the letter Miss Landsberger. The hotel was completely full and, assuming that the 'friend' was also female, had taken advantage and arranged for us to share a double room with twin beds. This gave us a problem, but a very small 'box' room was found for me on the top floor, while Evie got the double room to herself. We were guests for only two, or maybe three nights, but one was a Saturday, when a dance took place and we were able to dress up a little.

Thirty-five or so years later we revisited Dawlish along with our daughter Anne. The hotel we had stayed at was gone, replaced with a modern residential building, and there was twice as much traffic making the town much busier than before. The stream still ran down the center of the town.

♪

After our return from Dawlish, we started to make plans for our official engagement and wedding, along with plans for me to emigrate to South Africa. One night we received a message from Rollo and Eileen. They wanted to meet up with us to have a drink together. They suggested we meet at The Lass of Richmond Hill, which was by now our favorite pub/restaurant, because it was quite close to where Evie lived. When we arrived Eileen was all agog with her good news. She couldn't wait to tell us all about it. Then Evie broke in to the conversation and started talking about *our* good news. Young Rollo and I looked at each other and slowly sipped our drinks. "If I tell you our news," he said to me, "will you tell us yours?"

"Yes of course," I answered.

"Alright Eileen," he said, "what was our good news all about?" (pretending not to know!).

"We have set the date for our wedding," she said, "we're going to be married on January 5th 1963."

"I don't believe it!" said Evie, "Tommy and I are planning to marry on January 5th 1963, too!"

What a coincidence this was. Rollo and I, well into our thirties and the same age as each other except for three weeks, each with a girlfriend at least ten years younger, had chosen to marry not only in the same year and month, but on the same day. We were all absolutely flabbergasted!

We spent the rest of the evening talking, planning, and discussing, how and why we all arrived at the same day. Evie and I had chosen that particular day so that Evie's mother from South Africa could be at the wedding. I don't remember Rollo's reasons.

We celebrated Evie's twenty-first birthday on May 18th 1962 in the West End at a night club called the 'Talk of the Town', featuring Eartha Kitt, a famous black American singer. We had a marvellous time, Evie waving her left hand about as if she was conducting an orchestra, (showing off her engagement ring), and I watching her and thinking that soon she would be my wife.

We re-scheduled our wedding date after Evie's mother let us know that she couldn't, after all, come to the wedding. However, now Evie's dad could come if we changed the wedding date to August 11th 1962. So we did that. Our schedule was now the wedding on August 11th, followed immediately by a honeymoon train trip to Austria, Italy, and France. Then we were going to tie up all our affairs in London, resign from our jobs, and lastly, prepare and pack for our voyage to Cape Town.

Three weeks before the wedding was due to take place, Evie had not one, but two strokes of bad luck. The first was when she broke a fingernail whilst slamming the car door. I made the mistake of laughing and treating it as if it was unimportant. Well, it *was* important to Evie. However, the second piece of bad luck was really serious. One morning, while getting dressed for work, she pulled a muscle in her neck. The doctor recommended wearing a neck brace for the next six weeks. This reduced Evie to tears. "I'm being married in three weeks," she sobbed, "How can I walk up the aisle in one of those things? People will think I'm an invalid, and feel sorry for me." My mother gave support and assistance to a certain extent but Evie really needed *her* mother through this difficult period. She swore she would *not* wear that collar on her wedding day, and indeed she didn't, nor at any time on our honeymoon either. And her neck healed nicely on its own.

Our wedding took place in St Philip's Church, Kensington, and was conducted by the Reverend Selwyn Cox. He was a real old fuddy-duddy and fusspot. A few days before the ceremony took place, he insisted on having a full-scale rehearsal to make certain that we would have no glitches. He chalk marked the church floor, and worked out the relative angles where everyone would be standing. I don't know what would have happened if Evie's dad and the best man hadn't been standing forty-five degrees to, and slightly behind, the bride! He cautioned me seriously not to turn to watch the bride advancing down the aisle. "Too messy," he said. "Keep your eyes on the altar until I give you a signal." Then on the day of the wedding, he forgot to change his desk calendar in the vestry from the 10th to the 11th of August. The result was that Evie and I had our official photograph taken signing the marriage certificate with the wrong date showing on the calendar!

On the way to the church, I had a dose of the jitters. Ginger, who was my best man, hired a car to pick me up and deliver me to the church. When we got about half way there I asked him to slow down so that I could take just a little breath of air. That was all I wanted, just a stroll on the pavement for two minutes and then we would continue to the church. "Latch all the doors, Doris," yelled Ginger to his wife who was riding with us. "Keep Goodwin in this car at any cost." And with that he took off like a bat out of hell. He totally ignored the 30mph speed limit and went up to about 50mph or more. I knew he was not going to let me out so I relaxed and called out for him to slow down. He grinned at me through the reverse mirror, "We're going to church Tom," he said. I knew then in that moment that although we were kidding each other as only old friends can, he was going to fulfil his commitment and get me to the church on time whether I liked it or not.

The 'jitters' didn't last very long and they disappeared completely once I found myself in the calm, quiet atmosphere of the church. When the triumphant music started, I remembered to keep Reverend Cox's church tidy, and like a true soldier, kept my back straight, and my chin pointing forward until Reverend Cox's forefinger tapped on his prayer-book as a signal that I could move.

Evie looked truly wonderful; no wonder I wanted her as my wife. I remember thinking that any man would be satisfied at that moment. We had the organist play a piece, which was a favorite of ours ('Jesu, Joy of Man's Desiring' by J.S. Bach) and this brought forth some tears. After the wedding there was the traditional picture-taking session, and when the hustle and bustle had died down a little, Evie and I made our way to our chauffeur-driven car and I helped Evie into the back seat. The chauffeur started the engine and glanced in his mirrors in preparation to go. Evie and I were by now seated in the back of the car, when Evie squeezed my hand and said, "Are you happy, darling?" Before I could stop the words they were out. "I'll let you know in the morning," I blurted. The driver's head whipped round and he gave me a stern look but didn't say a word.

There was a reception upstairs in the hall of a pub called The Barley Mow, near the Thames, I think. We had paid for the food ahead of time but we hadn't paid for the drinks so I gave Ginger a lump sum of cash. With that he could estimate how long the bar would be open on our account, and when to close the bar and settle up. Evie and I left the festivities while the party was in full swing. Someone with a car drove us to the railway station where we caught a train to Dover. Our room at the hotel was booked in the name of Mr and Mrs Goodwin, which gave Evie quite a thrill. When we finally got settled in our hotel it was dark and we were both hungry. We bemoaned the fact that lots of food was left over at The Barley Mow while we had to buy more here for our supper.

Our European tour started that next morning with a ferry from Dover to Ostend in Belgium. We lost an umbrella in our hurry to get on the ferry, but popped into the Lost and Found office on the way back three weeks later and there it was.

Once in Belgium, we boarded a train going overnight to Salzburg. We should have booked a sleeper carriage for that part of our trip, but we didn't. That was an error. The train was packed to capacity and some people were even crowding into the corridors. We devised a little scheme whereby we could get some privacy. We dressed up in all of our finery, including Evie's fancy 'going-away' hat, and sat very close to each other. Whenever someone opened the door to come into our compartment, we cuddled up, and they could see that we were newly married and left us alone. However, it didn't really do us much good, as we had to sit up all night anyway!

Salzburg is the town in Austria where Mozart was born. It was also the home of Professor Doctor Hans Homma, and his wife Hansi. Doctor Homma, who asked to be called Hans, was head of the Medical School in Salzburg. He was a cousin of Evie's mother, so he became a relative of mine immediately.

Hans and Hansi drove us around the town in their Mercedes. Hansi did most of the driving, stamping her fat little legs on the brake, clutch, and accelerator as though there was no tomorrow. We got the grand treatment. We were driven to the best restaurants and were not allowed to put our hands in our pockets at all. They gave us two tickets for the Mozart Festival, which was for the night we arrived, and they had pre-paid our hotel room, so we were staying for free. In the early evening they reminded us of the tickets we had. "Mustn't be late," they said, "Those tickets are worth their weight in gold." Indeed, we heard later that those tickets had to be booked many months in advance.

We hurried as much as possible but still arrived after the music had started. "Sorry sir," said the usher, stopping us from going in. "Those who are late must wait for a suitable break in the music before being allowed to take their seats." When we asked the usher how long we would have to wait, he told us twenty minutes or so. We had a little conference and counted the amount of sleep we had missed the night before on the train. We could see our hotel across the street. "We could walk there in one minute," I said. "We are on our honeymoon," Evie said. "Oh heck," we both thought, "How about missing Mozart tonight? We really need some sleep." So we went. Do you know, I still have those tickets. They are a conversation piece and a curio, but they are way out-of-date. At breakfast the next morning, the Hommas asked us if we enjoyed the music last night and of course we had to say, "Yes, fine, excellent programme, we thank you both!" While we were in Salzburg, Hans and Hansi took us to the famous White Horse Inn for coffee, and to the *Schloss* (Castle) up on the hill, for dinner.

Our next stop on our railway tour was Vienna and we were to be met by a fellow called Mundl Kreuter. With Hansi's help we sent him a telegram telling him which train we would be on, and the time of arrival. Mundl, who was a life-long friend of Evie's mother, had offered us the use of his flat for a few days while his wife was out of town. He was to meet us at the station. He had very kindly offered us the master suite while he used the guestroom. There was a slight problem in that we didn't know him, or he us, and Vienna station was very large and complex. While we were still in London, Evie's mother had arranged for Mundl to send us a torn-in-half newspaper. The paper was a copy of a

Viennese publication called *Apotheker Zeitung* (Chemists' Newspaper). The idea was for me to hold up my half of the torn newspaper and march up and down the platform with it hoping for a middle-aged man to confront me saying, "Welcome to Vienna – I am Mundl." Mundl was supposed to do the same thing with his half of the paper and put it on show for *me* to recognize. Well, I am so glad that it wasn't rush hour! There were a couple of dozen people, coming and going all the time on a platform which was probably a quarter-mile long. Some of the people I was harassing looked belligerent, which I would also be if I were being pestered by some clown waving a piece of paper under my nose and chanting "*Apotheker Zeitung – Apotheker Zeitung!*"

After nearly an hour of trying to find Mundl (which seemed like trying to find a needle in a haystack) we came to the conclusion that something must have gone wrong. Luckily we had his phone number on one of Evie's mother's letters, so we called him. It turned out that he had never received our telegram because this was a local holiday, and the post office was closed.

Mundl was very entertaining. He took us around and showed us almost the entire city, keeping up a running commentary on every aspect, whether it was street, building, or park. One day while having lunch we talked about our plans for the future in South Africa. As we talked he watched Evie's every move and then he said a very strange thing. "If affairs had turned out slightly differently," he said, "I could have been your father." That was a surprise. He went on to tell us how, years before, he had had a crush on Evie's mother, but things didn't work out for him. He told us about the time that she promised to give him a *buss'l* (kiss) the next time that they met. When the next time arrived, she gave him a little chocolate, which was also called a *buss'l*. Apparently, they both enjoyed this little story for many years.

While we were in Vienna, Mundl took a snapshot of Evie and me, and that picture has always been my favorite. It's a slightly blurred photo showing us standing in front of a pond, dressed in casual holiday clothes and with our arms around each other. Our faces are radiant, full of happiness, love and hope for the future.

We took the night train to Venice, and arrived early in the day. We had not booked any hotels, rooms, or lodgings of any type, preferring to use a book that we had recently discovered. It was called *Europe on Five Dollars a Day*, 1962 edition by Arthur Frommer. With this book we were able to find many out-of-the-way, inexpensive and recommended hotels and B&Bs. We soaked up as much of Venice as we could in a couple of days, doing and seeing all that tourists are supposed to do. One thing we noticed about Venice was that there was a very large population of cats living in the city. I had never before seen so many in one place.

After Venice we had lots of fun deciphering Italian railway timetables. We also tried to find our way through Venice, Rome, Naples and Capri with the aid of numerous maps. It seemed as if we were forever hunting for something – either a railway station, restaurant, place of interest or hotel. We stood out like a sore thumb, probably because of our clothes, so we were targets for numerous voluble touts who promised us the moon if we would only go with them.

The end of our trip was heralded by a rowboat outing on the lake in Lausanne, Switzerland. Our last train stop before going back to London was Paris. In Paris we learned to say, "*le petit dejeuner*" when asking for breakfast, only to discover that some of the French speak better English than we do. From our Paris hotel we recounted some of the experiences that we had enjoyed on this trip. On 24th August Evie had celebrated my thirty-third birthday on the Isle of Capri while she was still only twenty-one. We had seen Naples with no problems, and we had stood where those Christian martyrs had died for someone else's fun. We didn't visit Pompeii, which was a mistake. The local mountain, Vesuvius, had blown its top on my birthday in AD79. Maybe on our next trip to Italy we will see the result.

Our honeymoon trip had taken about three weeks, and we had enjoyed the whole time except for once when we had had a disagreement over something or other. This was when we found it was so nice to make up.

CHAPTER 7

Adventures in South Africa

1962 – 1969

WE returned to London with about six weeks to go before our ship sailed for Cape Town on October 18th. Evie's current roommate was a South African girl, Claire, with the surname Smelt. Everyone made a joke because Claire Smelt! And she really did, by not bathing regularly. Claire had moved out of Evie's room while Evie and I were in Europe to leave the room available for Evie and me. I found a temporary job making large diameter steel cylinders to be used as boiler flues. It was as boring as heck but the pay was terrific, somewhere in the range of £35 pounds a week. It was just to tide us over until we left the country.

The building at 41 West Cromwell Road where we were living was originally designed as the home of a wealthy family. There was an upstairs and a downstairs, where a cook and a butler along with at least one maid would have worked. When space was needed to house all the visitors coming and going to the city of London, the building, along with its neighbors, underwent structural changes. These changes turned the building into several bed-sitting rooms, one of which Evie and I lived in for a short time. One day there was a knock on the door. It was a group of young male New Zealanders from one of the upstairs rooms who were travelling overland to South Africa. Evie gave them her mother's address, and we all promised to meet up with each other one day.

Every Saturday morning, the owner of the building, Major Busby, would pop his head around the door of our room to pick up the rent which we would leave on the table in an envelope. Every so often he would bring a little shovel with him to dig out all the half-crowns that we put in the slot to pay for the heat that we used. Our room was quite large with a hot and cold wash basin in the corner. When you walked out you found yourself in a foyer that led to the front door. All the other residents of the building had to walk across this foyer to enter or exit the building. This was the corner of the universe where Evie and I had spent so much time bidding each other 'good night' before we married. We joked about 'holding up the wall' while a never-ending stream of tenants came and went, some of them patting me on the back, and making noises of encouragement.

The reason we 'held up the wall' so often and for so long was because Evie's roommate Claire and her boyfriend commandeered the room to the point of being selfish. They were also a bit strange. I remember one time in particular, when it was pouring with rain and Evie and I were going to a movie which was due to start at about 7pm. Claire's boyfriend was already there in the room leaning on a wet umbrella at about half-past six. He and Claire were just looking at each other. Three hours later when Evie and I came back after the movie and a coffee we saw them in the exact same position as before, with the wet umbrella as well. At the time, they were engaged to be married. That's more than strange – it's weird.

Once back from honeymoon, Evie and I suddenly discovered that we had a lot of things to do. The first thing we thought of was the packing. But what were we going to pack? And in what were we going to pack it? Suitcases were not much use when moving from Southampton to Cape Town, so we hunted for and found a local shop which sold an assortment of trunks. The trunks had to be suitable for storage in the hold of a ship, so we played safe and bought steel ones. Three, if I remember correctly. Among the articles we brought with us were our stainless steel cutlery set (a wedding present from the Rollinsons), a set of twelve 33rpm records we had bought between us, and all sorts of sheets and towels. from my Mum and others in the family. We told anyone who cared to listen that bringing the records was a guarantee that we would stay together. As Evie said on one classic occasion, "We'd bought a set of records together, we *had* to get married!" In addition to sundry household items and clothing, I packed tools so that I could continue as a boilermaker, and the old car radio from my Hillman Minx.

We sent our trunks down to Southampton early to be sure that they didn't miss the boat. I had some interviews to take care of in order to sort out affairs such as car insurance, and then we were ready to go. We originally planned to go down to the boat by train, but the Rollinsons insisted on driving us down. Rollo and Eileen had only just returned from their honeymoon, having been married on October 6th. We took some farewell photos on the way down to the docks, which show the four of us all looking very happy. No wonder the Rollinsons looked happy – they were even more newly married than we were. However, the day was also tinged with sadness, because none of us really knew whether we would ever see each other again. I had known Rollo for nineteen years, and he was my best friend. But Evie and I were off on a new adventure, which gave us something to look forward to.

Evie and I stood on the deck of the RMS (Royal Mail Ship) *Pretoria Castle*. According to an extract from the log of October 18th the temperature was 54°F and the time we left Southampton was 4.21pm. There was a small brass band on the dockside playing old-fashioned tearjerker songs such as 'Auld Lang Syne'. Mum and Dad stood on the dockside waving us a tearful farewell along with Gladys and her family, Roy and his family, the Rollinsons, and young Carol. Someone handed me a paper streamer and while we held onto one end of it we tossed the other end to the family on the dockside. There were shouts back and forth from the sailors giving and receiving orders and then the ship started to move. Slowly and silently the ship moved away from the dock, first an inch then a foot then an arm's length. We rolled out the streamer until we reached the end and while we all gripped the paper streamer tightly, it snapped. This was meant to signify the breaking of the ties binding us to them. The figures and faces became smaller very quickly until after ten minutes they were gone.

♪

The voyage from Southampton to Cape Town took two weeks, from 18th October to 1st November, a distance of 6,011 miles at an average speed of 18.9 knots. That works out, by my figuring, to be approximately 20mph average for the whole trip. The ship (28,625 tons) carried 121 first class, and 468 tourist class passengers. In addition to these, of course, were the Captain, J.P. Smythe, and his crew. I don't know how many crew members there were but there must have been at least a hundred. The first class passengers were carried in the front (stem) of the ship while the tourist class had to make do with the rear (stern).

Evie loved being 'On Board Ship' and used the phrase as much as possible. Being On Board Ship, for her, was like 'Travelling North' would be for a motorcyclist starting on a long journey. We were a little restricted as far as space was concerned. In the tourist class there were four times the number of passengers in about the same, or a little less, space. We didn't care too much about walking space or lack of it. To get exercise we just did more laps of our part of the ship. We soon learned the rules for playing deck quoits and shuffleboard during the day, and canasta during the evening.

There was a swimming pool, which was filtered clean but had salty water. The baths were also supplied with salt water, which made it very difficult, even impossible, to soap up a lather while washing. However, there were showers that used fresh water, so Evie and I preferred those. To many of the English passengers, however, showers were considered foreign, and they still had to have their 'tub in'! We dressed in our best clothes, showing a bit of swank at every opportunity, especially at meal times, and dressed casually for activities such as Bingo, for instance, or propping up the bar.

When we were about three days out we arrived at the Portuguese island of Madeira, and anchored off shore. It looked to me as if we were about half a mile from the island which had a jetty and several transport vessels. The transports immediately began moving some of the passengers from our ship to the island, making the place what is called a 'tourist trap'. The island had a cliff a hundred or so feet high and a winding road, which looked difficult to climb. Evie and I opted to go to the island to take a closer look at the caves. We speculated on what it would be like to live in a place like that. "Rather romantic," said Evie with a smile.

"We couldn't live on romance – where would I find a job?" I said. By the end of the day, we agreed that Madeira was no place to settle and that Johannesburg would have more jobs available. We took a taxi ride around the island, ate some local food consisting mainly of fruit, and wandered through a bazaar looking for a memento that we could buy. We returned to the *Pretoria Castle* and left Madeira at the end of the day after spending the whole of October 21st there.

On October 25th we passed the RMV *(*Royal Mail Vessel*) Athlone Castle* on its return trip and waved frantically to the people on board. By now we were getting a rough idea of just how large the Atlantic Ocean is! Suddenly, those people on the other ship were our soulmates, real friends in this vast emptiness.

On the next day we crossed the equator and the crew put on a very amusing show for us. They dressed in all sorts of costumes, and as all kinds of characters including Davy Jones and Father Neptune. The action consisted mainly of throwing anybody and everyone within reach into the swimming pool, dressed or not.

While we were On Board Ship we got to know some of our fellow passengers who sat with us every day for breakfast, lunch and dinner. There were two other married couples, one lady by herself and one man on our table for eight. One couple were returning South Africans who tried to put my mind at ease as far as availability of work was concerned. This couple, Bill and Joan Leppan, painted a glowing picture of success in the industrial world of South Africa. According to Bill there was a drastic shortage of trained people, especially those trained in all branches of engineering. "If you served an apprenticeship as a boilermaker," he said, "then you will be in great demand in and around Johannesburg."

Bill produced some Johannesburg newspapers, which were admittedly way out-of-date – they had been picked up at Madeira – but as he pointed out, they gave us a good idea of what was happening in the area. In the first paper we counted fourteen advertisements for a boilermaker in addition to several advertisements for a foreman boilermaker, and many more for a welder. As we thumbed our way through the stack of newspapers, we noticed that the ads tended to repeat themselves.

One company advertising was named Cosine Engineering and they advertised at every opportunity. I made notes and jotted down lots of information not only regarding Cosine, but also about other companies who were looking for people. I noted phone numbers, addresses, products, and type of company. Instead of looking for a job, I was choosing! I knew that I could get a job of some kind and start earning money right away. I slept very well that night with absolutely no thought of being stranded on the other side of the world without money or a job.

I tended to have a problem with the movement of the ship. I suppose you would call it seasickness although I wasn't sick. To cure myself of feeling queasy, I would march around the deck in time with deep breathing exercises. During the day there was no problem. It was only at night that the queasiness, giddiness and sickness came over me. Evie had no problems with motion sickness at all and we made a joke of her cast iron constitution. When I took my evening 'constitutional' Evie would be down in our cabin getting ready for the night, and I would march to the rear deck of the ship. It was fascinating to watch the churning of water by the propellers and to feel the heaving up and down motion of the deck. Standing alone and facing the rear of the ship was a little scary because of the intense blackness. To describe the outlook as dark was the understatement of the year. There was no light at all until you turned to look forward, where you could see the lights of our ship.

While Evie and I were calmly making our way towards Cape Town in the autumn of 1962, Kennedy and Kruschev were getting involved in a blockade of Russian missiles to Cuba. We heard all the details on the radio broadcast, and what a relief it was to hear that the blockade ended peacefully.

On Wednesday October 31st 1962 we had what they called a Farewell Dinner. I still have a menu with an extract from the ship's log, and indeed this dinner was fit for a king. After dinner we had dancing until very late, and speeches by several people including the Captain. This was the culmination of the trip giving everyone a chance to bid their newfound friends goodbye.

When I woke the next morning I could feel that something was different. I tiptoed over to Evie's bunk-bed and saw that she was fast asleep and all mixed up with her blanket. It was quiet in the cabin, so quiet that

I could hear her breathing and beyond that nothing. I slipped on shirt, shorts, and flip-flops, picked up the cabin key and crept out to the corridor. I realised what it was that sounded so strange. There was *no noise* because the engines had stopped their incessant thud-thud-thud. For the first time since we left Madeira the engines were silent. We were being towed toward Cape Town bay by a couple of tugboats, and the view from our ship to Table Mountain was magnificent. I chatted to one of the crew members who told me that there was no 'table cloth' today. That meant there was no cloud covering the mountain, which makes it look like a table with a cloth on it.

We arrived in Table Bay on schedule, at 6am, and docked right away. Within a very short time there was a bustle which spread over the whole ship like wildfire. Several official looking men in what looked like custom's uniform came up the now-installed gang plank, and set themselves up with chairs and small tables. Each showed a sign that indicated his function, one was for returning South Africans, another for immigrants like myself and still another for foreigners and foreigners returning such as Evie.

I later joined one of these groups and stood in line. Each of the officials had one or two black helpers in tow to fetch and carry the tables, chairs, and various books, charts and paper work that was required. There was no doubt at all about who was in charge and this hit me in the first ten minutes. The whites were saying, "Hey, Kaffir do this" and "Hey, Kaffir do that", while the blacks were repeating, like a stuck gramophone record "Yes, my Baas. Yes, my Baas." The word 'Kaffir' was a derogatory term, similar to the insulting 'nigger', and I remembered that Bill Leppan had mentioned the subject whilst we were On Board Ship. "Race relations in this country are not like in other places," he told me. "One must start with an open mind and try to live by a very important concept: when in Rome do as the Romans do."

I eventually got to speak with the Customs and Immigration man. My name was in his book, along with all my personal information. I was welcomed as an immigrant to the country, and reminded that if I worked and stayed there for two years then my passage from England would be free. Whilst we were being interviewed by the officials, the ship was taken over completely by dozens and dozens of laborers. They were unloading, not only the ship's cargo, but also all the suitcases, boxes, and shopping bags that the passengers wanted removed from the ship. These laborers – I guess you would call them porters – were organised into groups of about ten men, each controlled by a leader called 'Boss Boy'. Porters and Boss Boys were all black. No white man moved into that kind of work situation. The white 'Baas' gave instructions to the Boss Boy, and the Boss Boy did the rest. This was quite some lesson that

I received on my first day!

The Boss Boy kept control of his boys at all times. Irrespective of age, all native men were called Boy, while native women were called Girl. The apparent weapon used to retain control of the natives was a short leather strap or whip called a '*sjambok*'. I say apparent because the Boss Boy made a big song and dance about the sjambok, cracking it like a whip but not wielding it with any force. Watching this performance was very similar to watching a group of animals performing in a circus. I felt embarrassed to watch.

We finished all that we had to do by mid-morning, with the exception of our trunks. They were supposed to have been taken from the ship's hold along with everyone else's, and stacked in alphabetical order in the customs shed. Our trunks were nowhere to be seen so I contacted some of the customs officials, and asked where my trunks might be. "You need to talk to the fellow handling 'G' for Goodwin," said one fellow. "But it looks as though the G's are all finished. There is the man you want. He's on his way home for the weekend so you'd better catch him before he goes." All this was delivered in a strange mixture of some kind of pidgin English and Afrikaans. "Oh boy," I thought, "what a mess. I hope they don't send our trunks back to Southampton."

It was about 1pm by that time, and suddenly a young couple came prancing up to us with shrieks and cries. This was Diana Gregson, an old school friend of Evie's and her boyfriend of the time, a fellow named Woter (pronounced Voter). Diana spoke with an accent similar to Evie's – kind of colonial, almost like an Australian. They were here to meet us. What a surprise! Diana, who lived in Johannesburg, was at university in Cape Town. She was taking courses and aspiring to be an opera singer.

When she and Woter heard my tale of woe regarding my trunks, they immediately started questioning the customs men in Afrikaans – a language derived from Dutch. Woter, being an Afrikaner was able to speak and understand this difficult tongue. The story became simple. Our trunks, when loaded into the ship very early, were placed at the bottom of the hold in Southampton. Our customs man was aware of this, and expected the trunks to be out in half-an-hour or so. In the meantime, he was on his way to get a cup of coffee and take a break. This was a relief and I would soon be able to supervise the loading of our trunks into the Johannesburg train and breathe a heavy sigh when the train was approved for leaving that evening (Thursday) at 7pm to arrive in Johannesburg on Saturday at 10am.

In the meantime, we had the rest of the day with Diana and Woter to get to know each other a little. Evie and Diana (known as Greg, short for her last name Gregson) started chatting immediately to catch up on the last couple of years and especially on details of our wedding. Greg and

Woter had the use of a car in which we went sightseeing all over Cape Town and the local countryside. We had to hurry because we were running out of time, having only six or seven hours until our Johannesburg train began its thousand-mile journey north.

Woter was a positive mine of information about South Africa, Cape Town, the Cape Province, the native Xhosa people who spoke with a clicking of the tongue, the many different tribes and races of people, until it made my head spin. He was an Afrikaner, a white African descendant of Dutch settlers who first arrived in the Cape in the 1600s. During our lively discussion he gave me a friendly warning about the resentment that is still sometimes harboured by the Afrikaners against the English. "They are still fighting the Boer War in some cases, " he said. We had a really wonderful day, all of us filled with promise and hope for the future and all excited about tapping into this growing country. For the moment, I had forgotten about the two-year limit we had set. For the moment.

Our steam locomotive started its journey on time and we were able to see some of the Cape Town suburbs before it got too dark. We had a sleeper carriage for the journey and this made things quite comfortable. When we awoke we found ourselves in the middle of the Karoo Desert. Outside the carriage everywhere was a kind of reddish brown, the colour of sand. The landscape in all directions was perfectly flat except for what looked like very tall vertical steel tanks dotted about. These piles of sand were a natural phenomenon but they looked as though a giant gardener with a fifty-foot shovel had formed. Possibly, at some time in the past, rains had washed away some of the softer material, leaving behind a rock-like residue about a hundred feet in diameter and two hundred feet high. I was fascinated by what I saw, especially when I noticed that the pattern went on and on for what seemed like forever.

We stopped a couple of times to take on water. Water is very necessary for a steam engine in the middle of a desert. There was another thing that I noticed on the way to Jo'burg. Lining both sides of the track, for mile after mile, were peach trees. They were not in good condition; some of them were wilting, but they were alive and growing. I figured out, and the porter confirmed it, that passengers had for years been throwing peach pips out of the windows. Leaks from the boilers and toilets from the trains did the rest.

Our journey took us past Kimberley, famous for its diamond mines which drew from Evie a comment about not wanting to live there if you paid her. On Saturday morning I shaved closely and cleaned up particularly carefully. I polished my shoes so that they shone and brushed my hair mercilessly until my head hurt. Today I was going to meet my mother-in-law for the first time and I wanted to make a good impression.

Mothers-in-law have a bad reputation so I was prepared for the worst. I knew that mine was born Baroness Elfreda Margot Rumler von Aichenwehr on July 15th 1912 in Vienna, Austria. She was the younger daughter of Baron Camill Rumler von Aichenwehr and his wife, the Baroness Lilli (nee Kopplinger). I was prepared to be quite in awe of her aristocratic heritage in view of the fact that I came from an extremely poor background. I was quite sure that *she* had never had to use a newspaper for a tablecloth, as we had had to do when I was a child. She was now called Elfreda M. Peiser. She and Evie's father, Harold Landsberger, had divorced when Evie was seven years old, and she had moved with Evie and her younger sister, Trixie, to South Africa. However, she had married again, and subsequently divorced her second husband, Fritz Peiser, after they had had a daughter together, Monica. At that time Evie was fourteen years old. I know that Evie has felt a lifelong sadness that she didn't have a normal upbringing in a family with both a mother and a father. She hardly remembers her time in America when she lived with her real father, and unfortunately she never got along with her stepfather. Before we were married, she told me that she was determined to *stay* married, because she would never want to put her own children through the same misery that she suffered. Many years later, our daughter Anne told us that she was so glad that we had never divorced. Anne at that time was about thirteen, and had quite a few friends who came from broken homes. Even at that age Anne could see the damage that divorce could cause, and she appreciated the fact that she had a stable and loving home.

Anyway, to get back to my first meeting with my mother-in-law Elfreda, or, as she preferred to be called, Elfy, who was living as a single parent with Trixie, Monica, and until recently, Evie. I had no problem recognising Elfy, a short, blonde, well-groomed woman who carried her fifty years so well. As we stepped off the train I noticed that in spite of the weather being cloudy and overcast, she was wearing sunglasses. Many years later I learned that this was to cover up the tears and emotion, which were bound to follow. Within minutes of meeting Elfy, I made one of my so-called jokes, which made me bite my tongue. In response to Elfy's inquiry, "I trust you have been treating my daughter well?" I answered, "Oh yes, I beat her every Thursday." I was so ready with my response that it sounded as if we'd rehearsed it. After a split second of silence we all burst out laughing.

Elfy and I became good friends from the word go. She delighted in being called 'the old battle axe'. This became a term of endearment between us with the passing of the years. She would give me presents for my birthday or Christmas and the card would be signed 'With love from the old Battle Axe'.

Elfy drove us to our new home from the station in her Hillman Minx, choosing the most scenic route even though it was out of the way. Elfy's Hillman Minx was a much newer model than my old car had been. It was much larger, a pale blue in color, and a convertible to boot. Mine had been black, and just an ordinary sedan. I must admit I was a little bit jealous. We finished our drive in front of the charming little cottage Elfy had rented on our behalf. The cottage belonged to Mrs Van Bruggen, or Mrs Van as we called her, who was an Afrikaans-speaking widow who lived with her college graduate son in the suburb of Kew. She owned three or four single storey dwellings, all sitting on the same plot of about three acres of land. She had, with the help of her son, and lots of cheap native labor, built the dwellings, brick by brick herself. She was a teacher; in fact Evie had at one time been in one of her classes, believe it or not!

Mrs Van was waiting for us when we stopped near the group of cottages. "This is the place that your mother said you would like to rent," she called. "If you don't like it there is another." We went through a gate, along a path through a flower garden, and there was the cottage in an orchard of peach trees. It was spacious enough, clean and freshly painted. There was a very large living room, two bedrooms, a kitchen with a large eating area as well as a separate pantry, and of course a bathroom. There was also a lovely covered veranda, where we could sit and drink our afternoon tea. The cottage was simply furnished with everything that we needed to start with. However, there were many things that we still had to buy to set up housekeeping, such as a broom, vacuum cleaner, and pots and pans.

Then the most urgent issue became job-hunting. Maybe the best plan was for me to get a local job temporarily, then take my time getting a permanent one later. The next thing we had to get was a car. Evie had a cousin who knew a man who sold cars. Maybe we could get a bargain. Then I remembered the newspapers I'd looked at On Board Ship and thought I must call Sammy Cousins of Cosine Engineering about a job. With our brains fully loaded, and completely exhausted, we slept our first night in our new home.

The first few months of our new life were so full of excitement and fresh experiences that I really don't know where to start. Some of the happenings were a cause for upset. Evie's cousin, one of our very few relatives, recommended a car salesman who had 'doctored' a car and then sold it to me. The engine needed new piston rings and a new main bearing, which I had to buy and put in myself. Luckily I had the know-how. I had trusted the dealer when I should have been more cautious. However, some of our earliest experiences were cause for pleasure such as our meeting with Austin and Hella. They were destined to become two of our best friends, and very soon.

I needed a phone to start the ball rolling about jobs for us both. Unfortunately, there was a waiting list of several months for a new phone, which made it very difficult to answer advertisements. Evie was lucky, as a friend of Elfy's had told her about a Japanese company that needed a private secretary, and she got the job right away. It was in the center of town, and Evie had to take two buses, and then walk another twenty minutes to her office. However, I was not so lucky. In order to make any phone call, I had either to beg someone who already had a phone, or find a public phone kiosk that hadn't been wrecked. Both methods were a darned nuisance.

The lack of phones in South Africa was matched by the lack of television. It was possible to get a phone if you waited long enough, but not a TV. I found it to be a refreshing change to be in a 'tellyless' environment, but I must say I was very surprised by it. TV wasn't banned, or against the law, but TV sets simply weren't available for sale. If you smuggled one into the country, it wouldn't do you any good because there were no programs or TV stations. The general theory was that the authorities didn't want the black population to see how blacks and whites treated each other in other countries. The law of apartheid (separateness) was in force while we were living there. It certainly wouldn't have done their policy makers any good if the blacks could see, for instance, a black actor climbing into bed with a white actress.

Within a few days, and after a bit of luck, I contacted Sammy Cousins. "Call me Sammy, none of that mister stuff here." I got to the location of his company, which was near the Benoni railway station. It was going to be a pretty long ride to work, if I wanted to stay living in Kew. The company consisted of two small buildings for the office staff, two secretaries and him, and a very large corrugated steel building that looked like an aircraft hangar. This place had a roof, but no walls, and no floor, just weeds and odd tufts of grass trying to grow out of the ground. It was called 'the workshop', and it covered about two acres of ground. I remember thinking that you could easily fly a plane into and out of the workshop. It was that big.

There were about a dozen men in and around the shop, all working on various projects made from steel sheets and plates. Whenever it rained while a wind sprang up, you could bet your boots that everyone in that workshop would get soaking wet. On the day in question, while Sammy and I were conducting our interview, it was hot. Almost unbearably hot. The men working there were wet with sweat, and they were constantly trying to dry themselves off with little towels. I tried to imagine myself being a part of the scene and I didn't fancy it at all. It looked as if most of their raw materials were stacked up in piles outside the shadow of the roof. When I inadvertently touched one of these piles on my circuit, I could feel the heat that the sun had soaked into it. Once the workers had dragged their materials into the workshop, under the roof and out of the sun, there was a definite improvement in the conditions but it was still far too hot for me to function.

I tried to imagine what it would be like in winter, working in a place like that. It probably wouldn't be too bad. Wintertime in southern Africa fell in June and July as we were south of the equator, and winter was regarded as the dry season. We got very little rain between May and August, just cloudless blue skies day after day. I came to the conclusion that winter would be fine for working outside, but not summer. Evie had described summer to me. It was the wet season, with thunderstorms dumping many inches of rain with what seemed to be clockwork precision, almost every afternoon.

Most people went to work carrying an umbrella in the summer. Then at about 3pm, clouds formed and lightning flashed heralding a tremendous storm by about 4pm. That, of course, was the signal that opened all the umbrellas! After the rain, the sun came out and all was peaceful again until the next afternoon at 4pm.

While being escorted around the workshop at Cosine Engineering, I decided I didn't want to work here, all things considered. I made up a little thank you speech for showing me around and told Sammy how I didn't think I could fit into this particular situation, so I would say good bye! I made for the gate, but he grabbed my arm and dragged me to his office saying to his secretary, "Sign Tom Goodwin up, he's coming to work for us tomorrow." It was as if he had suddenly gone deaf or crazy! One or the other.

"No," I said to the secretary, "I won't be here tomorrow," and I made my escape. On the train ride back to Johannesburg where I would get a bus to Kew, I went over the other possibilities on my list. There were five, maybe six companies listed and they all sounded desperate to hire someone like me. I got back to Johannesburg at 4pm in the middle of a tremendous thunderstorm. Evie was dead right with her timing.

I had to start back at the beginning with the telephone, having to wait the longest time just to get an open line. Then I made contact with a company called Airtec, and spoke to a fellow named Jack Ewbank who told me to come for an interview the next day. Then I called two more companies who were advertising for a foreman boilermaker. One of them was a lawyer; the other was a nurse! Then when I checked the phone numbers, the penny dropped. It was Sammy Cousins complete with camouflage. He had cajoled some of his friends or family to help with his advertising for a boilermaker. It looked as if he were flogging a dead horse; he wasn't very successful. I had one more brush with

Sammy on the phone, a day or two later when he answered a message that I had previously left for him. Neither one of us recognized the other's voice at first, until Sammy burst out, "Goodwin? Goodwin? Weren't you supposed to be starting work for me and you didn't pitch up?"

"No," I said, "I don't want to work for you, Mr Cousins."

"No," he said, "that goes for me too, don't bother asking for your job back!"

When I told Evie about this fiasco, we laughed like crazy, and hoped that all South African companies didn't behave that way. One company was OK as far as I was concerned, and that was Airtec Engineering where I had been successful with my interview. The works manager, Jack Ewbank, took me under his wing and helped me get started in this very foreign environment. He was one of the few English-speaking South Africans working there, which made him a crutch for me to lean on. Most of the other people were either Afrikaans-speaking, Portuguese, or German. The Portuguese were arrogant when speaking, or trying to speak, to an Englishman. The Germans were even more arrogant, but the Afrikaners! Well. Most of them were impossible. It really did seem as if the Boer war and conflict had never finished but was still continuing sixty or so years later.

I made two major errors whilst working for Airtec. One error was to defend the actions of the British authorities during the Boer or South African War, as it was sometimes called. That was a pretty bad mistake. What was even worse was to speak in a friendly way to the blacks assigned to me to help me as a 'mate' (now known as Kaffir Boys). That was unforgivable and not allowed under any circumstance. Every tradesman, whether he be a welder, driller, or boilermaker was assigned at least one, (sometimes more depending on the size and complexity of his current projects) Kaffir Boy. He would fetch and carry tools, wrenches and materials, and do the 'rotten' jobs, such as standing in line at the company store, or doing a clean up if necessary.

I couldn't help but notice that the mates, or helpers, were all black while the tradesmen, like me were all white. It was very easy to start up a simple conversation with my mate. He was a black fellow called Jonathan and he was as simple as a newborn babe. I noticed that whenever I spoke to him on a personal level, he looked uncomfortable almost to the point of squirming. He wanted me to give him an order such as, "Jonathan go to the store for more bolts" rather than a query like, "Did your son recover from his cold yet?". Jonathan calculated his replies very carefully when I spoke to him and on one or two occasions told me that the other white Baases didn't like me because I was too friendly with the Kaffirs. I have to plead guilty to being friendly towards all these new people that suddenly came into my life. However, having a friendly disposition towards some of them could obviously create enemies among the others.

I don't want to give the impression that all the Afrikaners or even some of them hated me as a person. They disliked me intensely for sure but that was only because I was English and one of the links to the Boer War. With my natural charm (ahem), I was able to get onto good speaking terms with several Afrikaners to the extent that we each brought Bibles and hymn books into work to compare English and Afrikaans Christmas carols. The relationship that typically existed between the Afrikaner and the black native (Bantu) was much more difficult to describe. The Afrikaner professed to be a father figure to the Bantu, but denied any kind of relationship beyond being a leader. The Bantu were extremely simple people most of whom had never been to school or received any lessons from anyone. After chatting one day with Jonathan, I discovered that he had never heard of Hitler, Churchill, De Gaulle, King George or any of a dozen well known politicians or entertainers. He certainly was not stupid nor was he foolish. He just lacked knowledge probably as the result of a lack of schooling.

Working at Airtec prepared me nicely for the trials of living in a multi national environment, and taught me how to react in many different circumstances. The Bantu were afraid of, and dominated by, the Afrikaners. The 'coloureds', known locally as 'Cape Coloureds' from the Cape Province, also dominated them. The coloureds were light brown skinned people whose ancestors were the offspring of the indigenous Bushmen and the white sailors who had landed in the Cape hundreds of years before. To complicate matters further there were many Bantu tribes such as Xhosa, Zulu, and others with unpronounceable names who were forever warring with other Bantu tribes.

In 1948 the vote had shifted in the national election from the United Party, supported by English-speaking voters, to the National Party, supported by Afrikaans-speaking voters. These Afrikaans voters, all white, represented about ten per cent of the population. The result of the election put the National Party (NATS) into power and freed them to start and pursue their policy of apartheid. The word 'apartheid' is an Afrikaans word meaning separateness. Taken by itself it's not such a terrible thing for some people to want to live separately from others. I've always been very comfortable living among English people and separate from Germans, or the French. However, apartheid as practised in South Africa since 1948 went a few steps further than that. A few 'homelands' were created, to which all the blacks, coloureds, Bantu tribes, etc were made to belong. This meant that all Bantu and others immediately became foreigners in South Africa and were assigned to one of the homelands. At the same time, all the blacks and coloureds were issued with a passbook that had to be carried at all times. This passbook ensured the complete control and domination of all the black and coloured people of South Africa.

Take an example of what could happen to someone like Jonathan under apartheid. He could forget to bring his passbook to work, and so turn around to go back and fetch it. This would mean walking through a white neighborhood where, away from the commuter time of day and alone, he would stand out like a sore thumb. Someone would pounce on him, and challenge him asking him how he had come to be walking through a white area when he should be in a factory somewhere, working. It would be almost certain that the police would pick him up and ask for his passbook.

In order for him to be allowed in that area by law he would have to show his passbook with the day's date, signed by a local resident giving a reason for him being in that area. This could be 'cutting grass' or 'washing windows'. In this case, Jonathan would have to admit that he didn't have a pass book with him, in which case, by the end of the day, he could be whisked away on a train, well on his way to Zululand, a thousand miles away. Meanwhile, I could be waiting for Jonathan to pitch up for work, wondering where the heck he is. This portion of my story reads like a fairy tale but unfortunately it has happened to both men (Boys) and women (Girls).

♪

I learned to put up with all the nonsense associated with the rules and laws related to whites, non-whites, and all the coloureds in between. I discovered that once you forgot politics and the plight of the non-whites, South Africa suddenly and miraculously became a wonderful place to live. Evie and I had arrived at the beginning of November, which coincided with the beginning of summer in that part of the world. The sun shone relentlessly on my little tomato and flower garden, and we got a short thunderstorm most afternoons. I settled into my job at Airtec and quickly gained a reputation for excellent workmanship in spite of the fact that I was an Englishman! The products being manufactured at that time were mostly pieces of equipment used in the gold mines.

We didn't spend much time with Elfy, my new mother-in-law, which was probably one of the reasons we all got on so well together! However, one day she offered to take us out to Witkoppen, a few miles out of Johannesburg. We were going to meet Hella and Austin. Hella was a friend of Elfy's and she lived in a flat in Johannesburg. She and Austin were at the time courting in the old-fashioned way, and planning some day to be married.

Austin was my age, thirty-three, within a few months and Hella was two or three years older. Austin's size and friendliness immediately impressed me. He stood six-feet seven-inches tall in his bare feet, and when we were introduced to each other, he wrung my hand until I thought it would come off. "Tommy," he roared in this strange South African accent, "welcome to Africa, welcome to Johannesburg, welcome to Witkoppen!" He was wearing the South African style shorts, shirt, and safari hat that seemed to be the local uniform, especially at weekends. "Elfy told me that you like engineering problems," he said. "Here's a problem that's got me licked, but maybe *you* can solve it."

The problem was really quite simple; the difficult part was actually doing it. Austin had recently purchased a six-acre plot of land in Witkoppen. Six acres is a fairly large piece of land, and of course the first requirement was to find water. There was no city water in the area so there was no choice. Austin would have to drill for water. He had hired a water diviner who walked about with his wooden divining rods for a couple of days. Eventually he claimed water to be underfoot at a particular location, which was at the high point of Austin's plot. There could be water underground in the form of a lake, or a stream and the water could be five feet down or a hundred! It sounded to me like a big gamble when Austin told me that he had bought a windmill and had it installed on the precise spot where the water diviner had claimed to sense the location of underground water.

Austin paid the windmill installer to bore for water, at the same time lining the borehole (well) with a steel pipe eight inches in diameter. It was then that he made his mistake. After the driller reached water at about 180 feet down, Austin decided to finish the job himself to save money. All that was required was to install an inner two-inch pipe inside the eight-inch pipe. This had to be lowered in twenty-foot sections, nine of them, until the two-inch pipe made contact with the water. When he had lowered four sections of the two-inch pipe by chain winch, somehow the pipe had slipped out of the winch and gone hurtling down to the bottom of the borehole!

So, when I arrived on the scene his problem was how to retrieve the pipe from the bottom of the well. There were a few inches of two-inch pipe protruding from the ground exactly beneath the windmill machinery, and the two-inch pipe that you couldn't see was way down at the bottom of the borehole. Austin and I tried for weeks in our spare time to get the pipe out of the borehole to no avail. "It's no good," said Austin, "we can never unblock that bore hole. We just have to measure twelve inches away from it and drill a new one." Austin was pretty upset at the loss of all the time, effort and wages, particularly the wages required for sinking a new borehole.

I told Jack Ewbank, my boss at Airtec, that I needed some pieces of scrap material and the use of a welder and grinder after hours. "No problem," said Jack, "take what you need." I busied myself in my spare time for a week, finally making a kind of bent ring, which slipped easily inside the eight-inch pipe. It was made in two parts like a pair of tongs, such as those used for picking up lettuce in a salad. I fabricated it in such a way that it hung off a chain, and when the chain was lifted, the tongs part pinched together and the more the chain was pulled, the tighter the tongs gripped.

One Saturday morning I met up with Austin at the borehole and showed him the contraption I had made. We attached a long length of chain to the gripper and dropped it down the hole. Nothing happened but a mark appeared on the gripping tool where it hit something on its way down, presumably and hopefully our two-inch pipe. Then for the next two hours we went through the same rigmarole: filing the bottom of the tool to make it sharper then dropping it, then hoisting it up, filing it, then dropping it. Suddenly something happened. We couldn't hoist the chain – it was too heavy. The tongs had finally gripped something!

We both started giving orders at once to the other, afraid that someone might upset whatever had started. Austin, being the stronger, straddled the borehole and gripping the chain, gave a long pull. "We have a heavy fish on the line," he said. "It's too heavy for me." I pushed a rod through the chain until it rested on both sides of our eight-inch pipe. That held the weight that Austin had just lifted. I had taken the liberty of borrowing from Airtec a machine called a 'CummerLong', which could be used as a hoist among other things. We rigged this up onto the windmill frame and when we operated the CummerLong, up came our chain. It took fifteen minutes to raise the top end of our two-inch pipe above the eight-inch. What a relief it was to see that little piece of steel, which I'd filed so carefully, all scrunched up and hanging onto the two-inch pipe by no more than a hair's breadth!

Now the rest of the job was easy. Taking twenty-foot lengths of two-inch pipe, one at a time and very carefully, we fed the remaining pipe down into the borehole making screw thread connections and linking the pump. The borehole problem had lasted at least a couple of months so the four of us became real buddies, bringing food and drink out to Witkoppen regularly. We often had what Austin called a *braaivleis*, which is literally 'grilled meat' in Afrikaans and barbecue in plain English. In the *braaivleis* we cooked *boerewors* which was farmer's sausage. Austin and I cemented a long friendship with that borehole, and Evie and Hella struck up a friendship too.

I discovered, in a few short months, that Africa is not necessarily a hot or even a comfortably warm place to be. As soon as the sun went down everything cooled quickly and we became thankful for the sweaters, jerseys and long trousers we had brought with us.

Now that the borehole was finished, the slightest breeze set the windmill turning and provided the main lever was 'on', water came pouring out. There was nothing on Austin's six-acre plot at this time. No trees or shrubs. Not even any weeds! "Now that we have water," said Austin, "I can do all kinds of things, I can even plan a house". The house that he referred to was called a *'rondavel'* – a round tribal hut with a thatched roof. With water available Austin was able to make and mix concrete for the foundations of his *rondavel*. He also decided to build what he called a 'dam', a twenty-foot diameter, four-foot deep concrete structure to hold the water that was, so far, merrily wasting itself until the windmill was stopped.

Austin didn't do all this work himself. While I was diligently working at my job at Airtec, he hired a local Bantu to do the heavy digging. This black fellow, who Austin promptly named Thunder Flash, was the best that could be found in spite of being extremely slow. He worked on digging various places for foundations and loosened the concrete-like earth. In spite of being slow, he was careful, relentless and methodical. I saw two pick-axes that had worn down to the shaft over a few weeks. Austin paid Thunder Flash wages by the day, in addition to allowing him to use a small plot, about a quarter of an acre, for his own use. Over a period of about six months, Evie and I visited Austin and Hella many times and saw the slow but gradual growth of the dam, the *rondavel* and various plantings such as apple trees and a kitchen garden. I find it difficult to re-create the comradeship that we all felt at that time, with Hella bringing cakes and cooked goodies, Evie and I fetching beer and wine whilst Austin brought some boerewors and chops that would be cooked on the *braai*.

The best time of day was what is known as 'Sundowner time'. This was when we would break open our first drink of the day, as the sun went down. With the sun went the heat of the day and we all huddled close to the warmth of the *braaivleis*. I remember very well Evie being astounded by the size of Austin's knees as we all squatted together. "They are as large as dinner plates," she would say. It was during one of these sundowners that Austin told me that although he was born in England, he regarded himself as an African. A white African who speaks not only English and Afrikaans (this is a bilingual country) but also portions of several Bantu languages. But being bilingual in South Africa didn't literally mean having the ability to speak two languages. What it really meant – with tongue in cheek – was having the ability to speak Afrikaans plus one other language. Elfy spoke English and German, but not Afrikaans. She was the perfect lady and summed up the language problem for me: "Afrikaans is not a language, it's a bloody inconvenience!"

In January 1963, I started a course in Mechanical Engineering at Veasey's Engineering College in Johannesburg. This was a part-time home study course that ran for three years. During this time we lived in Mrs Van Bruggen's cottage in Kew. We had two bedrooms, one of which I collared for my studies. One day Evie mentioned that she felt a bit lonely in the evenings when I was studying, and Elfy suggested that Evie give private lessons in Mathematics or Latin, which were Evie's best subjects in school. This way Evie would be occupied in the evenings, and would also earn a bit of extra money. So Evie advertised in the paper for pupils, and soon had a reply from a young Englishman called John Pau who wanted math lessons. John was a ladies' hairdresser who had become so successful that he already owned three hairdressing salons at the age of twenty-eight! The reason that he wanted to brush up on his mathematics was that he needed to be able to check up on the managers of his salons to make sure they were not 'cooking the books'.

On his first lesson he came to our cottage wearing tight purple trousers balanced by an orange shirt. We joked later about wearing sunglasses the next time John Pau came to our place! When he arrived, Evie introduced me and then took him into the kitchen where the lessons were to be held. I went to the second bedroom and continued with my engineering studies. I tried to hear what was happening in the kitchen but I couldn't as it was too far away; I had to wait until the end of the session.

Evie started the session by trying to discover what John knew. This was not difficult at all. He knew nothing about sums, plus or minus, or about multiplication, or about division, long or short, and when Evie started to talk about decimals and Rands and cents, his eyes glazed over. I had offered to help a little by preparing some problems for Evie to use, such as figuring how many gallons of paint were needed for how many square feet of wall surface. Evie was wasting her time talking to him about square feet. She had to go back almost to kindergarten level, and encourage him to recite the multiplication tables with "two times three is six, three times three is nine". Evie told her friends that she had secured a part-time job teaching a young man mathematics. After a couple of sessions however, she wanted to take the word 'mathematics' out of her self-appointed job description; it was too embarrassing. However, both he and Evie persevered and worked hard for a few months until he was able to correctly tabulate the various charges he used in his business.

We never saw John Pau's salons, but he did tell Evie that he was about to open a fourth one. We can only assume that his lack of math didn't interfere with his ability to curl and cut hair. I remember complaining to Evie that it took me a tremendous amount of energy to become an engineer while he achieved his success easily, in spite of not even being able to add two and two! It didn't seem fair.

I worked at Airtec for about a year and a half during which time I put up with the insults and aggravations thrown at me by the Afrikaner group. They eventually became threats about having my legs broken and warnings about how good my health would be if I were to work some place else. I don't really believe that I would have been attacked or injured in any way, I just got fed up with listening to all the threats. I decided to change jobs.

When I approached Jack Ewbank to tell him I'd like to leave, he was very sympathetic. "I know what's going on here," he said. "I was born in England too, which puts me into the same category that you're in today. However, did you notice that the Afrikaner treats me with respect?"

"Yes," I replied, "but I don't know why."

"Your problem," said Jack, "is that you treat the Kaffir as though he's your long lost brother. If you want to live in this country, you must alter your attitude towards the non-whites, or, to coin a phrase: when in Rome, do as the Romans do." I remembered hearing that little phrase before. I was to hear it again and again and again.

Jack tempted me to stay at Airtec a little longer by putting me onto the top rate of pay along with tradesmen who had served there for many years. He must have spoken to some of my colleagues too, because I noticed a distinct improvement in the attitudes of a few of the Afrikaners. Evie, who was still working in downtown Johannesburg for Mr Harada, asked me how I had got such a big increase in pay. I told her it was because my boss recognised how good I was at my job. Her reaction to that was, "Oh, go on with you!"

One of the more interesting jobs that I was involved in was in the production of a stainless steel ring about twelve feet in diameter, which was designed to have teeth (like a cog wheel) on the outside diameter and different sized teeth on the inside diameter. The idea was to change the ratio and speed of other wheels on the ring, rather like the gears on a three-speed bicycle. The outer ring was designed to shrink onto the inner one making a good joint with no welding distortion. The standard procedure was to heat the outer ring with a blowtorch allowing it to expand. Then, when it cooled down the outer ring shrank into its place. "Is that the best way, or the easiest, or the safest, or the cheapest way of doing that job?" Jack and several of the Afrikaners asked me.

"Yes, of course," I answered to all their questions. "I have shrunk a steel rim onto an iron wheel a few times using that method," I said.

"There is a better way," they all yelled. And they couldn't wait to tell me something I didn't know.

Jack explained that the shrinking process worked better and easier if, instead of heating the outer ring you cooled the inner one. Of course, you needed a heck of a lot of ice for this job, several wheelbarrow loads, but it worked like a charm. I had never before seen this reversal of the heat shrink process, but the whole of Airtec had. It was quite obvious that the process would work satisfactorily either way, provided it was possible to make a temperature difference.

I eventually left Airtec after about fifteen months, in March 1964, for three good reasons. Firstly, there was an ad in the paper for a "stainless steel specialist", secondly, the new company offered me a lot more money, and lastly – I was still having a hard time doing the things that Romans do. The company advertising for a stainless steel specialist was called Stanco. This was an abbreviation of Stan Nel Company. I discovered later that the owner, Stanley Nel, had made some kind of deal with Kestner APV, a well-known British process and chemical engineering and plant manufacturer. With an influx of money from Kestner APV, Stan Nel was able to manufacture any and all of Kestner's equipment, including fruit juice evaporators and heat exchangers. He had a brand new guillotine, capable of cutting an eight-foot wide by half-inch thick steel plate in one operation. There were several new, up-to-the-minute welding machines capable of handling all kinds of exotic materials including nickel and aluminium. This was a new workshop with no expense spared. The only thing missing was people.

When I marched into the shop for my interview (with a copy of the ad under my arm), I saw six Bantu. I had learned by now that they didn't count in the eyes of the Afrikaners, so I looked for the white people. I counted two, Stan Nel and Herbie. Stan was the boss, and Herbie was the staff. It looked like they were starting the business from scratch. The interview started smoothly with Stan asking me various questions, such as "Are you working now, and where?"

He also asked me if I was a welder, and I said "No, I'm a boilermaker but I can weld if need be." Then he asked me, "How come none of you Roi-Neks [Red Necks, a slang for newcomers to the country who get burned by the sun] can weld?"

I answered "Of course I can weld. I didn't say I couldn't weld. I just said I'm not a welder."

He went to the guillotine and cut several scrap pieces of various thicknesses. "There you go," he said. "I'm going for my lunch. Have these pieces welded and ready for my inspection when I return. Show me what you can do."

It looked as if getting this job depended on how well I could weld together these little bits and pieces! Some were thick, some thin. Some were stainless steel, some carbon steel. If I could practise for two or three hours on one of the welding machines I might have had a chance. Otherwise, my chances were slim. Very slim. After all, I didn't know the amperage required for setting the machine. What a shame, I thought, if I could stall him until tomorrow, maybe I could work something out, but I didn't know how.

I was suddenly aware of the other white fellow in the shop. He came over to me and held out his hand. "I'm Herbie," he said, "Herbie Hayton. I heard Stan giving you the third degree a little while ago. If you can weld even a little bit, I can show you how to set the welder to the right amps for each weld." It was as if he had read my mind. This was exactly what I wanted.

I took off my jacket, rolled up my sleeves, borrowed a pencil and paper from Herbie and made notes on exactly how many amps were required for each weld. In those days my memory was excellent, and I was able to commit all this information quickly to memory. After fifteen minutes or so, I was ready to start welding. Herbie made another set of test pieces for me to practise on and I carefully did my test for Stan Nel.

When Stan came back from his lunch he came to me immediately and studied my test pieces with a sour face. "Your Argon welding is up to shit," he said right away, "but your stick welding is not too bad. Can I take a chance on you?" Without waiting for a reply he said, "Start tomorrow morning, 8am".

I was so surprised I didn't know what to say. The words came to me in time and I gulped, "What about salary, wages, how much?"

"Fifty percent more than you get at Airtec," he said, indicating that the interview had ended.

♬

I worked diligently for APV/Kestner/Stanco for the next four and a half years, and although the period seemed to be placid, it was actually chock full of happenings and adventure. I have made a list of many of the things that happened, but have found it impossible to keep track of all our experiences. I may therefore jump around a little.

Evie and I continued to live 110 First Road, Kew, in Mrs Van's cottage. We put all of Evie's earnings into our 'nest egg', along with some of mine, and we lived on what was left. This wasn't much, but we had a very simple lifestyle and a very strict budget. During 1964 we cheated a little and used some money for a holiday. We decided to spend a few days at the Bushman Rock Hotel, a popular resort in the Eastern Transvaal. After studying the maps we decided it was less than a day's ride, so we could drive slowly and comfortably.

In order to get to Bushman Rock, we headed east into the mountainous area of the Transvaal. After driving for a couple of hours, we stopped at a viewpoint to take a look at the scenery and have a snack. The day was hot and very dry, so we were thankful for the flasks of water we'd brought with us. The mountain views were tremendous, and the clear blue sunny skies enabled us to see for many miles to the horizon. While I was playing with the camera, I noticed a very thin jet black line that looked as if it had been painted on the horizon with a paintbrush. We stared at it for a few minutes but neither of us was able to figure out what it was. We continued our drive, but half an hour later, Evie asked me to stop at the next viewpoint for another look at this strange phenomenon. When we stopped and looked at it again the black line was noticeably wider than before, about one inch at arm's length.

Suddenly we realised what it had to be. It was a cloud in the sky, moving towards us. It was the biggest cloud we'd ever seen. We decided to push on and keep going rather than turn around and go back. We continued on with our drive and watched as the black line went on to fill the sky. It became dark like midnight and I had to turn the headlights on. Then the rain came down with such a loud and vicious hissing noise that we could hear nothing else. We came to a section of road that had an avenue of trees on both sides. Three or four seconds after we had passed a particular spot, a tree crashed to the ground. I saw it hit the ground in the reverse mirror. It must have either snapped or uprooted. After ten or fifteen minutes of incredibly heavy rain it eased off to what would normally be classified as a heavy rainstorm.

During this onslaught of rain, I found a little piece of high ground for the car, so that it would be protected from the flood. Good old Volkswagen! The car performed like a champion, and kept on running throughout the storm. It turns out we were lucky to survive the storm on the way to Bushman Rock. On succeeding days, the newspapers reported a few people dead from drowning and several cars washed away with the drivers still inside. One noticeable fact in our drive was that we passed only a few cars on our trip; the traffic was very light.

That thin black line that crept up on us from the horizon had turned into a solid black sky that emptied water at a furious rate. Then, suddenly and miraculously, the sun was blazing, the sky was clear, and everything was the same as before. When we eventually got to the hotel the storm was gone, but it served as a subject of conversation for days.

The Volkswagen we were driving was a replacement for our Ford Anglia, stolen from us during a trip to the cinema in Johannesburg. We had been to see 'Those magnificent men in their flying machines', and when we came out after the movie the Ford was gone. It was the first and last new car we ever bought until Evie recently bought her new

Saturn. When the Ford was stolen, we found ourselves stranded in the center of Johannesburg, with the last few people driving home. I must admit I felt terribly nervous about being there, unprotected. If I had told a work colleague that I had taken my young wife walking in Johannesburg after midnight, they would have asked if I wanted to commit suicide. Really. It was that bad.

The Bushman Rock Hotel was more than just a hotel; it was a resort with lots of activities and relaxation, the best activity being touring and exploring the Kruger National Park nearby. This park, roughly similar in size to the state of New Jersey, was really a game reserve, which contained many of the indigenous wild animals of the area. The idea was to enter the park in the early morning, see the animals and take pictures, and then either get back to the hotel before dark (our choice), or book into a game reserve shelter. There were many shelters dotted around the park and they were designed to keep the people within the park safe from the animals. There were buffalo, elephants, crocodiles, as well as lions and snakes roaming loose in the park, so it was quite dangerous to be out after dark. Also, no one was allowed to get out of their cars while driving, whether by night or day. We had a few anxious moments one day that showed what a very good role that was.

We were driving through Kruger Park in line behind two other cars, and when they stopped, we stopped. We all looked out of the right hand windows and saw three springbok lying in the long grass. Then, looking out of the left hand windows we saw a full-grown lion coming up behind us. There were other cars behind us, so I expect the springbok didn't smell the lion because of all the exhaust fumes being pumped out. The lion, when he moved, took off with the speed of a rocket. He came past our left side, went past the front of our car and grabbed one of the springbok in his jaws before it was even on its feet. It seemed to me that the lion knew exactly what he had to do. He raised his head and swung the animal towards the car in front of us. The springbok died instantly, the lion dragged it away, and the driver in front suffered a badly banged up car.

During our stay at the Bushman Rock Hotel we met Eric and Riki Bouckley. It was Riki who first chanted, "Han Han Han Han-i-mol mol mol". This was a child's way of learning to say animal, she told me. They were both from London. Riki was a hairdresser and Eric was a tool and die maker. We became friends with them immediately and we all shared our ideas and thoughts about house building. Evie and I were saving like mad for our own house.

Eric was currently building his own house, brick by brick, according to the design of a local architect, and it was taking him forever. He and Riki planned a large family with everyone having his or her own room.

One of their major problems was that they had no children yet and Riki was already about thirty-five or so. Another problem concerned the house and its design. The roof was to be supported by eighteen-inch diameter wooden beams. This would give the inside of the house what Evie would describe as 'character'. However, after the beams were delivered and after Eric had hoisted them onto the roof (a big job), they were found to be contaminated with woodworm. They all had to be taken down and destroyed. Then they had to start again and buy new ones.

In addition to all this, Eric told us he hated his job. He said he would come home from work moaning and groaning about his boss and how badly the company was organised, and what a mess everyone was making of things. "Why don't you do something about the situation," Riki eventually asked, "instead of complaining to me all the time? Do something positive and change your job."

This must have triggered something in Eric's mind, because shortly afterwards he quit his job and started to take photos of houses for sale. He developed the photos and sold the pictures to the local Sunday newspaper. His new job – or new career – became an extension of a hobby that he'd been working at for years. He had never realised that he could earn money at it.

During one of our assaults on a bottle of Scotch, Eric told me how he had ended up in his other career as an automatic door technician. He was chatting to a friend who was the owner of a small apartment building. The main entrance to the building had a door that was controlled by a spring arrangement that automatically closed the door after you. At least, it was supposed to close, but it didn't. Eric's friend had been all over Johannesburg without success looking for a mechanic to fix it.

Eric, being naturally mechanically minded, took the contraption apart, found a broken spring which he promptly welded, and put the door together and presto! It worked. The only problem he encountered was the borrowing of an acetylene gas welder set, which took a few minutes. The building owner was overjoyed and was prepared to pay a large fee. Eric's response was "What are friends for?" Eric then got a flood of phone calls from people asking him to fix automatic closing doors. He was an overnight success, and was able to earn enough from this and taking photos to survive nicely. It's possible that Eric was the only fellow in southern Africa at that time to start a business based on the maintenance of automatic door closers. There's a moral there somewhere about being kind to your friend, or scratching his back, which was not lost on Eric.

The four of us had lots of good times at the Bushman Rock Hotel. We did some rock climbing, and Eric showed off by shooting his pistol and we had lots of picnics and took many rolls of photos. The Bouckleys were surprised that the Goodwins didn't have a gun or pistol, and the Goodwins were equally surprised that the Bouckleys did.

There was one other surprise that I discovered about Eric. He never read the daily newspapers and he claimed to be better off as a result. "Just look at the headlines," he would say, "and you'll find that the news is the same now as it was last week, last month, last year. The only thing that changes is the name of the person in the news." Strikes happen all the time; which union is on strike this week? A politician gave a speech last month and admitted this month that his speech was full of lies. "I don't read the papers," he went on, "or listen to the news on the radio, and then I don't have to pay attention to all this junk that gets churned out." I think that Eric would have loved to disappear over the horizon, and spend the rest of his life on a desert island. Our friendship with Eric and Riki spilled over after our holiday finished.

♫

Those of you who remember that I had planned to spend only two years in South Africa may now be wondering why Evie and I were talking about building our own house. I must admit that I had become very used to the way of life in Johannesburg – the beautiful climate, which was never too hot or too cold, the ease with which I had found good jobs, and the new friends we had made. I suppose it was a combination of all of these things, plus the fact that it would be so easy just to stay, instead of packing up again and starting all over back in England. I was quite happy to plan a future in South Africa for the moment, even though this was the same old country where apartheid was part of the law. I didn't like the politics, but for me it was a good life.

One day in 1965 we noticed a plot of land, a third of an acre, for sale on the next street. As I mentioned earlier, up until this point in time we had been putting all of Evie's earnings into a savings account and we lived on my salary. Slowly but surely our bank balance climbed until we were able to buy the plot of land. Every night and twice on Sundays we walked past what we called our 'dream house' at 75 Second Road, Kew. The plot of land was only two blocks from the cottage that we were renting, so it was very convenient for us. It also meant that we would not be moving out of the area, which was so handy not only for my job, but also for Evie's new job. But more about that later. In the meantime, we visited our new piece of property and continued dreaming, pointing out where our new house would go, planning a bedroom here, the kitchen there, until suddenly we were speaking of our house as if it already existed.

We bought a couple of sickles over the next few weekends and cut the weeds from shoulder-height down to the ground. Once the weeds were gone, we discovered an old well in what would be the back garden. Perfect for filling a swimming pool, we both thought. We started negotiating with a home building company called Everest Construction, and after many meetings with them, and many hours deciding exactly what we wanted and what we could actually afford, we signed a contract with them to build our new house. We had saved up enough for the downpayment, and we now applied for a mortgage from the Building Society. I must say that Evie had a ball while deciding on which design she wanted for our house. One of her new favorite words was 'character'. She would say, "If we move this wall a little that way, it will give the house more character." Or she would suggest, "Let's have some shrubs on the north-facing wall, as they will add character to the house." And so on. We were allowed to make certain changes to the plans up to the time when we signed a contract with Everest. Then changes would cost more.

While the builders were putting up our house, Evie and I measured approximately twenty feet by forty in the back garden, then hammered in some wooden pins so that the shape was finished as a rectangle with a curve at one end. This was the intended shape of our swimming pool, next to a plum tree, and fairly close to the water well. I took a spade, and cut all around the swimming pool shape. At this time, towards the end of 1965, I was still a relatively young man of thirty-six, very able and full of confidence, so I entered a period of intense activity with no problems at all. I put in a forty-hour week at Kestner's, then spent most evenings on my part-time home study, reading Veasey papers and solving Veasey engineering and mathematical problems for two hours. At weekends I busied myself with a spade and shovel, working on the pool.

Long before we even bought the plot of land for our new house, Evie had decided that she wanted to change jobs. She had been working in the center of Johannesburg as a secretary for a new Japanese company, and her role was mainly answering the phone, and taking messages for Mr Harada, her boss. After a while she got so bored that she started bringing books to work so that she wouldn't have to stare out of the window all day. In addition to the boredom, there was a long, tiresome commute in and out of Johannesburg every day. Evie knew that there were many office buildings very close to where I worked at Kestner's, so one Saturday morning she and I toured the area, and jotted down the names of half a dozen companies that looked suitable. Evie then wrote to each company, describing her secretarial skills, and indicating that she was looking for a job in the area. She got three replies, and her first interview was with a company called Superior Manufacturing Company, who made Kelvinator refrigerators and stoves. The company was only a five minute drive from where we lived, and only two streets away from where I worked. She was offered a job immediately, and it turned out that her boss was also a Londoner, from the same area that I grew up in. He even had a slight Cockney accent, just like mine.

We had a busy year during 1965 and '66. My part-time home study at Veasey Engineering College was coming to a close at the end of 1965, and I had to take exams in order to get a final certificate. After a few sleepless nights, and a struggle to remember all the formulas and conventions, I successfully completed the course. Evie was very happy that I had passed the exam, and insisted that we celebrate with dinner in a fancy restaurant. If it were not for Evie's participation in helping me with some of the tricky mathematics, I don't think I could have managed successfully to pass the exams.

While all these things were happening, in addition to following the floor plans of the house, we busied ourselves making more plans for carpets, curtains, and all the thousand and one components that a woman needed to turn a house into a home. In November 1965 our new house was finished and we were able to move in. We soon settled in, and of course wanted to show off our new home to all our family and friends. Elfy and Monica were the first to see the new house finished, and then we started inviting our friends over.

Diana Gregson (Greg), whom we had met in Cape Town several years before, was invited to tea one Sunday afternoon. She was still in training and practising in the hope of becoming a fully-fledged first class opera singer. Greg brought with her a boyfriend, Richard Fox, who had followed her all over Europe in the hope of eventually marrying her. I liked Richard from the time we first shook hands. He was an American, originally from Belding, Michigan. There was a kind of affinity between us that worked like magic. I was still working, with occasional help from a laborer, but mostly on my own, on digging out the hole for our swimming pool, which was to be three feet deep in the shallow end, and about ten feet deep in the deep end. Richard offered to help me at weekends whenever he could. We worked together with pick-axe and shovel to remove a particularly tough tree root in the way of the pool over several weeks, and when we finally got it out he said "Boy, doesn't that make you feel like Shane?" See the movie 'Shane' and you will know what that meant.

Richard and Greg often came to visit us, but their romance died a natural death after a while and Richard found other interests, along with a girl called Joan. Richard and Joan married and settled down, eventually having five children. Tragically, their marriage ended when Joan died of cancer. Richard took his young family back to his hometown of Belding in Michigan and raised them there successfully on his own.

Now that we were actually on the premises, I could devote more of my spare time to finishing off our swimming pool. The hole had been dug – twenty feet wide by forty feet long, sloping gently from three feet deep in the shallow end to ten feet deep in the deep end. Now I had to put in a reinforced foundation for the floor of the pool, which was to be made of concrete, as well as the walls, which consisted of a double layer of brick. After laying thousands of bricks to build the walls, with the help of African laborers, I then plastered both the floor and the walls to make them waterproof. The pool then had to be filled immediately with water, to prevent the plaster from drying out and cracking.

In the meantime, I had begged, borrowed or bought all the equipment needed to make the filtration plant for the pool. I assembled what I could in the shop at work, and then brought all the bits and pieces home, and built a pump room-cum-changing room near the deep end of the pool. The house was made of wooden logs and looked like a little Swiss chalet. Evie was thrilled. The pump worked like a charm, and kept the water sparkling clean. The following year, when the plaster was properly cured, we emptied the pool and painted the walls and floor a light blue. I put a nice stone edging around the pool, and I like to think that it looked like a really professional job.

With so many things going on, something really important for the Goodwin family was taking place, which changed our lives and our thinking drastically. Evie became pregnant, and a new baby was due to be born. This was the best news we'd had for years and from then on everything revolved around the new unborn child. This was, of course, before the advent of modern pre-natal testing, so we had to resort to guessing games. The only thing we knew for sure was that a baby would be born, at least one, maybe more. We sent letters to everyone we could think of: Mum and family in England, Evie's dad in the USA, and to anybody we thought might be interested. I even sent a note to Young Rollo, "We are expecting a baby, and it will be a boy called Stephen!" This was of course a guess on my part. Evie and I had been talking about our son Stephen, who would continue the family name of Goodwin into the future. For now, we had to wait and see!

While we were waiting, our new house started to go up by Everest Construction. It was to be a three bedroom, two bathroom solid brick construction house, with kitchen, dining room, living room and a separate garage. It had a tiled roof and an attached porch. There was also a tiny one-room apartment complete with a shower and toilet room labelled 'servant's quarters'. Evie and I agonised over whether or not to include that servant's room. We really couldn't afford it; we were scraping the barrel already, but at the last minute we decided to include it.

There was a South African law, which was being strictly enforced at the time, that a black person and a white person could not, under any circumstances, sleep under the same roof. This meant that if you wanted to keep a full-time servant at your house, then you had to provide separate accommodation under a separate roof for him or her. We reasoned that it would be difficult, if not impossible to sell the house at a later time if there was no servant's room. I reckoned that at least ninety per cent of the white population had a black live-in servant. So, although we had no servants ourselves, we decided to swallow hard and include the room as part of our house. (We did have casual labour to help out in the house and garden.)

The site for our new house was right on our route home from work, so typically we would stop to inspect the progress the builders had made each day. It was interesting watching the foundations being poured, then the walls and roof going up little by little. We watched, critically, every move that the builders made, making sure that everything went according to plan. We knew more about this house than the builders did after a little while and Evie could pinpoint every room and doorway in the house blindfolded.

At this time, Evie decided to continue working at Superior Manufacturing until the end of February so that she could have a few months at home before the baby was due around the middle of June. Two weeks before Evie was due to stop work, she ran me to work, as usual, then drove back home, and prepared for the day. After locking up the house, she went to work until noon. Normally she would have stayed in her office all day, but on this particular day, she decided to go home during her lunch break. As she walked toward the front door, she could see into the kitchen, and noticed that the fridge door was wide open. She was very puzzled, as she was sure that she would never have left it open. Then, on opening the front door, she looked down the long passage towards our bedroom, and saw that the door of the linen cupboard was open too. At that split second she realized, with horror, that someone had been in the house, and might, for all she knew, still be there! She quickly ran out of the house, and went next door to phone for the police and me.

We had been burgled some time between 9am and 12noon. Poor Evie was trembling and shaking when I got home. The very thought of strange, unknown people rampaging through our new house made both of us sick to the stomach. We decided not to touch anything until the police arrived. When they got there, they conducted a general examination, and a few facts surfaced. The burglars had known where Evie's two large suitcases were at the back of a wardrobe, and these had been opened up and filled with every scrap of my clothing. I was left with the clothes I stood up in and not a thing more.

The one detective motioned towards our double bed and asked me,

"Did they take your gun?" I told him I didn't keep a gun and asked why he had enquired. "It's very obvious to me," he said, "that the burglars came into this house knowing that the windows had recently been installed with new putty. This was how they got in. They also knew on which side of the double bed the husband slept." Evie and I got quite a shock when we heard this! How could they know? The detective pointed out that someone had pulled back the cover and pillow on the right hand side of the bed. "The husband of the household usually sleeps with his gun on his side of the bed," said the detective. "I assume that you sleep on the right side because he was looking for your non-existing gun there, of that I'm sure." It gave us an eerie feeling that they even knew which side of the bed we slept on.

Our burglar ignored Evie's clothing, but took all her jewellery, except for what she was wearing that day. We discovered that some sheets were missing, and a few towels and some miscellaneous items from the booze cabinet. But to top it all they added insult to injury by taking my old, dirty gardening shoes from the back door, where I normally kept them, and leaving behind their even older and dirtier worn-out shoes!

I was left with nothing to wear so I had to go shopping for underclothes, socks, shoes, and a suit. Fritz, Evie's former stepfather, came across with a host of re-usable items, such as suits, sweaters and shoes. Looking back on this episode makes me supremely happy that the thieves were out of the house before Evie got home. We regarded it as a lucky escape.

♪

Evie stopped work at the end of February as planned and stayed home knitting baby clothes in preparation for the new baby. One of the reasons she decided to stop work at that time was that she became eligible, after four and a half months' pregnancy, for a monthly maternity benefit check from the government. I don't remember how much it amounted to, but whatever it was it was very welcome. We were struggling to pay for our various necessities for our new house, such as curtains, rugs, insurance, as well as food! Our budget was rather tight at the time, and sometimes Evie would get to the end of the month and literally have no more than about a shilling in her purse.

Let me give you an example. There was a Portuguese greengrocer about one and a half blocks away where Evie shopped regularly for fresh vegetables, one of them being pumpkin. On one day in particular, among other things, she asked for a 'tickie' pumpkin. The tickie was a coin similar to a five cent American nickel. The shopkeeper carefully sliced off a piece of pumpkin, wrapped it in newspaper, and held it out to Evie, who immediately told the man, "That's not enough for my tickie." After haggling a little, the man reluctantly sliced off another wedge of pumpkin. Evie told me that every time she went she had to ask for a bigger slice.

Evie enjoyed these few months at home, knitting, reading and relaxing before the birth of the baby. Then, on Wednesday June 15th 1966, we all gathered at the Florence Nightingale Nursing Home: Evie, Elfy, Eric (complete with movie camera) and I to welcome the arrival of Anne!

I sent telegrams to family members telling of the good news that we now had a new member of the Goodwin family, and her name was Anne Goodwin. A telegram came back from Evie's dad, who was very happy to be a grandfather for the first time, which said, "Well done, Tom!" When Evie read that she nearly had a fit! What about the part *she* played in the proceedings?

Anne was a petite little thing weighing exactly five pounds, fifteen ounces, with light blonde fuzz on her head. I fell in love with her the moment I saw her and her tiny little fingers. "Wow," I thought, "this is my daughter." I was quite overwhelmed. Evie sailed through the whole procedure like a champion, and looked as lovely after the birth as she did on our wedding day.

Anne can best be described as a happy baby. She learned to smile at a very early age, and this was due, I am sure, to the non-stop care she received from her mother. Anne got only the best. There was however, one situation when she became quite unhappy for a couple of days. This was when Evie took Anne to the doctor for her three month baby shots. Anne didn't like that at all, and showed her displeasure by crying bitterly. "No problem," said the doctor. "She will recover very quickly from the injections in a day or two. However, if she keeps you awake at night give her a teaspoon of brandy." We gave her some brandy one night after she had been crying for some time and like a miracle, she slept through the night. The next couple of nights Anne cried again in the evening and we gave her some more brandy, and then we suddenly realised that Anne wasn't in pain from her shots at all. She just wanted her brandy!

She was a 'good' baby, sleeping through the night very quickly and fussing only when her nappy needed changing. I had finished the swimming pool in the garden by now and I can remember Evie setting the alarm to 4am so that I could spend two hours planting grass in the back garden before going to work. I was busy, busy. I also remember giving Anne her bath and shampoo, and 'dressing' her with a nappy and a large safety pin, as we did in those days. This time, as they say, was true quality time.

In the spring of 1967, we took Anne to England just before her first birthday, to be christened in St Philip's Church, Kensington where Evie and I had married five years earlier. The Reverend Selwyn Cox was still officiating, and as much of a fusspot as ever. He gave us a lecture in the form of a sermon, encouraging us to have more children, and assuring us that "God would provide".

This trip to England lasted about six weeks. Evie's dad, Harold, came over from the United States, and was thrilled to meet his first grandchild. Of course, it was easy to show Anne to the Goodwin side of the family. There was no travelling necessary except for an occasional hire car and rides we got from the Rollinsons and others who wanted to see Anne. We were very lucky to be able to stay in Mum and Dad's spare room in Benfleet Court, Haggerston Road. We certainly could not afford to stay in any kind of lodgings for six weeks, not even a bed and breakfast.

The weather during our six week trip was pretty rotten. It seemed to us to be raining all the time. We bought a well-worn secondhand stroller for a few pence at the local Kingsland Road market. Dad and I cleaned it up, adjusted and tightened all the screws and made it look like new. With this stroller we pushed Anne all over London and parts of southern England.

One Sunday, Anne developed a heavy cold with a cough and a runny nose. This was the first time that anything had happened to her, so we telephoned the local doctor, a cheery Scot who lived and worked two blocks away. It was his day off, and he didn't want to see any patients but Evie was very persuasive on the phone, so he told us to come along and he would wait for us. When we arrived at his office the doctor picked Anne up, made some goo-goo noises while he looked down her throat and studied her face and her nose. Then he bounced her on his knee, making her chuckle. "Tell me," he said, "is this your first child?" When we nodded, he smiled as he said, "In cases like this I usually treat the parents! Don't worry, look into your baby's eyes and you will see that she is perfectly healthy. She just has the sniffles." As he saw us to the door he said, "If your baby gets sick, you will know about it." Anne recovered from the sniffles after a couple of days.

Back in Johannesburg, we soon returned to our normal life. Stan Nel ran his workshop as a kind of figurehead, without doing any work at all. He managed to appear on the scene daily no earlier than about 10am, laughing and joking with the two pretty secretaries from the front office. He assigned all decisions to Herbie Hayton and me, so that his daily walk through usually consisted of a nod if he saw something different from the day before. He would scratch his chin and stop to give us a quizzical glance when he felt that something was out of place. Occasionally, he would give us a 'thumbs up' when he was pleased with the previous day's results.

A constant stream of workers used to parade past Stan Nel looking for a job. At first he kept the hiring and firing of workers as his own preserve, but after a few months he changed that. One day, he told me that I should henceforth have the title of Works Manager with, of course, a suitable increase in salary. I had to get rid of a few 'losers' that we had on the payroll, and I carefully hired some replacements with the experience of handling stainless steel, nickel and aluminum in addition to carbon steel, copper and other standard materials.

I finished up with a dozen men, all eager to build the high quality equipment that Kestner sold. After about a year of running the shop, I supervised the construction of a new workshop right next door, which effectively doubled the space available. The final team of a dozen workers was, of course, all white. I had a further twelve or so blacks who did menial tasks such as grinding, polishing and painting. I was quite surprised to discover that I often failed to take notice of the blacks. They were becoming a non-entity to me. I found myself going out of my way so that I wouldn't have to speak to them and run the risk of being called a 'Kaffir Boetie' (literally meaning a Kaffir Brother, but actually having the connotation of being a Kaffir sympathizer). I found myself beginning to treat them the way the Afrikaners did, and talk to them as if they were children. Half of my work team was made up of Afrikaners, including a Chris Prinsloo, a Labuschagne and a Van Niekerk as examples, with the rest being English-speaking South Africans.

There was also a Scotsman working for the company called George Taylor, who was responsible for figuring wages and salaries. George was a stern faced individual who cultivated an air of toughness in order to keep any hijackers away from Kestner, particularly twice a month on payday. Every two weeks he would collect the money from the bank in readiness for our fortnightly payment, during which time he kept up a non-stop barrage of threats and bluster, directed against anybody who happened to be in the area.

He would start a big show by marching out of the Kestner offices surrounded by four trusted black employees – big fellows – holding aloft a large, silver-colored pistol. He fired the pistol into the air three times and waved it towards anyone who might be watching. He then climbed into a waiting car, still protected by a black bodyguard, and was driven away to the local bank. Fifteen minutes later he returned, this time with a leather case strapped to his wrist. He then fired one more shot before entering the building. I saw George go through this performance many times. He was always welcome back to the office because he brought the wages; he never missed a trick.

There was another George, George Hamilton, an accountant who lives on in my memory. I remember one situation where we were gathered around a leaking heat exchanger with several other employees. It was a critical piece of equipment and it was my problem to fix it for a delivery next day. "Don't worry about it, Tommy," said George. "If we wait until tomorrow I'm sure it'll just rust up and stop leaking." No one wanted to tell him that the heat exchanger was made of nickel, a substance that doesn't 'rust up' like iron and steel. The company later gave him a reclining chair upon his retirement.

♫

Elfy continued living in Kew, and after one or two ventures when she bought and re-modelled old existing houses, she eventually settled and had a house built in Fifth Road, just a couple of streets from our new house. The house she had built was located on three-quarters of an acre, which was a double-sized plot. Once her house was built, there was an imaginary line running through her plot effectively turning it into two standard sized plots of three-eighths of an acre each.

She came to see us one day with a proposal concerning the spare plot. "How about this," she said. "I have an empty plot next to my house which is paid for, free and clear. Tommy, you will give your time and effort to build a house on that plot. We can go half each for all materials and native labor costs. When the house is finished, we can rent it to a tenant and we each get fifty per cent of what we make. How about that!" she finished with a flourish. Evie and I were more than surprised – we were flabbergasted! This was a chance to make a steady income, and possibly to get a lump sum of cash if the house were to be sold.

But my first reaction was to refuse point blank. "I can't build a house, I wouldn't know where to start," I lamented. Well, we talked about it, Evie, Elfy, and I, and they both gave me lots of encouragement, telling me that I had lots of brick-laying and concrete foundation experience from when I recently built our swimming pool.

"You will find it easy once you start," they said, "and laying bricks is laying bricks."

They convinced me to go ahead with it, and we agreed on some common sense ground rules. We ordered a truckload of bricks in June 1967 and a heck of a lot more over the next couple of months. I estimated about 30,000 bricks in total. I calculated the quantities of cement, sand and stone required for the concrete foundations and ordered it, then ordered doors, windows and plumbing fixtures. It seemed to be never ending. Elfy spent a lot of time making phone calls and following up with more phone calls until she almost went crazy. We didn't have any of the modern, sophisticated answering machines available today.

There was one time when Elfy and I disagreed on a detail of the joint project. The elevation of the foundation had to be level all the way around, so that if you stepped onto the foundation and walked, you would eventually come back to where you had started without stepping up or down. The house was situated on a gentle slope so that one side looked higher than the other, like an optical illusion. I had to walk Elfy a dozen times around that house before she would agree that my foundation was level!

The building of this house took nearly two years of my time and I discovered early on that I couldn't possibly handle the whole thing by myself. I was working full time for Kestner and so I singled out from their pay roll a native boy who was trustworthy, honest and smart. His name was Albert, and he was my right hand man from the beginning of the whole project. He was tickled pink when I told him my second name was Albert. We became friends, but on the surface only. I could never ever in a hundred years invite him to my house to visit. There was a law against it! When we passed each other in Kestner we each ignored the other. This was for our mutual protection. I couldn't ask him to work late in the evening, because his pass would have been invalid. In general, we worked Saturday, Sunday, and holidays, from sun-up to sun-down. I walked the three blocks to Fifth Road before breakfast and invariably Albert was already there at the building site with sand and cement (enough for the day) already mixed in the correct proportions. His toothy grin was always there along with his, "G'mornin' baas".

Within two minutes of my arrival, I was busy laying bricks and giving verbal instructions to Albert to shift ladders and bring enough bricks to enable me to continue our fast pace. If we needed help for any reason, he would disappear for half an hour, and then return with as many boys as we needed. I never had any problems with him or the boys he recommended. I had heard many horror stories from various South African friends and acquaintances about how lazy the Africans were, and how stupid and how sorry I would be to trust Albert, or any other native boy. However, my experience taught me otherwise. We became close, and as friendly as it was possible to be without breaking any laws.

Actually, there was not much chance of breaking laws by developing a friendship. A more likely problem would be if someone saw a friendship growing between a black and a white and decided to punish the culprits, perhaps with a brick through a living room window. I'd heard of this happening, and I didn't want it to happen to me. I'd rather be a safe coward than a beat up hero. However, I must give credit to Albert for being such a splendid helpmate to me while I was building the house.

While I was still working on the house, our good friends Austin and Hella decided to tie the knot and get married after a courtship of more than five years. Austin approached me one day in 1967, and asked me to serve as Best Man at his forthcoming wedding. I agreed, of course, and the happy event took place in Johannesburg. Over the last few years, a lasting friendship had developed between us and we were in the habit of visiting to keep in touch. Evie and Hella spent time analyzing knitting patterns along with baking and cooking procedures (both were knitting experts) whilst Austin and I talked about the latest design of well pumps, building problems and Austin's choice of fruit trees for his fast growing orchard in Witkoppen.

We always had some kind of background music playing during our visits, which used to end with the ladies serving coffee and cake. During one of these evenings, Austin played some organ music on his radiogram. It turned out to be a selection of pieces, written by Johann Sebastian Bach and performed by an organist named E. Power Biggs. That was a very enjoyable evening listening to Biggs make music, and we decided that next time we would have an evening devoted solely to music. During our first musical evening, there was no humming, no joke telling, and no gossip, just listening to the music.

We had a problem during the first couple of musical evenings, when the club consisted of only the four of us, Evie, Hella, Austin, and me. Anne was still very young and Stevie was not born yet. Our problem was what to do with Anne when we were having a musical evening at Hella's flat in Johannesburg. When we turned the music up, Anne awoke and started to cry. When we got to a comfort level for Anne the music was too soft and we couldn't hear it. We solved the problem by making Anne comfortable in her carry cot, then parking the carry cot in Hella's bath tub and closing the bathroom door. "No one is allowed to use the loo," Austin would say with a smile, "until the end of the evening!"

We so enjoyed our evenings of music that we decided to ask some of our friends if they would be interested in joining our little group. We found four couples who wanted to join, so we decided to lay down some rules and regulations.

The rules were very simple. Everyone took a turn, alphabetically, at being host. The host was responsible for choosing all the music for his or her evening, and for making a program. The whole evening was to be completely free of any and all kinds of talking, chatting, and whispering while the music was being played. Anyone breaking what we called the silence rule was banned from the club.

These musical evenings became an instant success and we were all amazed to discover how much music there was in the world to listen to. People began to play records that they had been given years ago as presents for Christmas or birthdays so that musical appreciation flourished. We were all encouraged to choose selfishly for our own musical evening. This way, relatively unknown music might eventually become popular, and some did! There was one restrictive rule: no Be-Bop, jazz or Ray Conniff-style popular music. Only music commonly known as 'classical' was to be used.

♫

As I continued to work on the house, one of the problems I came up against was the construction of the fireplace and chimney. I had to go down to the library and borrow a couple of books on the subject before I became familiar with it. I designed the grate in such a way that all the ashes could be removed through the outside wall, and not through the living room. That worked out fine, but the chimney gave me problems. Kneeling on the floor and starting above the grate, I laid a few bricks that represented the back of the chimney. These bricks had to curve towards me as they went up. Then they had to curve away from me as they went up further. At this point I laid some bricks representing the left and right side of the chimney, which were also supposed to curve as they went up. This was the point where everything fell down and I had to scrape the bricks clean and start afresh. I finally figured it out after about four hours of struggling and sweating. I had to regard the chimney as a brick arch, and build some supports accordingly. That day, I learned how to build a chimney; it's not easy.

There is only one way to find out if a chimney functions properly, and that is to light a fire in it. If the builder made a bad job then the house would fill with smoke and the draught would go down the chimney instead of up it. My chimney had its test after the house was completed, and our tenant family, John and Connie Rieben, moved in with their one-year-old son Chris. The Riebens were giving a party to celebrate moving into the house. There were about thirty people at the party including Evie, Elfy, and me. The festivity lasted until early evening, when it started to get a little chilly. John stood up and raised his hands for silence, starting to speak.

"Let me introduce my friend and landlord, Tom Goodwin. He built this house by himself with the help of only a licensed plumber, an electrician, and of course some African laborers. As you can see, the house doesn't look too bad. In fact, it looks like a professional job, not what you would expect from an amateur. The fireplace has not been tested yet, but this is a good opportunity to try it out." All the time he was talking, my stomach was churning. What if the chimney didn't draw and the house filled with smoke? This could be the worst embarrassment of my life. He scrunched up some newspapers, put them in the fireplace along with some kindling, some logs and a shovel-full of coal. There was a noise all around me and all at once I realised that the fire was alight and everyone in the room was clapping and applauding. As the fire burned stronger some of the people called out "Well done!" and "You did it!" This was the first, and maybe the only, time in my life when I was applauded by a room-full of people for doing a good job of work. Boy, did I feel good!

Elfy, too, deserved a lot of the credit for the success of this house. It was she who had drawn up the plans to her own design, including some very innovative ideas (for that time in South Africa, anyway), such as underfloor heating. She helped with the finishing of the kitchen cabinets and, of course, did all the running about, and made the phone calls. She later gave me a silver key ring (which I still treasure) with a picture of the house on one side, and 'The house that Tom built – June 67 to Feb 69' on the other.

While the 'house that Tom built' was proceeding nicely, Evie successfully became pregnant again and gave birth to Stephen Thomas Goodwin on June 11th 1968. Anne now had a baby brother almost exactly two years younger. Stevie, as he was called from the beginning, had a birth weight of six pounds and five ounces and was the happiest little fellow you have ever seen. He was born with the lightest fuzz of blonde hair on his head. He actually looked bald, which gave him a look just like his grandfather in America! He was christened when he was six months old at Saint Catherine's Church, Bramley, Johannesburg.

Evie told me of a moment that happened when Stevie was just four weeks old. She was holding him in her arms before a full-length mirror when their glances locked and he smiled at her. It is, apparently, a rare event for a four-week-old baby to recognize and smile at another person, even its mother.

By the time he was a year old, he was so chubby that he wobbled like a jelly when he laughed. It was Anne's job to make him laugh. We would say to her, "Make Stevie laugh, Anne," and she would jump up and down in front of him, and he would sit there and giggle and shake. It made us all laugh. Evie said that he looked like a miniature Buddha. By the time he was two, though, he had slimmed down, and that's how he stayed throughout his childhood.

Both Evie and I felt that our family was now complete. We had our little girl, and we had our son and heir. What more could we want?

I think I mentioned Fritz Peiser earlier in my story. Evie's mother Elfy had married Fritz after divorcing Evie's father. Elfy had gone to South Africa in 1948 with Evie, who was then seven years old, and Trixie, who was three, and married Fritz in Johannesburg. Unfortunately, after seven years, Elfy and Fritz divorced, making him Evie's ex-stepfather! He wasn't very prominent in our family, being an ex, but we visited him and his new wife, Jutta, and their four daughters, on many occasions. He was, apparently, quite wealthy, owning a large house on Scott Street where

Evie had once lived. All the children that Fritz could claim to belong to his family, had so far, been female. These included of course Evie, Trixie, his daughter Monica whom he had had with Elfy, and also an adopted daughter, Molly, from a previous marriage. So, when Stevie finally came along, not only was he the first male in this extended family, he was born on Fritz's birthday to boot! What a celebration there was.

At about this time, when Anne was two years old, she developed an intense liking for two of her toys. One of them was an old plastic wallet and the other a pink teething ring. She wouldn't listen to us, or take any notice unless she had these two items firmly clasped, one in each hand. She called one of them pee-boo, and the other was dub-dub. Evie and I were never able to figure out which was which, but I'm sure it didn't matter as long as Anne had her pee-boo and dub-dub.

Evie and I settled into a very pleasant lifestyle with the two children at 75 Second Road, Kew. We had the swimming pool to relax in daily and, to protect them from any accidents, I built a split pole fence around the pool area. This was mainly for Anne's benefit; she was becoming a 'tomboy', showing no fear of the water.

Saturdays and Sundays were special for us, as were holidays like Easter. I would get up early, before 6am and walk the couple of blocks to the house that Tom built. Then Albert and I would work like beavers till about 10am when Evie would appear, pushing Stevie fast asleep in his pram, with Anne bubbling over with joy, and trying to show me her pee-boo and dub-dub. Albert would then make himself scarce for a couple of hours, and Evie would unwrap our lunch, usually consisting of cold cuts, bread, fruit of some kind, and coffee. After the lunch was finished, Evie would take the children back home, and Albert and I would work for another long stretch.

♪

Living in South Africa, we were very insulated from the outside world, and were dependent for information on what the radio and newspapers chose to tell us. Both of these news sources were heavily biased in favour of the South African government, and the news we received was slanted to suit. I guess that was understandable. However, there were things going on right in our own country that never reached the news media and some of them were quite disturbing, as the following incident shows.

Evie and I often strolled up the street about two blocks from our house to where there was a fish and chip shop. There was always a group of people hanging about waiting for the next 'fry-up', and we sometimes stood in line and placed an order for some fish and chips. This, of course, made an excellent informal meal for us two or three times a month, as well as a good excuse for Evie to have a night off from cooking. We would then have coffee and cake, or something similar as a dessert.

One evening, as we walked up the street to get some fish and chips, we heard a loud commotion with people yelling and screaming and a dog barking. We saw a young white fellow holding the leash of an Alsatian dog. He was goading the dog to attack a young black fellow who was trying to get out of the shop, but was trapped in the shop doorway. The dog, which was inches away from the black man, was barking and snarling as if it was completely out of control. I hate to think what would have happened if the white fellow had let the leash go, or if the leash had snapped. As we stood transfixed, we heard the white man screaming threats at the top of his voice of what he would allow the dog to do. He was yelling with promises about what happened to cheeky Kaffirs who tried to enter shops ahead of white people. There were about a dozen or so people, all white, encouraging the dog owner to let go of the leash. Evie and I were so horrified that we turned around and quickly walked home.

That incident at the fish and chip shop was not isolated. Similar happenings took place regularly and frequently. I was always afraid that one of these outbursts would take place when Evie and the children might be vulnerable on the street. I decided I couldn't allow this to happen. For the last couple of years, Evie and I had had many discussions – one might call them conferences – about the future of the Goodwin family. So far, with hard work, and careful, diligent planning, we had reached what my Dad would call 'a respectable level'. We had fifty per cent of the house that Tom built, along with our house that had we paid Everest Construction to build for us. Our house, of course, had a pool that I had built in my spare time, and we also had a car and a telephone. By Cockney standards we would be considered wealthy. This was the financial side of our lives, which was backed up by the knowledge that I was now earning a decent salary and could support the family without having to rely on earnings from Evie. This meant, of course, that Evie could stay home and give her full attention to bringing up the children.

So we were, at that time, reasonably successful. All we had to do was to accept what was happening in South Africa, and become a part of it. But I dropped the proverbial bombshell a few days after Christmas 1968, when I told Evie that I didn't want the children to go to school in South Africa, or even to grow up there, and this meant only one thing; we would have to leave the country! For Evie, this was a very difficult thing to hear. And I had presented her with a tough decision to make. Her mother and half-sister would be left behind along with all her friends, including her oldest and one of her dearest friends, Dorothea Lulofs, whom she had met at the age of seven, soon after arriving in South Africa.

And even though Evie hadn't been born there, South Africa was the country she had grown up in and gone to school in. For her it was 'home'. But she could tell that I was quite determined to leave, and as she said, she really had no choice. She could insist that we stay, and live forever after with an unhappy husband, or she could agree to go, and try and make the most of starting a new life somewhere else. She felt that it was up to the wife to make the adjustments. This was before the time of women's lib!

We talked about leaving, and started planning all the things we would have to do. This wasn't an easy decision for either of us but we agreed that we were literally sitting on a powder keg. This theoretical powder keg could blow up at any time and when it did, (and I was sure it would), then I wanted us all to be out of there. The South African black and colored people were not going to put up with this kind of treatment forever. They would eventually assert themselves. There would be repercussions against the white population – of that there was no doubt in my mind.

Our next problem was where to go? Places like Russia, France or Italy would give us a language problem. New Zealand and Australia were so far away, and in those days people didn't just jump on a plane to take a trip, the way they do now. We knew that we would never be able to afford a holiday in England to visit my family, and the thought that I might never see Mum and Dad and the rest of the family again, to say nothing of our friends, put the idea right out of our heads.

Canadian winters would be too cold, and neither of us fancied living in Britain. Evie still had visions of young mothers hauling their laundry and their young children through the rain to the laundromat, and a lack of good jobs and high taxes frightened *me* off. The only place in the world that was acceptable to us both was the United States of America. Evie's father was still living in New Jersey so we thought we could go there first and then see what happened.

Evie was a citizen of the USA so we wouldn't have too much trouble gaining entry for the whole family. Any United States citizen was allowed, with no red tape, to bring his or her immediate family into the country, even if those members of the family were not US citizens. When the children had been born, I had taken the precaution of registering them as British subjects, so when I made application to emigrate to the USA, everything became very simple and the paperwork fell into line. We had one US citizen and three British subjects travelling together. I made the application around January 1969 and we started to make arrangements to sell the house.

We needed a real estate agent who would honestly show our house to the best advantage. We eventually settled on a company, and trusted them to get the best price for us as well as the best overall contract. Unfortunately, they seemed to take advantage of our naivety by encouraging us to accept a lower price than we might have been able to get, knowing that we were soon to emigrate. However, we had made a sizeable profit over the original cost of the land and the house, and this money became our nest egg for emigrating.

Now that the house was sold, we concentrated on selling all our furniture, curtains, and rugs, as well as our radiogram and electrical appliances. I wasn't worried about Stevie making the transfer; he was less than a year old, and was hardly aware of what was happening around him. However, Anne was nearly three years old by now, and she noticed everything, especially when all the household things around her started to disappear. Anne had a little red bicycle just made for a tiny tot like her. Her grandmother Elfy had given it to her and Anne loved it. I gave Anne a running commentary about the destination of her little red bike, all the while dismantling the bike and packing it into a small suitcase and making jokes about who was going to get to America first. She couldn't speak too well at this stage but she could understand everything. We put stamps on the case, addressed it to Evie's dad's house in New Jersey, left a screwdriver and spanner inside and hoped for the best when we posted it.

There was a flurry of events in the last few weeks before our departure. One of them was when our bank added 10 per cent to our bank balance by mistake. We were rich for about two hours till we had the bank change it. We were due to fly to London, and spend a week with my parents, as a sort of holiday, before continuing to New York. A dozen or more of our friends, many of them members of our musical evening group, promised us a farewell dinner at the Balalaika Restaurant, just outside Johannesburg. We had taken care of all of the miscellaneous details, tickets, passports, permits, income tax verification and a corrected check from the bank. Our house and car were sold and the money was in our account. We had moved in with Elfy temporarily to save hotel costs and we were now free to enjoy our farewell dinner.

For that dinner, we hired a mature trustworthy white woman to look after the children as Elfy had a previous engagement that night. Elfy was expected home early however, and said that she would pay the babysitter and then stay with the children until Evie and I got back from our dinner. We had a wonderful evening at the Balalaika (table Number 74 – the table number fell into my pocket on the way out and I still have it!). A couple from the group acted as chauffeur for us and Austin made a pig of himself with the oysters.

It was a brilliant moonlit night when we wended our way home. You really could read a newspaper by the light of the moon. But when we reached Elfy's house, we noticed that there was no car in the driveway. Either the babysitter or Elfy should have been there with a car parked in the driveway. We thought, 'Uh-oh, no babysitter, no Elfy, no cars! Panic stations!' Just as Evie started to whimper, "Where is Mom, where are the children, where is Mom's car?" Elfy came rushing out of the house in her bathrobe calling out in a stage whisper, "Don't worry, don't worry, I'm here and the children are both sound asleep." What a relief it was to discover that everything was all right. But where was Elfy's car? Well, if I gave you a hundred years you would not come up with the answer to that question. It was at the bottom of her swimming pool!

She had come home early, paid off the babysitter as arranged and had then noticed that she hadn't parked squarely on the concrete driveway. Without thinking, she opened the driver's side door and placed her shoulder against the doorframe of the car. Reaching into the car, she released the hand brake, intending to push the car back. Unfortunately, the builder who had originally built the concrete driveway had left it uneven, and on a slight slope. The car was too heavy for her to hold and it started to move forward. Within a few seconds she was pushed away as the door slammed shut and the car went rolling down the ever-increasing slope. There were three trees and the side of a shed in its way but miraculously the car skirted all these, finishing with a right hand turn that lined the car up with the long side of the pool. From there, it went into the pool with scarcely a splash, according to Elfy.

The next day, a reporter and a cameraman came out from our local paper and took pictures of this now famous car that went swimming at night. They also took some pictures of Anne as the car was being pulled out of the pool with a tow truck – Anne's first, but not last, picture in a newspaper.

♫

While all this was going on, I had kept my plans for leaving the country and leaving Kestners very hushed up, as I didn't want to lose my job until the last minute. It was at about this time, in early 1969, that I was promoted in my job at Kestner Stanco – from Works Manager in the shop, to Design Engineer in the drawing office. This was certainly a terrific boost to my career, as I had always wanted to graduate out of the boiler shop. I knew that I could handle any draftsman's job, and even many engineering problems, as I had had years of practical experience. This was to stand me in very good stead when I applied for my first job in America.

The head of the design and engineering department was Warren

Shackleford, who insisted on being addressed as Mr Shackleford at all times. Talk about old fashioned and Victorian: everything in his department had to be perfect, all the time. He was fond of bragging that the reason he was so successful was because he personally hand-picked every man in his team. This might, of course, have been his ploy to keep everyone loyal and on top of his job. This worked, as far as I was concerned, but it didn't work for Alec Scott. Alec, another Scotsman, and I 'clicked' as soon as I joined the design group. Alec called Shackleford, behind his back, of course, a 'jumped up draftsman trying to do a man's job'. Shackleford was at that time busy designing what he called a 'cara-boat' which was a cross between a caravan and a boat. He was hoping to put this unusual vehicle on the market and sell the design to people who were prepared to drive to a lake, spend time on the water, then drive back again.

Alec pointed out to me that all the time spent on the cara-boat design was paid for by the company. A swindle on a small scale. Alec told me of a time when Shackleford had advertised for someone to bring the copying and tracing of old drawings up-to-date, a drudgery usually undertaken by women who were known as Lady Tracers. After a short time, Shackleford, much to Alec's disgust, hired a German immigrant trainee who was unable to speak any English at all, except basics like 'good morning'. This fellow, whose name was Uhlrich Klempt, was expected to copy and trace complicated notes and drawings in English. Alec, who told me this story, finished by wondering, "If Shackleford needed a tracer, why didn't he employ one with tits?"

Alec and I worked together on various projects, and we spent time together discussing aspects of the same project. One day he called out to me asking what size I had made a particular pipe line that flowed from my drawing to his. It was lunch time, and he wanted to finish this section while it was still in his head. I walked over to his drawing table, and we looked at it together and pointed out different aspects of the design to each other, he tapping his drawing with a pencil, while I tapped it with a hard boiled egg that I had taken from my lunch box. "Be careful with that egg," he called out just as the egg smashed onto the drawing and the yolk and the white of my so-called hard boiled egg went running across his drawing. I could see immediately what had happened. When Evie made up my lunch bag that morning, she had picked up an uncooked egg from the fridge by mistake, instead of a pre-cooked hard boiled one!

"What did you do that for?" he shouted, frantically trying to mop up the mess with a handkerchief. "I've been working on that for two days."

"I didn't do it on purpose," I shouted back.

"It sure as hell looked as though you did," he replied. We were able to clean up and repair his drawing, and our relationship never suffered because of this episode.

Gert Gatje was a colleague in the drawing office who was transferred into the estimating group. He was German, and two years older than me. We often spent lunch time together swopping experiences. In 1945, Gert was an eighteen-year-old soldier in Hitler's fast declining army. The whole of Europe was in an awful mess, and the German army, among other things, was frantically trying to hold back the Russians. Everyone was on edge; no one wanted to be sent to 'the Front', which meant almost certain death. One bright sunny morning, Gert found himself in a platoon of about ten men sent on a patrol to a small town somewhere in Germany. There had been activity from the enemy (namely the British or Americans) during the previous night and his platoon was ordered to check out the situation. The ten men, in a crouching attitude, moved along the street, partially protected by low brick walls that marked the boundary of each property.

Gert called out to his sergeant, "I have terrible stomach cramps, I must go to the toilet."

The sergeant called back, saying, "Do what you have to do, then fall in behind the last man." Gert slipped into one of the gardens, relieved his tummy ache, and spent a few moments trying to adjust his trousers. He was about to join his other comrades when 'Ratatatatata' – a machine gunner opened fire and all nine German soldiers plus the sergeant were wiped out in a few seconds. Gert was the last man left from his platoon. He quickly made his way back to his company and reported to the officer in charge. This officer didn't believe Gert's story, accusing him of desertion in the face of the enemy and ordered him to be shot immediately. This would have been the end of Gert if another officer had not intervened on his behalf. "Don't kill the boy," he pleaded, "he was afraid – he was shitting himself. Can't you understand that?" Several others in the vicinity voiced their agreement and Gert was allowed to go back to his regiment. "I am lucky to be alive," he told me. "It is just as well that all us Germans are soft hearted." He said this with a wink!

When I did eventually give in my notice at Kestner, everyone told me they were very sorry to lose me. My boss, Mr Shackleford, told me that I would have had a great future with the company. When asked exactly why I was leaving, I just said that I was moving with my family to America to be near my wife's father. I couldn't tell them that I disliked the politics of the country. Politics was the one subject that couldn't be discussed with *anyone*, not even friends. Mr Shackleford gave me the names of some companies in America that they had had dealings with, one in Clearwater, Florida, and the other in Buffalo, New York. I felt that if I was unable to find a suitable job in New Jersey, I could always try and contact one of those two companies. Looking back on things now, we are certainly glad we didn't end up in Buffalo, where the winter lasts for about nine months!

♪

There was a difference of opinion among our friends when we discussed leaving South Africa. Most people thought we were foolish to leave, as they were convinced that everything would turn out for the best and that South Africa was indeed a good place to raise children. I disagreed most strongly, citing the fact that several members of the government, including the Prime Minister, Verwoerd, had said in public speeches on the radio that "the Kaffir is less than human", and displayed other racist attitudes. This sounded to me very much like the kind of rhetoric preached by Adolf Hitler in the 1930s, and we all know the results of that. I didn't want my children going to school to be taught by someone with this point of view, and even changing schools may not have helped. Even though Evie and I were quite liberal in our outlook, we knew that the influence that the schools and other people in South Africa would have on our children would probably be greater than the influence *we* would have. Children are always more likely to follow their peers, rather than their parents, especially when they are young. So we knew that whatever we did, the children would probably grow up with the same attitude as the majority of South Africans, and that was that the blacks were second-class citizens with no rights at all.

We lived in an all-white area, of course, and the children would have had to attend all-white schools. There were buses for whites, and buses for blacks. The cinemas were for whites only in our area, as were the municipal swimming pools and other sports facilities. There were counters for the whites at the Post Office, and counters for the blacks. This apartheid was everywhere, so how could the children possibly grow up in that sort of environment without thinking that they were indeed superior to the blacks, whom they saw only as servants, gardeners, or laborers?

I noticed that those who had no children were more likely to stay in South Africa, whereas the families with children were afraid to stay. Many of those families had no way of leaving, trapped by the fact that they had South African passports. Unless the men had very high qualifications, such as doctors or scientists, they would be unable to get into other countries. Evie and I might have considered staying had we not had the children, but we were extremely fortunate, as Evie had an American passport, and the children and I were British. We in fact had the minimum of *two* choices – we could either go back to England, or we could go to America or to any of the British colonies. But wherever we ended up, I just knew that I had to leave South Africa.

The day we left, at the beginning of August 1969, was charged with emotion. There were a couple of dozen people at the airport to see us off, and most of us were in tears and promising to write. Evie's family and old school friends and most of the friends we had made over the last few years were all suffering from some kind of emotional distress. Some of the men, myself included, put on sunglasses in an attempt to hide our tears, but it wasn't easy to hide the choking voices.

We then had to walk across the tarmac and climb the stairs into the plane. That was probably one of the longest walks of my life. Evie was crying her eyes out, and the children looked quite bewildered. However, once we were settled on the plane, we had to give all our attention to the children, and this took our minds off our very sad parting from family and friends. I can remember very well keeping Anne amused with crayons, making pictures on scrap paper and reading her three-page books again and again whilst Evie made Stevie comfortable in his carry cot, and fed him with special, gentle medicine to get him to sleep while on the plane.

I felt the hair on the back of my neck rise when I thought of us leaving South Africa. This was a tremendous relief in my mind, and I had a sense of well being and comfort that if we ever went back, it would be for a visit and not to stay. I remembered that originally, Evie and I had promised to spend the first two years of our marriage together in South Africa, and then have a rethink. Those two years had suddenly (so it now seems), turned into seven, and now was the time to restart before the children began school, and became tainted by apartheid. When our plane took off, I felt a great load lift off my shoulders.

CHAPTER 8

America, Here I Come

1969 – 1974

OUR plane journey to London en route to New York was uneventful and quiet, far different from the hectic pace we kept up the last time we emigrated. That was on the ship *Pretoria Castle* where the trip lasted two weeks, with non-stop entertainment and dining. This time the trip by plane was due to take some fourteen hours, with a couple of meals and snacks on the way. Things had certainly changed in the last few years. In 1962, almost everyone went by ship if they had somewhere to go, and hardly anyone went by plane. By 1969, more people were flying, especially if they wanted to get to their destination in a hurry, as we did. At one time we had considered taking a cargo ship to America; we had heard of some people who had done so. However, there were two drawbacks to this: one was that the trip took weeks and weeks; and secondly, there was no doctor on board. We didn't fancy traveling with two small children with no doctor around. And anyway, now that we had made the decision to go traveling to America, we wanted to get there as soon as possible.

We were having a stopover of about a week in London, which gave us a chance to catch up with all the local news and family gossip. It also gave us the chance to show our children to all and sundry; my parents, for example, had not yet met Steve. This was a really good opportunity to get all, or at least many, of the family together face to face.

Dad was now sixty-three and eligible for retirement and pension in a couple of years. His business, and therefore house, had been forcibly sold to the local council so that a school could be built on the site. So, that ancient dwelling that had provided shelter to many, many people since Dickens was a boy was finally removed. After forty years of 'making do', starting with Elderfield Road, Mum and Dad finally got a brand new flat in Benfleet Court with indoor plumbing! Mum was overjoyed with the flat and lost no time in coaxing Dad to start a flower garden in the back yard. "Then we can brighten the place up a bit," she said. Dad had recently obtained a part-time job as a gardener in Victoria Park and this income, along with what he got for his scrap iron business and a small enterprise dealing with pewter beer mugs, was enough to tide them over until their pension started. Mum and Dad would survive, and indeed did survive very comfortably in their new place.

My brother Roy, who had married Margie before Evie and I went to South Africa, now had two sons, David and Gary. He had a small house in Dagenham and worked for the Ford motor company. My sister Gladys and her family, Linda and the twins Tom and Carol, along with husband Lesley Davies, looked as if they were settling nicely in a flat in Poplar.

My baby sister Carol was now twenty-three years old (seventeen years younger than I) and married to Terry Wallis. The Wallis family came from just across the way in Braintree Street. Carol had two children, Michelle and Darren, who were each born within months of Anne and Steve. Another daughter, Lisa, was born later. As a matter of interest, many years later, Gladys's daughter Linda had five children, twin Tommy had four and twin Carol had six, making Gladys a grandmother fifteen times over. My sister Carol has a family of ten grandchildren; Michelle's had four children, Darren three and Lisa also three. I should write after all these numbers 'so far', because the totals may not be complete!

The last leg of our journey took us from London to JFK airport in New York and we arrived on August 17th 1969, just one week shy of my fortieth birthday. Was I brave? Crazy? Stupid? I had uprooted my whole family from one side of the planet to the other, with two children little more than babies and with no job or prospects. I had, however, a bank check for a sizeable amount of money from the sale of our house, and a very generous offer from my father-in-law! He had agreed to shelter us in his home in central New Jersey on our arrival until we could get ourselves organized. Getting organized meant taking care of at least three things. I needed a car, a job, and a flat, in that order. A car was necessary so that I could hunt for a job, and once I had a job, I would know where to look for a place to live.

Our arrival in New York was memorable for several reasons, the most important being the heat. This was before international airports coddled travellers with air-conditioned covered walkways from the plane to the terminal. We stepped off the plane down a portable stairway directly onto the tarmac. The tarmac was so hot that one could get a burn by accidentally touching it. In addition to the heat, there was high humidity. This turned the whole area into a steam bath, and made Evie very unhappy. If there is anything she dislikes more than excessive heat, it is high humidity. However, after a few minutes we were taken in tow by a very friendly immigration official who sang out "Welcome to the US of A – I have here all the paperwork required for the Goodwin family to enter, all I need now are signatures and you can go."

I was very impressed; there was a complete absence of red tape, which was probably helped by us being the only immigrant family on our plane. Evie helped too, I'm sure, by being a US citizen returning home.

Evie and I had made a tentative arrangement, whereby we would go directly to her father Harold's house, and stay with him in South Plainfield for a few weeks while we organized ourselves. Meanwhile, I would get a temporary local job so that I could learn more about American engineering methods. We were intending to try to settle permanently in, or near, Denver, Colorado, which is nearly two-thousand miles from New Jersey. We had heard from many people, including the Riebens, our tenants in the house that I built, that the climate in Denver was similar to that in Johannesburg, although they did get quite a bit of snow in the winter. However, Denver was a mile above sea-level, at 5,282 feet, and was in fact known as the 'Mile High City'. Johannesburg was about 6,000 feet above sea-level, so neither city had really severely hot summers.

Evie's sister, Trixie, met us at the airport, along with Harold, Evie and Trixie's father. Trixie had moved permanently to the United States in 1967 (she was also a US citizen like Evie) because she felt uncomfortable with the political situation in South Africa. She thought that America was an exciting country and she wanted to live in New York City. She told us how she had coaxed her dad to buy a larger more up-to-date Ford because, as she pointed out, his family had increased dramatically and his previous car was no longer suitable. Looking back on this period makes my head spin. How did we find the time to do all the things we did at an apparent snap of the fingers?

Harold had taken a couple of weeks' vacation time, and on our first day we set out with a pocket full of dimes for phone money to look for a car. Evie wasn't able to join us due to what was probably a bad cold, aggravated by the stress of moving. Harold and I had to take the children along with us, which made things a little difficult for choosing a second-hand car. We started out with a list of cars for sale in the local paper and phoned the first one on the list. Then, depending on what was said we either drove in Harold's car to look at it or scratched it off our list and phoned the next one. This method worked fine. We were able to judge whether the car was reasonable and worth looking at, and if not we went onto the next. We finished up, after looking at a dozen or more possibilities and discussing two dozen more, with a 1963 Chevrolet Nova 'Straight Six', and when we brought it home Evie declared it to be the best she'd ever driven.

A few days later, Harold took me to Cherry Hill, NJ where his cousin, George Skaller, lived with his artistic wife, Ruth. The company that George worked for, The Caddy Corp of America, needed designers and fabricators of stainless steel kitchen components and after a short interview with the company president, Mr Rothschild (no relation to the famous one), I was offered a job at $3.50 per hour. While we were out and about in the area we asked a local real estate agent to show us some houses. I knew that Evie may not approve of my choice completely but if necessary we could live and work and survive very well in Cherry Hill on this kind of salary.

After a couple of days' bed rest, Evie recovered sufficiently from her cold to spend some time with the children so Harold and I were able to concentrate on finding the best possible 'deal'. I had promised Mr Rothschild that I would let him know within two weeks whether or not I would accept his job offer. This gave me time to scout around to see what else was available. "I know a fellow," said Harold one day, "who is a sales representative who calls on dozens of engineering companies in the area. He would know which companies are looking for men like you." Within minutes, Harold had given me this fellow's phone number and his name, Fred Herstein. What a stroke of luck! Fred was a mine of information with knowledge of almost every engineer in and around New York City. One of the companies that Fred recommended was Ultra Dynamics in Paterson. "A good engineer needed," said Fred, "offering $175 a week, but they've been having racial problems recently in Paterson – you don't want to live there."

There were several names that Fred mentioned, all within about fifteen or twenty minutes of my father-in-law's place. One of these was Wigton Abbott, in the next town called Plainfield, and others called Power Flow in Linden, and Public Service Electric and Gas in Newark, also not too far away. I was able to make a few phone calls to some of these, and they all basically gave me the same story: send us a resumé and we will get in touch with you. There was also a Bowen Engineering who manufactured spray dryers. They needed a draftsman for $150 a week, and I remember spending lots of time at Kestner Stanco in Johannesburg, not only on the design, but also on the 'hands on' manufacturing of spray dryers. I would surely be of some use to Bowen Engineering. They were located on West Main Street in Somerville.

After helping me to analyze these companies with names and phone numbers, Fred Herstein left me to worry about them all. The first one I phoned was Wigton Abbott. The secretary, after making me wait a couple of minutes, told me that Mr Reis couldn't get to the phone right away, but if I could get to his office by 4.30pm, he would see me then. It was 4pm and I guessed that quitting time was at 5. I decided to go right away, so I brushed up and arrived at Bob's office early. The first thing Bob Reis said to me when we greeted each other was "Wow, I like your accent, you must be from England." He then described to me how he had been part of the American forces shortly after D Day, and I carried on the conversation telling him about my participation in the building of invasion barges in 1943. I had something in common with the Chief Mechanical Engineer of Wigton Abbott Corporation; we had both taken part, albeit a small part, in World War II!

"Well, what can I do for you, Tom Goodwin?" he asked, and I suddenly realised that Bob Reis didn't know what I wanted. So I started from scratch and told him how my father-in-law knew Fred Herstein and that Fred had recommended Wigton Abbott as an excellent company that may be in need of engineers, particularly mechanical engineers. I told Bob that I was fresh in the country and looking for employment. "Do you have a resumé?" he asked. I showed him a copy that Evie had recently typed up for me and he started to read. After a few minutes he started to chuckle and then the chuckle became a laugh. "This is different from any other resumé I've ever seen," he said. "Resumés usually start with the latest employment and then as they go on with more description they go further back in time. This one is the complete opposite. You started your resumé in 1943 and came to a temporary halt here in 1969."

"However," he said, raising a forefinger, "I can honestly say that I've never seen a more interesting resumé. If you wanted to attract my attention here today, you certainly succeeded." We then spent the next fifteen minutes discussing heat exchangers: how they should be specified for commercial standard, process, and/or food requirements and the various metals that could, should or even must be used for their manufacture. There are many different engineering designs and structures that can be used for the exchange of heat, the most common of course being the automobile heater and air conditioner, neither of which require a separate source of fuel.

He made an internal phone call asking his secretary to bring Mr Heinzer to his office for a short conference. Whilst we waited we chatted in a friendly fashion about this and that. He said to me, "Gerry Heinzer's our best boffin as far as commercial engineering is concerned. He's probably going to try to floor you with questions about lesser known subjects." Just then Gerry (everyone gets called by his first name in America) Heinzer arrived, and I had to sit on the hot seat for a little while. Gerry, a non-stop smoker, who bit his fingernails all the time, asked me many questions, not only about engineering methods, but also about common engineering knowledge. For example, he asked me the difference between a Process Plant and a Pilot Plant and under what conditions either one would be necessary on any given project or contract. As another example he asked what a Flow Diagram was and how I would interpret a hypothetical example of a flow diagram.

I borrowed a pencil and a scrap of paper from Bob Reis and made a tidy representation of a simple diagram showing the major components. I showed him a copy of a pump drawing I had made in Johannesburg and he was suitably impressed. At this point, Gerry was nodding vigorously at everything I said. As he left Bob's office he said, "I don't see any problems," and to me he said, "Good night."

"Well Tom," said Bob "Let's not beat around the bush. We'd like to have you on our pay roll. How does $200 a week sound for starters?" A quick mental calculation told me that this was my best offer so far. This would give Evie and me time to learn how the Americans operated before committing ourselves to going to Denver. Common sense told me that Evie would benefit from being fairly local to her sister Trixie in New York and her dad in South Plainfield, at least for a while. Ten seconds was all I needed to confirm that $200 a week was OK.

"When can you start work?"

"Blimey, you Yanks don't mess around do you?"

Bob told me to take two weeks to get organised with a house or a flat, unpaid of course, but I could take a loan against my first two weeks' salary if I needed it. "Just go to see Mr Olsen of Personnel first thing tomorrow morning," he said. "The company will loan you $400 at no interest." I thanked him but said it wasn't necessary. There was a general stir and a movement of people; it seemed like 5pm was quitting time after all. As I was about to leave, he called me back. "You've heard that old saying 'last man in is the first man out'? Well, it doesn't apply in this company!" I remember thinking that that was a strange remark for him to make.

Evie was overjoyed about my job. This meant, of course, that we would stay in the east for at least a year and be near Trixie and her dad. "What about the job in Cherry Hill?" she asked. The answer to that one was that there was no comparison between the two jobs. In Cherry Hill I would continue as a 'jumped up' plumber capable of organizing kitchens. But in Plainfield with Wigton Abbott I would continue as a 'jumped up' boilermaker, with a chance of finally becoming an engineer, not because of a university degree but because of my tenacity in finding the required knowledge from libraries and encyclopaedia (more about this later).

We went through the local newspapers like a dose of salts. All we wanted was a two-bedroom flat or apartment. Evie was on the phone for what seemed like hours, and then she found one. It sounded great, two bedrooms, kitchen and living room, $200 a month, next to a park and immediate vacancy. While Evie put the children to bed, I drove to the apartment to take a look and make sure it was a decent looking place. I spoke to the caretaker and confirmed that everything was all right and that I would bring my wife tomorrow to finalize the deal. Although it was late in the evening and quite dark I was able to get my bearings from a large lake across the street from the park. I should be able to find my way back from that, I thought.

The next day, Evie and I set out with the children to find the apartment house and we drove around the area for at least ten minutes before I had to admit I was lost! There was the park across the way, there was a building that looked like the one I saw last night, but where was the lake? Well, would you believe it? The lake was gone. It had disappeared! The caretaker later told us that when there is a very heavy rainstorm, the playing field next to the apartment building gets flooded and looks just like a lake, but it lasts only a short while; the water drains away very quickly into a stream in the park. I felt quite embarrassed that I had earlier insisted that this was not the place that I had been last night.

Evie liked the apartment, "As long as it's only temporary," she said, and we signed up for a short period, which meant we could move in immediately. One little snag of course was that we had no furniture. We could have used some of the beautiful stuff we had practically given away in Johannesburg a few short months ago, but that was now water under the bridge; we had to start afresh.

There was, at that time, an elderly couple living in Plainfield called Mr and Mrs Shimmel. We found them through the local newspaper. Those local papers were useful in those days, weren't they? The Shimmels were 'Snow Birds', which meant they travelled back and forth between NJ and Florida, taking advantage of the best weather every six months. In winter they lived in Florida, where the climate was comfortably warm, and in summer they lived in NJ away from Florida's searing heat. This meant, of course, that they had two homes, two cars, and they lived the life of very wealthy people.

When Evie contacted them she learned that their son in New Jersey had been divorced. As a result the Shimmels had decided to close their New Jersey home. When Evie and I discovered the scope of what was involved, we couldn't believe it. Everything in their apartment was for sale. We had been advised to buy cheap second-hand furniture so that when we made the trip to Denver we could leave it behind. It would be far too expensive to ship it the 2,000 or so miles, so we were prepared to buy 'junk' furniture. However, the things that the Shimmels were offering for sale were far from junk. In addition to items such as armchairs, bookshelves, and a complete roomful of bedroom furniture, there were lots of miscellaneous bits and pieces. Brush and pan sets, bucket, scrubbing brush, all the things we needed, and some that we didn't, such as a beautiful oil painting copy of Renoir's 'The Boating Party' which we fell in love with and bought anyway.

Mrs Shimmel, after raking through a couple of shelves, discovered some toys to keep Anne and Steve amused. In the meantime, the four grown ups discussed each item in turn with Evie making a list and Mr Shimmel and I fixing the price of each item that Evie wanted.

At one stage of the proceedings, Mr Shimmel called out, "Ah, I nearly forgot," and from a drawer he retrieved a camera. "I bought this for $150 about a year ago and never used it. Will you give me five dollars for it now?" There were so many bargains in that apartment that we were tempted just to buy the lot. This wasn't possible because we didn't have enough space in our comparatively small apartment to fit all the Shimmels' stuff in. When we finally called it a day, we had enough for our needs except for a dining-room set, (theirs made Evie shudder), and various carpets and rugs that were all the wrong color. I tried to coax Evie into accepting some of the floor coverings, especially since the Shimmels were giving most of them away for free.

Evie was not to be tempted. "If it's the wrong color then it won't fit in with my color scheme," she said. I had to agree. Purple, red and orange were not our colors!

♪

I found it very easy to settle down to my new life. Not only did I have a new country to think about; I also had a new job in a company filled with people wanting to talk to the 'new guy'. Evie didn't have this last benefit. Her job (if you could call it that) consisted of putting together a new home whilst dealing with unfamiliar shopping practices, and looking after a three-year-old and a one-year-old. She volunteered some of her time to the local YWCA to keep herself busy, and to get an opportunity to talk to some grown-ups. The Y, as it's known, provided a baby minding service that gave young mothers like Evie a chance to get away from their youngsters occasionally.

Evie had a tough time getting settled and finding new friends for herself, something I didn't have to consider or think about. In Wigton Abbott there were about 200 employees, of which about half were mechanical engineers and the rest architects and electrical engineers. There were another fifty or so clerical workers and another group in the printing department. I had access to a large proportion of all these people if only to say 'good morning' to. I didn't have to make any effort to find friends or acquaintances, but Evie did.

There was one person with whom Evie struck up a fairly close friendship and that was Jane Mann. Jane and her husband Tim lived with their children next door to the Seligmanns, who were very close friends of Harold. Esther Seligmann knew from Harold that we were going to stay with him with our two small children, until we could get settled in our own home, and she also knew that Jane had a crib that her three-year-old no longer used. She asked Jane whether she would be willing to lend the crib to us for Steve, who at that time was not yet old enough for a proper bed. Jane very kindly agreed, even though she had never even met us. This kind gesture gave us a good idea of how generous the Americans could be. After we had settled in at Harold's place, Evie telephoned Jane to thank her for the loan of the crib, and as they were about the same age, and had children of similar ages, they became friends. Finally, we also met Jane's husband, Tim. At that time he was learning to play the clarinet, and practising daily, sending Jane out of her mind! Jane retaliated by taking classes in pursuit of a degree in psychology.

I settled in at Wigton Abbott very nicely under the guidance of Al Bowne. He and I were, in theory, supposed to report to Gerry Heinzer. Gerry spent most of his time with the air conditioning group and the newly purchased computer. The computer was mounted on a large truck outside the building and needed more than a few engineers to run it and to analyze the results, which printed out in what appeared to be a foreign language. At that point in time, all the engineers and designers working in Wigton Abbott worked out their calculations with the aid of a slide rule or a book of logarithmic tables. In the accounts department, people were using adding and subtracting machines. Multiplication machines were rare, and a division machine was almost unheard of. We didn't know that just a few years down the road there was destined to be an explosion. Very soon, the calculator would become capable of figuring the most complicated arithmetic instantly. Not only that, but the technology evolved so fast, and the cost became so cheap, that for the cost of a calculator worth only a few dollars a bright ten-year-old could solve mathematical problems that previously were almost impossible for anyone to work out.

However, the calculator paled in comparison with what eventually became known as the personal computer (PC). The PC seems to me to be limitless in its capabilities. I'm trying to discover in my mind exactly what a computer can do, and the only thing I can think of is that it can do anything you want it to.

My first project for Wigton Abbott was a chemical plant for Beecham Pharmaceuticals in Piscataway. I was expected to figure out, after a couple of meetings with Beecham engineers, exactly what pieces of equipment would be required, and what size or capacity would be needed for each piece. I also had to make drawings showing the locations of all the tanks, pumps, and pipe lines required, co-ordinating the position and situation of equipment of other disciplines such as electrical requirements.

I found it necessary to pay several visits to the local library at night in order to come up with estimated heat loads for chemicals that were unfamiliar to me. The Beecham engineers, of course, believed that I had this information under my hat. They never knew when I met them that I had studied and learned this the previous night at the library. Al Bowne sat in one of the meetings I had with the Beecham fellows. After the meeting he gave me a warning. "Don't give away all your information; these Beecham fellows are picking your brains so as to look good to their boss."

I couldn't believe that Al said that. I couldn't believe that a couple of fellows, each the owner of a degree in chemical engineering, should ever want to pick *my* brains. I remembered Gert Gatje in Johannesburg, who escaped death so closely during the war by having to excuse himself from the rest of his unit. "You would be surprised," he told me once, "how many people there are who don't really know how to do their job."

While I was getting my feet wet in American engineering, my family settled into our apartment in Plainfield. It was cold outside. Boy, was it cold. As the year 1969 wound slowly down, the outlook for Evie in our apartment became rather bleak. These so-called 'garden' apartments consisted of several two-story apartment buildings, with lawns and pathways in between. Evie, an outdoor person and used to the warmth of Johannesburg, wrapped herself and the children in heavy winter clothing and spent some time in the gardens. This was an attempt to meet up with other young mothers. However, the weather was so cold and windy that she never saw a soul outside to talk to until the advent of spring.

One Saturday, in January, Evie, Harold, and I took the children across the street into the local park. Anne led us to the kiddies' slide, then to a lake that was frozen so hard that a five-ton truck was able to drive right across without cracking the ice. We made our way to one of the picnic tables where we all gathered together. "Come along everyone," called Evie, "let's have some tea and biscuits. Grandad, will you have milk in your tea?" And with that she swept up an imaginary cup and saucer in her left hand, and an imaginary teapot in her right. Steve stared at Evie, then at me, then at Harold, looking for the cup and saucer. I hoisted Steve onto my lap asking if he would like a biscuit or maybe a glass of milk? Steve reached over the table while Anne roared with laughter as she pretended to hand them to him.

Steve was mystified by the whole business, and tried vainly to pluck a biscuit or a glass of milk from the air. Anne danced around the table pretending to hand out tea and biscuits to everyone. Of course we all responded, until Evie called out, "OK, tea is finished, everyone must do the washing up." Anne couldn't wait to hustle over to Steve so that she could show him how to scrape some snow from the ground and do a hand washing motion. Steve seemed quite surprised to find the 'washing up' to be ice cold but he didn't care. He was only too happy to find something that was real and solid. We dried Steve off, put him in his stroller and fed him some real milk. This was better, this was more like it; after all he was less than two years old.

It must have been soon after this pretend children's tea party that I got a phone call from Colorado. Long distance. Who did I know who would call me from Colorado? It was John Rieben! He and his family still lived in the 'house that Tom built' in South Africa. He was calling to send us greetings and to welcome us to the United States. Evie and I took turns on the phone, so that we all, including Connie, got a conversation with everyone else.

"I have some good news for you," he said. He told me that he had been in contact with some colleagues in Denver, and had told them what my qualifications were, and that I would be interested in relocating to Colorado. He told me that there were five companies willing to interview me right away. Two of them were prepared to pay my fare to Colorado for the interview. This was all very exciting, and Evie and I spent many hours trying to decide what, if anything, we should do.

Within a few days of this news there was an unpleasant surprise. The Boeing works in Seattle had cut back its workforce drastically. This meant that many thousands of engineers of all types had been thrown out of work. This was very bad news for me. Instead of feeling confident that jobs were plentiful in the far west, my attitude changed literally overnight into feelings of doubt about my ability to secure and hold some kind of position against such tremendous competition. I had a mental picture of me trekking around the country, from Seattle to San Francisco to Denver, competing against men with university degrees and other qualifications that I didn't have.

Evie and I took stock of our position and counted our blessings. We were renting a very comfortable apartment, we had acquired some excellent furniture which, although second-hand, was now in brand new condition (due mostly to Evie's abilities as a homemaker). We had a lump sum from the liquidation of the South African house and would have another from the house that Tom built. Our ambition was to settle in Denver, the mile high city, but we agreed that 'a bird in the hand is worth two in the bush'.

We decided to 'stay put', especially since Wigton Abbott had recently started including pink slips with their salary checks to certain people. I remembered what Bob Reis had told me during our interview. His statement had been something about 'the last man in not necessarily being first out'. I cornered him at a quiet moment in his office one morning to ask him about it. "You have nothing to worry about," he told me. "We are at present getting rid of what we call dead wood and there will be more, the economy tells us that. However, you are not included in the pink slip brigade. We intend to keep you on our payroll no matter what happens."

Evie was quite impressed when I related this to her. "It would be foolish now to quit your job on the chance of getting something better," she said. "You may get a job with more money, but that doesn't mean you'll keep it. At Wigton Abbot they like you, you've made an impression. Let's stay here."

We stayed.

♪

In July 1970, Elfy came to visit. The main reason she came was, of course, to see us all, but she also offered to look after the children, and me, for a week so that Evie could take a short vacation and have a rest. Harold's friends Esther and O.H. (pronounced 'Oh Hah') Seligmann were quite wealthy, and among other things owned a small ranch in a place called Jackson Hole, Wyoming, in the mid-west. They offered to let Evie stay there for a week as a break from the children. The place was fully furnished with everything necessary for a holiday stay including blankets, towels, cups and saucers, with a launderette and diner within a short walking distance. This was the first time that Evie and I had spent any time apart and we both agreed later that absence does make the heart grow fonder.

While Evie was away I spent my time at work, and with Anne and Steve. This was a time when I got to know them a little more. Bedtime was the best time for having fun. I created a character called Big Blomp (that was me) who would fall on the carpet trapping one or both of them and making a hideous 'aagghh' noise. Then, with hundreds of giggles, they had to try to escape. After everything became quiet I got into the habit of telling a story and instantly their eyes focused on me in anticipation. Anne's favorite was about a rabbit that lived on a farm and was always hungry for carrots. Steve didn't mind what the story was about, he usually fell asleep pretty fast, probably from the droning of my voice.

In the evenings, after the children had gone to bed, Elfy and I chatted about this and that, and played some of the gramophone records that Evie and I had bought originally in England, taken with us to Johannesburg, and finally, to the US. I remember one evening reminiscing about things we had done and places we had been to (Elfy had ridden a camel in Egypt; I had driven a tank in Germany) and we got onto the subject of Evie's birthplace. What a coincidence it was that Evie was born in Muhlenberg Hospital, Plainfield, about 250 yards from where we were sitting! She had come full circle.

One of the subjects that Elfy raised during our marathon chatting session was a bicycle. "Do you remember," she said. "I gave Anne a little red bicycle before you came here. Whatever became of it?" I took her down to the garage and pointed to a small suitcase in the corner. "It arrived by mail a few weeks ago in that suitcase!" I told her. She was quite surprised that a bike could be dismantled and made small enough to be sent half-way around the world by the post office. I told her how Anne and I had worked together, first packing and posting it, and later making a trip to the post office to retrieve it. When we got the suitcase to our apartment, we opened it up and found inside it, not only the bike in pieces, but also the screwdriver and pliers that I had packed in Johannesburg and forgotten about. Anne couldn't wait to get on the bike. The garden in between the apartment buildings was criss-crossed with concrete pathways that were perfect for little children to ride on. Steve later went into competition with Anne with a wheeled push toy called 'The Green Machine'. That toy kept me working till nearly 2am as I tried to assemble it for Christmas Day. I managed to complete the blasted thing in time to enjoy breakfast with a smile.

The economy in the USA continued in a downward trend following the slump affecting the Boeing works. President Nixon ordered a ninety-day freeze on wages and prices and other measures to curb inflation. All of this made very little difference to Evie and me. Shortly after starting work, we had taken the precaution of investing our nest egg in a banking vehicle called Federal Land Bank. It was giving about 4 or 5 per cent return on our money and was regarded by everyone as safe.

The big item for discussion during 1970 at Wigton Abbott was, "Who will get laid off this week, who will get a pink slip?" Each week, several people lost their jobs, but on each pay day, not only was my job still safe, but on two occasions I actually received a pay increase. Bob Reis told me that Beecham officials had praised my work on the chemical plant that I was handling. Wigton Abbott, as a kind of 'middle man', showed their appreciation of me in a very satisfactory fashion. They raised my pay!

There came a time, around the beginning of 1971, when Wigton Abbott had laid off enough engineers. They wanted to keep a remaining core of desirable employees on their books in readiness for the time when contracts would be more plentiful. I was in that core. However, as times got tougher and contracts more difficult to come by, stronger measures became necessary. Some of Wigton's engineers were loaned, temporarily, to other companies, so as to be 'on tap' as much as possible and ready to be called back on to Wigton work.

I was 'farmed out' to Henderson Construction in Somerville, where I engineered some site work and drainage ditches on the United Parcel Service property. The secretary at Henderson was very small, very young, and very pretty. She looked about twelve years old and drove a car that looked like an aircraft carrier. She was about the only person I remember from Henderson.

After a few months I was sent on loan to Dick Brady, a one-man business which knew everything about anything in the mechanical and engineering trades. Dick, whose company name was John R. Brady Associates, lived and worked in Staten Island, New York. He told me that he was intending to move to Oldwick, a small village in New Jersey, in July. When the time came for the move to take place, he said I would be invited to continue working for him on a permanent basis. Dick was very concerned about ethics, and would never want to 'steal' me from Wigton Abbott, but Dick's wife, Ruth, had no scruples about the matter. She acted as go-between for Dick and me, and while on vacation in Florida, she successfully persuaded me over the phone to join Dick's company as an estimator. I was virtually finished with the contracts I had been involved with at Wigton, so I felt no guilt when I gave them a month's notice. Although they were sorry to see me leave, they wished me all the best for the future.

1971 became quite a busy year for the Goodwin family. Now that we had given up, at least for a while, the idea of settling in Colorado, we gave serious thought to moving out of our rented apartment, and investing in a house. We had had some previous experience at house buying, but that was in another country and under apartheid laws.

Evie and I worked out a system in which she drove me to work with the children in the car. Then, leaving me at work, she drove back with the children to our apartment to begin her day. Her day consisted of contacting real estate sales people and checking out the houses for sale. Most of the properties she was shown, by the ever-eager sales people, were either close to being slum dwellings, or were more like Buckingham Palace. Occasionally, there was a likely candidate that looked decent and was affordable, and these I got to see in the evening after work. There was always a problem of one kind or another, however, until Evie found a district called Piscataway in central New Jersey.

Piscataway was about thirty miles south of New York, about fifteen or so from Wigton Abbott and less than fifty miles from the seashore. The Township of Piscataway was founded in 1666 by eight families who had moved to this part of New Jersey from the area of the Piscataqua River in New Hampshire. The Piscataqua River flows into the Atlantic Ocean at the town of Portsmouth, New Hampshire. The name 'Pascattaway' had been used during the 1600s in New Hampshire, and is believed to have derived from the Lenni Lenape Indian language, meaning 'great deer river'. Indeed, the western border of present-day Piscataway lies along the Raritan River. The township covers approximately nineteen square miles, and the population is now approaching 50,000. In 1971 many parts of Piscataway were very rural, but of course, many of the farms have since been sold to housing developers.

A builder was putting up a row of houses just off Custer Street and the houses were just what we were looking for. There were three or four spaces left so we had a small choice of location. When we sat down with the salesman to work out the financial details, we discovered that the price quoted was the 'bare bones' price. The realistic cost of one of these houses became the base price plus a few thousand dollars for things like storm windows, which were essential in New Jersey. This was a big disappointment for both of us because everything about Custer Street fitted our requirements so nicely.

Next morning, Evie dropped me off at work and contacted a saleswoman to start the process again. Anne and Steve were familiar with the rigmarole and played quietly with their toys in the back seat of the saleswoman's car. The saleswoman (I believe her name was Jenny) asked if the house had to be new. She told Evie of a fourteen-year-old house, built in 1957, which was for sale a couple of miles away from Custer Street. It had everything that we wanted including a one-acre plot of land, and it was on a dead end street. Best of all, it was quite a few thousand dollars less in price than the house in Custer Street would have ended up being. Evie called me at the office that day to tell me all about it; she couldn't wait. At 5pm, when Wigton Abbot quit for the day, she was sitting outside the office with the children in the car and the engine running. Of course, we high-tailed it immediately to 215 Wyckoff Avenue, Piscataway to meet the current owners, the Ackeleys.

Mr and Mrs Ackeley were a pair of fusspots who had been painting and polishing their house for years in preparation for the next owner. We quickly realised what a gem this house was. Everything was clean, and in tiptop condition. The only complaint I could make was that the dining room was pink. I didn't like that but a gallon of paint would quickly rectify it. The Ackeleys had recently sold the house, but the sale had fallen through and they were now negotiating for another house in another state. This meant, of course, that they had to get rid of this one. Quickly!

They were asking forty thousand dollars. We countered thirty-two. They asked again for thirty-six and a half. Sold! We couldn't stand the pressure. We could have bought the house for a little less, but, looking back on it now it makes almost no difference. We didn't have enough to enable us to pay the whole thing in cash so we had to take out a mortgage. We had a checking and a savings account at our local bank, called the Plainfield Savings Bank. We both thought that this would be a perfect place to apply for a bank loan. So one afternoon, I took an hour off work and strolled downtown to the bank.

As I arrived at the bank, I was surprised to see Tom Benwell through the revolving door entrance. Tom was the Office Manager at Wigton. I greeted him with a "Hello, Tom, fancy meeting you," and a smile. It was his job to ensure the smooth running of all departments, including paper delivery and whatever else was required in an engineer's office. He smiled back at me and said, "Actually, I'm Tom's brother, George. But don't be embarrassed – practically everybody mixes us up. You certainly aren't the first." Well, I didn't think two people could look so alike. Tom and George were brothers who looked the same, but one worked in the bank. I couldn't tell the difference between them. "Now that we've got ourselves organised," said George, "can I help you?" I told him my story, requested a bank loan, and within ten minutes I was filling in forms and signing documents. Everything went according to plan.

After a number of years the Plainfield Savings Bank changed hands and became the Savings Bank of Central Jersey. This, in turn, eventually became the Starpoint Savings Bank, and then the Dime Savings Bank. Then, it was taken over again, and became the First Fidelity Bank. The last change took place when First Fidelity became First Union Bank in the mid-90s. This whole sequence took place between 1969 and 2000, with six banks down. I wonder how many changes will take place during the next thirty years?

We soon took possession of our house and moved in on April 24th 1971. I could see that the actual move was going to be a tough assignment for all of us. Evie had use of the family car, I rented a U-Haul truck for the day and I managed to coax three or four of my colleagues and newfound friends from the apartment complex to help. There was no one to look after the children and we needed a diversion for them. A couple of days beforehand, we paid a visit to a toy store, and bought a combination swing and slide set. This was the wisest move we made so far. During the day of the move, the children looked after themselves, wore themselves out, and laid down for a nap, in that order. We managed to move all of our possessions and furniture, including the old piano Harold wanted to get rid of, into the house in one day.

We had our first visitors while we were still messing about with pictures, curtains and mattresses. They were Bill and Jeanette King, our neighbors from next door on the left, and they were intent on making us welcome, no matter what. They were carrying gifts for us including the proverbial cake. They also gave us a couple of shrubs for the back yard. We were overwhelmed. However, what turned out to be the best gift of all, was the fact that they had a fourteen-year-old daughter, Cindy, who loved children, and was very keen to babysit for Anne and Steve. The children just adored her, and couldn't wait for Evie and me to go out on a Saturday night so that they could have Cindy over. Whenever Cindy babysat during the day, she would take the children to her house next door to see all her animals – she kept rabbits and guinea pigs and hamsters, as well as a couple of cats and three or four dogs. We felt perfectly comfortable leaving the children with Cindy. She was reliable and gave all her attention to the children, so we knew that they were quite safe. In fact, Cindy became a good friend too, especially to Anne, who corresponded with her long after Cindy married and moved to the other side of the country.

After we had been in the house a couple of months, Evie organised a birthday party for the children in June, as Anne turned five and Steve turned three. It was at this party that Evie introduced a game called 'topfschlagen', a German word which translates as 'hit the pot'. This game originated in Austria, where Elfy played it as a young girl. The game was played as follows:

The children would stand in line to await their turn. A pot was placed, upside down, about twenty feet from the starting place and a toy or candy was hidden underneath it.

The next child in line was blindfolded and given a big wooden spoon.

A grown-up would then spin the child around a few times to slightly disorient them and would then point the child towards the pot, and say, 'go'.

The child would then crawl forward tapping the spoon on the ground until the child hit the pot with the spoon (encouraged in the right direction by the others).

Then the child would take off the blindfold, turn the pot over and claim the prize.

The game was very popular because everybody was a winner and got a prize. The prize could be varied to suit the particular age of the child. The best part for each child came when the pot was found and whacked. If you ever decide to organize *topfschlagen* for your youngsters and their friends, don't use your best pot. Or your best wooden spoon! In fact, the Goodwin birthday parties became so popular because of this game, that mothers told Evie that their children talked of nothing else for weeks, and kept asking when the next Goodwin birthday party would be. None of the children had ever played a game like *'topfschlagen'* before, and none of them ever played it at any other birthday parties. Anne and Steve were very proud of their unique parties.

♪

At the beginning of July 1971, I left Wigton Abbott and started with Dick Brady in his new office in Oldwick. It was an easy twenty-minute ride from the house via Route 287 and Route 78 to a little village nestled in the countryside. Both of these roads were interstate highways, with easy access to both NYC and Philadelphia. They were also brand new roads, built in the last few years. There was, at that time, very little traffic along these two roads, making my ride to work almost a pleasure.

On my first day with Dick Brady, I found my way off Route 78, and into the village of Oldwick. Within about three or four minutes, I discovered that I was driving *out* of Oldwick. This place wasn't very big, there weren't any traffic lights, but they did have a crossroads. Turning my car around, I drove back up the hill and pulled into Dick's driveway. His house was quite large, built in the Victorian style, and the property behind the house consisted of about two acres of lawn and woods, with a salt lick in the middle. The salt was for the deer that ran free in the area. Close by the salt lick, there was a two-story building that had at one time been a dwelling, but was now an office. There was an outside stairway attached to the side of the building, and heating and air condition equipment for comfort.

When I arrived, Dick was in the small parking lot, chatting with a woman in her early forties, about my age. This was Rose Wickham, secretary for Dick's company and 'in charge' of all filing, typing, medical insurance, records, and all correspondence required for the efficient running of an engineer's office. Rose and I got on well together, managing very well when Dick was away on one of his several trips to Florida.

I learned that Dick had recently suffered the loss of his first wife Lillian, leaving him with two young children: Mary Alice, who was three months old at the time, and Jonathan who was three. Dick had married his second wife, Ruth, before I went to work for him on Staten Island, and they had a very happy and stable family. Ruth had some family down in Florida, which explained their frequent trips there.

I had a colleague at Dick's in addition to Rose. He rode a motor cycle into Oldwick from Staten Island every day wearing a black leather jacket and a beard. Jimmy Megna maintained it was his beard and biker uniform that made him a target on the highway for the police patrol. "Look at you," he complained to me once after picking up two speeding tickets on his way to work. "You're Mr Nice Guy on your way to work, you wouldn't be speeding or carrying any drugs. They look out for people like me on purpose; young, unshaven, doing maybe two or three mph over the limit, and looking as though I don't really want to belong to your stuffy society. I belong to the hippie society that began at

Woodstock." He then went off into a tirade against everyone in authority, except Dick, Rose and me. I don't remember exactly how it went, but luckily he would always shut up in time to start work.

At some point in 1972, my old colleague from Wigton Abbott, Norman Neilson joined the company. This was the first time in my working career that I had ever worked alongside the same person at two different companies. Little did I know that it wouldn't be the last, however. But more about that later. Norman and I had always got along well, so it was a pleasure to have him work in the office with me. Often at lunchtime, we would sit down to a game of chess. Neither of us was very good at the game, but we enjoyed the challenge. Sometimes I won, sometimes he won, but it didn't matter. We played because we liked each other's company.

Dick's work consisted mostly of cost estimating for other engineers, doing budget estimates for architects and others, and any other engineering work such as monitoring the progress of existing contracts and making sure that contractors built a job that conformed to the drawings and specifications. Norman's specialty was plumbing design, while I worked on the HVAC (heating, ventilation, air conditioning) and process parts of the contracts. However, Dick had a clientele of a dozen or more companies that used him regularly as an estimating and checking service. One of these went by the name of CUH2A (Collins, Uhl, Hoisington, and two Andersons). They were located on Route 206, just outside Princeton, and it was always a pleasure to combine a trip to CUH2A with a trip to the J.B. Redding Company.

J.B. Redding was a very successful plumbing contractor serving the Princeton area and all the university buildings. Princeton University had its own engineers who provided drawings and specifications for the various items of work required. J.B. Redding acquired a set of bidding documents that included drawings and specifications that were handed over to Dick for processing and figuring. Dick would analyse the whole bid package and come up with a total price for the job. This would include equipment, labor, piping systems, and anything that should be included in the price, and would cost money. A typical example would be hiring a police officer to keep traffic flowing whilst a road was dug up in order to install underground piping. Dick had to be very careful to include in his price the cost of any miscellaneous items required to start and finish the contract, as well, of course, as taxes and profit.

J.B. Redding provided lots of work for us, making for a good relationship between the two companies. Whenever we were successful on a bid that they asked us to figure for them, they got the contract. To sum up very briefly, everyone was paid on results. On one occasion, Mr Redding asked us to bid a desirable job on the Princeton campus. He also asked if one of his new employees, a budding estimator, could sit in at the crucial meeting we would hold on bid day. This meeting was a kind of last-minute check to be sure, among all sorts of things, that the number of man-hours required to complete the job was reasonable and the union rate of pay was correct. Mr Redding's new employee, a young fellow named John, needed the experience of finalizing a contract.

When bid day arrived, Dick and I got to Princeton early. We went over the estimate slowly with a fine tooth comb for John's benefit. After about an hour of talking and discussion in which we mentally took the job apart, and then rebuilt it, we reached a point of being almost finished. "What did you learn, John?" asked Mr Redding. "Did any of that information soak into your head?" There was no reply. "Did you hear what I said, John, are you paying attention?"

I sneaked a look at Dick; he was smiling broadly. "John is having his afternoon nap," he said, "He's out for the count!" And so he was. I had never before heard of anyone attending a pre-bid meeting and falling asleep half-way through. In fact I would have thought it impossible had I not seen it myself. John was given short shrift, and finished the day as an ex-employee of the J.B. Redding Company.

During the same period, Dick and I worked as a team for a company in Philadelphia. The company was called Synergo, and they were an architectural outfit with an engineering branch. Synergo was a large company (many times larger than J.B. Redding), handling several million dollars' worth of business a year. In order to get in on some of this, we started our day with a one-hour drive to Philly in Dick's Cadillac, picking up coffee and doughnuts on the way. The last thing Dick yelled as we left the office was, "Call up Fritz, and tell him we left half an hour ago." Fritz was our main contact with Synergo, and we lived by an unwritten law: no matter what happens, keep Fritz happy!

Fritz always welcomed us with the same lament: "Boy, am I pleased to see you. This place is going nuts." Fritz was in charge of mechanical contracts, which embraced HVAC, plumbing, and process design. He invariably smothered us with drawings from various in-house contracts which were in the process of being engineered and drawn up by his crews. Our job was first and foremost to check for accuracy, and secondly to take a good hard look at what had been drawn and accomplished so far to see if the same result could be reached by using less material, or different materials. Dick and I worked well together and were able to weave magic onto these drawings, and save lots and lots of dollars that others would not see. Synergo was of course the recipient of these savings and Fritz was happy to rush Dick's billing through the accounts department.

On one memorable occasion, we found ourselves working together on the same contract on the fourteenth floor. We had all the information we needed except for one particular set of drawings which was being used by someone on the fifteenth floor. "It's only one floor up," I said. "I'll nip up and get it."

I went to the elevator, pressed the button and waited. After a few minutes my patience ran out and I decided to walk up. I went into the stairwell, nipped up the stairs, and pushed the door. The door wouldn't open. "Oh darn it," I said to myself. "Now what?" I tried to open the door again, but it wouldn't budge. It was locked shut.

There was a little window in the stairwell door and by standing on tiptoe I could see the fellow I wanted to speak to, so I rapped on the window to get his attention. I guess he couldn't hear me, because he didn't look up. By now I was getting a bit fed up, so I decided to go back down to the fourteenth floor. However, much to my horror, I found that *this* door was locked as well. I realized that the stairwell doors had a one-way lock on them and you couldn't get out without a key.

I took a look through the window, and there, completely oblivious, was Dick working away, and probably wondering where the devil I was. I had no alternative but to go down the stairs, floor by floor, until I reached the bottom. I tried the stairwell door at each level, fourteen, thirteen, twelve...until I finished up on the garage level where, at last, I was able to get into the elevator, which took me up to the fifteenth floor. I picked up the roll of drawings I had originally gone to retrieve, and when I finally got back to the fourteenth floor with them under my arm, I heard Dick say, " Hey Tom, it's 12 o'clock. There's a restaurant on the fifteenth floor. How about if we quickly nip up there for lunch? It's only one floor up – let's take the stairs." You can imagine my expletive!

♫

We had two very special visitors in 1972. After months of telling each other that there was nothing in the bank left over for luxuries, Evie and I dug a little deeper and found enough in our budget for two return tickets from London to New York. We invited Mum and Dad to come and visit us for six weeks on a no-cost (to them) holiday in October. This sounds like a very simple arrangement, especially since we planned to stay close to home and not have any long range touring plans. But the preparation for this visit was not simple at all. There was some painting to be done, windows and storm windows to be cleaned, and two cars to be serviced (Evie by now had her own car, a white Opel). We tried to make our house look as nice as possible for the impending visit.

Anne and Steve were all agog and kept asking when Grandad and Nanny were coming. They knew that their sleeping arrangements would be changed temporarily, but I didn't hear any complaints or fuss from them about it. We squeezed both children's beds into Anne's room for my parents and rigged up camp beds and sleeping bags in Steve's room for the children. They wanted me to set up the tent for them in the back yard, but we talked them out of that one.

The getting out and setting up of the folding camp beds reminded us of our holiday the year before, when we went camping in the Acadia National Park, Maine. The kids really loved the excitement of camping out doors, and living rough. We did too, until the last day of the holiday when it rained non-stop from morning till night, continuing through the night. In the morning, it was still raining, and everything was wet. After getting Evie and the children into the car, I started folding and packing our stuff. Luckily, I had with me some waterproof rubber boots, a plastic coat and sou'wester hat. The children watched as I trudged through the mud, dropping our things into little rivers made by all the rain, unable to keep a straight face for laughing. Then it all became a game. I dropped something into the mud, throwing my hands up in despair, and the children shrieked with merriment. The last thing for me to pack was the tent and Evie offered to help me with that. It was very large, very wet and *very* heavy. Well, it didn't make any sense for two of us to get wet so I left her in the car. It was as much as I could manage to fold it up, lift it onto the roof-rack of the car, and tie it into place with ropes. We had managed to keep a couple of towels relatively dry so we were able to dry off a little for the ride home. That had been our previous experience of camping as a family and I guess this was what the children expected when they saw the folding camp beds come out for my parents' visit.

The visit turned out to be very pleasant for all of us. It was October, 'autumn' for Dad, and 'fall' for the Americans. Dad commandeered what he called the garden, and what most Americans called the back yard. The weather, for most of the visit, was what is called an Indian Summer, when there has already been a frost, but then the weather turns warm again. You really have to experience one in order to appreciate it. Dad and Mum both organised themselves with deck chairs close to the strawberry patch. Dad found work to do by weeding, turning the earth over, and generally behaving like a gardener. "Tom," called Mum on one occasion, "You be careful with all that digging, you're not used to it any more." Dad sank into his deck chair, giving me a wink, and mumbling to any one who would listen, "There she goes, trying to rule my life. I'm in my sixties and she is still telling me what to do."

Mum wanted to help around the house, but Evie refused point blank. "This is your holiday," she said. "Relax and enjoy not having to do anything." Neither Mum nor Dad lasted more than a couple of days with no duties and nothing to do around the house. Eventually Evie found a job that Mum could do at her own pace – she gave Mum the set of silver cutlery that Elfy had given us when we left South Africa – and asked Mum to clean each piece, about one-hundred-fifty in all. That kept Mum busy for a while. Dad, of course, busied himself not only with the gardening, but also with my tools and machines. He spent some time cutting the grass with what he called the 'motor mower'. This was the ride-on mower that I'd bought from Mr Ackeley for $100 when it was worth three times that. Dad also spent time in the garage, and to see all my gear hanging on the garage walls as neat as could be made him proud. Whenever people came to visit, he would invariably offer, "Come and see my son's garage, you won't find a better selection of tools anywhere."

During this six week visit, Dad and I discussed the fact that there was no connection between the house and the garage even though they were under the same roof. If we came back from a shopping expedition in a rainstorm, or, worse, a snowstorm, we had to get out of the car, open the garage door, and bring the shopping out into the rain in order to get it into the house. This was nonsense, we said. There ought to be a door connecting the garage with the dining room. On the garage side, a four-step stair would be required to get from garage level to house level. Evie thought it would be a wonderful idea to install a door to the garage. "It would certainly make my life easier," she said. "Just be careful when you start cutting into my dining room."

Dad and I worked out what materials we needed and drove to the local timber yard to fetch them. Then we started sawing, cutting, drilling, and hammering. It was like old times working side by side with him. I remembered years ago, in the scrap yard of 82 Braintree Street, when he showed me how the teeth of a hacksaw blade must always look forward. He hadn't changed much over the years, showing me construction methods as if I were still a boy! We both had fun during that time, and, more importantly, the door was a huge success. Mum got a little worried about him overdoing it so we had to postpone painting for a couple of days. Incidentally, the door, step, and handrail have all survived to the present day making them thirty years old with no repairs as yet. Were Dad still alive, he would be very, very pleased.

♪

A lot of things happened in and around 1973 and '74. Some were good, some not so good. One of the good things was that Trixie invited Evie on a short holiday overseas with her. In order to make this trip work, we had to make some kind of arrangement for the children to be looked after while I was at work. That was no problem; our neighbor across the street, Pat Byrne, had two children the same age as ours so she offered to help out and be available when necessary.

Evie and Trix were planning to meet Elfy in Florence where she was travelling with a friend. Evie and Trixie first flew to France. Evie had visited both France and Italy previously during our honeymoon trip, but that was a different kettle of fish. To set this visit in motion, Evie and Trix took an overnight train from Paris to Florence, discovering to their horror that men and women shared the same sleeping compartment. Evie told me later that there was no way she was going to change into her pyjamas, so she had to sleep in her brand new travelling outfit!

After five lovely days in Florence with their mother, they took a train to Milan, and hired a car to Lake Como, taking in some of the most beautiful scenery ever. They finished their trip by going to Paris to see the sights. They had lots of fun and interesting adventures along the way.

Another exciting event, a real milestone in Steve's life, took place when Steve started kindergarten – Big School! – in September 1973. He now took the bus to school, leaving the house at about 11.30am because he went to the afternoon session. However, he came home on the same bus as Anne, which he thought most exciting. His school days had started in earnest. Anne was now in second grade, and an old hat at riding the school bus.

The worst thing to happen in 1973 was that Evie developed a slipped disc that worsened as time went on. It started in July, and gave her much pain and suffering, confining her to bed for weeks. After gingerly making a partial recovery, she had to retire to her bed again in November with a relapse of the slipped disc.

This was most worrying for all four of us. Not only did we have to deal with Evie's delicate back, but we had to somehow take care of the children while I was at work each day. In July, while the children were home during their summer vacation, we quickly made arrangements with a local reputable summer camp called Mommy Baabs. The children were not at all happy with this situation, they hated Mommy Baabs, but we had no choice. Then, in November, we were able to get by with me taking some time off work, and friends and neighbors helping with the children after school.

Shortly after, in February 1974, Evie suffered her severest attack of slipped disc yet. It was so bad that we phoned for the Rescue Squad who sent an ambulance to take her to hospital. After a week I was able to bring her home, and this time we decided to get some outside help with the household chores. It was again a very difficult time for all of us, not least because the country was at that time going through a gasoline shortage, and all motorists were on gasoline rationing. To add to my misery, I was working at a company in Newark that Dick Brady sent me to, about twenty miles from home, so I was using more gas than usual. As we were only allowed to take $3 worth of gas every second day, I spent hours lining up at gas stations while I was desperately needed at home. It was a tough time to get through, but somehow we survived.

Finally, this whole trying period came to an end when my car was drowned. Let me explain how *that* happened!

We had snowstorm after snowstorm during the winter of 1973–74, and the snow banked up and became thicker and thicker over the whole area of Watchung Mountains. One particular day, I was driving to work along the aptly named River Road when I noticed that the weather had suddenly turned warmer, and the snow was beginning to melt. I didn't worry about it. There were cars behind and cars in front and everything looked all right, so I kept on driving.

River Road runs parallel with the Raritan River, and has been known to flood occasionally after a heavy rainstorm. As I approached the railroad underpass, I saw that the road was indeed flooded about six inches, but with cars in front and behind, I didn't have much choice, so decided to go through the underpass. A car was coming the other way, at a pretty fast pace. It created a surging wave in the water that splashed over my car. I remember thinking I was lucky the windows were closed, when, at that precise moment the engine stalled, and I came to a stop.

I tried the key, but nothing happened. No engine. No horn. No lights. Nothing.

I opened the car door and saw that the water was about ankle deep. I didn't quite know what to do. I didn't fancy spoiling my shoes, socks, and trousers by stepping out into this ice cold water. I tried to figure out what had happened but the only thing I could think of was that the battery had short-circuited itself, and some of the electrical fuses had blown. I certainly had no desire to get out and start fiddling with fuses. I knew what I had to do.

I took off my shoes and socks, rolled up my trousers, grabbed my brief case containing details of my current work with Dick, and stepped into the freezing water. I splashed along for about fifty feet until I found a dry area. The hankies that I habitually carry now came in handy to dry off a little. Then, with a glance at my trapped car, I marched up River Road and hiked back home. Evie got a scare when I pitched up at home. "What happened?" she asked. "Where is your car?" After we had talked about the situation, we decided that I would take Evie's car to work, and ask a local gas station which had a tow truck, to retrieve mine.

I went straight away to the gas station and asked the attendant to have someone tow my car out of the underpass. Giving him a set of keys, I promised to touch base with him before the end of the day. "Don't worry about the car," he said, "We will take care of it."

I guess it was a busy day for people who had tow trucks, because it was early afternoon before I could get through to the gas station attendant to ask him about my car. "Sorry, Mr Goodwin, we were not able to find it, it was gone." I couldn't believe the car was gone. Where had it gone? Where *could* it have gone? Maybe someone with a tow truck had stolen it? I quit work early and drove to the underpass. When I got there I couldn't believe my eyes. The whole brick underpass designed to carry trains overhead, nearly twelve feet high, was completely under water. If anyone wanted to go along River Road from one side of the underpass to the other, they would have to use a boat. Or swim!

Later, it was discovered that the sudden thaw had created havoc all over New Jersey. When I spoke to the tow truck man, he told me that the water had risen so fast after the thaw that several cars had been trapped on the wrong side of the underpass. He also told me that the police had been there and had taken charge of the situation. The cars stranded in the underpass had been taken to a junkyard, and that's where I found my car, my beautiful Chevrolet. The engine, gearbox, and rear axle were filled with water, and the interior had some ice in it. "How much do I owe you?" I asked the man, preparing to write a check.

"Nothing," he said. "I'll keep the car in payment for towing it here and you don't have to worry about it any more."

"Oh no," I said. "This is *my* car and I would like you to deliver it to my address. What is the charge?"

Well, he couldn't believe that I actually wanted him to tow my soaking wet, filthy car, full of mud and debris, back to my house. It had turned colder again, and he warned me that if the water froze inside the engine, I would have to replace the engine, which would be quite expensive. Once again I tried to explain that this was *my* car, and I wanted it back. He eventually accepted my $30 check and towed my car to the house, where I soon started to strip it, dry it and work to bring it back to being serviceable. I did, in fact, have to replace the engine, so I bought a reconditioned one and installed it myself. I bought new seat covers, and cleaned and polished as much as I could to make the car look nice again. Thank goodness Evie was still not driving, so I was able to use her car every day for work. By the time she had recovered from her third slipped disc, all the work on my car was finished, and I was able to give her back her Opel. And believe it or not, I still got another 50,000 miles out of that old Chevy!

♫

The rest of 1974 was, by comparison, a wonderful year. Both children were in the local school system, and apparently, enjoying the experience. Evie's discs eventually, after a bit more agony, settled into their correct locations, and all seemed OK provided she was careful about sudden movements. I was still working for Dick Brady in the office in Oldwick and really enjoying it, along with my pay check. It was also the year that Elfy invited us to visit South Africa. In addition to all these things, Stephen came close to meeting Santa Claus, and I started to learn to sing. Yes, sing!

About our trip to South Africa. Elfy had bought some gold Kruger Rand coins when they were first issued by the South African mint. They had greatly increased in value, so she sold some and used the profits to pay for our four plane tickets to Cape Town, where she was now living. She suggested that we come for Christmas and New Year, and then fly up to Johannesburg to visit all our old friends there. Evie told me that she burst into tears of joy when she first read Elfy's letter offering us all the trip. She was *so* excited to be going back home again, and spent the next six months preparing. At this time Anne was eight, and Steve six, and we arranged with their respective teachers for them to have some extra time off school to visit the country of their birth.

Our destination was Cape Town, with a change of planes first at Johannesburg. Elfy met us at the airport in Cape Town and chauffeured us to our hotel. From this time on she gave us a really super holiday, showing us Cape Town from a visitor's viewpoint. She lived in a small, comfortable apartment in one of Cape Town's suburbs. She now regarded Cape Town as her home since leaving Johannesburg a year before.

Among her bridge-playing friends was a special friend, Gerhard Freund, who had in 1936 taken part in the Olympic Games in Berlin. Gerhard had been a member of the German Ice Hockey team. It is strange that I hated Germans as a race for a large part of my life, yet I never met a German I didn't like. He and I met when Elfy, Evie and the children went shopping. He had served as a German soldier in the First World War, which made him ancient in my eyes. He was out walking with a comrade one day when a British sniper's bullet struck down his comrade. Gerhard survived that day. When I met him he was looking forward to his ninetieth birthday. I wrote a short poem for him and kept a copy. Here it is. It is the only poem from my pen.

A Poem for Gerhard

1890, 1900. Marching through the years.
    I've seen a lot of life my dear, I've also seen some tears.
Tsar of Russia, Wilhelm Kaiser, poor unhappy crew;
    Chaplin, Churchill, Marlene Dietrich kaleidoscoping through.
I fought against the British, and did my bit with pride;
    Friend and foe, some lived, some died – one fell by my side.
I've been in the land of the sun so long I now can call it home,
    But I haven't lost my itchy feet, I still would like to roam.
Perhaps to the good old USA; if not, I'll think of friends
    'Cause happiness is friendly thought, that's where
Our future tends.

Gerhard was a chess enthusiast. He challenged me to a chess match on the beach while the women and children were otherwise engaged. I was, and still am, a rather poor chess player, so I prepared myself for a crashing defeat. Imagine my surprise, then, when I won the first game in about ten moves. The next game had a similar ending and I won hands down. He wasn't very happy about this. I could see that I would have to manufacture a win for him to save him embarrassment. He was about eighty-five years old, so it wouldn't be easy. I played again as black, the same as both games before, and I decided to make a clumsy move, making it easy for him to take my queen. Then I would capitulate, making him the winner with me congratulating him, and he with a respectable loss.

However, before I could even do *that*, he made another error. As soon as he realized it, he knocked the pieces over 'by mistake', and claimed the game. "Hard luck, Tommy, you almost won that game but I was a little too tough for you." What could I say? I simply let him get away with it.

One day during our visit I broke a tooth and had to drive into town in search of a dentist. I found a fellow who repaired the tooth for me, and temporarily capped it. When I drove back to where Evie and I had agreed to meet at the municipal pool, I parked the car and strolled slowly along what we English used to call the 'front' or seaside. I found myself on a very large, elevated walkway where one could lean on a railing, and look down on a swimming pool of gigantic size.

This pool was arranged in such a way that it was fed from the ocean. It was a salt-water pool. It took me a while to catch sight of Evie and the children from the distance among all the many hundreds of white blobs out there. I was looking for a large white blob and two small ones. While I was looking, I noticed only one black face among all the so-called privileged whites, and I wondered what he was doing there. After all, there were signs everywhere in two languages designed to keep him away from the water, and indeed, away from the whole area. I realised straight away that he was working! He was carrying deck chairs for the white madam. That's why he was there: for the increased comfort of the white people. That odious apartheid law that had driven us away from South Africa was getting up my nose again.

I leaned, along with a couple of hundred black people, on the railing that overlooked the water, and the feeling struck me that sooner or later they would rebel and drive the whites into the sea. I did not want to be there when it happened.

Gerhard invited us all to Christmas Eve dinner. It was going to be at his house and Evie and Elfy volunteered to help with the cooking. I offered to carve the turkey, but Gerhard refused, saying, "No, Tommy, I must cut some very special pieces, the pieces that Santa Claus liked so much when he came to visit me last year." Every one at the table stopped talking to look at Gerhard. Stephen's eyes popped open, along with his mouth, and his face changed color. Anne, who had been primed ahead of time, sat and waited for something to happen. Gerhard, without the children seeing, suddenly rapped his knuckles on the table very hard, looked towards the porch behind a heavy curtain and called loudly in a hoarse whisper, "Who's that!". Everybody jumped, and Evie and Anne purposely dropped their spoons on the floor with a loud clatter. Stephen, with a very white face, jumped off his chair and ran across the room. Gerhard, being very nimble for his age, got to the curtain first and grabbed it with two hands. Gerhard shook the curtain, making a lot of noise, and talking as if somebody was behind the curtain, saying "Santa Claus, Stephen is here. Let's put his toys under the tree," and, "Was he a good boy last year?" Stephen was absolutely convinced that Santa came to visit us that Christmas Eve. He kept repeating, "Santa Claus, Santa Claus". We all joined in the fun, squeezing each other onto the porch, and pointing out some of the downtown lights, asking, "Is that Santa's sled we can see?"

Stephen, now full of importance, with his little face quite pale, marched up and down the room, chanting, "See, Anne. I told you," as she pretended to be convinced. I reckon this was the happiest and most boisterous Christmas Eve that I've ever spent, before or since.

After two wonderful weeks in Cape Town, we flew to Johannesburg to visit family and friends there. Our good friends Eric and Rikki had invited us to stay in their huge house, and we gratefully accepted their offer, as we could never have afforded a hotel. We spent some lovely hours with Hella and Austin at their plot at Witkoppen, which had really blossomed in the years that we had been away. Evie's former stepfather Fritz and his wife hosted a large cocktail party at their beautiful home in Waverley for all of our friends and family, as we could never have seen everyone in the short time that we were there. I stayed only a week, and then flew on my own to London to see Mum and Dad, Carol, Gladys, Roy, and everyone else. I was amazed at how mild it was at that time of year in London. The roses in Dad's garden were blooming like mad, and it was only the beginning of January.

Evie and the children spent that second week in Johannesburg visiting all Evie's old school friends, and she told me how proud she was when everyone admired how well-behaved Anne and Steve were, and how friendly too. I was the first to arrive back in New Jersey, and when I picked up Evie and the children from the airport, I could see how much Evie missed the beautiful climate and her friends in Johannesburg. It took her quite a while to get used to being back in Piscataway, but once she got involved with all her usual activities, she soon settled in.

Anne graduated with a BS degree in Business Management and Marketing from Montclair State College in the spring of 1989

Celebrating my 60th birthday, August 1989

Trixie and her husband Burt 'N.' Dorsett, at our house for Christmas, 1989

Evie's parents, Harold and Elfy, in Sarasota, Florida, where they both retired, 1989

In front of the 'School of Music' in Oxford in 1991; I've played the piano, fiddle, piano accordion and harmonica, sung in choirs and given music lessons

Two boilermakers reunited; with Andy Robertson in Scotland, 1991

Prioress House, where I lived as a child; taken on a visit to London in the early 1990s. The coal man used to hump coal to the top floor and put it in the bathtub

The back of Prioress House; we lived in the top flat on the right. The remains of the bomb shelter our family used can still be seen

Revisiting my old school where the class picture (shown earlier) was taken in 1939 before I was evacuated to Oxford

My family together for Christmas, 1992

Taken on my 65th birthday at Steve's house, 1994; note the festive tie!

Steve and Kris were married on October 8th 1994 in Cranbury, New Jersey

The proud father of the groom

Many happy hours have been spent with friends at the bridge table, on the golf course and in the church choir. Back row from left: Kathleen Appleby, Alan Appleby, Cleone Dill, Ellis Dill. Front row from left: Erna Pharaon, Rosemary Boden, Fred Boden, 1994

At Trixie and Burt's apartment in New York City, mid-1990s. I taught myself to play the piano in the style of Irving Berlin – using only the black keys!

My sisters, Carol and Gladys, in the mid-1990s

Anne marries Dave on 15th July 1995 in Abingdon, England

My office while I was working for Ted Whitehouse; I learned to use the computer for this, my last job

The happy gardener in retirement. My working life spanned 52 years continuously from 1943 to 1995

With Rollo in Snowshill, Cotswolds, England; still best friends after almost 60 years, 1997

Ready for the next 35! Celebrating our 35th Anniversary on the deserted beach in Cape May, 1997

Three Wise Men; with Ginger and Rollo in Abingdon, 1999

Rollo and I celebrating our 70th birthdays; with Evie and Eileen at the Upper Reaches Restaurant, Abingdon, 1999

My sister Carol and her husband, Terry, at the party

Tom, 5'11", Austin, 6'7", and Rollo! Austin and Hella Horn were visiting from South Africa and joined us for my 70th birthday party

The largest birthday present I ever had, from the children for my 70th. The hot air balloon was about half-way inflated here

Steve's son Garrett, on his 3rd birthday in August 2001

Garrett with his sister Grace, Easter 2002

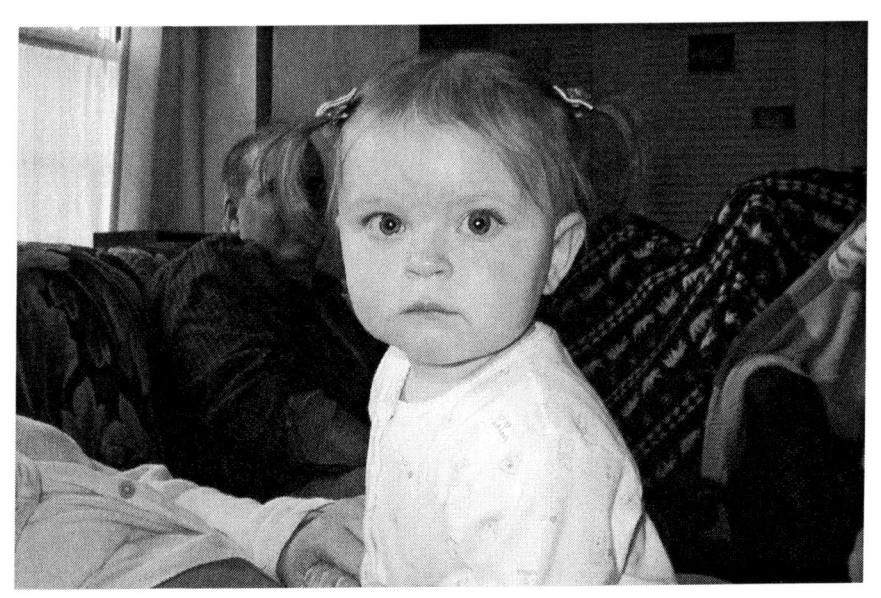

Grace at 10 months, 2002

Anne's children, Henry and Jane, Easter 2002

Jane, at 15 months, 2002

Returning from feeding the ducks with Henry, at Abbey Meadows in Abingdon, 2001

My den, where the seed for the book germinated and I began writing in 1995

Working on the last chapter on my new computer, 2002

Sorting out the pictures for the book with Anne was a wonderful trip down memory lane, 2002

Steve works as a Petroleum Pipeline Operator; he trained as an electronics technician and started working for Colonial Pipeline in Woodbridge, New Jersey in 1990

Relaxing in the new sunroom

CHAPTER 9

Working for a Living

1975 – 1980

EVIE and I played bridge for relaxation and, I guess, for fun. We had taken bridge lessons at the local Bound Brook High School a couple of years previously, so we understood the rudiments of the game, and were able, occasionally, to put together a bridge game with other couples living nearby who wanted to learn the game. Bridge was similar many ways to Solo, and to Solo Whist which I had played many years before in London. This helped me pick up the game pretty fast, and Evie, who is by nature a smart cookie, learned just as quickly.

As some people already know, bridge is played by four people, and each four get their own table. So, if you take part in a three-table game, twelve people will be taking part. There came a time early in 1975 when some of the neighborhood players moved away, and Evie and I were invited to take their place. All the players lived locally, and the games were arranged to take place once a month on a Saturday night. Of course, each couple took a turn at being host/hostess, and served coffee, cakes and drinks. It was all very pleasant and low key, and with twelve people in the house there was a constant hustle and bustle and soft hum of small talk. A couple of months after our return from South Africa, it was our turn to host three tables of bridge at our house.

For some reason, I was not only in a very good mood (being a Saturday there would have been no work the next day), but I was also behaving in a boisterous manner, singing little snatches of the famous Italian song 'O Sole Mio'. Steve and Mary Jo Tyler, neighbors from two blocks away, were sitting at a table with Evie and me so they got the full rendering close up. Evie objected to the noise, saying the Tylers didn't want to listen to it. "That's all right," said Steve, "You can sing very well. Let's hear some more." There was a little more banter around our table about my singing but Evie silenced all my remaining backchat with a single glance my way!

The evening continued until a little before midnight, with everyone thanking us for a wonderful time and hoping for better cards next time. Next morning, Evie took the children to Sunday School as usual, and I stayed home. We had followed this habit every Sunday morning ever since Evie spent time in the local hospital with her bad back. A visiting priest, Father Englund, had seen that she was a patient there and had introduced himself as the Rector of St Paul's Episcopal Church of Bound Brook. He invited Evie to bring the children to Sunday School on a regular basis and to sit through the service and sermon while she was waiting for them. Bound Brook wasn't far from where we lived, just a few minutes by car, so she decided to do that. Evie had wanted for some time to give the children some religious education, and this seemed like the perfect opportunity. The Episcopal Church in America is the same as the Anglican Church (Church of England), which is the church Evie belonged to.

At the end of the service, with the organ music playing behind them, everyone started to leave and formed a line by the front entrance. Father Englund took up a position by the door, shook the hand of each and every parishioner, and exchanged a few words as they went out. When it got to Evie's turn he beamed broadly. "Ah, Mrs Goodwin, I hear that your husband is planning to join our church choir." Well, as Evie described later, she almost swallowed her back teeth. She knew she would *never* be able to get Tommy into a church! We laughed about this for a while after she told me, then forgot about it.

Two months went by, and out of the blue came a phone call. It was from Father Englund and he wanted to talk to *me*. I couldn't imagine what he wanted to speak to me about but I answered him directly and as politely as possible with a "Can I help you?" approach.

After discussing my general health, he got down to brass tacks. "The Bishop is coming to visit St Paul's in the spring to officiate at the graduation of the confirmation class," he said. "This is a happy period for all of us, and to make the moment even more outstanding, we are planning to have our choir sing some special anthems to mark the occasion. Will you join us in singing for the Bishop's visit?" My first reaction was to refuse the offer, claiming no knowledge of the Episcopal Church or its music. I told him that I had not the slightest idea of how to read music. I pleaded ignorance on a grand scale. For Father Englund, it was as if I said nothing. Every time I pleaded to be released from having to sing for the Bishop, he came back at me, saying how he had it on the best authority that my voice was excellent and only needed a few evenings of practice to 'brush up'. Eventually I had to give in to him. In spite of not being familiar with any of the music, or the prayers, or any of the protocol that takes place in a church, and not being able to read music, he made me promise to join the choir on a temporary basis until after the confirmations and the Bishop's visit. "Watch the other choir members," he said, "take your cue from them."

As for reading the music, he told me to watch the little black dots on the music sheet. When they go up and down, you do the same. I wasn't quite so simple that I needed advice like that. Before closing the phone conversation, I asked him who had mentioned my name in reference to this business. After humming and hawing for a while, he told me. It was Steve Tyler. Then I remembered my outburst a few weeks earlier at the bridge table. This is what you get, I thought, for fooling about like that. When I contacted Steve, he defended himself by saying it was a shame that my singing ability was being wasted. Darned cheek on his part, I thought, to uproot my spare time like that, but oh well! It was only for a few weeks and then I wouldn't have to waste my time studying church music, hymns, or anthems especially for Bishops. That, at least, is what I thought.

♪

Dick Brady and I continued to work as a team during 1975, complementing each other, and figuring the cost of various projects. The most important of these was Johnson & Johnson (J&J). J&J was a real presence in central New Jersey, spending huge amounts of money on office buildings and pharmaceutical and drug manufacturing facilities. J&J manufactured drugs of all kinds, and I guess it was pretty obvious to everybody that an up-to-date research facility was not only required, it was necessary. With a tremendously lucrative business on the doorstep, everyone wanted a piece of the pie, and that, of course, included the Brady Corporation. I remember one Saturday morning I got a phone call from Dick. Someone from J&J had called him and wanted a budget estimate to build a mechanical room-cum-boilerhouse on Route 206 in Raritan. This was with a view to building a future research facility in Raritan Township.

The architect in charge of the whole project was chosen to be Wigton Abbott, my first employer in the US. The Brady Corp would be responsible to Wigton Abbott for scope of work, billing, etc. Suddenly, there was a lot of work to be done in several disciplines. The architectural portions of the various sub-contracts, such as earth moving, steel framing, bricks, concrete, and glass were handled by what are called general contractors, or GCs. Our expertise lay rather in the mechanical trades which were labelled heating, ventilating and air conditioning (HVAC), plumbing, and process. For these contracts we had more work than we could handle.

That Saturday morning phone call was the beginning of a period of a lot of work. The Philadelphia work had to continue as it was our bread and butter, and now we also had stacks of cost estimating and preliminary mechanical designs to take care of for J&J.

For the J&J project it was just as well that I was paid by the hour for any time I worked over forty hours a week, because my work week increased quite a lot. There was a mechanical contractor named Elling Brothers, who Dick had worked for in the past, and in no time at all we were on their payroll for part of our time. Elling Bros set up a double-sized trailer for me at the job site, and this was where I worked, a quarter mile from Route 202, and a couple of miles south of Somerville Circle. I enjoyed working at the job site for the better part of a year, on and off. Dick took me to Philadelphia occasionally to massage Synergo and keep Fritz happy. I spent some of my time at Elling's main office in order to take advantage of their new computer system. This system added up the cost of all the components required in any particular system, including man-hours of labor, making adjustments to allow for the different unions involved.

I was not, however, impressed with Elling's new computer. There were other computer systems on the market at the time which were easier and friendlier to use, but who was to know, at that time, which ones would be better for our application! There was a second modern technological system that was in its infancy along with the computer and that was the copying, printing fax machine. This had great potential, but, like the computer, it was ahead of its time. It was primitive by today's standards, but very useful for me in my job. In estimating the cost and availability of a special item manufactured, say, in California, I had a real problem getting the specifications to a rival in, say, Winnipeg. A contract could be won, or lost, depending on my ability to get the correct information to the correct guy, even if he was fast asleep in bed. But the fax took the guesswork out of a lot of bids.

My relationship with Dick was the best I'd ever had with an employer, and it was a terrible pity that it temporarily ended in 1975 when his second wife, Ruth, died of cancer. He took it very badly; this was his second wife lost to cancer in a very short time. His two youngsters were motherless again and it was no surprise that his business suffered drastically. This was, for Dick, a bombshell indeed, and in fact the suffering spread to Dick's other employees when we all suddenly became jobless.

A company called C.F. Braun was advertising for engineers and both Norman Neilson of Wigton Abbott and I contacted them. Norm's resumé didn't quite fit the bill, so he went for employment to a mechanical contractor. However, my upside down resumé that Bob Reis had laughed at a few years ago was good enough to get me an interview with the manager of C.F. Braun. Before that, though, I was interviewed unofficially by Lucille Baker, one of the very few women working at Braun. She handed me three small books, written by Mr C.F. Braun, the owner of the company. "You may want to familiarise yourself with these books before your interview," she said, "especially those pages I marked with an asterisk. They provide information about things like dress code, and how we expect our people to behave."

She gave me a small smile as she elaborated. "The clothes you are wearing today," she said, "although there is nothing wrong with them, would not be suitable. Sports coats, leisure suits and sweaters are out of place." I was wearing a sports coat. "And our men choose white, pastel or soft-colored dress shirts, avoiding plaids, broad stripes and other bold patterns on their ties." I was wearing a colored tie. I asked her outright what would happen if I came to work wearing a purple and red tie and a yellow shirt! "I don't know," she said, "but you would probably lose your job!" Lucille arranged an interview for me with Bob Fursdon a few days later. "You may keep the books," she said, "as they contain a lot of information about the company that is very useful. Mr Braun wrote them to be used as a guide to good living and pride in oneself."

Well! I'd never heard of a place where a fellow could lose his job if he wore the wrong color shirt to work. But I didn't know whether I was attracted to this company or not as the benefits were exceptional, including medical and life insurance, profit sharing, a modern restaurant for 300 people, and numerous activities, including bowling, bridge, and golf.

When I discussed this with Evie, she was all for it. She immediately started to plan a couple of preliminary new suits, and the Sears catalogue was consulted for style and color. I curled up in a corner, protesting that I didn't have a job with Braun yet, and in any case, I wasn't sure I wanted to work for such a fussy company.

C.F. Braun & Co was housed in quite an imposing building, or, rather, group of buildings. It was known as the Murray Hill Engineering Office; their head office was located in Alhambra, California. It consisted of several buildings spread over a few acres of parkland and garden. There was an underground system of tunnels used for maintenance, joining all the buildings together. These tunnels could be used by anyone on rainy days, or, indeed during any kind of weather and any day.

I arrived for my interview at the appointed time, and was met by Bob Fursdon who immediately started to grill me on my knowledge of the manufacture of polypropylene. This was followed by a question and answer session dealing with high and low pressure steam, tracing, and insulation. The conversation gradually shifted from my ability as a design engineer to me as a person. One question he asked me, that I remember to this day, went something like this: "On a scale of one to ten, Mr Goodwin, how would you rate yourself?" I gave him an answer instantly – "Nine, because no one is perfect!" If he was at all surprised by my quick-wittedness, to say nothing of my confidence in my own abilities, he made a good show of hiding it. My answer seemed to please him, however, because his manner changed and he became much friendlier.

I was taken on a grand tour of the establishment, starting with the dining facilities (everyone's pride and joy), and then marched quietly along corridor after corridor, some of which ended with a stairway leading up or down. I thought it would be only too easy to get thoroughly lost. I mentioned this to Bob, and he pulled a map from his pocket. "Here," he said, "you need one of these. Some people have been working here for years, and they still get lost."

The corridors throughout the building were covered with what looked like a very expensive heavy carpet and every fifteen feet or so there was a door into an engineer's office. Each engineer sat in his office, in a clean, tidy atmosphere, his jacket hung in his wardrobe, not on the back of his chair. I mentioned to Bob that the whole building was so neat and impeccable it was as if the place was poised, waiting for inspection by someone. "Yes," he said. "We encourage tidy personal habits, because that leads to good work concentration and more effort in the job."

I was offered a job with C.F. Braun at a substantially higher salary than I had been earning with Dick Brady, and in spite of some of the fusspot rules in force I enjoyed the experience. On one occasion, I saw a group of individuals being escorted through the buildings. I remember thinking how scruffy they looked. They were visitors, and visitors, of course, could dress as they pleased. I realised from my reaction to them that I had been brainwashed into thinking like the company.

I was assigned to a job on a polypropylene plant for the Northern Company in Morris, Illinois. The first task was to draw the whole plant at three eighths to the inch. Then, a model maker constructed a complete model of the plant at half an inch to the foot. This pinpointed all the buildings and structures on the site, as well as the steel framing and platforms to carry all the piping. Then the piping was made and installed on the model. This was when work at C.F. Braun became fun. Part of my job now consisted of making the piping, (the 'works' of the model), at the scale of half an inch to the foot. This was a scale model indeed.

I had never made a scale model before, but I took to this job like a duck to water. This made up for the Meccano erector set that I never had as a boy. The piping that I installed was made of plastic tubing of the appropriate scaled-down size, in other words, a six inch pipe on the model was in reality a quarter inch diameter.

In addition to the site drawings and model making, I also made detailed isometric drawings of the whole project, bit by bit. An isometric is basically a three dimensional sketch as opposed to a standard two dimensional drawing. There was, at this time, a new machine on the market capable of automatically drawing an isometric, but most people had a tough time making it work as it wasn't yet ready for the market.

I found isometrics easy to draw, so easy in fact, that I quickly gained a reputation for being *the* iso sketcher at the company. No one could do them better or faster. One of the design engineers, who was incidentally earning quite a bit more than I was, due to his possession of an engineering degree, approached me one day. "Hey, Tom," he said, "I have to make some iso's and I'm having some difficulty with them. Would you mind giving me some help, but don't let on to the other guys that you're teaching me."

I couldn't believe it! Here was a man, technically my senior, asking me for help to carry out what was to me a standard procedure. I thought this was a bit of a cheek, but I felt flattered by it. I gave him some quick advice: serve an apprenticeship as a boilermaker, and then get lots and lots of experience in the workshop and design office. Then isometrics may come to you as second nature.

♫

During the 1970s and into the 80s we watched the children grow, and, during the summers, at least, we had lots of fun with them. A couple of years after we moved into the house at 215, we joined a small, private swim club, called the Wynnwood Swim Club, which most of the families in our neighborhood belonged to. Wynnwood is the name of the area in Piscataway where we live. We paid an annual fee, and had the use of the large Olympic-size pool, the baby pool and the picnic grounds. Every summer the Board of Directors of the swim club organized various barbecues and picnics and other events to get all the members of the club together. The club was a real godsend during the long summer school holidays, because it gave Evie a place to go to with the children where they could play with their friends, and Evie could spend time with the other mothers.

On a typical day, Evie would do all her daily chores, including lunch and a short nap. Then she would drive Anne and Steve down to the swimming pool where they would spend the longest time in the water while Evie soaked up the sun and read all kinds of books. This idyllic and quiet situation lasted until Daddy came home. On the very hot days, I shifted my schedule around so that my workdays started early and finished early. On those days, I used to get home around 4pm, put on swim trunks, and leaving my car in the garage, ride my bicycle the one mile journey from the house to the pool.

Then the fun would start. Evie, being careful not to wet her hair, would slowly and majestically dip into the shallow end amid calls from a dozen or so children saying, "There goes the Big Dipper!" When we had all had enough of the water, Evie would unload the picnic items from the car and lay out a cold supper for us. This we enjoyed until the bugs, mostly mosquitoes, started to bite, making the pool and picnic area very difficult to stay in. When we started to slap ourselves, we knew it was time to get back to the house, which of course had protective mosquito screens on all the windows.

Evie and I arranged to picnic as often as possible during the summer, but most times we had no choice, during bad weather or wintertime, but to eat inside. It was very difficult for us to teach the children table manners when for the last few weeks they had been cavorting around the pool with our blessing.

We invariably ate dinner with Mozart or some other well-known composer as background music. If this was not enough to acquire a smooth dinnertime with no giggling or jumping about, we drew attention to the Renoir painting, called 'Luncheon of the Boating Party', which hung on the dining room wall behind Steve. "How many men are in the picture?" we'd ask. "How many ladies? How many people are wearing hats? How many bottles on the table?" And on and on. The children became thoroughly familiar with all the characters shown in the painting, and what the characters were doing.

This was usually sufficient to calm everyone down so that we could proceed with dinner. However, there were times when the children just would not behave, and for those times I reserved the Wooden Spoon. No, I didn't hit them with it, I just stamped my way to the kitchen growling "That's it, now you've had it." Then I made a big noise rattling the knife drawer and came back thumping the palm of my hand with a very large wooden spoon which I gently placed on the dining room table whilst giving them a hard look. You should have seen their eyes! The mere threat of the wooden spoon always worked to give us a pleasant dinnertime. Eventually, they learned to behave, and, I'm proud to say, acquired very good table manners, without the wooden spoon. By then they also knew a little about art and music appreciation, too.

We really enjoyed the summers, Evie and I, spending lots of our time at the pool with the children, soaking up the sunshine, and watching as Anne learned to swim, and then became a member of the Wynnwood Swim Club swim team. She became a very good swimmer, equally adept at the four different strokes – breaststroke, backstroke, butterfly and freestyle, and was a valued member of the swim team for years. Our swim team competed against other teams in the area and the competition was fierce. The Plainfield Swim Club was our arch rival, and we often swam against them. It was cause for celebration whenever we beat them for we were both near the bottom of the league and if they were bottom then we would not be!

Steve wanted to swim for the club but as Evie told him, "First pass the test set by the life guard, and then you can join the team." According to swim club rules, all non-swimmers must pass a test before being allowed into the deep end. The test consisted of swimming one length of the pool, unassisted; swimming one width of the pool under water, also unassisted; and treading water for one-and-a-half minutes. Steve ran over to the lifeguard, Mrs Rivers, calling for a test. The first thing she told him was, "No running, otherwise I won't give you the test until tomorrow!" Now the strange thing was that Steve didn't know how to swim, but he so wanted to be able to swim in the 'big' pool, that he was determined to take the test. He was a stubborn little boy (I wonder who he took after?), and we didn't want to discourage him, so we went along with it all convinced that he wouldn't be able to do it. Imagine our astonishment when we watched him do the width under water in very good time. Then, when he swam the length, he was only able to do it in the doggie-paddle style, but he did it to the cheers of everyone watching. Then, without being allowed to take a break, he completed his one-and-a-half minutes of treading water. We couldn't believe it. The word quickly buzzed around the pool that he had just turned six years old and had passed his swim test. Mrs Rivers said she had never before seen such determination in a boy so young. When he came out gasping and gagging, he asked Mrs Rivers, "Did I pass?"

"Of course you did," we all shouted.

Anne started right away coaching him. She thought it would be a dead cert that he would get onto the swim team. After all, she was a little older. She was eight!

We had made a substantial donation to the club, which made us part-owners, about one hundredth, so we could come and go during pool opening hours. Apart from reading library books at the pool, Evie's favorite pastime was chatting with and getting to know some of the ladies who lived in Wynnwood. She made many friends down at the pool, and gradually got to know not only which people lived on a particular street, but also which house they lived in.

One day, one of Evie's acquaintances at the pool, Dorothy Lange, with whom Evie is still friends, asked, "Excuse me, but did I hear you say you were from South Africa?"

"Yes," said Evie, "I grew up there."

"Well," Dorothy said, "we have a South African woman living on my street, on Wynnwood Avenue. You may like to meet her. She recently moved here from New York City with her husband, who is a musician." Evie expressed an interest and said that maybe one day they could get together.

No more was said then, but that night as Evie lay in bed, some little shred of memory came to the fore. Evie told me the next morning that the cogwheels had started up in her brain and she suddenly realized that a girl she had gone to boarding school in Johannesburg with had moved to America after leaving school and married an American fellow who was a musician. She began to wonder whether this could *possibly* be the same person. When she went down to the pool that afternoon, she asked Dorothy about this woman. "Is this South African woman tall?"

"Yes," replied Dorothy.

"And is she blonde?" Again, the answer was yes. Evie mentioned that she had gone to boarding school with someone who fitted that description, who she knew had moved to America, and married a musician.

Dorothy then said, "I know this woman's maiden name, because she runs a small business from her home under her maiden name, and it is written on the mailbox. It is 'Emery'. Well, Evie says that she just broke out in goose bumps because this was the girl she had gone to school with. She could not believe that out of only about twenty-five girls in her senior class, two of them had ended up in a small town in New Jersey, just two streets away from each other. Talk about truth being stranger than fiction!

Needless to say, we arranged a meeting with the two couples, and became friends with June (Emery) and her husband Jay Shanman. We often played bridge together on a Friday night, or went swimming in their enormous pool. Their house was much larger than ours, because Jay was six feet six-and-a-half inches tall, and weighed about 240 pounds, so he *needed* a large house. We always thought that this was one of the strangest coincidences we had ever come across.

♪

As the year 1976 approached, the whole country became caught up in the fervor of celebrating the 200th anniversary of independence from Britain. Practically every city, town, and village was planning a huge celebration on 4th July, with fireworks like never before. I decided to get into the swing of things, and during the spring of that year, I planted a flowerbed of red and white tulips, and blue grape hyacinths. Most patriotic! We as a family were a mixed breed at that time. Evie was a US citizen; I was an Alien/Permanent Resident holding a Green Card, as were both children. However, the children were also South African citizens because they had been born there. And to add to the confusion, the children were also British subjects, as I had registered them with the British Consulate in Johannesburg when they were born. This was my right as a British citizen – my children could be British no matter where in the world they were born.

At that time, in 1976, we had been in America for about the same length of time that we had been in South Africa (seven years), but here I felt as if I really belonged. I certainly had no intention of moving to another country again, and the children might just as well have been Americans, listening to their accents. This was the place I had chosen to settle in, and this would be where we stayed. In fact, both Steve and I would eventually become American citizens, but more about that later.

♫

You'll remember that it was Father Englund of St Paul's church in Bound Brook who was instrumental in getting me started as a singer in the choir. He had begged and pleaded and argued with me until finally I agreed to take part in a choir performance for the local Bishop. Then he left me alone to get on with it.

At that time, the church choir had approximately four ladies singing soprano, four singing alto, four men singing bass and one tenor. The men were way out of balance, but no one wanted to sing tenor, and I, being a believer in safety in numbers claimed to be a bass. I might have been able to sing tenor, but what happened if Jim Risberg, our only tenor, fell sick or took a day off or something? I would have had to sing as a soloist. I would rather hide myself among all those basses, so that's what I did. Jim was a fine tenor capable of being heard above the other men, and he was always on key in spite of what others were doing.

At some point in 1976, Evie and I went to listen to a concert given by a choral group called Schola Cantorum, led by Lou Hooker. They were singing their hearts out, and they sounded, all forty or so of them, professional. Evie noticed a note on the back of our programme asking for volunteers to join the group. 'If you are interested', the note said, 'please come and audition next week'. "Why don't you try out?" Evie asked me. "This is a much better group than the church choir, and you have started to enjoy the singing on Sundays, and the practices on Thursdays."

We talked about it for a couple of days, with me saying that I couldn't in a million years sing like that, and Evie telling me that I wouldn't know till I tried. Eventually I became curious to see whether I could really fit into the Schola Cantorum or not. I went to the audition, and found myself in the middle of a large group of people, all singing in harmony with each other while following the scales that were being thumped out by the pianist. Lou Hooker kept everybody in time with a wave of his hand. He wandered up and down the rows of singers, cocking his head from side to side, obviously listening to everyone as he passed them by. He stopped us frequently, then restarted, sometimes the altos, sometimes another group. He would continually ask the chorus to sing or not to sing, raise a note or lower one, all with a slight nod of his head or lift of a finger. I was beginning to realize that there was more to concert singing than met the eye. I passed the audition, and was invited to join the group.

When a conductor takes control of a chorus of voices, there is an unspoken language between them, and then, music happens! Lou Hooker was the only conductor in my memory who could raise goose bumps on the back of my neck simply by raising his hands in anticipation of creating a chord.

I sang with Schola Cantorum and St Paul's for many years in the bass section until Jim Risburg, our one and only tenor at St Paul's, collapsed and died on the golf course. The following Sunday I was approached by the choir leader temporarily to fill the empty space created, "Just for a week or two until we get ourselves organized." How could I refuse? I sang tenor not only with St Paul's, but also later with Schola Cantorum and discovered that it was easy for me; I was a natural. I was sorry I hadn't made the switch before. While I was busy practising and singing with St Paul's every week, the children were still going to Sunday School, while Evie attended the service. She also became very active with the Episcopal Churchwomen, and was at one time invited to serve on the Vestry. This was when both Evie and I decided to become official members of the Episcopal Church, and we were both confirmed together with about a dozen other adults. Both Anne and Steve were confirmed in their early teens, and Anne became a staunch and very active member of the youth group.

♪

I spent a year working for C.F. Braun. Everyone was a bridge fanatic and tried to get as many games played in the one-hour lunch period as possible. Most of the players were pretty bad and regarded the play just as fun, with almost every bid doubled. Getting to lunch required using the underground system of tunnels. However, I learned quickly never to forget to bring my jacket. ('C.F. Braun people must be fully dressed at all times except when in their office, when a jacket may be removed and hung in the wardrobe provided.') If you forgot your jacket, they wouldn't let you into the dining hall. That could mean a five or ten minute delay until you got your food on the table, the cards shuffled and dealt, with your partner growling, "Two no trump – where the hell have you been?"

One day, I went on a tour around the site looking for the nearest toilet room. I found one fairly close to my office and as luck would have it, there was a water fountain right there. I marked the location of the fountain on my office map and thought it a good idea to remember where it was. A couple of days later, an inter-office memo was delivered to my office. Everybody got one, and it had to do with the water fountain I had recently found. It was noted on the map as Number P7. The memo went something like this: "Water fountain Number P7 is recessed into the wall, and has a hinged door which is arranged so that the fountain cannot be seen when not in use. Please ensure after using the fountain that the door is kept closed. This will keep the area neat and business-like."

After a few days, another memo came out on the same subject, begging us to close the fountain door after drinking from the water fountain. It seemed that half a dozen fellows contrived to leave the door open on purpose whenever they walked past, because now the door was left open all the time. The building manager was then seen giving instructions to two maintenance men at 5pm, and by the next morning at 8am, a self-closing spring had been installed. The door was shut. It was shut so tight that nobody could open it without grazing his knuckles. Several people made it their business to complain, so the spring was removed and the door left open. This state of affairs continued for a week or two until one morning it was discovered that water fountain Number P7 was gone. Someone had worked late the night before and removed the whole thing – the fountain, the door, and even the wall. The Management were determined to show exactly who was in charge. This was the company I now worked for, a company which removed water fountains and where a fellow had to put on a jacket and tie in order to go to the toilet!

One year, I told myself. For one year I'll work here. Then I shall rethink. I enjoyed the year, which went like wildfire. At least, I enjoyed the job, especially the part where I built a scale model of the polypropylene plant. One of the projects being engineered at this time fell behind, so overtime was introduced. Not much. Just one hour in the morning and one hour at the end of the day. We had no choice about this – the overtime was mandatory, and let me tell you, after a couple of months, I was exhausted. I seemed to spend all my time either getting to or from work, or being *at* work, and I was really resenting it.

The money was welcome at time-and-a-half, but I fell sick at this point and spent a day or two in bed to try and recover. My boss criticized me for not working, and especially for not working overtime. This was the last straw! I decided to quit. I had already made the decision to leave after a year's service. The year was up, and I was getting fed up with all the crackpot rules and regulations that were still in force. When I handed in my notice, Bob Fursdon, my Supervisor, summoned me to meet him immediately in the dining hall. There we sat down to a marathon session on why I wanted to quit my job. He used every verbal trick he could find to coax me into staying, but it was of no use. By the day's end, he had accepted my resignation. I felt quite sorry for him because he now had to explain to his boss how and why I was leaving the company.

Then my lucky streak clicked in. I call it the Goodwin luck. I received two phone calls just after I had handed in my resignation to C.F. Braun, one from my old boss, Dick Brady, and one from Bobby Wortman, who was the President of Elling Bros. They were both offering me a job – both of them wanted me on their payroll! These offers couldn't have come at a better time, as now I wouldn't have to go looking for another job. After giving it a lot of thought, I decided to go back and work for Dick.

♫

The second half of the 1970s seemed to pass at an ever-increasing pace. Maybe this was the result of approaching fifty, and then actually attaining it. My brother Roy died of cancer in 1978 and I felt a little guilty that I didn't find the time or the money to attend his funeral in England. Roy and I had never behaved like true brothers to each other and there was room for improvement over the years. However, neither one of us made the effort to get together, so I guess we both paid a penalty.

My cousin Jimmy, along with his wife Iris and son Mark, paid us a visit in 1978. We played a lot of croquet on the back lawn, and discovered that Anne, closely followed by Steve, was the best croquet player on Wyckoff Avenue. Our visitors were not used to the strong summer sun that we in New Jersey take pretty much for granted. Mark, who was eighteen, suffered from the heat more than anyone else did. We took him down to the swimming pool to douse him and try to cool him off but that didn't help much. He was overheated from the time he stepped off the plane until he was on his way back to England.

As they grew, both of our children were very involved in many and varied extra curricular activities. Anne took dance lessons for several years. She joined the local Girl Scouts and spent a lot of her time playing softball. Swimming, summer and winter, was high on her list of activities, during which time she won several medals. Anne was a member of the church youth group and the choir at St Paul's, and also belonged to the High School choral group and drama club. She was one of a select group of students inducted into the High School Honor Society for having consistently good grades. She had many friends, and seemed to have endless energy, as she also had various part time jobs after school, such as working at our local drug store and babysitting. She seemed to have a real love for life, which she has to this day.

Speaking of energy, I have to mention Steve who became a veritable ball of fire with his activities. For several years in succession, I took him on various canoeing, fishing, and camping trips. This was something that Steve and I could do as father and son. We lived a little rough, and toilets were hard to find. We lived off baked beans (which we called 'shirt lifters') and coffee, sauntering about like cowboys. We learned to prepare and bring with us enough small logs from 215 to make a decent-sized campfire. I played old-fashioned music on my mouth organ and we pretended to be in Wyoming. The canoeing was tough when it was shortly after a rain. Sometimes we had to carry our canoe around the bridge for safety's sake. Many years later Steve told me he still remembered these outings, and he has very fond memories of them. Closer to home, he joined the Boy Scouts, played baseball and soccer, and took part in swim team races. His swimming culminated with him being awarded a gold medal for the age ten-and-under breaststroke at the year-end championships.

Thus happened all the excitement around the house, and with the children, throughout this period. However, there was, you might say, a hidden force at work. The glue that held it all together. She who must be obeyed! (This is a famous line from the hit British series 'Rumpole of the Bailey'.) The family member who cut a thousand sandwiches, and made a thousand dentist and doctor appointments for us. This hidden force did so much, drove thousands of miles to make sure that we all got to the right place at the right time, whether it was soccer or baseball or dance lessons, or whatever. Evie is her name.

Over the years, she also became involved with quite a few organizations. Soon after our arrival in the US she joined the Women's Club of the YWCA of Plainfield, and after a few years became President of that club. After we had moved to Piscataway and joined St Paul's Church nearby, she became a member of the Episcopal Churchwomen (ECW), a group of ladies who met once a month to organize various functions, such as rummage sales. She became Treasurer of the ECW a year or so after joining, and stayed in that position for eleven years. Evie is such a logical person that it's no surprise to me that they didn't want anyone else in that post. She also served for three years on the Vestry of St Paul's, so besides taking care of the house and us, she gave her time to the community too.

After analyzing the last couple of sentences, I come to the inescapable conclusion that mine was the easy job that finished each day at 5pm. Evie often had chores or duties that took her well into the evening, but I never heard her complain. She always seemed to be very contented with her life.

♪

Throughout all these years of carrying on with our ordinary lives, I was of course concentrating on earning a living. I had decided to leave C.F. Braun in 1977 and go back to work for Dick Brady. He seemed to have recovered from the trauma of losing his second wife, and I felt a certain amount of loyalty to him, because he had always been so good to me and my family. I was thinking specifically of the time when Evie was in bed with her bad back, and Dick had said to take off as much time as I needed to take care of things at home. He never deducted any money from my pay check when I took time off, so I felt that in some way I wanted to pay him back. I knew that he valued my work and really wanted me to go back and help him rebuild his business, so that is why I decided to go and work for him at that time.

For the first year or so, things seemed to go quite well. However, being such a small company, Dick was unable to offer his employees a pension scheme. When I approached him about this (after all, I was now getting on for fifty, and had to start thinking about the future), all Dick was able to do was to give me an increase so that I could start my own retirement savings account. The government had recently started a scheme that allowed people to put a certain amount into a non-taxable account called an IRA, (and that does *not* mean the Irish Republican Army!), which stands for Individual Retirement Account. I started putting as much money as I could afford into this account, but as we were really living on a very tight budget it didn't seem to amount to much.

It didn't take long to get back into the swing of things at Dick's. He was getting a lot of work from many of his old sources, including Elling Bros in Somerville, and we were very busy. In fact, many nights I worked late to try to catch up with the workload. The working conditions at Dick's facility were vastly different from those at CF Braun. Dick's office building was at one time a stable at the back of his house which had been rebuilt into a two-story apartment. Some time later the apartment was rebuilt and fashioned into a large modern office. There was a spiral staircase inside linking the two levels together. I remembered that when I was laid off a year before, I had built that staircase for Dick, and it was still giving good service. The main entrance into the office was a regular staircase running in one length from top to bottom on the outside of the building. The whole place had a folksy charm about it, which was at the same time old-fashioned and modern.

I remember working late one evening on a project in the dead of winter. It had been snowing but Dick had swept the area, and had gone out for the rest of the day. I thought it might be a good idea to take my project home with me in case I couldn't get to work the next day on account of the snow. I gathered up all the things I would need: a set of rolled up drawings and a booklet of specifications that I was working on, together with my electric calculator. I turned off all the lights, latched the door at the top of the outside stairway, and because it was dark, gingerly stepped out onto the little platform. As I started going down the stairs, my foot slipped, and I skidded down with the back of my head hammering every step as I went down.

I reckon I went down about twelve steps until I stopped with rolled up drawings under one arm and calculator under the other. I was lying on my back, and waiting for the pain, afraid to move. I remember thinking that if you break your back or neck you are likely to wind up paralyzed without feeling it or even knowing about it. Not feeling any pain may be a bad symptom. I opened my eyes and tried to move. That was when I saw the pointed icicle hanging directly over my head from the eaves above. It was about three feet long and tapered like a spike. A thought went through my mind like wildfire; if the spike came down, it could penetrate my head like a spear. Then the ice would melt, leaving no trace of what caused my death. Would anyone ever be able to figure it out? Believe me, I was up and out of there before you could say 'Jack Robinson'! The following day Dick insisted that I have a thorough check-up at the local hospital, with X-rays and all. Thank goodness I wasn't hurt in any way. What an experience.

While I was working for Dick we picked up a contract dealing with Aquaduct Race track. The owner of Aquaduct had hired an architect to arrange for a large portion of the stadium, which was open to the wind and rain, to be closed off with glass windows. This was in addition to installing several rooftop-heating units for the comfort of the punters. Each week a meeting was held to review the status of the contract, and to discuss problem areas, such as availability of materials. I wrote minutes of these meetings and kept the owner informed about what was happening. Each week I distributed copies of the previous week's minutes, and there was only one complaint from one of the contractors. He objected to my use of a tape recorder at our meetings. "That's funny," I told him, "I don't use a recorder, I just remember everything that was said." He was very impressed.

When the job was finished, one of the contractors invited everyone to a gala lunch to celebrate the opening of the new facility. There were seven of us, by now friends, who were in a party mood. This was the first day of racing, and someone suggested we make a bet. After about fifteen minutes of haggling, we came up with the details. Everyone put in $2 making $14 bet money. One of the fellows put himself in charge and suggested we do a daily double, which is picking the winner of the first race with everything going onto the winner of the second race. Instead of trying to pick winners, we picked numbers. What numbers? Who knows? Someone shouted, "Use our table number, forty-four", so we did. Number four had to win the first race, and number four had to win the second race.

"Not much chance," we were saying, when suddenly we heard a general hubbub indicating the start of the first race. All seven of us were seated in the main dining room, and there were monitor TVs all around us on the walls. Our horse, number four, was in the middle of the pack. Then it was gaining on the others. Then it was in the lead. We all cheered it on lustily, as it won the race. Whew! What excitement. All we had to do was wait half an hour till the next race. Some fellows talked about abandoning it, but no one did. We all waited. We gathered up our things in readiness for a fast getaway, and eventually they were off. Our horse went off like a rocket and won the race hands down. It was so easy, or so it looked. For our $2 bet we each received $110. To get our pay-out we lined up facing our man with the money and he rattled us off one at a time: Tom – $100, plus a ten; the architect – $100, plus a ten; the electrician – $100, plus a ten; and so on, until he had handed out all the money. I put the money away and when I got home I put the $100 dollar bill into one hand, and the $10 dollar bill into the other, and told Evie to choose one. Guess which one she chose? She has a nose for money – of course she chose the $100 bill! This incident was cause for much merriment over the years.

My second stint with Dick Brady lasted for about four years. This time, my reason for leaving his company was that after a while the business seemed to stagnate. We had been doing a lot of work for Elling Bros in Somerville, and Bobby Wortman, the President of Elling, approached me more than once, and indicated that he would very much like to have me on his payroll. Every time I said no, until about the end of 1979, when I realized that I needed to give some serious thought to my future. We had been doing a lot of work for Elling Bros over the years, so I often saw Bobby Wortman at meetings in his office. He would pull me to one side, telling me what a great company Elling was, and one time he even showed me the details of his IRA pension, which was very impressive, compared to the one I had recently started for myself. Elling Bros, a company in business since 1922, offered stability, a pension, and security. As Bobby so succinctly put it to me one day: "Hank said to tell you, Tom 'Sh— or get off the pot'!" (Hank Flower was one of the directors of Elling Bros)

After much soul searching and discussion with Evie I reluctantly handed in my notice to Dick. I did this by calling him and asking him to have a drink in the local bar that evening. We sat down together and discussed my future. His attitude was supportive: "Go to Elling, that's your best bet." We parted on a friendly handshake, both knowing that in the future, he and I would be on opposite sides of the fence, struggling for the same contracts.

♫

I started work for Elling Brothers in February, 1980. I was in a very happy frame of mind hoping to stay until retirement. Settling in at Elling Brothers was easy. I knew just about everyone, including my old friend and colleague Norman Neilson, with whom I had worked first at Wigton Abbott in Plainfield, and then at Dick Brady's in Oldwick. Norman, too, had been unhappy with the job he had found after leaving Dick's in 1975, and when offered a permanent position with Elling Bros, he had taken it. This was now the *third* company that I was working in with Norman – what a strange coincidence! The computer I had to use held no horrors for me. Luckily, this was well before everything started to get complicated with mice and email.

Cliff Elling was the owner of the company, but did not run the place. The running was done by Bobby Wortman, the company President. Cliff went under the title of Chairman and Founder. Bobby was one of those amazing people who could achieve anything and make it appear commonplace. At the age of thirty-eight he was already boss of the company, which at that time was worth several million dollars. Bob's grandfather had at one time worked for the company and Bob himself had served an apprenticeship there as a plumber after starting as a truck driver. Bob's beautiful wife and four kids came to the office occasionally. He was a volunteer fireman for Somerville and handsome enough to make any man envious.

When I joined Elling Bros the whole company was undergoing a facelift. Some of the workshop and storage space was being obliterated to make room for half a dozen or so urgently needed offices. Bob held a mini-meeting to decide the layout of who went where – and why.

Bill Ballantine, a draftsman, made a preliminary plan, and after some thought he placed Dorothy Banker right next to Bobby Wortman. Dorothy was a pricing clerk who knew the price of almost everything. If she didn't know a price, she could get it. You might say she was an invaluable member of the team, but unfortunately she just never stopped talking. When Bobby saw the layout of the plans he just about exploded. He sent Dorothy on a false errand before starting to berate Bill. "You can't put her next to me," he said, "she never stops talking! Don't you know I've been putting up with her for ages? This is my chance to move her as far away from me as possible." All of us in the estimating department had to hide our smiles. Dorothy was a very nice person and no one wanted to upset her, but oh boy, could she talk!

This conversation was taking place at a time when women's liberation was already well entrenched. Some of the ladies working at Elling Bros, such as Tricia Garay, Jo Hann, and Dorothy, objected to being referred to as 'girls' as well as being noted as 'Miss' or 'Mrs', preferring 'Ms'. (Evie always said that 'Ms' stood for 'Missed'!) We had to be extra careful not to give the impression that we were favoring the men over the women; now everyone was equal. Unfortunately, some were more equal than others but how could you tell them that? Anyway, Bobby had the seating plans drawn up with Dorothy way down at the end of the corridor, and that was the way it had to be. She just had to accept it. *But*, now she was right across the corridor from *me*!

Elling Bros was a mechanical contractor which did not undertake actual engineering work. Typically, all the engineering had been taken care of ahead of time. From now on, my job consisted of taking pre-engineered drawings, and figuring the cost of building a facility. That part was known as the bid. If I was successful with my bid presentation, then I got to re-draw any parts of the job that needed it, and analyse any cost-savings ideas that I might notice on the job. An example might be to cut the cost of labor involved in the assembly of some parts in the field.

Bobby hated salesmen with a passion. Whether they were salesmen or saleswomen, he didn't like to deal with them. He would see a particular car through his office window, and recognize it as belonging to a salesman on the prowl. "Tell him I'm out," he would yell to Jo Hann. "Give him Tom Goodwin's number, and tell him Tom's in charge of all company purchasing and buying until further notice."

There was a particular vendor who wanted to make a sale on a Johnson & Johnson contract that we had. This was concerning some specialized ball valves with built-in complicated controls which were to be made from a high quality stainless steel. The salesman's name was Compoli, to which I quickly added 'Ball valve' making him for evermore Ball Valve Compoli. Everyone took to his new nickname, even Bobby, who was seen discussing the fine points of our contract with Ball Valve Compoli. There were a few hundred of these special valves required for our contract, each costing an average of about $100. A fine sub-contract in anyone's language that Ball Valve Compoli landed for his company.

One day Bobby came to work with a stiff neck, and spent half an hour trying to limber up. The stiff neck persisted into the third day, prompting me to give him some friendly advice. "Don't sleep in a draft, and if that doesn't work, go see your doctor." Well, nothing worked – not the home cures, not the doctor, not the advice. No one knew what this pain in his neck was. A trip to a local specialist solved the problem immediately. He had cancer of the worst kind. His body was riddled with it and it was so bad that two specialists gave him only one year to live.

Everybody was absolutely devastated. How could this happen? I can't find words to describe how we all felt; the shock of knowing that Bobby Wortman was going to die of cancer within a year was just too much for us to handle.

But the one person who handled the situation with the least amount of fuss was Bobby himself. He quickly developed a habit of commandeering one of our Johnson & Johnson contracts, along with the designer in charge and threw himself into the job, saying, "We might as well work". I got caught a couple of times on these late-night forays, sometimes not getting home until midnight. He and I might be trying to figure out the size of a water pipeline, and in the midst of our calculations, he would glance at me with a smile saying, "This really is fun isn't it, Tom?" I thought he was incredibly brave to carry on like this.

Bobby knew that he was dying, and managed to put on a brave front to all of us at work. However, the time came when he was too ill to come into the office any more, and a pall fell over Elling Bros. Here was a young, vibrant man, not yet forty, with a beautiful wife and four lovely children, and within a year of finding out that he had cancer, he was dead. There were a couple of hundred mourners at Bob's funeral, including all of Elling Brothers, all the volunteers from two fire houses, and many of his relatives and friends. It showed what a likeable, popular fellow he had been.

CHAPTER 10

Family Ties

1981 – 1995

THE 1980s started with excitement from Evie's side of the family. Her sister Trixie, who was four years younger and had never been married, tied the knot with a wonderful fellow whom she met through a mutual friend. At that time, Trixie was living and working in Washington, D.C. and her future husband was living and working in New York City, so for a while they had a long-distance romance. However, when they decided that they were serious about their relationship, Trixie moved to New York, and on March 1st 1981 they were married in Burt's beautiful apartment in Manhattan. Elfy was there for the Christmas holidays and extended her stay in order to be there for the wedding. Monica came over too, bringing Elfy's family of three daughters all together at one time – a rare event.

During the wedding ceremony, Burt was called on to state his complete name, which he did: 'Burt N. Dorsett'. After the wedding I asked him what the 'N' stood for. Burt told me, "When I was undergoing a medical exam to join the Army, the recruiting sergeant asked me that same question: 'What's your middle name?' When I told him I had no middle name, the sergeant marked a large 'N' on my form. He said, 'Everybody gets a middle name in this man's army so I'll put you down as 'N. for No Name'." Ever since then we have jokingly called him Burt 'N. for Nothing' Dorsett!

In 1983, Elfy sent Evie a plane ticket so that she could visit Johannesburg. Evie was to leave in February, mid winter in the US, but mid summer on arrival. She had been checking the New Jersey weather forecast carefully for a week before her trip, and it was going to be cold with some snow, but nothing to worry about. Evie always suffers a little from nervousness (as I do) when faced with a long overseas plane trip coupled with the threat of bad weather. A big snowstorm started on the day before she was due to fly out of JFK airport, and it continued with such fury that the airport was forced to close for the first time ever! Evie called the airline and found that her flight had been cancelled, of course. Now what?

Later in the day the airline called back, and said that if she could be at the airport by 8am the following Monday morning, a plane would be available. We left the house before 6am on that Monday, and I dropped Evie at the terminal. When she finally reached Johannesburg she telephoned me to tell me of her safe arrival. She said that only about twenty of the original two-hundred passengers had turned up for this flight, and they had the whole plane to themselves, with each passenger having three crew members to look after them. It was sheer luxury! So something good *did* come out of this situation. The only unfortunate part was that Evie lost two days of her stay with Elfy, as she had to return on the date originally scheduled. However, she had a wonderful time visiting family and old school friends, whom she had not seen since our visit there at the beginning of 1975.

She took another trip to Johannesburg, again at Elfy's invitation, in 1986, and told me on her return home how much things had changed in South Africa since her visit three years earlier. Every house now had a six-foot high brick or concrete wall around it, topped by barbed wire or bits of broken glass. Every house, of course, had a burglar alarm and half-a-dozen locks on the front door, and most had two or three guard dogs as well. In fact, the houses had become fortresses. We were glad that we were no longer there – it would have been like living in a prison. We had become so used to living on our one acre property with no fences or other barriers, where we all just cut our own lawn up to our boundaries, and where you could look along the back gardens for miles with nothing but trees or shrubs in the way. The view from our back garden is just like a park. How lucky we are.

♫

The 1980s continued with excitement from the children. They both graduated from Piscataway High School, Anne in 1984 and Steve in 1986. They had each completed all grades and were ready to start thinking about college. A few years earlier Evie's dad had given us a donation for the children's college, so we had most of the money we needed earning interest in a savings bank.

To make up for any shortfall, Evie went back to work and earned a surprising amount of money working as a secretary in a sales office. She also took calls as a Customer Service Representative whilst working for Brother International. That was an interesting job, and Evie did very well at it. Brother sold electric sewing machines, electric typewriters, and electric word processors. Evie's job was to handle incoming calls from people who had purchased electric typewriters or word processors, and give them help and assistance over the phone when they needed it.

This meant that she had to know the typewriters and word processors very well, and if not, she would have to be able to pinpoint the customer's problem, quickly find the relavant catalog, and talk him or her through the problem. Being a good talker, she had no problem with this!

Our family holidays had consisted, for several years when the children were young, of trips to Chincoteague, Virginia where we played in the sun, set up our pop-up tent trailer, which was our way of circumventing expensive hotel bills, and tracking the famous ponies. The ponies, running free, are descendants of some which escaped from a shipwrecked Spanish ship many years ago. This famous group of animals continues to grow on Chincoteague Island and gets culled every year to keep the number within limits. There is a yearly round-up and the result of that was an auction. We always planned our trips to miss the large crowds that invariably turned out for the auctions.

We didn't spend all our holidays on Chincoteague Island. As the children became teenagers, we found a little beach resort in southern New Jersey, near the end of the Garden State Parkway, called Wildwood Crest. It became ideal for us when we found a reasonable hotel about 100 feet from the sea with no hurly burly from vendors or sales people. From Wildwood Crest to the busier resort of Wildwood as the crow flies was about a mile or maybe a little more. We developed a daily ritual that pleased all four of us. Anne and I woke early from our sleep and marched energetically along the beach and boardwalk north to Wildwood. Evie and Steve slept late and drove to Wildwood later where we met together for brunch.

There was a trolley service between Wildwood and Wildwood Crest that the children got to use as they got older. At first Evie and I worried that they would get lost, or, worse than that, meet up with undesirables. Then I remembered my youth when I had a free hand wandering around London with no supervision. I suppose teenagers and youngsters in general all act the same, from generation to generation, even if the result seems risky, to us clever grown-ups. Independence is what they really wanted, and don't we all?

Anne started her independence by going to college after graduating from high school. "You can go to any college you like as long as it's Rutgers." This was my standard approach, which was a joke to coax the children into the local State University. Rutgers State University was located a couple of miles away from our house which meant students could live at home and shuttle back and forth for classes. We were residents of New Jersey and eligible for certain benefits because of that. However, Anne chose to go to Montclair State University where her best friend, Laurie, was also going, which was still a State University, but was too far away for her to live at home. She was sprouting wings. Home was no place for her to stagnate.

Anne graduated in 1989 with a Bachelor of Science degree, the first Goodwin from my family to do so in the 20th century. Anne had paid her dues in more ways than one. She worked part-time as a waitress to help with college fees and general expenses, as well as working the summers as a receptionist at a local hotel and in other temporary jobs. Halfway through her degree she dearly wanted to do a semester in Leeds, England under a reciprocal student exchange arrangement. We nervously agreed that she should go and be let loose among many millions of eligible Englishmen. Or maybe she would come back with green hair? That didn't happen. She learned to drink warm beer English style and found the time to go and stay with my mother, Rhoda and visit with her cousins. She took the required classes, learned a little about the English and their habits and travelled around England, Scotland, Wales and Ireland. I believe she had the time of her life that semester; it was well worth the time, effort, and money expended.

After living at college in the dormitories for a couple of years, Anne rented a room in a house in Montclair, then lived in Bloomfield and later Clifton with her friend, Heather. During her last summer break from University, Anne and an old high school friend, Traci, drove nearly 2,000 miles to Denver, the city where Evie and I had nearly moved to when we first arrived in America. They rented a house, found part-time jobs and travelled around the Rocky Mountains and neighbouring states, returning two months later exhausted but exuberant from their trip.

After graduating from university in the spring of 1989, Anne wasted no time writing a resumé and securing for herself a marketing job for a company in northern New Jersey that manufactured and sold ophthalmic lenses, contacts, and frames. She was all set for a successful and comfortable life by the time she reached the age of twenty-three. But, like her mother and father before her, she had itchy feet, and wanted to travel. She decided to move to England for a while and in early 1990 set off with her bags to stay with my Mum in Hackney. Travel was now getting easier and places were more accessible to the traveller. When I was a little boy, Scotland was a long way away and Spain was completely out of sight. Travellers now organize hiking holidays to take them all over Europe to places like Italy, Greece and Germany. The world wasn't so open for inspection by all and sundry until at least the 1980s. The ordinary British youngster, the ones like me who would normally go to Blackpool or Brighton for holidays on a motor cycle, experienced a drastic change when Europe opened up.

Anne lived with my Mum in Hackney, in the East End, for a few months, spent time getting to know her English relatives and explored more of the country before finding a permanent position with a company in Hammersmith. She moved to a shared house in west London and settled happily into her new lifestyle.

Steve, however, wasn't even sure that he wanted to go to university when he left high school. One of his problems was that he didn't know what he wanted to do. During his years at high school, he worked after school hours at various part-time jobs, such as washing cars, cutting lawns, and pumping gas, but of course none of these were good for lifetime careers. One thing Evie and I definitely were not going to do was force Steve into something that he didn't want to do. We knew that this could be a recipe for disaster, because of something that was said to me by our dentist, Dr Stephenson.

The four of us used Dr Stephenson, a dentist from Plainfield, for any and all dental work required. He had been dentist to Evie's dad since the 1950s, so he had great references. I found him, like all other dentists, very difficult to talk to, or hold a conversation with. It usually went, "Good morning doctor, how are you these days?" Then all that I could manage to say was "ga ge ga ga", until he finished working on my teeth, then goodbye till next time! This was hardly the environment to have any kind of talk, so I was completely surprised when, one day, he opened up and started to talk about his son.

His son was a college drop-out who refused to study for any of the professions that Dr Stephenson and his wife wanted. The Doctor became incensed when his son worked as a landscape gardener, which was a fancy name for someone who cut other people's lawns. He wanted his son to follow in his footsteps so to speak, or at least go through the motions of becoming a professional of some kind, a dentist, doctor, lawyer, an engineer, even a teacher. But to be a nothing was more than he could bear. He told me he envied me for not pressuring my son into a career he did not want. We had given Steve free rein (Anne too, as a matter of fact) to choose a university and a career for himself. I couldn't believe that this well-to-do, professionally successful man actually envied *me*. I must admit that I left the dentist's office that day feeling really chuffed!

Steve kept his eyes open, even when he watched TV, for ideas of what to do. One day he saw an advertisement for a local college called De Vry Technical Institute, which was offering, amongst others, a course to become an Electronics Technician. The course was split into smaller parts than a regular university. It could be extended to include an engineering portion, but the best part of all (in Steve's opinion) was that the course was 'hands on'. Right after graduating from high school, Steve had attended Middlesex County College nearby, and taken some business and accounting courses. That was when he decided that he did not want to spend the rest of his life sitting behind a desk. At De Vry, he would be learning to troubleshoot and repair all kinds of electronic circuits and machinery, and learn how they worked. From this course he would later have an entry, if he wanted, into engineering. De Vry guaranteed that every student finishing the course would, with De Vry's help, find employment. Steve approached us about this course and after we discussed the financial aspect, we gave him the go-ahead to sign up for it immediately.

While Steve was studying for his diploma from De Vry he stayed with us, in his same bedroom, surrounded by all his old things. His classes were all either in the afternoon or the evening, so he managed to find a part-time job at a supermarket in the morning so that he could earn some money for his expenses. He was a hard worker, and got all A's in his courses. We honestly believe that that was due to the fact that he had found something that he liked to do. He had not been forced into this; he had chosen it himself, and it made a lot of difference to his attitude. He became very relaxed and easy-going. Towards the end of his studies, he made a promise to Evie and me that he would move out one year after finding his first full-time job.

One evening Steve asked me to help him to manage his money, and that is when I showed him how to make a budget. We sat down at the dining-room table, and made a list of all his monthly expenses. We then subtracted that from his monthly pay check, and I told him that what was left was for him to spend on anything that he wanted, such as movies, new tapes of music (this was before the days of CD), gifts for girlfriends (ha, ha), and anything else that he wanted to buy. Evie and I insisted that he give us some money towards rent and food, just to teach him that there would be nowhere he could live for nothing. He did not know this at the time, but we were actually putting this money away, and when he finally moved out, we gave it all back to him in a lump sum. Was he surprised! He was able to buy himself a double bed, as well as carpeting for his new bedroom, which was in a townhouse in Woodbridge that he was going to share with three other fellows.

After finishing at De Vry, Steve quickly found a job which he really enjoyed (and where he met his future wife, but more about that later), and after his first year was up, he clubbed together with three of his friends and rented a four bedroom townhouse. They each had chores to do, which they all swore to keep to on a stack of bibles. They were all decent blokes, and behaved pretty much as they should. Unfortunately, one or two of them became a bit lazy, and Steve and one other friend found themselves doing most of the housework. When their lease was up at the end of their first year in the apartment, Steve decided that he had had enough of living with other people and found his own one-bedroom apartment here in Piscataway. It was nice to have him closer to home again.

For the first time in twenty-four years, Evie and I were alone in our house! Steve rented a truck to move some of his furniture to his apartment, and he and his friends all mucked in to help each other with carpets, rugs, and chairs. He was disappearing in a puff of smoke, promising to keep in touch with us, and call often, and suddenly he was gone. There were no dry eyes at 215 Wyckoff Avenue that day, but we consoled ourselves by remembering that Steve would be only twenty minutes' drive away in Woodbridge, and Anne was less than an hour away from us in north Jersey, still at Montclair State University.

We had the memories. This was our baby, Stevie. The one who demanded that he be called Steve at the tender age of eight. He showed them! When playing in the All Star Baseball Championships, he showed all the other kids how to steal a base. Then, when everyone was blaming each other and looking the other way he stole another one, and this one was home plate and he had scored a run! No one else had ever done that. No one else had had the determination and drive that Steve had shown. Evie and I had delightful memories; not only of Steve, but of Anne, too, both of whom provided cause for pride in our family.

♪

As mentioned earlier, from the mid-1970s onward, I took part in many concerts. In a few I sang bass, in the choir of St Paul's Church. Then, after the death of Jim Risburg, I inherited the tenor slot in the choir and I also changed to tenor in the Schola Cantorum. I was never good enough to get up front and sing solo. I didn't have the nerve or the courage. I took part in dozens upon dozens of concerts during these years, most of them in a choral group at Rutgers University, called Musica Sacra. I had joined Musica Sacra when Lou Hooker retired, and the Schola Cantorum group disbanded. Musica Sacra was a prominent group in this area and I felt very privileged to sing with them. There were a few occasions when I sang duet with one of the ladies, but that was rare.

Of all the concerts that I took part in, there were two that were really special for me, both of which were performed before a paying audience. The first was in 1989, when I was singing in the Rutgers Musica Sacra group. At that time our leader was a well-known conductor, Richard Westenberg, who came out from New York City once a week to take our rehearsals. One evening he announced that for our next concert we would be performing the Mass by Dave Brubeck, and that Dave Brubeck himself would conduct. You can imagine how thrilled and honored we all were, and we practised like mad. The Brubeck performance and rehearsals gave us all an opportunity to meet Dave Brubeck in person.

When I shook him by the hand, I realized that this was the first time in my life that I had met a truly world-famous person.

The second memorable concert took place in Carnegie Hall, New York City, in February 1992. This was a performance of Bach's St Matthew Passion, also conducted by Richard Westenberg. I sang in the tenor chorus with great success in both of these concerts. However, at the Carnegie Hall concert, there was one slight hitch. The St Matthew Passion is very, very long (over three hours), and I found out afterwards that my very good friend, Fred Boden, who had made a special trip into the city together with Evie, and his future wife Rosemary, had slept through about three quarters of it. Only afterwards did he confess that he didn't really like classical music all that much, especially choral music. He had only come to see me sing in one of the most famous concert halls in the world.

I realized at the time that I was quite possibly unique in one way, in that I was probably the only former boilermaker to take part in both of these performances for paying audiences. I wonder how many boilermakers, present or former, can match this? None, I bet.

♪

We continued to live in the same old house on Wyckoff Avenue, and year after year we counted our birthdays and anniversaries, birthdays and anniversaries. In 1987, we were due to celebrate our 25th, or Silver wedding anniversary. This was to be a special celebration in more ways than one. First of all, it was a milestone in our marriage. Secondly, and perhaps even more meaningful, it was going to be the fulfilment of a vow that we had made in 1962 to the Rollinsons. As we were about to embark on our voyage to South Africa, we promised Rollo and Eileen that wherever in the world we might be we would make every attempt to celebrate our Silver wedding anniversaries together.

Evie and I always assumed that we would go to England on a visit sometime during 1987 to celebrate this special anniversary. The Rollinsons had also been married in 1962, in the October, so the two couples would be celebrating their Silver anniversaries in the same year. When Rollo and Eileen had driven us to Southampton to catch the boat to South Africa, we were all very sad to be parted, especially Rollo and I. He was my best friend, and neither of us knew when we would see each other again. Evie and I were going to start a new life in a new country, and we didn't know when we would be able to go back to England to see our family and friends. We didn't have much money, nor did Rollo, so we knew we couldn't just take a trip when we wanted to. This was when we made the promise to meet up again in twenty-five years. Little did we know that at that time we would be living in America.

As it turned out, we had actually seen Rollo and Eileen a few times during the years on trips back to England, such as when we had taken Anne there to be christened in 1967, and on our way to live in the States in 1969. As we approached 1987, the year of our 25th anniversary, we started thinking about taking a trip to England so that we could be with Rollo and Eileen. When we mentioned it to them, we were pleased to hear that they wanted to come *here*. They told us that they had always wanted to visit America, and would come for our anniversaries. When we asked them if there was anything special that they wanted to do or see here, they said that they would leave it up to us. As they would have to spend quite a bit of money on airfares, we decided to do something within driving range to keep expenses down. We decided to show them the beautifully restored colonial village of Williamsburg, in Virginia, which we had seen some years before. We would then stop for a couple of days in Washington D.C., on our way back, to show them the capital. We suggested that they come after the heat and humidity of the summer, so we planned the trip for September, after all the children had returned to school.

Young Rollo and Eileen flew over from England to join us for a few days in our house, and then we all drove together down to Williamsburg. We learned a lot of history about the early days of the settlers. On one of our tours, our guide, a young woman of about twenty-three, was leading our group of about thirty tourists into the original Legislative Chamber where the colonial law makers once met. She wanted to demonstrate how they were chosen. She asked us all to stand and follow her instructions. First, she asked all the women to sit down. Then, anyone who was not an Episcopalian (Anglican) was asked to sit down. Then, anyone who was not British, sat down. After all the shuffling and commotion had died down, we discovered that only Rollo and I were left standing. Poor old Rollo was really nervous to be on show like that; he hated having attention drawn to him. What the guide was trying to demonstrate was that if we had come over here a couple of hundred years earlier, we would have been the only two out of that whole group eligible to govern.

It turned out that Rollo and Eileen enjoyed their visit to America so much that they decided to try and come again three years later. So it was that in 1990, we – or rather Evie – arranged a holiday for the four of us. We drove to Niagara Falls in Canada, sleeping each night at a different bed and breakfast. Once again we had suggested that the Rollinsons come in September, not only to miss the heat of the summer, but also the crowds of families with young children.

Evie and I had heard that New York State was very beautiful, with large tracts of forests, many lakes and rivers, and some spectacular scenery. We decided to travel off the main highways in order to see some of this scenery. Evie did a lot of research and found some b&b's for us, each of which would give us a comfortable day's driving, and would still give us time to explore the surrounding countryside. We had different people looking after us every day, and, of course, daily, we had a different adventure. On the first day of our trip, we were a little early for our b&b, as we had been told not to arrive before 3pm, as the couple who ran the b&b both worked as teachers, and no one would be at the house. After we had stopped for lunch, and checked our map, we realised that we still had two hours to kill before we could show up at the b&b, and we were only about twenty minutes away from it. We were just wondering what to do when we passed a sign on the side of the road that said 'Museum'. Evie said, "Hey, let's go and take a look. We've got some time to spare, and this will give us something to do." So, we decided to take a look.

When we drove in, we discovered that this Museum was actually a small, rather shabby, cluster of wooden huts, trying desperately to pass itself off as a replica of Williamsburg. There were a dozen or so small buildings meant to show how the colonials had lived in the 1700s. We wandered around the place and amused ourselves for a while. We poked our heads into one or two of these buildings, and in one of them, there was a woman, dressed in the clothes of the 1700's, who almost pounced on us as we walked in, and told us quite firmly to "sit"! We didn't quite know what she was up to. We thought maybe she was waiting for some more people to come in, and then she would give us a tour of the building. Little did we know that we were in for a thirty-minute lecture! She proceeded to tell us, in minute detail, all about the building we were in – every plank of wood, every nail driven into the walls, the uses of every cooking utensil – until our eyes began to glaze over.

She then started talking about all the exhibits on show in the whole complex, and how old they were. She said she would be happy to answer all our questions and show us how people lived and worked in previous centuries and "Oh, you come from England, welcome to the USA..." Whew. We could not stop her from talking.

We suddenly realized that we were practically being held captive, and we decided it was time to go. We stood up and made for the little door, mumbling something about having to go to the toilet. Well, she wanted none of that. "But you haven't seen the upstairs yet," she said with a smile. We just ran! "Cor Blimey," said Rollo as we drove away. "If that is what museums are like, please don't take me to any more." It became a standard joke among the four of us – Evie and I would teasingly point out any museum that we saw, and Rollo would wince. Forever after that, he always went out of his way to dodge museums if possible!

Once again we had a wonderful vacation with them, and once again they said that they wanted to come back for another holiday three years later. However, it actually turned out that they came in 1994, a year later than planned, as it was the year Steve and Kris got married. Right after the wedding, the four of us went down to Disney World in Florida, and had a great time.

We arranged to meet together again in 1997, and take a trip to Boston, Mass. This trip, unfortunately, had to be postponed when Rollo's car broke down and he had to replace it, using up most of the money he had saved for his holiday in America. However, as we had already booked the hotel, Evie and I took the trip anyway by ourselves. As a joke, we went out of our way to find every single museum in and around Boston – and there were dozens of them! We took photos of every building that had the word 'museum' on it and compiled a booklet of these photos. We sent this to Rollo, telling him that that was what he would have to look forward to seeing when he came the next year! We all did the Boston trip in 1998, parking my car in the parking lot of our b&b and taking the local underground to the tourist spots. We showed Young Rollo how diligently we had picked out all the museums for him. As Evie reminded him, "We all know how much you love museums!"

♪

Sadly, Evie lost both parents in a short span of time. Elfy died on February 12th 1990, and Harold died on December 1st 1991. Elfy had left South Africa for good at the end of 1986 and settled into a beautiful retirement home in Sarasota, Florida. Harold, after leaving South Plainfield in 1978, had also settled permanently in Sarasota in a comfortable retirement home, which happened to be quite near to the one that Elfy eventually moved into. Florida was, and still is, a haven for elderly people. The weather is hot in summer, and mostly warm in winter; there are also certain tax advantages, and for older people, that's enough to make Florida desirable.

Even though Elfy and Harold had been divorced for many years, they had always regarded each other with respect. After all, they had two daughters and two grandchildren in common. Whenever Elfy visited us here in America, she and Harold saw each other and were on friendly terms. When Elfy moved to Sarasota, Harold offered to drive her around, as both Evie and Trixie felt that Elfy should not try and drive on the wrong side of the road, especially as her eyesight was not too good. This was certainly a great help to Elfy because when she first moved to the retirement home, she had to buy furniture and other things, and she also occasionally needed to be driven to doctors.

One day, in March 1989, after Harold had taken Elfy to her doctor's appointment, she invited him to lunch. When they were sitting at the table, Elfy asked Harold if he knew what day it was. He answered "No". Elfy told him that if they had still been married, that day would have been their 50th wedding anniversary. When Elfy later told us about that, we felt that it was really ironic and quite sad. Here were two people who had been divorced for over forty years, but had lived to see their Golden wedding anniversary, while there were so many other couples who had been happily married, but where one of the partners had not lived to see this day in their marriage.

Elfy had for many years expressed a desire to be cremated upon her death with the ashes placed in an urn in the family grave in Pitten, near Vienna in Austria. Evie and Trixie took time out to satisfy this wish. They took the urn containing Elfy's ashes to Pitten, and placed it, along with others of her family, in the family grave. There it still lies. Evie's father, too, had wanted to be cremated, but his request was to have his ashes scattered in the sea, just beyond Sarasota in the Gulf of Mexico. He had come to love this town, so had made arrangements with a company that took care of this sort of thing.

♫

In 1983, my Dad had died at the age of seventy-seven, far too young in my opinion especially as I now, nearly seventy-three at the time of writing, consider *my* age creeping up slowly but surely. I had lived away from my Mum and Dad for many years, but I still felt an intense sadness at his passing. I was glad that Evie and I had taken the opportunity to take Anne and Steve to London to celebrate Mum and Dad's Golden Anniversary four years' earlier.

The year 1996 was especially tough for the Goodwin family, when my mother died at eighty-seven, and my sister Gladys died at the age of sixty-five. Mum had always been the rock of the family, for as long as I can remember. She was a tower of strength not only during the war years, but before that too, when she had to struggle with virtually no money. It was a sad day when I got the news from Carol that she had died.

This now leaves only me, the oldest of the four Goodwin children, and Carol, the youngest, in this particular branch of the family.

♫

One of the highlights of the last decade of the 20th century was that Evie reached the magnificent age of fifty, in 1991. She took it very well in spite of the fact that she thought about it a lot. We thought it a good idea to get the four Goodwins (Evie, me, Anne, and Steve) together to celebrate the birthday. It was not always easy to get all of us in the same place at the same time. As Anne was already living in London, we thought that it made sense to celebrate the birthday there. We wanted to go to England to visit Anne anyway, and to see my mother, my sisters and friends, so we decided to give Steve a plane ticket to London so that we could all be there together. When Ron and Eileen heard that we were going to be there for Evie's birthday, they immediately offered to hold a big birthday party, right on the day, as that year Evie's birthday fell on a Saturday. Saturday night is always a good night for a bit of a booze-up!

During this trip, Evie and I paid a visit to Scotland to a small town called Broughty Ferry near Dundee, to say hello to my old buddy Andy Robertson whom I had worked with at Fraser & Fraser in London. Andy lived alone since his wife's death, but made us welcome promising, "A fine Sco' ish breakfast while ye stay in my hoose". This turned out to be porridge boiled the night before with added salt. With the boiling, the porridge became quite hard. Evie, predictably, opted for toast and honey! While we visited with Andy, we did lots of sightseeing, including visiting the famous St Andrew's golf course. I enjoyed sitting in the evening with Andy reminiscing over all the good times we had had so many years before, when Andy had worked in London.

We had only been back in London for a few days when Steve was due to arrive. At twenty-two, this was the first plane trip that he had ever made on his own. He had come with us on visits to South Africa and London before, but had never flown on his own. I don't know whether *we* were more nervous, or he was! On the day that he was due to fly in, early in the morning, Anne and I were going to meet him at Gatwick Airport. We took the underground there, and we were shocked to see so many police officers, strolling back and forth and all carrying machine guns! This was not the England that I remembered as a boy, and we couldn't figure out what was going on. When we finally found Steve he told us that he had been waiting there for about fifteen minutes and he was very nervous about all the police with their guns. Even in America the police don't patrol the airports with guns. I told Steve that they must be worried about an IRA attack. Wrong! There was a soccer crowd who could riot if their team lost. The stakes were high. This match was a Cup Final, which was to take place later that day, Evie's birthday. The Cup Final in soccer is like the World Series baseball final or the Super Bowl in American football. The only difference is that, believe it or not, the British soccer fans can get really nasty, whereas the Americans are more laid back, and even though they may shout and holler a bit at their teams, they rarely throw things or get into fights. I think the British soccer fans have a very bad reputation all over the world.

We had a wonderful time with Steve, introducing him to Kew Gardens, Oxford, and the English countryside via a bus trip. He was fascinated with the gargoyles that were attached to the centuries-old buildings all over Oxford. Each gargoyle was carved from stone, and we had a lot of fun climbing the stairways to get to the top and the sides of the buildings where these gargoyle carvings were fixed. All in all we had a terrific time together. This was a special occasion, and I know that Evie was very glad to have her two chicks by her side, if only for a short period of time.

♪

From the time I first arrived in the United States on August 17th 1969, until I became a citizen on September 30th 1993, I was a resident alien and holder of a Green Card. For those twenty-four years I was allowed to live and work in the US with all privileges except voting. I kept my British passport of course and continued as a British subject until I decided to become a US citizen. I remember when I first came here I wouldn't have been able to hold both British and American citizenships, and there was no way that I would have given up the Union Jack, so to speak.

However, at some time the law changed, and some of my British friends here took US citizenship, assuring me that they were still able to hold on to their British passports. Being a bit of a doubting Thomas, (Evie always says that my mother named me well), I put off taking the plunge, but eventually I was persuaded that I wouldn't have to give up my British passport, so I applied for citizenship. Steve decided to apply also, so that we could both take the oath at the same time. By this time, Anne was living in England, so she was no longer eligible to apply.

On September 30th 1993, I took the Oath of Allegiance to the United States of America, and became an American citizen. I have a little memento of the occasion on my desk, given to me by Evie in the form of a knife-shaped letter opener. It's solid brass and stamped with my initials and with the date I became a citizen. Unfortunately, it gets used less and less as the mail gets more and more sophisticated, but I keep it just to look at and touch. I regard myself now as American even though I don't sound like it. I still occasionally get a request to "say that again", as my funny accent is still there.

♪

There are many golf clubs in New Jersey, scattered all over the state. We in Elling Brothers took advantage of this fact, and played as much as possible while the weather permitted. Most times we played on Saturdays and Sundays – Norman Neilson, Harold Straub, Bob Vecchio, and other fellows who could find the time – but occasionally we played on company time. This amounted to taking a day off, and these days were very welcome and usually a Friday. On these days, we sometimes played against other companies and groups that had connections with mechanical trades. Some of these were local and were remembered from previous golf tournaments.

I remember one day when our tournament was due to be played at a very exclusive club, the Baltusrol Golf Club. This is a very exclusive club. The Elling Brothers contingent arrived early, giving us time to check out the facilities. All the staff from Elling had been invited to what amounted to breakfast, lunch, drinks and dinner, along with at least eighteen holes of the finest golf you could find anywhere. We sauntered past the practice-putting field, on our way to the dining room and bar, when we heard a cry from Norman: "Where is Dorothy?" Several of the fellows had seen her drive into the club, but nobody had seen her in the club house. Harold said, "Don't worry about her, she'll find her way". Bob Vecchio, who regarded himself as being in charge because he was department head at the time, said we ought to try to find her.

I volunteered to go, and set off at a slow jog trot around the various buildings. After a fifteen-minute hunt I found her leaning against a sign that said 'No Entry For Women, Men Only'. "Help," she called when she saw me, "I can't get through. The whole place is filled with half-naked men, and the club officials won't let me in." Well, there was no problem when we explained to the club officials; Dorothy had taken a wrong corridor and had finished up in the middle of the men's changing area.

"This doesn't mean no women allowed anywhere," I told her. "The sign was meant to show the extent of the men's/women's changing areas." Poor Dorothy. Not only was she the only woman in the Elling Brothers group, but she was the only woman in the whole of the golf club!

Apart from that little mix up with Dorothy Banker and the changing rooms, the day went well. Baltusrol was one of the better courses that we were privileged to play on, but there were many others that we were treated to by the company. One little incident comes to mind that I find quite amusing. We had played against another mechanical engineering firm all day, and at the dinner that evening, the Chairman handed out various prizes to the players. One was for the best (ie lowest) score, one for the person who had hit the most birdies, one for the person who had hit a 'hole in one', and so on. After covering all the categories, the Chairman still had one prize to hand out, so after thinking for a minute, he asked, "Who had the *highest,* (ie worst) score?" Well, guess who *that* was. You're right – yours truly! It takes a lot more than the worst score in golf to upset me, so without embarrassment, I walked up to the podium and took my prize – a beautiful cashmere sweater that I still wear. It is a nice memento of those days playing golf.

♪

The period at Elling Brothers was the longest time I ever spent at one company. The years spent working there spanned from February 1980 till January 1992. My job had become ho-hum almost to the point of being boring, but at least it helped pay the rent. At one time I was even invited to teach as an adjunct professor. The subject was 'Estimating for Mechanical Engineers' and I was recommended by Clifford Elling to teach at Fairleigh Dickenson University. In spite of my nervousness I did very well with the class, teaching half a dozen sessions. In fact, many years later, just after I had retired, I was again asked to teach at a local college, but this time I would have needed to show proof of an engineering degree, so that project fell through.

I enjoyed working at Elling Brothers, and had no intention of leaving before my time to retire had come. However, I was in for a rude awakening one Friday at the end of January 1992, when my boss came in and told me that I, together with my immediate supervisor and two other employees, was being made redundant. Although this was a huge shock, it was not altogether unexpected. The country had been in a severe recession for a couple of years, and Elling Bros, like many other engineering firms, had been laying off employees for many months. Being the bighead that I was, I was sure that *I* would not be laid off!

Here I was, sixty-two years old, with no job. And believe it or not, that very day Evie had given in her notice at her part-time job because she was not very happy there. I was already at home when she got in from work, and at first she thought that the reason I was home so early was because I had had to deliver some drawings to a company near our house. I often did that, and then came straight home instead of going all the way back to the office, especially late on a Friday afternoon. When I told her that I had lost my job, she almost fainted. She immediately called her boss, and asked if she could withdraw her resignation, and he said yes. So at least we would have a little bit of money coming into the kitty.

I had, of course, to find myself another job after being laid off from Elling Brothers. Evie and I were in a real panic, as we still had a mortgage on the house, all the other bills to pay, and, as there is no national health system in this country, we had to pay for our own health insurance. The latter took all of Evie's income, so that meant we had nothing coming in for food or anything else. I needed a job in a hurry. But who was going to employ a sixty-two-year-old during a recession? I started making phone calls to anyone I could think of on the first Monday after being laid off. I rushed down to Radio Shack, our local electronics store, and quickly bought an answering machine, the first one that we'd ever had or used. Now I wouldn't have to sit by the telephone all day waiting for someone to call me back.

I soon discovered that I was not the only engineering designer or estimator looking for a job. Everyone was looking for a job. I tried to lean on fellows who I thought would be certain to help but there were no vacancies. I resigned myself to having to open a portion of my pension and use some of it. However, once again the Goodwin luck kicked in. Word had gotten around that Tom Goodwin was no longer with Elling Brothers, and was looking for a job. On the Thursday after being let go, I got a call from someone who told me about an opening at a company called Roy Kay. I immediately called them, and set up an interview for the following afternoon. When I walked out of there the next day at around 6pm I had a job. When I told Evie, she couldn't believe it. I had been out of work for exactly one week!

Roy Kay was located in Freehold, NJ, about forty-five minutes from the house. Roy Kay was not only the name of the company; it was also the name of the owner. He knew me from several years before when Roy Kay had done some work for Dick Brady. Oh boy! What a small world we live in. But I was not happy in this job for several reasons, although I was successful in landing two contracts for the company, each one being worth close to a million dollars. That fact alone should have enticed me to stay, but it didn't. My problem, or rather my main problem, had to do with the fact that most of the work originated in New York. Not the NY that you and I know as tourists, which is the island of Manhattan, but the surrounding areas where the industry and commerce and slums are. To do my job efficiently, I would have to come and go through some of the real bad parts of NY. This job gave me a much-needed income, and meanwhile I got to look out for something else. I stayed at Roy Kay for a few months without problems but I noticed that some of the other estimators 'nursed' me in attempts to make me stay. One in particular was Ron Smith.

He and I helped each other by filling in appointments that were necessary in and around Brooklyn. Ron often took care of some of these for me, explaining that, as he was a black guy, he would be able to slip in and out of the bad areas without being noticed. This embarrassed me but, as Ron predicted, "If you go out into that concrete jungle looking like that, you won't last a day. You won't even be able to find a safe parking spot!"

After I had been working at Roy Kay for about three months, I got an unexpected phone call. It was from someone called Ted Whitehouse. Ted was the owner of Somerset Mechanical Contractors of Ringoes, near

Flemington, NJ. He had a reputation for being tough, self-made, wealthy and successful in the mechanical trades. His company was no stranger to me. When I had worked at Dick Brady in the early 1970s, I had worked on a couple of estimates for Ted, on a sub-contract basis. I now wondered why he was calling me; the last time we had met and spoken together was almost twenty years before. He asked if I was the Tom Goodwin working for Roy Kay and I answered yes. He then asked me if I was happy in my work or whether I would like a change. My answer, of course, was "It all depends". He suggested that we get together as soon as possible so that we could interview each other at one sitting. We agreed to meet the following Saturday morning at his office. Evie was very happy at the prospect of me leaving Roy Kay. She knew how unhappy I was there. That night, after the phone call, we talked about my chances late into the night.

I discovered that Ted's office was about thirty-five minutes from my house and an easy ride through the countryside. His house sat on about ninety acres of farmland scattered with woods and gardens. There was a large building with an adjoining barn some distance from the main house. I assumed that this was the office and workstation. I drove to the large building, parked next to two or three cars and made my way in. A young woman greeted me with, "Hello, Tom, nice to see you again." What a coincidence. This young woman had been a parishioner at St Paul's Episcopal Church when I had been singing regularly in the choir, and she had been attending church. This was the last person I expected to see. Kathy Kintner, that was her name. I remembered it in time.

She showed me upstairs into the largest office I had ever been in, and there I found Ted Whitehouse with Bob Fox, the vice-president of the company. The walls of the office were covered with trophies of all kinds of animal heads, mostly deer with huge antlers. I couldn't help gaping at this show of a hunter's prowess, which caused him to smile. "I hunted and shot all these animals on my land," he said. "Every animal tells a story. I won't bore you today with animal stories, let's start with interviews."

Ted asked me if I had any questions about the company. I did have a question, but it wasn't about Somerset Mechanical. I was curious to know how Ted knew that I wasn't working for Elling Brothers any more, and Ted told me he had found out from Hank Flower, of all people. Hank, as you may remember, was a director of Elling Bros, and he had told Ted that if Ted was looking for someone to work for him, he couldn't do better than hire Tom Goodwin. That was a feather in my cap, after the terrible blow of being let go by Elling. Then it was Ted's turn. He started off by stating bluntly what he required of me and where each person in the company stood. He said my job would be to find suitable contracts that were out for bid and figure out how much it would cost for us to build them. Then I would work closely with Bob Fox to negotiate the price if necessary. Bob would deal with the owner and supervise the progress of the job. Kathy would take care of all correspondence, the fine print on contracts, and all billing and wages. Ted would contact various unions and be responsible for hiring the right number of tradesmen at the correct rate of pay. He would also be responsible for the mark-up of any and all jobs along with the right to cancel anything. "After all," he said, "I am the boss."

There was a set of drawings lying on Ted's desk. "Let's pretend this is a job to bid," he said. "How would you go about bidding it?" I pretended to be a teacher and carefully explained how I would go about preparing the bid. I could see from their questions that they were impressed with what I had to say about mechanical construction. One item not covered was a computer.

"Who takes care of that?" I asked.

Ted and Bob immediately disclaimed having anything to do with computers. "I tried to turn one on once," said Ted! They both hastened to assure me that I would be put on a computer course in Orlando, Florida, to bring me up to speed with their equipment.

At this point, clearing his throat and nodding his head, Bob said, "Yes!".

Ted, reaching out his arm, shook my hand and said, "Salary will be same as Roy Kay plus ten per cent. Medical benefits paid for." Kathy, who had been taking notes, now asked if she should make arrangements for the computer course. "All right," said Ted, "take care of it. Return air ticket, hotel for a week, computer course for a week. Oh, and $100 expenses." As an afterthought he said, "Why not take your wife along and regard the trip as a mini-vacation?" Well, I was absolutely staggered. I could not believe my good fortune in finding an employer like this. He gave the impression of doing things right no matter what the cost. I reckon this was one of the best Saturdays I ever spent. Both Ted and Bob Fox were the friendliest people I had met for a long time.

When I told Evie about our proposed trip to Orlando she immediately started thinking about what clothes to wear and what things to pack. We got through that and had ourselves a very happy holiday. The computer school was right across the street from our hotel and also close to the shops for Evie. We did some sight-seeing including visiting Sea World, Disney World and the Epcot Center.

When I explained who did what at Somerset Mechanical to Evie, she was surprised at how small the company was. There was me, Ted, Bob, Kathy, and an outside man, who I believe was called John. If we needed any more help, we hired them by the day. I was now working in a situation where everyone was on trust, and no one felt junior to any others. Many times I would find myself alone in the office. I would arrive in the morning to find a note from Kathy telling me that she would be in one place, and Ted and Bob somewhere else. This sometimes left me alone until lunchtime. If I needed some particular help, such as finding a phone number, then I'd had it. I should have asked the question the night before. The environment was terrific, with every window showing a view that would be fantastic under any circumstance. This was just an office, and Ted was justifiably proud of what he had built and created. The house Ted lived in was built around the late 1700s, with Ted and his father building the office, barn and workstation later.

Lots of New Jersey townships have formed what they call Historical Societies in order to protect certain buildings and houses dating from the 18th and 19th centuries. Even if you are the owner, if you have a house deemed to be 'historical', you have to get approval from the Historical Society before any changes can be made. This tends to work most of the time, but occasionally the society goes overboard. Then it's called the Hysterical Society!

Ted Whitehouse's house was on the historical register, and it had a very interesting feature. In the kitchen there was a hidden trapdoor in the floor, just large enough for a man to crawl through. The original owners had made this trapdoor for slaves escaping from the South. It led to a cellar underneath the house, and was instrumental in helping escaping slaves make their way from the Southern States to the Northern States during the Civil War. The secret trapdoor still exists and of course it is never used now, but it's interesting from a historical viewpoint.

The three and a half years that I spent working for Ted Whitehouse were the last and, in some cases the best, of my working life. The reason for this was that there was no pressure; Ted was a very laid-back person even when work was scarce. The first person in the office each day made coffee and picked up the phone messages from the night before. This set us up for the day. At first, we were busy bidding successfully for several local jobs at the Hunterdon Medical Center, Carter Wallace, and the BASF plant. However, as time went by, work became difficult to get. It was around 1994 that Ted began thinking of selling his business. Not the house and property, just Somerset Mechanical.

This year, 1994, was the year I was going to turn sixty-five, which was the usual retirement age. When Ted asked me, when I first started working for him in 1992, whether I would be retiring on my sixty-fifth birthday, I had said no, because I had felt that I would like to work as long as possible. However, now in 1994, with there being less and less to do in the office, Ted came up with the suggestion that I might like to work only when there was a job to do. I would be paid on an hourly basis, and would thus be able to sort of 'ease' myself into retirement. This sounded like a wonderful idea, and it would kill two birds with one stone, so to speak. I would still be earning money, but would not be working a full forty-hour week, unless there was a really urgent job to finish. In the meantime, Ted was going to put out some feelers to see whether anyone was interested in buying his company.

We called this 'easing into retirement' and Ted had some words of advice regarding retirement. "When married men decide to retire," he said, "their two main problems become flowers and colors". Ted warned me to not give any opinions regarding the suitability of any flower or color if asked. The safest plan is to mumble, "Yes, dear," or, even better, simply gaze at the sky.

I postponed retirement, but developed the habit of taking Mondays and Fridays off each week. Ted found a buyer for his business in Parsippany in the summer of 1995. One of the conditions of sale was that Ted would guarantee to put in a set number of hours for this company for two years. This was a kind of 'settling in' period. The buyer was also keen to get *me* on his payroll, but by now I had had enough. The drive from Piscataway to Parsippany (northern New Jersey) was more than I wanted to make. My last job finished in October 1995. My first job had been in August 1943 as a rivet boy holder-up. My working life had spanned fifty-two years continuously. Now I had to take note of the colors of the curtains, and the flowers!

Never mind the colors. What about tomorrow? For over fifty years I'd been going through a daily ritual. Get up, shave, and go to work, always working out how many working days until the next long weekend, and complaining that vacations were not long enough. Well, now I had one long enough. Finally. When I started work in Fraser's boilershop on my birthday in 1943, I felt as if I were doing something worthwhile. However, after working for about ten years in the shop, first as an apprentice, and then as a tradesman boilermaker, I came to the conclusion that I could do better. On looking back and seeing dozens of errors and mistakes being churned out by the drawing office, I knew that I could certainly do no worse. My ambition was to leave the shop and 'step up' to the drawing office. Any drawing office!

After several attempts to get a position as a draftsman, or a trainee draftsman, I eventually realized that I was up against the old English stumbling block of class distinction. People from Europe and USA may not realise that class distinction is alive and well in most parts of England today. People describe themselves, and each other, as middle class, upper class, or working class. I found it was impossible to break out of working class (boiler shop) and into middle class (drawing office).

I know that I could never aspire to upper class, this was reserved for Lord and Lady Muck! The people I applied to knew I was from the working class as soon as I opened my mouth. I couldn't fool an Englishman about my class or breeding or lack of it. The war interrupted my education for five years. When I should have been studying mathematics, or history or English, I was on the evacuation trip, or working on invasion barges. As I'm reviewing my past working life here I can see now some reasons why I have gaps in my general knowledge.

However, I *was* able to break out of the factory in South Africa, so that by the time I moved to America, I was what was considered a 'white collar worker'. I took that three-year engineering course while in Johannesburg, and this stood me in good stead in the United States. And although I never earned a fortune, I was always able to provide for the family, and with the 'Goodwin Luck' I was never out of a job for more than a week. It seems strange now that my working life spanned fifty-two years – the time certainly went by fast.

My one fear when I eventually retired was what would I do with myself all day. I imagined getting up in the morning, having breakfast and reading the paper, and *then what?*! I could see the days stretching endlessly in front of me for the rest of my life, but that is not what happened. Soon after my last contract for Ted Whitehouse, I bought a simple old-fashioned word processor, and letter by letter, started writing this book, something I had wanted to do for many years. I had never learned to type, so it is by the 'hunt and peck' typing method that this has been written. Over the years my speed has improved, and I work on a computer now, but it is still very slow compared to a real typist, like Evie.

And of course, there have been other past-times besides writing, like playing golf with Steve or my old buddy Fred Boden, working in the garden in the summer time, and taking trips to England to visit Anne. And even occasionally sitting and reading a book, which is what Evie always claimed I had longed to do all those years that I was working. She always says, "Go ahead, that's what you have been waiting for – to have the time to read." So, looking back on my working life, I would have to say that it was successful.

♪

You could say that the 1990s were a romantic period filled with weddings. My old buddy Fred married Rosemary. Anne married Dave, and Steve married Kristina. Then there were the Rollinsons' children; both Graham and Jane got married. It seemed like our whole calendar was taken up with weddings. Not that I'm against marriage as an institution. Evie and I are still going great guns after forty years together. Of course, we've had a few ups and downs during this time but most of our problems were due to me missing birthdays or anniversaries. This is unforgivable. Especially missing an anniversary! Every husband should make a big fuss over his wife's birthday and an even bigger fuss over their (not *her*) anniversary. Life would instantly become more pleasant for him. I learned this from personal experience, the hard way.

The story of how Anne met Dave began back in February 1990 when, less than two weeks after Elfy died Anne went to England for an extended visit. She gave up her job in the US and embarked on a period of work and travel in Britain and Continental Europe. Anne was entitled to live and work in the UK; her British passport issued in Johannesburg at her birth was valid and permanent. These two happenings, coming so close together, were traumatic for Evie. Her mother died and her daughter moved to another continent, all in a few short weeks.

After living and working in London for over a year, Anne took a holiday to the Greek island of Paros in August 1991 and while she was there she met David Hall. He was also on holiday. Anne, at that time, was living in Ealing, west London and Dave was from Grove, near Oxford. A few telephone calls were all that were needed to kindle a long distance friendship between them. Anne brought Dave home to the US for the first time during Christmas that year. We wondered at the time, "Is this serious? Is she bringing home a beau?" It was much too early to tell; he was a pleasant young man with a good sense of humor. This was our first meeting with our future son-in-law.

In August 1992 Evie and I went to London for the wedding of Jane, Rollo and Eileen's daughter, to Dave Parry. While we were there Anne told us that she was thinking of coming back to New Jersey later that year for an extended visit. So in the fall of that year, she came home to stay with us, and visit friends on the West Coast in California and Washington. She missed Dave, but wasn't sure where her future would be: in England or in the United States. She tried to find a job here in the US, working for a charitable or 'do good' organization. "If I'm going to work forty hours a week," she concluded, "I might as well do some good in the world." She wanted her time and effort to count for something. The country was coming out of its recession, and jobs were available, but Anne found nothing that was really suitable for her.

Then, just a few days before Christmas, Dave called from England and told her that he had been offered a six-month contract to work in Holland. He would be working for Phillips in Eindhoven, and asked Anne if she wanted to go there with him. By this time Anne had realised just how much she missed him, so she jumped at the opportunity. She immediately called the airline, and changed her return ticket. What excitement! Anne could hardly wait to be with him again. She flew back to England to pack up some more of her belongings, and in the New Year she and Dave started their stint in Holland. In May 1993, on our annual visit to England, we took a side-trip to Eindhoven to visit them in their tiny apartment. We had a wonderful time. As Anne was only doing casual work, she was able to show us around. We visited the charming city of Delft, and also spent a day in Amsterdam, where we visited the Anne Frank Museum (very, very moving), and also the red-light district. Evie had to cover my eyes at times!

1993 was also a very special year for Steve; it was the year that he and Kristina got engaged. While he was working for ABB Kent, in 1990, he met Kristina James. They became good friends right away, paying visits to various places like aquariums and museums. I remember thinking that she was going to be a really good influence on him so long as they stayed together. I suppose there was no fear of them breaking up. After their engagement, they hunted out a beautiful single-storey house in Hightstown, NJ and combining their resources, bought it. Settling into the house proved to be easy for them – after all, Kris had attended school in Hightstown as a youngster and teenager so for her it was like coming home.

Evie and I threw a little dinner-party to mark their engagement, and took lots of photos of the group. We took Kris and Steve singly and together dressed in their best and Steve wearing a tie. Then there were Linda and Carlton, Kris's mom and dad, who were divorced but coming together for the sake of the photo session. We had to get Steve to take Evie and me finishing with various groups and double shots. We bragged about how these photos could last for a hundred years (at least) and show how these two families would undoubtedly grow in the foreseeable future. When Evie tried to take the film out of the camera she couldn't move it so she popped into the camera shop nearby for some help. The camera man glanced at our camera, turned it over and grinned. "Lady," he said "There is no film in this camera." Evie told me later that day that this was her most embarrassing situation ever. Now she had to call everyone and tell them that all the wonderful shots we had taken were made with an empty camera. Evie claimed full responsibility but that wouldn't be fair. We all touched the camera a little during the course of the evening so we were all to blame.

Steve and Kris married on October 8th 1994, and Anne came over to the US to take part in the celebration and to be a bridesmaid. They were married on a beautiful fall day at St David's Church in Cranbury, New Jersey. Kris's father, Carlton James, delivered a wonderful speech at the reception in praise not only of his daughter, but also his new son-in-law, reducing all the guests in the Forsgate Country Club first to tears and then to laughter and merriment. Kristina looked absolutely beautiful, and we could see that Steve was very happy. They made a wonderful couple. I just hoped that the photographer hadn't forgotten to put film in *his* camera!

We knew at this time that Anne and Dave were not coming to live in the USA. During our summer visit to England in 1994 to see Anne, she invited Evie and me to the flat that she shared with Dave in Abingdon. She said, "Why don't you come for a few drinks on Friday evening?" Our party consisted of, in addition to Evie and me, Lorna, Dave's mother, and Gerry, Lorna's friend. We were a party of six who were getting to know each other. After a little while, when we were all on our second drink, we noticed that Anne and Dave had slipped out of the room. Then, coming back into the room, and looking decidedly sheepish, Dave and Anne called out, "Surprise". Anne was holding up her left hand and showing an emerald and diamond ring on her engagement finger. There was a deluge of tears and smiles. They were engaged! Then Anne said, "We have another surprise for you!" That was when, I called out, "I don't want to hear about it!" Everyone laughed. Anne told us that she and Dave had bought a house in Abingdon – they had signed the papers the day before. *That* was the second surprise. More hugs and kisses! When we went out to the pub for dinner later we had a wonderful, celebratory meal.

Anne married Dave Hall on July 15th 1995. There was an incredible amount of planning to do and traditionally the mother of the bride organizes a lot of this. Of course, with Evie and me on the other side of the Atlantic it wasn't possible to have us make arrangements; Anne herself planned all the details, the wedding, the bridesmaids and their dresses, the reception and food and drink for the guests. Evie and I helped as much as we could by telephone and with several checks from our bank balance. About a week or so before the wedding we flew over to England to help with any last minute things that needed attention. A few days later Steve and Kris flew in, as they were both in the wedding party. The night before the wedding we took part in a rehearsal and welcomed several of our friends who had come to celebrate with us. There were people from the USA, from the continent, from Scotland, all dressed up in their finery for the wedding of Anne and Dave. About eighty people attended the luncheon reception right after the ceremony, and 120 people took part in the evening dance.

On the morning of the wedding, Anne and Dave's house was buzzing with activity and with last-minute arrangements and touches. Anne and I were the last two to be waiting for the hired car to take us to the church. Some neighbors, seeing Anne and me at her doorway, started cheering and wishing her 'good luck'. Needless to say, Anne looked absolutely stunning in her simple cream wedding dress. She had used some of the silk flowers from Evie's wedding veil in her own veil. All of a sudden, Anne burst into tears. It was just too much for her. I didn't know what to say or do. Anne, most likely understanding why she would cry on a happy day like this, said something that sounded like 'kitchen' and 'brandy'! With Anne sniffing and weeping slightly, we made our way to the kitchen where I poured two stiff brandies and Anne repaired her make up. We went back to the street door where she faced the picture-taking neighbors with smiles of happiness.

Our car came and we got to the church with a little time to spare. Music was emanating from the church organ. Anne by now had recovered her composure. Then I heard a couple of bum notes from the organ! I remembered that during the rehearsal, the organist had shown a tendency to doze off half way through the proceedings. As he dozed more and more, so his head drooped more and more, until his ear played a couple of notes that did not belong. That apparently woke him up because his head jerked up cutting off the bad notes. At that point he started to droop again setting off the same bad notes. This went on like a stuck gramophone record until he suddenly burst, with a flourish, into 'Here Comes the Bride'. He could play, and play well. Maybe the fact that we was about ninety years old had something to do with his performance.

The music played at Anne's wedding reception was mostly the standard modern stuff that all the youngsters go crazy over nowadays. Very few polkas or two steps, and even fewer waltzes. "C'mon Dad," cried Anne, "this is 1995, get with it." I got with it to the best of my ability, but I really wanted to do a Strauss waltz with my daughter on her wedding day. To ensure that this would happen, I had made a cassette tape of a couple of the better-known Strauss waltzes ahead of time. Anne and I also took the time to practise the one-two-three time required to dance the waltz. She learned the steps under my guidance and we danced for the longest time at the wedding, spinning and whirling alone on the dance floor. This was one of the high points of my life, but I had to be careful not to fall. I was no spring chicken any more. I was past retirement age and had to behave accordingly.

The wedding celebration continued as if there was no tomorrow, and a good time was had by all. Among the older guests were many of our friends including Rosemary and Fred Boden, Cleone and Ellis Dill, Evie's sister Trixie and her husband Burt, Evie's uncle Henry and his wife Betty, all of whom had flown over from the United States. Andy Robertson (my favourite Scot), the Rollinsons, as well as guests from Dave's side of the family were also there. I was gratified to see that so many of our friends had turned out to take part in this celebration in spite of the cost of plane tickets and hotels.

Rollo and I had each had a son and a daughter, and so far three of our four offspring had married. The last of the four children was Graham, Rollo's son, and in 1998 he and Marie Murphy were married in a civil ceremony in a hotel in London, with a very nice reception to follow. On our usual visit to Anne and Dave during 1997, Graham and Marie had taken a day off work to come and visit us in Abingdon, especially to invite us to their wedding. Both Evie and I were very touched by this, and of course we said that we would be there. So, in 1998, we planned our visit to England to coincide with the wedding.

CHAPTER 11

The Retirement Years

1995 – 2000+

AFTER retiring in 1995, I realized that I would be able to do anything I liked – within reason, of course, and if I could afford it! One of the things that had been nagging at the back of my mind for forty years was the thought that I had never made the trip to New Zealand that I had wanted to do when I was in my twenties. So when Evie said, "Celebrate your retirement. You've earned it, and you've been talking about going to New Zealand forever," I decided that maybe she might be right. Our friend Rosemary, who had grown up in New Zealand, was planning a trip there with her new husband, Fred Boden, and she suggested that we go with them, so that she could show us around the country. But more about that later. Let me tell you why I had been hankering to go to New Zealand for over forty years.

In the 1950s, I met up with a sheetmetal technician named Garth, who had applied to emigrate to New Zealand. At that time, anyone from Britain who had some sort of trade or profession could emigrate to one of the British Commonwealth countries such as Australia, South Africa, Canada or New Zealand. If they agreed to stay and work for two years at least, their fare would be paid for. Many people emigrated after the war and when Garth told me that he had applied to go, I immediately said that I would like to go with him. We talked about it, and learned that after two years, the immigrant tradesman was free to stay or to return home, owing no money. This sounded like a very good idea, something like a busman's holiday that would last for two years.

I went to New Zealand House and signed up accordingly. I deliberately kept it to myself and didn't tell a soul, just in case I was talked out of it. I knew that there would be a lot of opposition, especially from my family. Wouldn't you know, a woman who lived on Braintree Street worked for New Zealand House and the first thing she did was accost my mother: "Did you know your Tommy is emigrating to New Zealand?" With my secret out in the open, I found it difficult to survive the onslaught that erupted, especially from Mum. To keep the peace, I cancelled my application and stayed in England. As it turned out, Garth came back two years later, married his previous girlfriend, and as far as I know still lives in England.

So here I now was, forty years later with the opportunity to go to New Zealand with Evie and some good friends. How could I resist? I started looking at the maps and reading up about the country in the encyclopaedia. I discovered that New Zealand and the British Isles were approximately the same size, with about the same number of people, all English-speaking, of course. It was going to cost more than we wanted to spend, but we budgeted to suit and found the trip to be do-able. Our friend Rosemary had grown up in New Zealand and as a young woman had travelled extensively around both the North and South Islands. Who better than she to show us all the sights? At the time, her husband Fred was still working as an engineer at Castrol. Rosemary, too, was still working, but they both arranged to have the time off, and we made our plans to leave on December 21st 1996, for approximately three weeks.

I met Fred in 1989, after giving a performance with the Cantabile Chamber Chorale. He was a friend of one of the singers from the Chorale, and he had come to listen to our concert. After the concert, we were all invited to our friends Kathleen and Alan Appleby's house for a post-concert celebration. At that time, Fred was new to the area, having just moved from Louisiana to work at Castrol here in Piscataway. He had recently been widowed. Evie and I got to talking to him, recognizing a fellow Brit. He was originally from the north country of England. It was at that same party that he met our friend Rosemary, who had also come to the concert, and who he would later marry.

We discussed the various routes available to us and started to book tickets for our trip to New Zealand. Besides the four of us, Rosemary's daughter, Catherine, who was in her early 20s, was to come with us as well. There would be no friction or problems of any kind with Fred in the group. Fred and I were really good friends. He and I often played bridge partners against Evie and Rosemary and even though our bridge was atrocious we managed to hold our own against the ladies. Fred was quite a character, with an immense capacity for remembering old-fashioned English songs and poems. He and I thought nothing of breaking out into song suddenly, at the bridge table, with songs such as 'Showing Young Maidens the Way' (Fred's favorite, which he would sing with a lecherous voice), or 'Sam, Sam, Pick up thy Musket'. Or maybe 'Brown Boots' (when everyone wore decent black or mourning suits). Fred knew the words of most of the songs, and I would follow him with all of the music and some of the words.

Anyway, back to our preparations for our trip. Rosemary was a mine of information when we got down to planning our itinerary. As she knew New Zealand well, she was able to suggest many special places and picturesque spots that she thought we might enjoy. She organized all of the bookings of hotels, the rental car, the ferries, the internal flight from the South back to the North Island, right from her computer here in New Jersey. She was an absolute wiz on the internet! No wonder she was one of the owners of a very successful company – she had a wonderfully organized mind.

Our trip from New Jersey to New Zealand was not quite as uneventful as we had expected. It turned out that Fred had left his green card behind, which was as important as losing his passport. He didn't confess to this until we were well over the Rocky Mountains – and Rosemary would gladly have thrown him out of the plane! However, once we arrived in Los Angeles they were able to contact a friend in New Jersey, who located his card, and it was forwarded to him in New Zealand, so a situation that seemed to be a disaster resolved itself and ended well.

When we arrived in Auckland to start our three week trip, we were made to feel very welcome by Rosemary's family. They had invited us to spend Christmas Day with them, as we were not due to leave for our tour of the country until after the holidays. I shared the driving with Rosemary, neither Evie nor Fred being keen on driving on the wrong side of the road. We saw many out of the way and beautiful places that the standard tourist would never find. Rosemary took great delight in finding mountain passes and peaks that she had first seen as a teenager. Many were found on our map and one in particular was marked with a kind of headstone, decorated with a poem carved in the rock. She recognized it instantly and was able to quote what had taken place a couple of centuries ago. We soon learned about the very large population: of sheep of course! The Islands boasted more sheep than people, we discovered.

One of the more memorable occasions for me was spending New Year's Eve in Queenstown in the South Island. It is a beautifully located town on a lake, surrounded by mountains. We had decided to spend the evening in the hotel. We had dinner in one of our rooms, and then Rosemary, Fred, Evie and I played bridge until midnight. I cannot remember what Catherine chose to do. New Year's Eve was celebrated with fireworks over the lake, and the next day, a lone piper played his bagpipes on the edge of the lake, wearing his Scottish kilt, which apparently he did every New Year's Day. I can remember coming down to breakfast on New Year's Day and seeing a row of clocks above the reception desk showing the times in different cities around the world. I was amazed to realise that for us, it was 10am on 1st January 1997, while in New York City, they hadn't even celebrated New Year's Eve yet! Even though I knew why this was so, it still seemed so strange to me. Time isn't always what we think it is.

All too soon, our three week holiday came to a close. We spent our last day in Auckland on our own, as Rosemary, Fred and Catherine left separately to spend a few days in Hawaii. Evie remarked that the center of Auckland reminded her very much of Johannesburg in the late 1950s, and she wondered if we had made a mistake by not moving to New Zealand when we left South Africa in 1969. She liked the rather slow, old-fashioned look and attitudes of the country. However, at the time, we realized that if we had moved to either New Zealand or Australia, we might never have seen my family in England again. We couldn't have known at that time that one day people would be flying all over the world at the drop of a hat. That was one of the forks in the road that we took, and we made our decision, for better or worse – mostly better, I would say.

At the end of the day, we took ourselves to Auckland airport, checking cases, tickets, and passports. It was dark outside, and quiet. We were the only plane waiting on the tarmac. Evie and I held hands tightly as we always do on lift off, and waited. After ten minutes we were still sitting there, and we began to realize that something was wrong. We wanted to go; our arrival time in Los Angeles was scheduled to be only two hours before our plane to New Jersey was due to take off, and we would have to go through customs and immigration and get to another terminal for the plane to Newark. We had better get going soon, we thought, otherwise, when we got to LA our connecting plane would be gone. Oh what a mess that would be! Then, after what seemed like an interminable wait, we heard our pilot. After clearing his throat he said, "We are now ready for take off. We had a slight problem with the fuel lines, but that is now alright." We had a visual image of having slight problems with our fuel lines whilst flying over some thousands of miles of Pacific Ocean. Let me tell you it wasn't pretty!

We arrived safe and sound in LA, but we did miss our connection. The airline gave us a hotel room overnight and we had to wait for the next plane to New Jersey. From that point on everything was all right. Fred, Rosemary, and Catherine, who were not with us on this leg of the journey, had missed all the fun and excitement that we had had. But despite the slight hitch, I think that the trip to New Zealand was probably the most exciting one of my life.

♪

Once we had returned home from New Zealand in January 1997 and recovered from our jet lag, we soon settled into our normal routine. When the warmer weather came, I was able to go outside and start pottering around in the yard. Gardening, believe it or not, can be classified as being a major part of my lifetime activities. When we first moved into 215 Wyckoff Avenue, I could climb the ladder to the roof and survey the whole property. Our house was easily recognizable from the street. That was because of the hedge. The hedge is a beautiful yew that runs the length of the property. The original owner planted it and obviously put some decent soil at the roots because it thrived. We moved into the property in April 1971, so I have been nursing my hedge for about thirty years. I cut and trim twice a year, which means that I have trimmed and fussed with this hedge about sixty times. Spring and fall I do my trimming. I graduated to using an electrical hedge trimmer a long time ago and that's all I use. People walking and jogging past often call out in praise, "How do you make it so straight?" My answer is that it's a boilermaker's secret! There are other hedges in and around the property, but they are less imposing. Nevertheless, I give them just as much time and care as I do the hedge along the street, and this keeps me occupied and happy. Whenever I have nothing to do, and start to bother Evie, she tells me to go and check the hedges, and see if they need trimming. This gets me out of her hair!

When we first moved in to 215, there were two beds of strawberry, one of rhubarb and several grapevines in the back garden that had been planted by the previous owner. Most of the rest of the property was taken over with grass and shrubs. The whole property, measuring 200 feet square had hedges all over the place but very few trees in the back. In fact, the back part of the property looked like a football field, and Evie was not very happy with that. So I started planting seedlings and small trees at regular intervals, and today, more than thirty years later, we are reaping the benefit of the beauty and the shade these trees provide. In fact, sometimes people say the back yard looks like a park, and this, of course, makes me feel quite proud.

One of the best trees in the back is one that almost did not survive. When we first moved in, Evie often cut the grass if I was working long hours during the week. We had bought a ride-on lawnmower from the previous owner, and I taught Evie how to use it. One day I came home from the office to find Evie with a stricken look on her face. She told me that she had a confession to make – whilst riding up and down on the lawnmower, she had left it too late to swerve around one of my newly-planted trees and had ridden right over it and chopped it down to about three inches high. She told me she had actually considered packing a suitcase, in case I told her that I would choose the tree over her! Anyway, I left that little stump in the ground, and just put a fence around it for a few months, and today it is one of the best trees in the garden. Where it was cut off, it grew in two branches, so it is a permanent reminder of which tree it was. We still have a good laugh about that.

I found it very comforting to be able to go traipsing off into my one-acre lot to plant some seeds, trim a bush, sift a few square feet of soil to make a flower garden, and sometimes to hide! From several vantage-points on the roof I was able to see into all four corners of the property, and watch out for things happening that should not be. One of these things, for instance, was the woodpecker that was probably the toughest contender to challenge me regarding ownership of my house. He (or was it she?) came back year after year to try to make a nest, first in some dead wood in a tree close by, and then on a loose board outside the pink (main) bathroom. Each year I won the battle but each spring he/she came back to torment me with hammer blows at 5am.

The carpenter bees, too, caused me many a headache. They came in squadrons, sending out spies on the wing. They were called carpenter bees because they liked to bore into wood, and our house was of wood construction, covered with wooden shingles, which is very common in this part of the country. The carpenter bees were forever trying to make nests in the soft wood trim of my house. At one point, they began to attack people at the front door of the house, and that I couldn't live with. I had to resort to poison. I eventually discovered that changing some of the wood trim on the apex of the house to plastic was something these carpenter bees didn't like. They could not bore into plastic so they simply went away. Eventually, I won the war against most of the pests that appeared from time to time to plague me. I poisoned the ones that tried to get into the house and I had to learn to live with the rest.

I had inherited a small patch of beautifully fertilized soil that had been the previous owner's vegetable garden, so I decided to carry on and plant tomatoes, squash, lettuce, and a few other vegetables. Little did I know what a struggle this would become. First of all, all these delicious, free vegetables attracted the rabbits and the groundhogs, who had a ball. Even turtles came and helped themselves! Then I had to battle Mother Nature – either we had too much rain, and the vegetable patch got flooded and everything rotted, or we didn't have enough rain, and the heat of the sun dried everything up. It turned out that I was working for my family in the office during the day and in my free time I seemed to be working to keep the rabbits and other animals fed.

Evie, too, took a turn at growing things. She loved to have fresh flowers in the house, as we had had in South Africa, so she planted a flower garden at the back. However, she could not stand the humidity during the summer, and found it was too much to keep the flowerbed going, so we eventually just planted evergreen shrubs that took care of themselves. It was in this flowerbed that I planted my 'bicentennial' garden in 1976 for Evie and the children. The red, white and blue flowers came back each spring for quite a few years, but eventually they died out. Now we add color to our garden by putting hanging baskets of impatiens or geraniums in the trees, and putting urns of summer flowers by the front door. This is a job that I leave completely to Evie, as I follow my old boss' advice, and never get involved with flowers or colors. I think that if the Ackeleys were to come back today and see our beautiful property, they would be quite impressed.

♪

One of the promises I made to myself while I was still working had to do with making music. Or, rather, trying to make music! I could already play the piano on the black notes (in the key of F sharp) but that was like cheating. I wanted to play. Properly. As if I knew what I was doing. To this end, I engaged Barbara Rogers to give me weekly lessons on the piano as I now had the spare time. Barbara was accompanist to the Cantabile Chorale where I was singing so it was almost like belonging to a large family.

Barbara gave me lessons from September 1995 until September 1999. But she and her family then moved out of state relocating the source of the lessons and (as it turned out) stopping my foray into music. This effectively cut off any thoughts I might have had about one day being able to really play. However, I had found it very difficult to retain the details of the lessons. Five, six or seven-year-olds are able to make their fingers and thumbs dance up and down the keyboard with their eyes shut. This nearly 70-year-old, however, could not make the magic flow at all. I had left it too late. I should have had some lessons in 1939; instead I was evacuated to Oxford due to the war. However, some of the expertise Barbara taught me still lives in my mind and I run through various exercises just for fun.

At different times in my life, I have played not only the piano, but also the violin, which I taught myself, although I play very, very poorly. I also played the mouth-organ, and at one time the piano accordion. Unfortunately my piano accordion disappeared while I was doing my National Service, and I never replaced it. I have always had a love of music and making music, and it was our mutual love of classical music that helped bring Evie and me together. We still enjoy going to concerts today.

Some time during the 1990s I received a phone call from Bill Wagner, the brother-in-law of a friend of Evie's. Bill was a member of a church choir, was singing bass, and was not doing too well at it. He needed help from someone who could guide him into the correct notes. He was prepared to pay me for this help. How much would I charge? I explained to him that I wasn't a music teacher, so there would be no fee. I sang in a chorus for pleasure just as he did. If he cared to come to my house the following Thursday evening, bringing his choir music with him, I would be happy to review it and help him in any way I could. This turned out to be a long-term relationship, which began with us analyzing relatively simple hymns and Christmas carols and graduated to pieces like Handel's Messiah, and that tough old nut, Brahms Requiem.

Many of Bill's original problems I believe were due to a lack of confidence in himself. Even though his singing has improved dramatically, we still get together most Thursdays to dig into the current piece of music that he is working on. Evie always serves us coffee and cake when Bill first arrives, and as a token of thanks, Bill gives us an enormous hamper of goodies at Christmas, as well as a very special bottle of Scotch for me.

♪

Very close friends, for me, have never been plentiful. At the age of ten I lost track of the people around me when I was evacuated to Oxford. Then, after a very short time, my new friends in Oxford disappeared, and I was presented with a new group of friends in London. Later, when I emigrated to South Africa, and later still to the US, the penny dropped. Friends are few and far between and should be looked after accordingly. There are friends of mine, like Rollo, who go back almost sixty years. I also made a life-long friend of Austin Horn, whom I met in Johannesburg in 1962. More recently, I had a good friend whom I unfortunately only knew for a short while – about ten years. His name was Fred Boden, with whom we travelled to New Zealand.

Fred and I became great friends in a very short time, and after Fred retired we spent a lot of our free time on the golf course, trying to play golf, but actually only improving our swearing! In 1998, he was stricken with cancer, which he fought tooth and nail, but sadly he died from it on October 10th 1999. Many people gathered in Rosemary's house to pay their respects to Fred. Rosemary asked me to deliver one of the eulogies, which I did. Several other people also spoke, sharing anecdotes and stories concerning Fred. It was a very, very sad day. My friend was irrevocably and finally gone. I had to try to remember how it had been with him, and not dwell too much on how it would be without him.

♪

One of my lesser interests was playing the card game bridge. I must admit that although I liked the game up to a point, I really only persevered with it because Evie liked it. It was an activity that we could do together with another couple and have a nice social evening. Usually the other fellow and I would have a couple of Scotches, and this of course would affect my game, for the worse unfortunately. However, most of our friends didn't take the game too seriously, so we would have a good time.

In all the years that I have been playing bridge – and that is almost thirty years – only two or three games really stand out in my mind, probably because I was on the winning end for a change. One of these games took place about twenty-five years ago, when we played with Evie's old high school friend June and her first husband Jay. We had a rule that husbands and wives did not play as partners, so whatever silly thing one of them did, the other one couldn't yell at them. This way there were no divorces! So I always played with the other husband, and Evie with the other wife.

One evening June and Jay came over to our house, and on one hand Jay opened one diamond. I looked at my hand, and bid five diamonds! Jay almost fell off his chair. (For anyone not familiar with bridge, this was a huge jump in bidding, and a pretty ridiculous bid to make). As he had to play the hand, I had to put *my* cards on the table (I was now the 'dummy'), and as soon as he saw my cards, he started ranting and raving and saying, "How could you bid five diamonds? I'll never make this hand," and on and on he went.

I got up and went to look at his cards, and I said, "Move over and let me play the hand. I'll make it."

Jay said, "Right, if you can make five diamonds, I'll buy you dinner." Well, needless to say, I made it. How, I'll never know. Jay kept his word, and a few weeks later he and June took us to a very smart restaurant in Princeton for a slap-up meal.

One other moment of glory at the bridge table comes to mind, and I think this is one that Evie will also never forget, as she was on the losing end. We had gone on vacation to a lovely beach resort in Delaware with our friends Cleone and Ellis Dill, who are both excellent bridge players. Unfortunately, it poured with rain for about three days, so we weren't able to go down to the beach, which Evie and I love to do. We like to sit and watch the ocean, reading and taking the occasional stroll along the water's edge. As it was, we were stuck indoors, so what to do? Play bridge, of course. As always, I played partners with Ellis, and Evie played with Cleone. Without going into all the bidding and playing details which some people may not understand, let me just say that I ended up 'setting' or defeating a contract that Evie and Cleone had come to. Evie had to play the hand, and in fact it was her bidding that had gotten her into the contract. Her partner had really only been a passive participant, so all the blame, if the hand wasn't won, went to Evie.

My partner, Ellis, and I defeated the contract, although I held most of the good cards that caused Evie and Cleone to lose, and by doing so they lost 2,800 points. That's *two thousand eight hundred points*! I think that must be some sort of record. To lose a couple of hundred points is already quite a lot. To lose over 2,000 thousand points on one hand is tremendous. In fact, Evie likes to boast that she doesn't know anyone who has lost as many points in one hand as she has; she seems quite proud of that. (And for those of you who do play the game, Evie was down five tricks, vulnerable, doubled and redoubled!) So even though I do not distinguish myself at the bridge table, I have had my moments of triumph.

♫

My seventieth birthday was due on August 24th 1999, and Evie and the children insisted that we celebrate this momentous event in style. They wanted me to have a big party, but with part of the family in this country, and part in England, where would the party be? If we had a party here in New Jersey, then of course I would want Anne to be here. And if the party was in England, then I would want Steve to be over there. And then of course there were my friends in America and England, especially Rollo, who would turn seventy just three weeks after I did. On our visit to England in 1998, Rollo, Eileen, Evie and I had talked about having a joint celebration for our seventieth birthdays, but again the question arose: where? It would mean that both the Rollinsons, and their two children and their families flying over here if the party was in America. That would not have been very easy for them to manage.

So, what to do? In the end, we decided to have *two* parties – one in England, where I could be with my English friends and family, and then later on, I would have one in New Jersey. We started thinking about the party in England. Rollo and I had great ideas of inviting all sorts of old friends and acquaintances from our apprenticeship days at Frasers, and hiring a hall in London for a big bash. But once we started thinking about all the ramifications, we decided that that would just be too complicated. And expensive, too! So, in the end, we decided to invite just our close families to a dinner at the Upper Reaches, the poshest restaurant in Abingdon. We set the date for Saturday, September 4th 1999. We paid for Steve to fly over for five days, so that I could have both my children with me. Unfortunately, Kristina was unable to come over as by this time she and Steve had presented me with my first grandchild, a boy called Garrett Thomas Goodwin, who would be turning one just two days after I turned seventy. Kris felt that it would be too difficult for her and the baby to make the journey for such a short stay, and she was greatly missed at the dinner.

However, it turned out that the dinner in Abingdon was actually the *second* celebration I had, because just before we flew over to England, I had a joint birthday party with Garrett – he for his first birthday, me for my seventieth. We met here at my house and I opened my presents sedately, while Garrett ripped the paper off his! We then had lunch, and Evie brought in a Carvel ice cream cake (a tradition in the Goodwin family for birthdays), with a candle in the shape of the number '1' on it. When Garrett had blown that out, Evie took the cake back to the kitchen, and brought it out again with a candle in the shape of a number '70' on it. Talk about economical!

The dinner in Abingdon was the next celebration. There was yet to be a party here at home, but that wasn't until early October. In Abingdon, Evie had booked a room at the Upper Reaches Hotel for the cocktail hour, in case of inclement weather, and had also reserved a large table in the dining room for our dinner. She had made all the arrangements while on a visit by herself to see Anne earlier that year, so by the time we arrived at the end of August, everything was laid on and organized. Besides Evie and me, my side of the family was represented by Anne and Dave, who had a 9-month old baby, Henry, my second grandchild, and Steve, as well as my sister Carol and her husband Terry. Then there was Rollo, Eileen, Graham and Marie, Jane and Dave and their daughter Danielle. We also had two very special guests from South Africa. It turned out that my good friend Austin Horn and his wife Hella were visiting England at the same time that we were there. I hadn't seen Austin for twenty-five years so I asked Rollo if he would mind if there were two people at the dinner who were not actually family members. He said, no of course not, so Hella and Austin also came to the dinner.

The evening turned out to be exceptionally warm for that time of year, and believe it or not, also quite sunny, and so we were able to have our cocktail hour outside on the terrace of the hotel, which was so much nicer than being indoors. At that time of the year, early September, it stays light until around 8.30pm, and everyone stood around making toasts to me and Rollo and enjoying their drinks and hors d'oeuvres. Eventually we moved inside, where we had the dining room almost to ourselves. We enjoyed a slap-up meal, where there were more toasts, lots of jokes and laughs and stories, and the exchanging of presents. It was a party I'll never forget.

Talking of presents, unbeknownst to me, there had been a lot of whispering about my birthday present every time Evie spoke to Anne or Steve on the telephone. I found out later that this had been going on for quite a few months before my birthday. After all, I had reached the biblical age of three-score-and-ten, and darn it, I deserved something special! It turned out that they had been discussing what to get me, wondering what to give the man who had everything – ha, ha. Evie had already decided that she wanted to get me a new camera, as our old one had recently broken.

But what about Anne and Steve? They needed ideas, and Evie was at a loss. One day Anne called with a fantastic suggestion, which she wanted to be kept a secret. She wanted to know what Evie thought of the two children giving me a ride in a hot-air balloon while we were all in England? At first Evie told Anne, no way, she was not having her husband doing anything that dangerous. Anne said, "Hey, this is for Dad, and he would love it." She suggested that Evie try and sound me out without giving anything away, which Evie managed to do. It seems that I told her that I wouldn't mind doing something like that, probably thinking that it would never happen. Little did I know! I do remember asking Anne one day what she was getting me for my birthday, but she was very secretive, and all she would say was that she couldn't post it to me, as it wouldn't fit into the letterbox, or even a delivery truck, or a plane.

My first clue to what my birthday present might be came when Anne met Evie and me at Heathrow when we flew in at the end of August. Before we even got into the car for the ride back to Abingdon, Anne showed me a drawing of a huge hot-air balloon with four little people inside, each representing one of the Goodwins. I couldn't for the life of me figure out what she was trying to tell me, so she had to explain that this was to be my present – a ride in the balloon. I must admit I was a little apprehensive, especially as Evie refused point-blank to come along. She was certainly not going to put *her* life in danger! Anne said that I should think about it, as she could always cancel the reservation. She gave us a brochure with all the details, and Evie called the company to find out more about the ride, especially the insurance side! By this time, Steve had arrived from America, and both he and Anne tried to coax Evie into going. I had decided that I would take a chance and go on the ride.

When the day came, it turned out to be one of the most glorious autumn days England had seen for years. The golden sun shone out of a cloudless blue sky, and there wasn't a breath of wind. Perfect conditions for a balloon ride, we were told. Our ride was scheduled for 6pm, and was to leave from a small field next to a pub near Abingdon called The Dog House. Rollo and Eileen had already arrived in Abingdon for the birthday dinner, and they drove out to see us off. All day Evie had been mulling over whether she should go or not, and in the end it was the weather, of all things, that encouraged her to go. When would she ever get another opportunity to go for a balloon ride over the Oxfordshire countryside with both of her children on such a perfect evening? Never. So in the end, very apprehensively, she climbed into the basket along with Anne, Steve and a slightly nervous me!

The pilot was a very experienced man who did his best to reassure Evie that nothing would go wrong. He told her not to look down at the ground as the balloon rose, and apparently this worked. We all looked out straight ahead of us as we left the ground (except Anne who was busy taking pictures of our journey), and from then on it was like a dream. We floated over the farms and villages around Oxford and looked down on the toy cars and toy houses below us. What a ride! After landing roughly in a farmer's field, a car drove us back to The Dog House, where the pilot broke open a bottle of champagne, and gave us all a certificate to say that we had taken this trip. That night in my dreams, I could still hear the whooshing sound of the gas and air operating the balloon. What a wonderful idea for a seventieth birthday gift – certainly one that I would never have thought of myself.

When we returned to the United States after this memorable trip to Abingdon, Evie organized yet another party for me, here at home. This way I was able to share this milestone with my American friends. We invited about twenty-eight people to a buffet supper, which was held in the beautiful new sunroom we had added on to the back of the house the year before. Evie decided to really splurge and organised outside catering. Once again I was very spoiled with some lovely gifts, the nicest one being told that I didn't look anything near seventy! I had now had three celebrations for this special birthday. I think Evie wanted to make sure that I didn't forget how old I was!

♫

At the end of 1999, there was a big hullabaloo about the Y2K (Year Two-Thousand) bug. Many people believed that when the clocks in all the computers and other automatic machines turned over from midnight on December 31st 1999, to one minute after midnight on January 1st 2000, there would be dire consequences. There was a fear that computers wouldn't be able to accept the new date as they are only programmed for 19— dates. All these machines and computers would start whirring and buzzing and suddenly break down, and we would not have any lights or water or telephones. Even things like food deliveries might come to a halt, and all over the country people were talking about stocking up with bottled water, firewood, flashlights and batteries. It got to be so ridiculous at one point, that we didn't know what to believe.

It so happened that on December 31st 1999, Evie and I were playing bridge at the Dills' house. Ellis Dill's birthday is on December 31st, and almost every year since we met the Dills we have celebrated both his birthday and New Year's Eve together. That year, TVs were turned on early, and the commentators were showing us how the whole world was anticipating the unknown consequences of the clocks turning over to January 1st 2000.

As the countdown progressed and we got closer to midnight, we all sat there holding our breaths. What would happen? Ellis knew what would happen. *Nothing*! He had been telling us this for months. And he was right. The lights stayed on, there were no sirens blaring or rockets falling or anything else that wouldn't have happened on a normal New Year's Eve. Ellis bounced out of his seat calling for more champagne and bridge, saying that now we had that fiasco out of the way, maybe we could all get back to reality. Happy New Year!

♫

When I first thought about writing down the story of my life, I had no idea that it would turn into such an enormous project. The idea came to me soon after arriving in the United States from South Africa, and lay dormant for a long time. However, now that I look back, I can see that I would never have been happy unless I had recorded, on paper, some of my life's experiences. I felt a great need to do so. Not only had the children often asked me about my early years, but many of my friends had expressed an interest, especially those in the USA who had not lived through the war in England, let alone emigrated twice to a foreign country. When I said in the Preface that I needed to satisfy my own selfish ego, I meant what I said. I wrote this book for *me*, first and foremost, but with future generations of the Goodwin family in mind. There have been many times when I wished I could have known more about my parents' grandparents, but unfortunately I learned very little about the earlier generations when I was growing up.

I actually started making notes about this book while I was still working, but it was only when I retired, and was able to devote most of my time to writing, that I started putting my life story down on paper. We had bought ourselves a simple computer, and on this I started typing, literally with two fingers. When I said that writing this book would be a challenge, little did I know how true this would be. The challenge lay more in finding the letters on the keyboard, than finding the words to say. It has been a labour of love. I have persevered over the years, and now I find myself winding down to one of the most pleasurable times of my life – that of being a grandfather.

When Steve and Kris told us that they were expecting their first child, due to be born in August 1998, both Evie and I were overjoyed. This would be an entirely new experience for us. We had many friends who were already grandparents, and we had listened to their stories and admired their grandchildren, as any good friends would do. However, we secretly yearned to have grandchildren of our own, and now at last, our wish was to be fulfilled. And it was not long after we learned about Steve's first child, that Anne and Dave told us that they were expecting a baby, due in December 1998. Our cup runneth over.

Neither Steve nor Anne wanted to know the sex of their babies, so we were kept in suspense until the last moment. I'll never forget the excitement of that early morning phone call, when Steve told us that Kris had safely delivered a baby boy, called Garrett Thomas Goodwin. The date was August 26th 1998. Do you know the first thing that Evie and I did? We ran to the toy store and bought every little 'boy' toy that we could lay our hands on! Well, maybe that is a bit of an exaggeration, but we really hadn't been able to buy anything because we didn't know whether it would be a boy or a girl. This joyful moment was to be only the first of four – as three other grandchildren followed in fairly quick succession.

On December 8th 1998, Anne and Dave had a little boy called Henry Gerald Hall in Oxford, England. It was very difficult being so far away at such a time, but we took a trip to Abingdon the following February to get to know our second grandson. Then Anne and Dave announced that they were expecting their second child, and on February 2nd 2001, Jane Megan Hall put in her appearance, also born in Oxford. Now Anne and Dave had their 'pigeon pair'. This is a saying in England when parents have one child of each sex. Evie and I had had our pigeon pair, and now Anne and Dave did too.

In the meantime, Steve and Kris also told us they were expecting again, and on July 3rd 2001, Grace Lili Goodwin arrived. Another pigeon pair. The Goodwin luck was certainly in evidence here. What more could each of our children wish for? All four babies are healthy, beautiful, smart, and all those other qualities that grandparents attribute to their own grandchildren!

I was already in my thirties when I married, and well into my sixties when I first became a grandfather. Little did I know that these four little bundles of joy would bring me so much pleasure, and would instil in me such feelings of pure love. It was something I had not felt before.

You might say that I have now accomplished my goal of recording my life story for the children, their children, and other members of the Goodwin family. It is, after all, for them as well as for myself that I have written this book. I have lived to see the Goodwin name carried on, and can count that as one of my many blessings. I hope that when they read my book it will give them an insight into the times in which I lived, and also give them a feeling of being part of the family. And most of all, I hope they feel that now they know me better.

THE END

Afterword

I ENJOYED writing this book; it became a major hobby of mine. I developed a habit of drinking a small Scotch during the late afternoon, which Evie kindly served me as the sun went down; this was leftover from the ritual of the South African 'sundowner'. The drink would then see me through until the end of that day's writing.

In many ways I miss my daily sessions of writing in the mornings and afternoons, but once I had written the final sentence, I felt a sense of relief that, come what may, I had put all my thoughts down on paper.

There is one major note that I would like to bring to the readers' attention. While the text was still being edited, Evie and I decided to return permanently to England. We made the decision after much thought and the reasons are many and varied. We sold our property at 215 Wyckoff Avenue and with the proceeds bought a little house about two miles from Anne in Abingdon, near Oxford. For me it is like coming home.

T.A. Goodwin
Abingdon, England
2002

Thomas Goodwin (formerly Godwin*) — Keziah Day

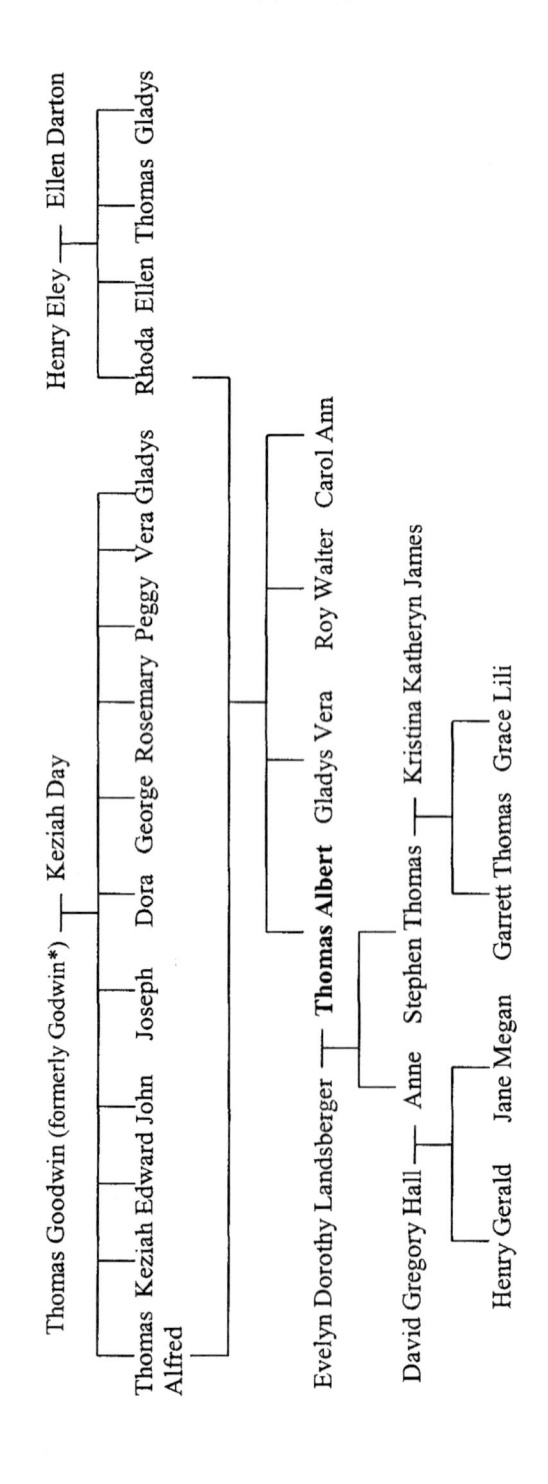

Thomas Keziah Edward John Joseph   Dora George Rosemary Peggy Vera Gladys
Alfred

Henry Eley — Ellen Darton

Rhoda Ellen Thomas Gladys

Evelyn Dorothy Landsberger — **Thomas Albert** Gladys Vera   Roy Walter Carol Ann

David Gregory Hall — Anne Stephen Thomas — Kristina Katheryn James

Henry Gerald   Jane Megan   Garrett Thomas Grace Lili

*Thomas Godwin (whose brother was a priest) changed his name to Goodwin when a young man

286

English – American Dictionary

English (or explanation)	American (or explanation)
afters	dessert
Autumn	Fall
box room	very small bedroom
braces	suspenders
BT	British Telecom
bungalow (house)	ranch (house)
café	diner/luncheonette
car park	parking lot
caravan	camper
chemists	pharmacy
chuffed	delighted
coast	seashore
Cockney	person born in East End of London, within the sound of the Bow Church bells
conkers	game played with horse chestnuts
cooper	barrel maker
Copper	Police Officer
Cor blimey	My goodness
council flat	subsidised housing
cul de sac	dead end
curriculum vitae	resumé
cut	canal
draughts	checkers
East Ender	someone who lives in the East End of London
Estate Agents	Real Estate Agents
fag	cigarette
flat	apartment
football	soccer
fortnight	two weeks
frock	dress
garden	yard
git	jerk
governor	boss at work
gramophone record	phonograph record
grumble	complain or moan

harmonica	mouth organ
holiday	vacation
Jerry	slang for Germans, used during the war
lift	elevator
long bow	large bow
magic lantern	old fashioned cinema
main line station	railway station
mate	helper (at work), or buddy/friend
maths	math
Members of Parliament (MPs)	Congressmen
motorway	highway
nappies	diapers
off licence	liquor store
oil shop	hardware store
pavement	sidewalk
petrol	gasoline
picture palace	cinema
pictures	movies
pint (of beer)	mug (of beer)
posh	elegant
public house/pub	bar
publican	bartender/manager
punter	gambler
queue	line
quid	a British pound (sterling)
RAF	Royal Air Force
redundancy notice	pink slip
registration plate	licence plate
row house	town house
school mate	school friend
Sister	Head Nurse
spectacles	glasses
sweets	candy
three R's	reading, (w)riting and (a)rithmetic
tin	can
toff	well educated / wealthy people
underground	subway
Union Jack	British flag
vicar	rector
wireless	radio